Hakikat Kitabevi Publications No: 21

MIFTAH-UL-JANNA
(Booklet for Way to Paradise)

Written by
Muhammad bin Qutb-ud-dîn Iznikî

Revised by
Hüseyn Hilmi Işık

English version by
Hakîkat Kitâbevi

Eighth Edition

Hakîkat Kitâbevi
Darüşşefeka Cad. 53/A P.K.: 35
34083 Fatih-ISTANBUL/TURKEY
Tel: 90.212.523 4556–532 5843 Fax: 90.212.523 3693
http://www.hakikatkitabevi.com
e-mail: info@hakikatkitabevi.com
AUGUST-2020

Indroduction to
Booklet for Way to Paradise

Allâhu ta'âlâ sent Prophets "alaihim-us-salâm' to His born slaves so that they should attain happiness, comfort and peace in the world and in the Hereafter and lead a brotherly life by attaching their hearts to one another, and for the purpose of teaching them how to perform their duties as His slaves. Through those select people, the highest of mankind in all respects, He let His born slaves know the best way of living. He announced that Muhammad ''alaihis-salâm', the highest and the aftermost of His Prophets ''alaihim-us-salawât-u-wa-t-teslîmât' is the Prophet of all people that will be living all the world over until the end of the world. In His grand heavenly book named the **Qur'ân al-kerîm** and which He revealed to this most beloved Prophet of His through an angel piecemeal in a proces of twenty-three years, He declared His commandments and prohibitions. Because the Qur'ân al-kerîm is in the Arabic language and provides extremely subtle teachings and ultramundane pieces of knowledge beyond the grasp of human mind, Muhammad ''alaihis-salâm' explained the entire book, from the beginning to the end, to his Sahâba ''alaihim-ur-ridwân'. He said: **"Anyone who explains the Qur'ân al-kerîm in a way at variance with my explanations will become an unbeliever."** Islamic scholars, who heard from the Ashab-i-kirâm the explanations made by our Prophet 'sall-Allâhu 'alaihi wa sallam', made them clear and plain enough to be understood by everybody and wrote them in books of Tafsîr. These scholars are called the scholars of Ahl as-Sunnat (or Sunnî scholars). Books which the scholars of Ahl as-Sunnat wrote by compiling semplars of explanations from the Qur'ân al-kerîm and our Prophet's 'sall-

TYPESET AND PRINTED IN TURKEY BY:
İhlâs Gazetecilik A.Ş.
Merkez Mah. 29 Ekim Cad. İhlâs Plaza No: 11 A/41
34197 Yenibosna-İSTANBUL Tel: 90.212.454 3000

ISBN: 978-975-8883-27-1

Allâhu ta'âlâ 'alaihi wa sallam' utterances, which are called **hadîth-i-sherîfs**, are called books of **'Ilm-i-hâl**. People who want to acquire true and tenable knowledge of the **Islamic religion** which Allâhu ta'âlâ teaches in the Qur'ân al-kerîm have to read these books of 'ilm-i-hâl.

The original title of the book, **Booklet for Way to Paradise**, which we are currently presenting, is **Miftâh-ul-Janna**, which means **The Key of the Gate to Paradise**. It was written by Muhammad bin Qutb-ud-dîn Iznikî 'rahima-hullâhu ta'âlâ', who passed away in Edirne in the hegiral lunar year 885 [1480 A.D.].

Profound Islamic scholar Sayyid 'Abd-ul-Hakîm Efendi 'rahima-hullâhu ta'âlâ' (1281 [1865 A.D.], Bashkal'a, Van – 1362 [1943 A.D.], Ankara, Turkey) stated: "The author of the book entitled **Miftâh-ul-Janna** is said to have been a pious person. It will be useful to read it." Therefore, we have published the book. The explanations here and there in the book and which have been added within brackets are citations borrowed from other books. They are by no means expressions of personal views and comments. May Allâhu ta'âlâ protect us all against separatism and disunion, which are the inescapable consequences of falling into the traps set by Islam's enemies lying in ambush and their treacherous, heretical, lâ-madhhabî, reformist-minded accomplices under Muslim names, some of whom pass for men of religion! May He unite us all within the Madh-hab of **Ahl as-Sunnat**, the one and only way of following and adapting ourselves to His beloved Prophet 'sall-Allâhu ta'âlâ 'alaihi wa sallam'! May He bless us all with a way of life wherein we love and help one another! Âmîn.

[When a person is about to do something, first a khatara (idea, thought) comes to their heart, so that they intend to do that thing. This intention of theirs is called **niyya(t)**. This person then orders their limbs to do that thing. The person's ordering the limbs is called **qasd** or **teshebbus** (attempt). The limbs' doing the work is called **kesb**. The heart's work is called **akhlâq** (conduct, behaviour). There are six places whence the khatara comes to the heart: Khatara that comes from Allâhu ta'âlâ is called **Wahy**. The Wahy comes only to Prophets' hearts. Khatara brought by angels is called **ilhâm** (inspiration). The ilhâm comes to Prophets' ''alaihim-us-salawât-u-wa-t-teslîmât' and sâlih (pious) Muslims' hearts. Khatara given by sâlih Muslims is called **nasîhat** (counsel, advice). The Wahy, the ilhâm, and the nasîhat are always good and useful. Khatara coming from the devil is called **vasvasa** (doubt, misgiving); khatara that comes from one's own nafs[1] is called **hewâ** (carnal passion, sensual fancy); and khatara imbued by evil company is called **ighfâl** (seduction, deception). Nasîhat (counsel, advice) is given to anybody. The vasvasa and the hewâ come to disbelievers' and fâsiq[2] Muslims' hearts. Both of them are evil and harmful. Things that Allâhu ta'âlâ likes and approves of are called **good** things, and those which He dislikes are called **fenâ** (bad, evil) things. Because Allâhu ta'âlâ is very compassionate, He has declared good and bad things in the **Qur'ân al-kerîm**. He has commanded to do the good things and prohibited the evils. His commandments and prohibitions are called, collectively, the **Ahkâm-i-islâmiyya**. If a heart follows the counsel provided by good company and reason and thereby adapts itself to the Ahkâm-i-islâmiyya, it will become pure and full of nûr. It will attain happiness and peace both in this world and in the Hereafter. A heart that disobeys the Ahkâm-i-islâmiyye by following the nafs and the devil, which in turn is the result of believing the misguiding oral and written statements made by evil people and zindiqs, will become dark and rotten. A pure heart full of nûr will relish obeying the Ahkâm-i-islâmiyya. A heart that has become dark will enjoy following evil company, the nafs, and the devil. Allâhu ta'âlâ, being very compassionate, creates a pure heart for each and every newly-born baby all the world over. Afterwards, parents and evil company make their hearts dark like their own hearts.]

---

[1] Malignant force innate in man's nature.
[2] Sinful, disobedient Muslims.

BOOKLET for WAY TO PARADISE

Al-hamd-u-lillâh-illedhî je'alenâ min-et-tâlibîna wa lil'ilmi min-er-râghibîna wa-s-salât-u-wa-s-salâm-u-'alâ Muhammadin-il-ledhî erselehu rahmatan lil'âlamîna wa 'alâ Âlihi wa Ashâbihi ajma'în.

ISLAM
ALLAH EXISTS AND IS ONE

[Allâhu ta'âlâ created all beings. Everything was non-existent. Allâhu ta'âlâ, alone, was existent. He always exists. He is not a being that came to existence afterwards. If He had been non-existent before, there would necessarily have been a power to create Him. For, nonexistence of a power to create something nonexistent entails the continuation of the nonexistence of that nonexistent thing, so that it can never come to being. If the owner of power to create it existed, then Allâhu ta'âlâ is that eternal being who possesses the power. Conversely, if it should be argued that that creative power as well came into being afterwards, then it will have to have been created another power, which in turn perforce leads to an infinite number of creators. This, however, means nonexistence of a beginning for creators. Nonexistence of the earliest creator results in nonexistence of the creation that it would have effected. When the creator is nonexistent, then all this material and spiritual creation that we see or hear around us will have to be nonexistent. Since material beings and souls do exist, then they must have a single and everexistent creator.

Allâhu ta'âlâ first created simple substances, constituents of all material beings, and souls and angels. Simple substances are termed elements now. There are a hundred and five elements known as of today. Allâhu ta'âlâ has created, and is always creating, every substance and every object from these hundred and five elements. Iron, sulphur, carbon, oxigen gas, chlorine gas are an element each. Allâhu ta'âlâ has not stated how many million years ago He created these elements. Nor has He let us know when He started creating the earths, the heavens and the living beings, which are products made up of these elements. Everything, living or non-living, has a certain life-span during which it stays in existence. He creates it when the time comes, and annihilates it when its life-span is over. He not only creates something from nothing, but also creates something else from another thing, slowly or all of a sudden, and as the former comes into being the latter ceases to exist.

Allâhu ta'âlâ made man from lifeless substances and a soul. Man had never existed theretofore. Animals, plants, genies, angels had been created before that earliest man. That first man was named 'Âdam (Adam) "alaihis-salât-u-wa-s-salâm'. And from him He, (i.e. Allâhu ta'âlâ,) created a woman. From these two did the entire mankind multiply. We see that all things, living and lifeless ones alike, are changing. Something eternal would never change. In physical events, states and forms of substances are changing. Yet chemical reactions change their essence and nature. Substances are ceasing to exist, while other substances are coming into existence. In nuclear events, on the other hand, even elements disappear into energy. This process of all things' coming into being from one another can not be an eternal process without a beginning. They have to have issued from the earliest substances created from nothing. For, eternal means without a beginning.

Enemies of Islam disguise themselves as scientists and say that men were created from monkeys. They say that an English doctor named Darwin said so. They are liars. Darwin (Charles [1809-82 A.D.]) did not say so. He propounded the struggle of survival among living beings. In his book entitled **The Origin of Species** he wrote that living beings developed traits that best suited their environments and thereby underwent some insignificant mutations. He did not say that one species changes into another. In a meeting that British Association for the Advancement of Science organized in Salford in 1980, Prof. John Durant of Swansea University said that Darwin's evolutionary explanation of the origins of man has been transformed into a modern myth, to the detriment of science and social progress, that the secular myths of evolution have had a "dramatic effect on scientific research," leading to "distortion, to needless controversy, and to the gross misuse of science." He concluded that Darwin's theory has now come apart at the seams, leaving behind heaps of ruinous and disingenuous thoughts.[1] These statements which Prof. Durant

---

[1] Dr. John Durant (University of Swansea, Wales), as quoted and cited in "How evolution became a scientific myth" "New Scientist," 11 September 1980, p. 765.

made about his compatriot are among the most interesting answers given to Darwinists in the name of science. The innermost reason that lurks behind the present attempts to imbue people at a certain cultural level with this theory of evolution is sheer ideology. They bear no scientific motives. The so-called theory is being exploited as a tool for the insinuation of materialistic philosophy. The argument that man evolved from the monkey has no background in knowledge. And it is all the farther from being scientific. It is not Darwin's argument, either. It consists in the fibs of ignorant enemies of Islam quite unaware of knowledge and science. A man of knowledge or a scientist can not make such ignorant and ridiculous statements. If a university graduate leads a dissolute life and forgets what he has learned in school instead of carrying on with his studies in the science he has majored in, he can never be a man of knowledge or a scientist. What is even worse is his taking a pet aversion to Islam and attempting to scatter his mendacious and spurious words and writings in the name of knowledge and science and thereby ending up as a base and treacherous microbe harmful to society. In that case his diploma, title and position will become ostentatious traps to be exploited for hunting young people. Sham scientists who spread their own lies and slanders in the name of knowledge and science are called **impostors of science**.

What Allâhu ta'âlâ wants from people is that they should live in comfort and peace in the world and attain endless felicity in the Hereafter. For this reason He commands useful things that will cause felicity, and prohibits harmful things that will cause perdition. If a person, regardless of his being religious or irreligious, a Believer or a non-believer, adapts himself to the Ahkâm-i-islâmiyya, i.e. the comandments and prohibitions of Allâhu ta'âlâ, knowingly or unknowingly alike, the degree of the comfort and peace they will attain in this worldly life will be in direct ratio to the quality of their obedience to the system of rules. It is identical with the maxim that anyone who takes the right medicine will recover from illness or malady. The current success that many an irreligious and atheistic person and people have been enjoying is due to their working in a manner that would be approved by the Qur'ân al-kerîm. Attaining the eternal felicity by obeying the Qur'ân al-kerîm, however, is possible only if the obedience is done knowingly by a Believer.

The initial commandment of Allâhu ta'âlâ is to have **îmân**. And **kufr** is what He prohibits before any other vice. Îmân means to 'believe the fact that Muhammad ''alaihi-s-salâm' is the final Prophet of Allâhu ta'âlâ. To him did Allâhu ta'âlâ impart His commandment by way of 'Wahy'. In other words, He revealed His Ahkâm-i-islâmiyya to him through an angel, and he in turn explained all of them to people. The Word which Allâhu ta'âlâ revealed through an angel is called the Qur'ân al-kerîm. A book that contains an entire written text of the Qur'ân al-kerîm is called a **Mushaf** (a copy of the Qur'ân al-kerîm). The Qur'ân al-kerîm is not the personal statements made by Muhammad ''alaihi-s-salâm'. It is the Word of Allâhu ta'âlâ. No human being is capable of making a single statement equal to the perfection in its verses. The rules taught in the Qur'ân al-kerîm, collectively, are called **Islam**. A person who believes all of them with his heart is called a **Mu'min** (Believer) and a **Muslim**. To dislike even a single one of them is called **kufr** [animus towards Allâhu ta'âlâ]. Belief in the Rising after death, the existence of genies and angels, the fact that 'Âdam ''alaihi-s-salât-u-wa-s-salâm' is the father of the entire mankind and the earliest Prophet, is only the heart's business. These facts are called teachings pertaining to **îmân** or **i'tiqâd** or **'aqâid**. As for the practices that must be observed and the prohibitions that must be avoided both physically and with the heart, it is necessary both to believe them and to do them or to avoid them. They are called teachings of **Ahkâm-i-islâmiyya**. Belief in them also is within îmân. Practising or avoiding them is **'ibâdat** (worship). It is worship to observe the Ahkâm-i-islâmiyya by making niyya (intention) first. Commandments and prohibitions of Allâhu ta'âlâ are called the **Ahkâm-i-islâmiyya** or the **Ahkâm-i-ilâhiyya**. Commandments are called **farz** (or fard), and prohibitions are called **harâm**. As is seen, a person who denies and despises a single one of these duties becomes a **kâfir** [enemy of Allah]. A person who neglects them although he (or she) believes them does not become a kâfir; he (or she) becomes a **fâsiq** (sinful) Muslim. A Mu'min who believes Islam's teachings and practises them to the best of his abilities is called a **Sâlih Muslim** [good person]. A Muslim who obeys Islam and loves a Murshid for the purpose of attaining the grace and love of Allâhu ta'âlâ is called a **Sâlih** [good] person. A Muslim who has attained the grace and love of Allâhu ta'âlâ is called an **'Ârif** or a **Walî**. A Walî who serves as a means for others also to attain this love is called a **Murshid**. All these selected people, collectively, are called **Sâdiq** people. All of them are sâlih people. A sâlih Believer will never go to Hell. A kâfir (enemy of Allah) shall definitely go to Hell. He shall never go out of Hell and shall be subjected to unending torment. If a kâfir has îmân (becomes a Believer), his sins will be forgiven outright. If a fâsiq person makes tawba and begins to practise the acts of worship, he will never go to Hell, and will go directly to Paradise, like sâlih Believers. If he does not make tawba, he will either be forgiven and directly go to Paradise, by attaining shafâ'at (intercession) or without any means in between, or be burned in Hell as much as he deserves on account of his sins and enter Paradise thereafter.

When the Qur'ân al-kerîm was revealed, its grammar suited with the Arabic language spoken by the people of that time, and it is in poetic form. In other words, it is metrical like poetry. It abounds with the delicate subtleties of the Arabic language. It excels in the Arabic sciences of belles-lettres such as Bedi', Beyân, Me'ânî, and Belâghat. Therefore it is very difficult to understand. A person who does not know the delicacies of the Arabic language can not properly understand the Qur'ân al-kerîm, literate as he may be in Arabic. Even people erudite in those delicacies were unable to understand it, so that our master, the blessed Prophet, explained most of it. Rasûlullah's 'sall-Allâhu 'alaihi wa sallam' explanations of the Qur'ân al-kerîm are called **hadîth-i-sherîfs**. The Ashâb-i-kirâm 'ridwânullâhi ta'âlâ 'alaihim ajma'în'[1] conveyed the teachings that they had heard from our Prophet 'sall-Allâhu ta'âlâ 'alaihi wa sallam' to younger generations. In process of time hearts underwent a gradual darkening, so that new Muslim converts attempted to interpret the Qur'ân al-kerîm with their parochial mentalities and shorts sights, thereby deriving meanings disagreeable with the explanations of our master, the Prophet. With the enemies of Islam provoking the cleavages and fissures, there appeared seventy-two wrong and heretical credos. Muslims who hold such aberrant credos are called **people of bid'a(t)** or **people of dalâla(t)**. All the seventy-two groups of bid'at shall certainly go into Hell, but, being Muslims, they will not stay eternally in Hell; going out of Hell, they will enter Paradise. If a person's belief disagrees with one of the credal teachings clearly stated in the Qur'ân al-kerîm or in hadîth-i-sherîfs, that person will lose his îmân. He is called a **mulhid**. A mulhid thinks he is a Muslim.

Islamic scholars who learned the teachings of i'tiqâd, i.e. credal tenets correctly from the Ashâb-i-kirâm 'ridwânullâhi ta'âlâ

---

[1] Please see the book entitled SAHÂBA 'The Blessed' one of the publications of Hakîkat Kitâbevi, Fâtih, Istanbul, Turkey.

'alaihim ajma'în' and wrote these correct teachings in books, are called scholars of **Ahl as-Sunnat** 'rahmatullâhi ta'âlâ 'alaihim ajma'în'. They are scholars who attained the grade of ijtihâd in one of the four Madhhabs. These scholars believed only as they learned from the Ashâb-i-kirâm, rather than attempting to understand the meanings in the Qur'ân al-kerîm with their own minds and views. They spread the true way that they learned from our Prophet, rather than following their own understanding. The Ottoman State was a Muslim State, and they held the Sunnî creed.

As is understood from what has been written so far, and as is written in many a valuable book, for being safe against disasters in the world and in the Hereafter and to lead a comfortable and happy life, it is necessary to hold an îmân taught by the scholars of Ahl as-Sunnat; that is, to learn their credal tenets and to believe them all. A person who does not hold the Sunnî credo will become either an **ahl-i-bid'at**, i.e. a heretical Muslim, or a **mulhid**, i.e. a kâfir (disbeliever). The second duty of a Believer with true îmân and correct i'tiqâd is to become sâlih, which means to attain grace and love of Allâhu ta'âlâ. With this end in view, one should acquire the Islamic teachings pertaining to what must be done and what must be avoided, physically as well as with the heart, and live accordingly. In other words, one should perform the acts of worship. Scholars of Ahl as-Sunnat explained the acts of worship in four different ways. Hence, the four (Islamically authentic) **Madhhabs**.[1] Because the points whereon they differ from one another are few and on insignificant matters, and since the same credal tenets bind them together, they both sympathize with one another and pay respect to one another. Each and every Muslim has to practise their acts of worship in obedience to one of these four Madhhabs. That a person who does not adapt himself to any one of these four Madhhabs will have abandoned the (only true way called) Ahl as-Sunnat is a definite fact, which is written (also) in the chapter entitled 'Dhebâyih' of Ahmad bin Muhammad bin Ismâ'îl **Tahtâwî**'s 'rahmatullâhi ta'âlâ 'alaih' (d. 1231 [1815 A.D.] annotation to 'Alâ'uddîn Haskafî's 'rahmatullâhi ta'âlâ 'alaih' (1021, Haskaf – 1088 [1677 A.D.]) book entitled **Durr-ul-Mukhtâr**.

If a kâfir (disbeliever) says, "I have become a Muslim," he is to

---

[1] The four Madhhabs pertaining to Islamic practices and which Islam authorizes are: **Hanafî**, **Shâfi'î**, **Mâlikî**, **and Hanbalî**. Details about these four Madhhabs are available from the publications of Hakîkat Kitâbevi in Istanbul.

be believed, regardless of whether he is one captured in warfare or one who says so during peace time. But then he will have to immediately learn the **six essentials of îmân** and believe them. Thereafter he will have to learn and observe Islam's commandments called farz (or fard) and its prohibitions called harâm whenever they become incumbent on him (or her), and whenever they have the opportunity to do so. If they do not learn them, or if they slight and neglect a single one of them although they have learned them, they will have overlooked the religion of Allâhu ta'âlâ. They will lose their îmân. People who lose their îmân like this are called **murtadd**s (renegades, apostates). Of murtadds, the ones who disguise themselves as religious people and thereby misguide Muslims are called **zindiq**s. We should not believe zindiqs or their lies. As is written in the hundred and sixteenth page of the Turkish version of the commentary to the book entitled **Siyar-i-kabîr**,[1] and also in the final part of the chapter dealing with a disbeliever's nikâh (marriage contract prescribed by Islam) of the book entitled **Durr-ul-mukhtâr**, if a person has reached the age of puberty without having professed Islam and without having conceived in his mind that he is a Muslim, if that nescience of his has been because of not knowing Islam and not as an indulgence in worldly interests, then he will be judged to be a murtadd (renegade, apostate). It is written in the final part of the chapter dealing with a disbeliever's nikâh of **Durr-ul-muhtâr** that when a Muslim girl who is married with (an Islamic marriage contract termed) nikâh reaches the age of puberty without having known Islam, her nikâh, (i.e. Islamic marriage contract,) becomes null and void. [In other words, she becomes a murtadd.] Attributes of Allâhu ta'âlâ will have to be coached to her. She will have to repeat what she hears and say, "I believe them." Ibni 'Âbidîn 'rahima-hullâhu ta'âlâ' explains this matter as follows: "When to girl is small, (i.e. below the age of puberty,) she is a Muslim, since her religion is to be named after that of her

---

[1] That book was written by Muhammad bin Hasan bin 'Abdullah bin Tâwus bin Hurmuz Sheybânî (Imâm Muhammad) 'rahmatullâhi ta'âlâ 'alaih' (135 [752 A.D.], Wâsit – 189 [805 A.D.], Rey), one of the greatest Islamic scholars educated by Imâm Abû Hanîfa 'rahmatullâhi 'alaih'. Shems-ul-aimma Abû Bakr Muhammad bin Ahmed 'rahmatullâhi 'alaih' (d. 483 [1090 A.D.]) wrote a commentary to the book, and the commentary was rendered into Turkish by Khwâja Muhammad Munîb Efendi of 'Ayntab (d. 1238 A.H.).

parents. When she reaches puberty she will no longer be dependent on her parents' religion. When she reaches puberty in a state of nescience in Islam, she becomes a murtadd. If a person who does not believe the tenets of Islam although he has heard them utters the Kalima-i-tawhîd, i.e. if he says, "**Lâ ilâha il-l-Allah Muhammadun Rasûlullah**," he will not become a Muslim. A person who believes the six tenets expressed in the credo that reads; "Âmentu billâhi..." and who says, "I accept the commands and prohibitions of Allâhu ta'âlâ," is a Muslim. Hence, each and every Muslim must have their children memorize (the six tenets of Islamic credo in) the expression, "Âmentu billâhi wa Melâikatihi wa Kutubihi wa Rusulihi wa-l-Yawm-il-âkhiri wa bi-l-Qadari khayrihi wa sherrihi min-Allâhi ta'âlâ wa-l-bâ's-u-ba'd-al-mawt haqqun Esh-hadu-an-Lâ ilâha il-l-Allah wa Esh-hadu-anna Muhammadan 'abduhu wa rasûluhu," and teach them its meaning well. If a child does not believe these six tenets or one of Islam's commandments and prohibitions and does not say that it believes them, it becomes a murtadd, and not a Muslim, when it reaches puberty. Detailed information on these six tenets is available from the book entitled **Belief and Islam**, (one of the publications of Hakîkat Kitâbevi in Istanbul.) Every Muslim should read that book, have heir children as well read it, thereby consolidating their îmân, and do their best so that all their acquaintances as well read it. Accordingly, we should take utmost care so that our children should not be raised as murtadds. In the early stages of childhood, we should teach them îmân, Islam, 'abdest (ablution), ghusl, and namâz![1] Parents' primary duty is to raise their children as Muslims.

It is stated as follows in the book entitled **Durer wa Ghurer**:[2] "A man who has become a murtadd must be told to become a Muslim. His doubts must be clarified and eliminated. If he asks for a term of respite, He will be kept in prison for three days. If he makes tawba, (i.e. repents for his grave sin and begs Allâhu ta'âlâ for forgiveness, promising Him that he shall never commit that gravest sin,) his tawba will be accepted. If he does not make tawba, then he will be put to death by the (Muslim) judge. A woman who becomes a murtadd will not be killed. She will be imprisoned and

---

[1] The fourth fascicle of **Endless Bliss**, one of the publications of Hakîkat Kitâbevi, enlarges on these teachings.

[2] Written by Muhammad Molla Husraw 'rahmatullâhi ta'âlâ 'alaih', the third Ottoman Shaikh-ul-islâm.

kept in prison until she becomes a Muslim. If she flees to the dâr-ul-harb, she will not be a jâriya as long as she is in the dâr-ul-harb. If she is captured she will become a jâriya. When she becomes a murtadd her nikâh will become null and void. All her property will get out of her possession, (i.e. it will no longer be her property.) It will be her property again if she becomes a Muslim again. When she dies or flees to the dâr-ul-harb [or becomes a murtadd as she is in the dâr-ul-harb], her property will become her inheritors' legacy. [If she has no inheritors, the property will be inherited by people who have rightful shares from the Beytulmâl.][1] A murtadd cannot inherit property from another murtadd. Property earned by a murtadd as he (or she) is a murtadd will not be his (or her) property. It will be fey for Muslims. (**Fey** is defined in a subchapter headlined **THE DISBELIEVER'S MARRIAGE** and appended to the twelfth chapter of the fifth fascicle of **Endless Bliss**.) All her social transactions such as buying and selling, rental agreements, and gift-givings, will become bâtil. (Please see the thirty-first chapter of the fifth fascicle of **Endless Bliss** for 'bâtil'. They will return to their former state and become sahîh if she becomes a Muslim again. She will not have to make qadâ of her former acts of worship, with the exception of hajj, which she will have to perform again." The first three acts of worship that a new Believer has to learn how to perform are to make an ablution, to make ghusl, and to perform namâz.

The six essential tenets of îmân are: To believe that Allâhu ta'âlâ exists and is One, and (to believe) His Attributes; to have îmân in, (i.e. to believe,) Angels, Prophets, Heavenly Books, events that will happen in the Hereafter; Qadâ and Qadar. Later on, we shall explain each and every one of them separately.

In short, we must observe Islam's commandments and prohibitions both with heart and physically, and our hearts should be on the alert lest they should sink into ghafla (oblivion, unawareness, lethargy, torpor). If a person's heart is not vigilant, [that is, if he does not keep in mind the existence and greatness of Allâhu ta'âlâ and the flavour of the blessings in Paradise and the vehemence of Hell fire,] it will be very hard for that person's body to adapt itself to Islam. Scholars of (the Islamic science called) Fiqh (and which teaches Islam's commandments and prohibitions) convey fatwâs, (i.e. answers provided by authorized Islamic

_____

[1] Please see the first chapter of the fifth fascicle of **Endless Bliss**.

scholars for Muslims' questions concerning the ways of performing their acts of worship.)[1] It devolves on men of Allah to make them easy to practise. The body's adapting itself to Islam with alacrity, ease and willingness requires the heart's being pure. However, if a person attributes importance only to heart's being pure and the behaviour's being nice and yet cold-shoulders physical obedience to Islam, then he is a **mulhid**. Such peoples' extraordinary accomplishments, [such as informing about the unknown and curing invalid people by breathing on them,] are called **istidrâj** and will drag both the owners of the accomplishments and their admirers down into Hell. The symptom of a heart that is pure and a nafs that is mutmainna [docile] is the body's adapting itself to Islam willingly. The pretext, "My heart is pure. Look to my heart," put forward by people who do not adapt their sense organs and bodies to Islam, is empty words. By saying so, they are deceiving themselve and people around them.]

ATTRIBUTES of ÎMÂN

Scholars of Ahl as-Sunnat say that îmân has six attributes:

ÂMANTU BILLÂHI: I believe that Allâhu 'adhîm-ush-shân exists and is One; I have îmân in it.

Allâhu 'adhîm-ush-shân exists 'and is One.

There is not a sherîk or nadhîr for Him. (He does not have a partner or a likeness.)

He is munezzeh (free, exempt) from mekân (place). (He is not at a place.)

He is muttasif (qualified) with His Attributes of perfection (Kemâl). He has Attributes of Kemâl (or Kamâl).

He is free and far from attributes of imperfection. They do not exist in Him.

Attributes of Kemâl exist in Him. And attributes of imperfection exist in us.

Attributes of imperfection that we have are deficiencies such as being without hands and/or feet and/or eyes, illness and health, eating and drinking, and many another similar imperfection.

Attributes possessed by Allâhu 'adhîm-ush-shân are Attributes

---

[1] Sources whereon the fatwâ is based are to be appended to the fatwâ.

of Kemâl such as His creating earths and heavens and all the divers creatures –living in the air, in waters, on the earth and underground–, His keeping all the time in existence so many creatures some of which we know and an incomparably greater number of which we are not even capable of conceiving –on account of (the human) mind's limited capacity–, His giving rizq (food, sustenance) to all these creatures, and His other Attributes of perfection. He is qâdir-i-mutlaq (the almighty). Each and every creature is a work from the Attributes of Kemâl of Allâhu 'adhîm-ush-shân.

There are twenty-two attributes that are about Allâhu 'adhîm-ush-shân and which it is wâjib for us to know. Also, He has twenty-two other attributes which are muhâl (inconceivable, impossible for Him to have).

Wâjib means necessary. These Attributes exist in Allâhu 'adhîm-ush-shân. Attributes that are muhâl do not exist in Him. Muhâl is the opposite of wâjib. It means: "cannot exist".

There is one Attribute that is called sifât-i-nafsiyya about Allâhu 'adhîm-ush-shân and which it is wâjib for us to know: **Wujûd**, which means "to exist".

The evidence to prove by tradition that Allâhu 'adhîm-ush-shân exists is Allâhu ta'âlâ's qawl-i-sherîf (blessed statement) which reads: "**Innenî Enallâhu**." The evidence to prove it mentally is that there definitely exists a creator who created all these beings. It is muhâl for Him not to exist.

Sifât-i-nafsiyya means that the Dhât (Person) without Him and He without the Dhât cannot be conceived or thought of.

There are five Attributes concerning Allâhu 'adhîm-ush-shân that are termed Sifât-i-dhâtiyya and which are wâjib for us to know: They are (also) known as **Attributes of Ulûhiyyat**.

1– **Qidem** (or Qidam), which means that there is not a beginning for the existence of Allâhu 'adhîm-ush-shân.

2– **Baqâ** means that there is not an end for the existence of Allâhu 'adhîm-ush-shân, which is also called wâjib-ul-wujûd. Its evidence by tradition is the third âyat-i-kerîma declared by Allâhu ta'âlâ in the Hadîd Sûra (of the Qur'ân al-kerîm). Its mental evidence is that if His existence had a beginning and/or an end He would be incapable and imperfect. And an incapable and imperfect being in turn could not create others. Then, it is muhâl (impossible for His existence's having a beginning or an end).

3– **Qiyâm bi-nafsihi**, which means that Allâhu 'adhîm-ush-shân does not need anyone in His Dhât, in His Attributes, or in His Deeds. Its evidence by tradition is the final âyat-i-kerîma of the Sûra of Muhammad ''alaihis-salâm'. Its mental evidence is that if He did not have these Attributes He would be incapable and imperfect. Being incapable or imperfect is muhâl concerning Allâhu 'adhîm-ush-shân.

4– **Mukhâlafat-un-lil-hawâdith**, means that Allâhu 'adhîm-ush-shân is unlike anyone, in His Dhât (Person) as well as in His Attributes. Its evidence by tradition is Allâhu ta'âlâ's declaration in the eleventh âyat-i-kerîma of Shûrâ Sûra. Its mental evidence is that if He did not have these Attributes He would be incapable and imperfect. Being incapable or imperfect is muhâl concerning Allâhu ta'âlâ.

5– **Wahdâniyyat** means that Allâhu 'adhîm-ush-shân does not have a sherîk (partner) or a nadhîr (match, like), neither in His Dhât, nor in His Attributes or Deeds. Its evidence by tradition is Allâhu ta'âlâ's first âyat-i-kerîm in Ikhlâs Sûra. Its mental evidence is the fact that if He had a partner all beings would be non-existent. As one of them willed to create something, the other one would will not to do so.

[According to the majority of Islamic scholars, **Wujûd**, which means existence, is a distinct Attribute. Accordingly, there are six Attributes under the appellation **Sifât-i-Dhâtiyya**.]

SIFÂT-I-THUBÛTIYYA

There are eight Attributes that are wâjib for us to know concerning Allâhu 'adhîm-ush-shân and which fall into the category termed Sifât-i-thubûtiyya: Hayât, 'Ilm, Sem', Basar, Irâda, Qudrat, Kalâm, Tekwîn.

The meanings of these Attributes are as follows:

1– **Hayât** means that Allâhu 'adhîm-ush-shân is alive. Its evidence by tradition is the initial part of Allâhu ta'âlâ's two hundred and fifty-fifth âyat-i-kerîma in Baqara Sûra. Its mental evidence is the fact that had Allâhu ta'âlâ not been alive these creatures would not have come into existence.

2– **'Ilm** means that Allâhu ta'âlâ has knowledge. Its evidence by tradition is Allâhu ta'âlâ's twenty-second âyat-i-kerîma in Hashr Sûra. Its mental evidence is the fact that Allâhu 'adhîm-ush-shân would be incapable and imperfect if He did not have knowledge. Being incapable or imperfect is muhâl (impossible) concerning Allâhu 'adhîm-ush-shân.

3– **Sem'** means that Allâhu ta'âlâ hears. Its evidence by tradition is Allâhu ta'âlâ's first âyat-i-kerîma in the Isrâ Sûra. Its mental evidence is that He would be incapable and imperfect if He were without hearing. It is muhâl concerning Allâhu 'adhîm-ush-shân to be incapable or imperfect.

4– **Basar** means that Allâhu 'adhîm-ush-shân sees. Its evidence by tradition is, again, Allâhu ta'âlâ's first âyat-i-kerîma in Isrâ Sûra. Its mental evidence is that Allâhu 'adhîm-ush-shân would be incapable and imperfect if He did not have seeing. Being incapable or imperfect is muhâl concerning Allâhu 'adhîm-ush-shân.

5– **Irâda** means that Allâhu ta'âlâ wills. Whatever He wills happens. Nothing takes place unless He wills. He has willed (the existence of) beings and created them. Its evidence by tradition is Allâhu ta'âlâ's twenty-seventh âyat-i-kerîma in Ibrâhîm Sûra. Its mental evidence is that He would be incapable and imperfect if He did not have willing. And being incapable or imperfect is muhâl (impossible, contrary-to-fact, out of the place) concerning Allâhu 'adhîm-ush-shân.

6– **Qudrat** means Allâhu 'adhîm-ush-shân's being almighty. Its evidence by tradition is Allâhu ta'âlâ's hundred and sixty-fifth âyat-i-kerîma in Âl-i-'Imrân Sûra. Its mental evidence is that He would be incapable and imperfect if He were not almighty. It is muhâl for Allâhu 'adhîm-ush-shân to be incapable or imperfect.

7– **Kalâm** (or kelâm) means that Allâhu 'adhîm-ush-shân has speech. Its evidence by tradition is Allâhu ta'âlâ's hundred and sixty-fourth âyat-i-kerîma in Nisâ Sûra. Its mental evidence is that He would be incapable and imperfect if He did not have speech. And being incapable and imperfect in turn is muhâl concerning Allâhu 'adhîm-ush-shân.

8– **Tekwîn** means that Allâhu 'adhîm-ush-shân is creative, i.e. (He has creating power, so that) He creates. He, alone, creates all from nothing. There is no creator other than Him. Its evidence by tradition is Allâhu ta'âlâ's sixty-second âyat-i-kerîma in Zumar (or Zumer) Sûra. Its mental evidence is that He has a stupendous variety of creatures on earths and in heavens, and He is the sole Creator of all. It would be kufr, (i.e. it would cause one to lose one's îmân,) to say, "creator," about anyone besides Him. Man can not create anything.

Allâhu 'adhîm-ush-shân has eight Sifât-i-ma'nâwiyya (non-material attributes) that are wâjib for us to know: Hayyun, 'Alîmun, Semî'un, Basîrun, Murîdun, Qadîrun, Mutekellimun (or Mutakallimun),[1] Mukewwinun.

The meanings of these blessed attributes are as follows:

1– **Hayyun**: Allâhu 'adhîm-ush-shân is alive.

2– **'Alîmun**: Allâhu 'adhîm-ush-shân knows with such knowledge as 'ilm-i-qadîmi (eternal knowledge).

3– **Semî'un**: Allâhu 'adhîm-ush-shân hears with a hearing which is eternal (sem'i qadîm).

4– **Basîrun**: Allâhu 'adhîm-ush-shân sees.

5– **Murîdun**: Allâhu 'adhîm-ush-shân wills with an irâda-i-qadîmi (eternal will).

6– **Qadîrun**: Allâhu 'adhîm-ush-shân is almighty with His qudrat-i-qadîma (eternal power).

7– **Mutekellimun**: Allâhu 'adhîm-ush-shân has speech, which is kalâm-i-qadîm (eternal speech).

8– **Mukewwinun**: Allâhu 'adhîm-ush-shân is creative, and He creates all.

Attributes that are muhâl concerning Allâhu ta'âlâ are antonymous with the aforesaid attributes.

WA MELÂIKATIHI: I believe also the angels of Allâhu 'adhîm-ush-shân; I have îmân in them. Allâhu 'adhîm-ush-shân has angels. He created them from nûr (radiance, light). They are jisms (bodies). [The jism (body) mentioned in this context is not the jism mentioned in books of physics.] They do not eat or drink. They do not have sex. They get down to earth from heavens and ascend back to heavens. They appear in different guises. They are never disobedient to Allâhu 'adhîm-ush-shân, be it as long as a wink, let alone sinning like us. Among them are muqarrabs[2] and Prophets.

WA KUTUBIHI: I believe also the (heavenly) Books of Allâhu 'adhîm-ush-shân.

Allâhu 'adhîm-ush-shân has Books. There are one hundred

---

[1] Alternative transcriptions in Latin alphabet have been intended to help the reader to acquire as accurate as possible pronunciations of the technical terms.

[2] Please see the fifth level of wara' in the first chapter of the sixth fascicle of **Endless Bliss** for 'muqarrabs'.

and four Books named in the Qur'ân al-kerîm. A hundred of them are small Books. They are called 'Suhuf'. And four of them are major Books. **Tevrât** (or Tawrât, Torah) was sent down to Hadrat Mûsâ (Moses) ''alaihis-salâm', **Zebûr** to Dâwûd (David) ''alaihis-salâm', **Injil** to 'Îsâ (Jesus) ''alaihis-salâm', and the **Qur'ân al-kerîm** to our Prophet Muhammad ''alaihis-salâm'. **Could not Answer**, one of our publications, provides detailed information concerning the books entitled **Torah** and **Bible** and which are being read by today's Jews and Christians.

Of the hundred suhuf (plural form of sahîfa, which in turn means 'sheet' or 'page' or 'tablet', literally), ten suhuf were sent down to 'Âdam ''alaihis-salâm', fifty suhuf to Shis (Seth) ''alaihis-salâm', thirty suhuf to Idris ''alaihis-salâm', and ten suhuf to Ibrâhîm ''alaihis-salâm'. All of them were brought down by Jebrâîl ''alaihis-salâm'. The Qur'ân-i-'adhîm-ush-shân is the final one of all the heavenly Books that were sent down. The descent of the Qur'ân-i-'adhîm-ush-shân took twenty-three years, piecemeal and in âyats, and its rules shall survive till the end of the world. It has been protected from abrogation, [i.e. from becoming invalid,] and from human interpolation, [i.e. from being changed or defiled by mankind.]

WA RASULIHI: I have îmân also in the Prophets ''alaihim-us-salawât-u-wa-t-teslîmât' of Allâhu 'adhîm-ush-shân.

Allâhu ta'âlâ has Prophets ''alaihim-us-salawât-u-wa-t-teslîmât'. All Prophets are human beings. 'Âdam ''alaihis-salâm' is the first Prophet, and our Prophet, Muhammad Mustafâ 'sall-Allâhu ta'âlâ 'alaihi wa sallam' is the final Prophet. Many other Prophets ''alaihim-us-salawât-u-wa-t-teslîmât' came and went between these two. Allâhu 'adhîm-ush-shân' knows their number.

There are five attributes that are wâjib for us to know concerning Prophets ''alaihim-us-salawât-u-wa-t-teslîmât': Sidq, Amânat, Tebligh, Ismat, Fetânet.

1– **Sidq**: All Prophets ''alaihim-us-salawât-u-wa-t-teslîmât' are faithful in their word. Whatever they say is true.

2– **Amânat**: They never commit a breach of trust.

3– **Tebligh**: They know all the commandments and prohibitions of Allâhu 'adhîm-ush-shân and convey them to their Ummats.

4– **Ismat**: It means to be far from committing sins, grave and venial ones alike. They never commit sins. Prophets ''alaihim-us-salâm' are the only group of people who are sinless. [Shiites, however, say that there is yet another sinless group of people.]

5– **Fetânat**: It means that all Prophets ''alaihim-us-salawât-u-wa-t-teslîmât' are wiser than other people.

There are five attributes that are jâiz (permissible, possible) for Prophets ''alaihim-us-salawât-u-wa-t-teslîmât' to have: They eat and drink; they become ill; they die, (they are mortal,) they migrate from one world, (i.e. this world,) to the other world, (i.e. the Hereafter;) they are not fond of the world.

There are twenty-eight Prophets whose blessed names are given in the Qur'ân-i-'adhîm-ush-shân. There is a scholarly statement saying that it is wâjib for everybody to know them.

Names of Prophets ''alaihim-us-salawât-u-wa-s-salâm':

'Âdem, Idris, Nûh, Shis [Seth], Hûd, Sâlih, Lût, Ibrâhîm, Ismâ'îl, Is-haqq, Ya'qûb, Yûsuf, Mûsâ, Hârûn, Dâwûd, Suleymân, Yûnus, Ilyâs, Elyesa', Zulkifl, Eyyûb (or Ayyûb), Zekeriyyâ, Yahyâ, 'Îsâ, and Muhammad 'salawâtullâhi 'alâ nebiyyinâ wa 'alaihim'. There was a disagreement over the names of Uzeyr (or Uzayr), Loqmân (or Luqmân), and Zulqarneyn. Some (of the Islamic scholars) said that these three people and also Hidir ''alaihis-salâm' were Prophets, while others, (i.e. other Islamic scholars,) said that they were Awliyâ. It is written in the thirty-sixth letter of the second volume of Maktûbât-i-Ma'thûmiyya[1] that there is a convincing scholarly traditional citation stating that Hidir ''alaihis-salâm' was a Prophet. As is stated in the hundred and eighty-second letter, Hidir's ''alaihis-salâm' appearing and doing things in the human guise does not show that he is living. Allâhu ta'âlâ has allowed his soul as well as the souls of many Prophets and Awliyâ to be seen in the human guise. Seeing them does not show that they are alive.

And also, what is incumbent upon you is to say, "I am, al-hamd-u-lillah, a descendant of Hadrat 'Âdam ''alaihis-salâm' and one of the Ummat (Believers, Muslims) of the Prophet of the latest time, Muhammad ''alaihis-salât-u-wa-s-salâm'." Wahhâbîs deny the fact that 'Âdam ''alaihi-s-salâm' was a Prophet. Therefore, and also because they call Muslims 'polytheists', they are kâfirs (disbelievers).

---

[1] Written by Muhammad Ma'thûm Fârûqî 'rahmatullâhi ta'âlâ 'alaih' (1007, Serhend – 1079 [1668 A.D.], the same place), the third son of Hadrat Imâm Rabbânî 'quddisa sirruhumâ'.

WA-L-YAWM-IL-ÂKHIRI: Also, I believe the Day of Rising; I have îmân in it. For, Allâhu ta'âlâ has informed us about it. The Day of Qiyâma(t) begins when people rise from their graves. It continues until people go to their places (which are either) in Paradise or in Hell. All of us shall die and thereafter come back to life. Paradise and Hell and mîzân [Scales] and the bridge of Sirât and hashr [assembling] and neshr (or nashr) [leaving the place of hashr to go to Paradise or Hell] and torment in grave and being questioned by the two angels named Munkar (or Munker) and Nekir (or Nakir) are all haqq (truth). They will definitely be experienced.

WA BI-L-QADAR-I-KHAYRIHI WE SHARRIHI MIN-ALLÂHI TA'ÂLÂ: I believe also that all the past and future events, good and evil one, alike, have taken place and will take place with the taqdîr of Allâhu 'adhîm-ush-shân, that is, suitably with His knowledge and decree in eternal past, and with His creating them at their destined times and with His writing them in the Lawh-il-Mahfûz;[1] I have îmân in it. There is never a doubt in my heart.

Esh-hadu an lâ ilâha il-l-Allah wa esh hadu anna Muhammadan 'abduhu wa rasûluh.

And also, my Madhhab in i'tiqâd, [i.e. in tenets to be believed,] is the Madhhab of **Ahl as-Sunnat wa-l-jamâ'at.** I am in this Madhhab. The credal tenets held by the other seventy-two groups are wrong and heretical. They will go to Hell.

[Muslims who love all the Ashâb-i-kirâm ''alaihim-ur-ridwân' are called (the grup of) **Ahl as-Sunnat.** All the Ashâb-i-kirâm were learned and 'âdil Muslims. They attended the sohbat, (i.e. blessed togetherness, presence,) of the Master of the entire humanity, (i.e. Rasûlullah,) 'sall-Allâhu 'alaihi wa sallam', and assisted him. Even a Sahâbî who attained the least of that (most valuable) sohbat is higher than a Walî who is the highest of all the Awliyâ and yet who is not a Sahâbî. The hâls experienced at a single one of the sohbats and tawajjuhs of that Darling of Allâhu ta'âlâ and the kemâls (perfections) attained under the effect of his blessed looks and breaths have not fallen to the lot of anyone who did not attain that presence, that fortune of closeness. All the Ashâb-i-kirâm 'ridwânullâhi ta'âlâ 'alaihim ajma'în were secured against

---

[1] Please see the thirty-sixth chapter of the third fascicle of **Endless Bliss**.

indulgence in the desires of their 'nafs'es[1] as soon as they attained the first sohbat (of Rasûlullah). We have been commanded to love them all. It is written as follows in the initial pages of the commentary to the book entitled **Shir'at-ul-islâm**:[2] "Talk as courteously as possible about any of the Ashâb-i-kirâm "alaihim-ur-ridwân'. Never speak ill of any of them." As for the seventy-two (aberrant) groups: Some of them carried the matter too far, while others were remiss in it; some of them put their trust in mind, while others fell for philosophy and Greek philosophers. Thus they practised things that were not in Islam and which were even contrary to Islam. They embraced bid'ats, (i.e. beliefs and practices that had nothing to do with Islam and which had been invented in the name of Islamic beliefs and practices.) They abandoned the Sunnat, i.e. Islam. There appeared people who resented Islamic celebrities such as Abû Bakr as-Siddîq and Hadrat 'Umar 'radiy-Allâhu 'anhumâ', the highest ones of the Ashâb-i-kirâm according to the ijmâ' (unanimity of Islamic scholars), –in fact, the resentment felt by some of them would not sidestep the blessed name of our Master, the Prophet "alaihis-salâm'. There appeared people who denied the fact that our Master, the Prophet, had been taken up to heaven both physically and spiritually on the night called Mi'râj, (which is explained in detail in the sixtieth chapter of the third fascicle of **Endless Bliss**.)

It is so appalling to see some *soi disant* contemporary Islamic scholars dismally serving as mouthpieces for the group called **Ismâ'îliyya**, the most harmful of the seventy-two groups (of bid'at). They are striving to misquide and poison the innocent young generations by writing and spreading various destructive lies such as that the blessed male and female ancestors of our Master the Prophet were disbelievers and that our blessed Master the Prophet "alaihis-salâm' had been immolating sacrificial animals before idols before he was designated as the Prophet, and adducing some Shiite books to support their misrepresentations. It can be seen clearly that the aims of such defeatists is to undermine the Islamic religion, to steal the îmân of young people, and to blemish them with disbelief. An âyat-i-kerîma in the Qur'ân al-

---

[1] Please see the forty-third chapter of the second fascicle of **Endless Bliss** for 'nafs'.

[2] Written by Muhammad bin Abû Bakr 'rahmatullâhi ta'âlâ 'alaih' (d. 573 [1178 A.D.]). Its commentary was written by Ya'qûb bin Sayyid 'Alî 'rahmatullâhi ta'âlâ 'alaih' (d. 931 [1525 A.D.]).

kerîm purports: "**A person who interprets the Qur'ân al-kerîm in accordance with his own mind will become a disbeliever.**" Islamic scholars had adab (polished manners, as taught by Islam). They would talk and write with diligence. They think hard lest they should say something wrong. Talking without reserve, e.g. attempting to voice one's wrong and aberrant personal views and opinions in the name of Islam instead of derving true information from the **Edilla-i-shar'iyya**, i.e. from the four major sources of Islamic knowledge, is not something that an average Muslim do, let alone an Islamic scholar. We must deem the destructive and belief dirtying words and writings of such ignorant people who have not realized the greatness of our blessed Prophet 'sall-Allâhu ta'âlâ 'alaihi wa sallam' or of the Ashâb-i-kirâm 'ridwânullâhi ta'âlâ 'alaihim ajma'în' as lethal venoms.

A Persion line in English:

I shudder like a willow leaf if they should assault my îmân.

May Allâhu ta'âlâ increase the love of His beloved ones in our hearts. May He protect us from falling into the inferno of loving His enemies! The symptom of îmân's existence in a heart is its loving the beloved one's of Allâhu ta'âlâ and its resenting His enemies.]

There are four Madhhabs in 'amal (Islamic practices, acts of worship, deeds and actions): They are the Madhhabs of Imâm a'zam (Abû Hanîfa), Imâm Shâfi'î, Imâm Mâlik, and Imâm Ahmad bin Hanbal 'rahmatullâhi 'alaihim'.

It is necessary to adapt oneself to any one of these four Madhhabs. Madhhabs of all four of them are true and right. All four of them are within the Ahl as-Sunnat. We are in the Madhhab of Imâm a'zam. Muslims in this Madhhab are called **Hanafî**s. "The Madhhab of Imâm a'zam is thawâb[1] and right. There is the likelihood as well that it may be incorrect. The other three Madhhabs are incorrect. There is the likelihood as well that they may be correct," we say.

And also, îmân's staying with its holder permanently without leaving is dependent upon six conditions and causes:

1– We have had îmân in the ghâib. Our îmân is in the ghâib

---

[1] The word 'thawâb' is used both as an adjective and as a noun. When a certain behaviour is thawâb, it means that Allâhu ta'âlâ likes it very much and in the Hereafter He will give rewards for it.

(unknown, unseen), not in the zâhir (known, seen). For, we have not been able to see Allâhu 'adhîm-ush-shân with our eyes. However, we have believed, we have had îmân as if we had seen Him. We have never had any doubt as to it.

2– On the earth and in heavens, among human beings, genies, angels, and Prophets "alaihim-us-salawât-u-wa-t-teslîmât', there is not a single creature to know about the ghâib. Allâhu 'adhîm-ush-shân, alone, knows about the ghâib, and He imparts whatever He wishes of the ghâib to creatures that He chooses. ['Ghâib' means (something) which cannot be perceived with sense organs or understood by calculation or experimentation. The ghaîb can be known only by those to whom He imparts the ghâib.]

3– To know harâms as harâms and to believe them as such.

4– To know halâls as halâls and to believe them as such.

5– Not to feel secured against the torment of Allâhu 'adhîm-ush-shân, and to always fear Him.

6– Not to give up hope of the compassion of Allâhu 'adhîm-ush-shân no matter how sinful you are.

If a person does not fulfil one of these six conditions although he may fulfil five of them, or if he fulfils one of them and does not fulfil five of them, that person's îmân and islam will not be sahîh.

There are forty [40] things which may cause a person with îmân at the moment to lose their îmân later:

1– To hold a bid'at, which means to have a flaw in one's îmân. [A slightest deviation from the credal tenets taught by scholars of Ahl as-Sunnat will cause the deviator to become either a heretic or a disbeliever. If a person denies something that is compulsory to believe, that person becomes a kâfir (disbeliever) outright. It is **bid'at** or **dalâlat** to deny something that is not compulsory to believe. A bid'at or dalâlat may cause its holder to die without îmân.]

2– Îmân that is weak, i.e. îmân without 'amals (compulsory practices or acts of worship).

3– To let one's nine limbs abandon the right way.

4– To continue committing grave sins. [Therefore, Muslims should not take alcohol, and Muslim women and girls should not show their heads, hair, calves, and wrists to nâ-mahram[1] men.]

---

[1] Please scan the twelfth chapter of the fifth fascicle of **Endless Bliss** for detailed information about terms like 'mahram' and 'nâ-mahram'.

5– To cease from gratitude for having been blessed with Islam.

6– Not to fear the likelihood of going without îmân to the Hereafter.

7– To perpetrate cruelty.

8– Not to listen to an adhân-i-Muhammadî that is being performed in a manner prescribed by the Sunnat. [A person who slights an adhân being performed likewise becomes a disbeliever outright.] (Adhân-or azân-and how to perform it in a manner prescribed by the Sunnat, i.e. by Islam, is explained in full detail in the eleventh chapter of the fourth fascicle of **Endless Bliss**.)

9– To disobey one's parents. To harshly refuse their orders that are suitable with Islam and which are mubâh.

10– To swear oaths frequently even if they are true.

11– When performing namâz, to neglect the ta'dîl-i-erkân at rukû' (bending the body during namâz), at qawma (standing upright after rukû'), at two sajdas (prostrations during namâz), and at jalsa (sitting upright between two sajdas). Ta'dîl-i-erkân means to stay in tumânînat, i.e. motionless for as long as a time during which one could say, "Subhân-Allah."

12– To think that namâz is something unimportant and not to attach importance to learning it and teaching it to one's family and children, and to prevent others from performing namâz.

13– To drink hamr [wine] and any other hard drink that intoxicates when imbibed in a large amount; the same rule applies even if the alcohol taken is only a little.

14– To get Believers into trouble.

15– To make a false show of being a Walî or being learned in Islam. To represent oneself as a religious man, a preacher, without acquiring the teachings of Ahl as-Sunnat. [False religious books written by such liars should not be read. Their sermons and speeches should not be attended.]

16– To forget about one's sinfulness; to take it lightly.

17– Arrogance, i.e. to take too much pride in oneself.

18– 'Ujb (self-admiration), i.e. to admire one's learning and piousness.

19– To be a munâfiq, i.e. hypocrisy, double-facedness.

20– Covetousness; to be jealous of one's Muslim brother.

21– Not to obey the commandments of the government or of

one's master (even) when their commandments are not against Islam. To revolt against their commandments that are against Islam.

22– To say that so and so is a good person without putting that person to the test.

23– To be an inveterate liar.

24– To avoid scholars. [Not to read books written by scholars of Ahl as-Sunnat.]

25– To grow one's moustache longer than the limit put by the Sunnat.

26– For men to wear silk. It is permissible to wear synthetic silk or material woven with silk weft and cotton warp.

27– To be a habitual backbiter.

28– To cause trouble to one's neighbours, even if they are disbelievers.

29– To show too much anger over worldly matters.

30– To receive and pay interest.

31– To boastfully wear garments with sleeves and/or skirts too long.

32– To practise sorcery.

33– To never visit one's mahram relative who is a pious (sâlih) Muslim.

34– To dislike a person liked by Allâhu ta'âlâ and to like people who (you know) are trying to defile Islam.

35– To bear grudge against one's Muslim brother for longer than three days.

36– To make fornication a habit.

37– To commit sodomy and not to make tawba[1] thereafter. Sodomy (liwâta) means to insert one's dheker into another person's anus. Dheker (penis) is the organ which a man uses for urination. The female organ used for the same purpose is called ferj (vagina).

38– To perform the adhân (or azân) not at times prescribed in books of Fiqh and/or not in a manner dictated by the Sunnat,

_____

[1] To make tawba for a certain sin or for one's sins means to repent for it or for them, to beg Allâhu ta'âlâ for forgiveness, and to promise Him not to commit it or them.

and/or not to show due respect upon hearing an adhân being performed in a manner agreeable with the Sunnat.

39– When you see a person committing a munkar (harâm), not to perform 'nehy' (or 'nahy'), [i.e. not to dissuade that person from doing so,] by using an elegant language, although you have the ability to do it.

40– To condone Islam's prohibitions being committed by women who you have the right to give advice, such as your wife and daughter(s); e.g. their going out without properly covering their heads, arms, and legs, or ornamented and/or perfumed as they are.

Îmân means the tongue's declaration and the heart's confirmation of the facts which Prophets have conveyed from Allâhu 'adhîm-ush-shân. And **Islam** means to have îmân in Muhammad ''alaihis-salâm' and to practise ('amal) his teachings.

Also, **Dîn** and **Millat** are synonyms. **Dîn** or **Millat** means the i'tiqâd, i.e. credal tenets, which Prophets brought from Allâhu 'adhîm-ush-shân.

Islam or **Ahkâm-i-islâmiyya** means the 'amal, i.e. practical tenets, which our Prophet 'sall-Allâhu ta'âlâ 'alaihi wa sallam' brought from Haqq ta'âlâ.

And also, îmân-i-ijmâlî (summarized belief), which means to believe briefly, will be enough (for a person to become a Believer, a Muslim). It will not be necessary to go into detail or to know îmân in detail. A muqallid's îmân, which means a person's belief without understanding, will be sahîh, (i.e. valid, sound.) Details, however, is required in some matters.

There are three levels of îmân: Îmân-i-taqlîdî, îmân-i-istidlâlî, and îmân-i-haqîqî.

Îmân-i-taqlîdî (imitative belief). A person with this level of îmân does not know farz (or fard), wâjib, sunnat, or mustahab. They imitate their parents in their belief and acts of worship. Îmân held by such people is precarious.

Îmân-i-istidlâlî (inferential belief). A person with this level of îmân both knows farz, wâjib, mustahab, and harâm, and obeys Islam. They are both knowledgeable and communicative concerning tenets of belief. They have learned them from religious teachers and books. Îmân held by such people is firm.

Îmân-i-haqîqî (true, genuine belief). If the entire creation came together and agreed on the denial of their Rabb (Allâhu ta'âlâ), a person at this level of îmân would not deny (Allâhu ta'âlâ). There would never be an iota of doubt in their heart. Their îmân is identical with the îmân of Anbiyâ (Prophets). This level of îmân is higher than the other two levels.

Also, Islamic rules pertain to 'amal (practices, acts of worship), not to îmân (belief, credo). Îmân, alone, would suffice for entering Paradise. Yet it is out of the question to go in there only with 'amal, (i.e. by practising acts of worship.) Îmân without 'amal is acceptable. 'Amal without îmân, on the other hand, is useless. Acts of worship performed, pious acts done, and alms given by people without îmân will do them no good in the Hereafter. Îmân cannot be donated as a gift to someone else, while the thawâb earned by way of 'amal can be gifted. One cannot give or write an instruction concerning îmân in one's last will. Yet one can instruct one's inheritors to perform 'amal on one's behalf (after one's death). A person who neglects 'amal will not become a disbeliever. But a person who abandons îmân or who takes 'amal lightly will become a disbeliever. A person with a good excuse ('udhr) or who is unable will be absolved from 'amal. But by no means will any person be absolved from îmân.

There is one îmân which all Prophets conveyed to their ummats. Yet they differ from one another in their rules, dispensations, and religious practices.

Also, there are two kinds of îmân. One of them is îmân-i-khilqî, and the other kind is îmân-i-kesbî.

Îmân-i-khilqî is the born slaves' saying, "**BELÂ (Yes),**" at the time of the 'ahd-i-mîsâk (solemn covenent).[1]

Îmân-i-kesbî is the îmân acquired and professed after reaching the age of puberty. Îmân of all Believers is the same. Yet they differ in 'amal.

Îmân is farz-i-dâim (always compulsory), whereas 'amal becomes farz (compulsory) when its time comes.

Îmân is farz both for the disbeliever and for the Muslim. 'Amal is farz only for the Muslim.

Also, there are eight categories of îmân:

Îmân-i-metbû' is the îmân of angels.

Îmân-i-ma'sûm is the îmân of Prophets.

---

[1] Please see the third paragraph of the first chapter of the book entitled **The Rising and the Hereafter**.

Îmân-i-maqbûl is the îmân of Believers.

Îmân-i-mawqûf is the flawed îmân of holders of bid'at.

Îmân-i-merdûd is the mendacious îmân which munâfiqs pretend to have.

Îmân-i-taqlîdî is the îmân of people who have heard it from their parents and not learned it from religious teachers. Such people's îmân is precarious.

Îmân-i-istidlâlî is the îmân of a person who knows Mawlâ-i-mute'âlî by inferring His existence from evidence. That person's îmân is staunch.

İmân-i-haqîqî. A person with this îmân would not deny their Rabb (Allâhu ta'âlâ) even if all the other creatures agreed on the denial of their Rabb, and there would never be an iota of doubt or hesitation in that person's heart. As we have stated earlier in the text, this kind of îmân is the noblest of all.

Îmân bears a three-fold import:

First, it saves one's neck from the sword.

Second, it saves one's property from (taxes called) jizya and kharâj.[1]

Third, it saves one's body from everlasting Hell fire.

"**Amantu billâhi ...**," is also called Sifât-i-îmân or mu'minun bih or dhât-i-îmân or 'asl-i-îmân, on account of its grandeur and honour. (It is the expression of the credal tenets of Islam and reads on as follows: "**... wa Melâikatihi, wa Kutubihi, wa Rusulihi, wa-l-Yawm-i-âkhiri, wa bi-l-Qadari, Khayrihi wa sharrihi min-Allâhi ta'âlâ, wa-l-ba's-u-ba'd-al-mawt, Haqqun esh-hadu anlâ ilâha il-l-Allah wa esh-hadu anna Muhammadan 'abduhu wa Rasûluhu.**")

Also, there are two medârs for îmân, i.e. points of time whereat it becomes compulsory (for one) to have îmân: Age of discretion and age of puberty.

Also, there are two reasons for îmân: Creation of all beings and revelation of the Qur'ân al-kerîm.

Also, **there are two kinds of evidence**: Delîl-i-'aqlî (mental

---

[1] Please scan the eleventh and the twentieth chapters of the first fascicle, the thirty-third chapter of the second fascicle, the twenty-first chapter of the fourth fascicle, the first and the twelfth chapters of the fifth fascicle, and the first chapter of the sixth fascicle, of **Endless Bliss**, for jizya and kharâj.

evidence) and delîl-i-naqlî (evidence by tradition).

Also, **îmân has two rukns** (principles)**, 'asls** (origins): Ikrâr-un bi-l-lisân (professing it with the tongue) and tasdîq-un-bi-l-jenân (confirming it with the heart). And there are two conditions stipulated for them:

The condition stipulated for the heart is that it should not harbour any doubt or hesitation, and the condition pertaining to the tongue is one's awareness of what one says.

Also, is îmân a creature? It is a non-creature with respect to its being a hidâyet (guidance) from Allâhu 'adhîm-ush-shân. On the other hand, it is a creature from the point of view of its being the born slave's confirmation and declaration.

Is îmân a collectivity, a singular whole, or a plurality?

It is a collectivity in the heart and a plurality in the limbs.

Yaqîn means to know the Dhât of Allâhu 'adhîm-ush-shân with His Kamâl (or Kemâl).

Khawf means to fear Allâhu 'adhîm-ush-shân.

Rejâ means not to give up hope of the Rahmat (Mercy, Compassion) of Allâhu 'adhîm-ush-shân.

Muhabbatullah means to have affection for Allah and His Messenger 'sall-Allâhu ta'âlâ 'alaihi wa sallam' and the Islamic faith and Believers.

Hayâ means to feel ashamed before Allah and His Messenger 'sall-Allâhu ta'âlâ 'alaihi wa sallam'.

Tawakkul means to entrust all one's matters to Allâhu ta'âlâ. To put one's trust in Him when beginning to do something.[1]

Also, what are called Îmân, Islam, and Ihsân?

Îmân means to believe all the facts stated by Muhammad ''alaihis-salâm'.

Islam means to perform the commandments of Allâhu 'adhîm-ush-shân and to avoid His prohibitions.

Ihsân means to perform one's acts of worship in a manner as if you were seeing Allâhu ta'âlâ.

Îmân; its lexical meaning is 'positive confirmation'. In Islam, it

---

[1] The thirty-fifth chapter of the third fascicle of **Endless Bliss** enlarges on tawakkul.

means to believe and confirm the six credal tenets.

Ma'rifat means to know Allâhu ta'âlâ to have the Attributes of Kemâl and to be far from atributes of imperfection.

Tawhîd means to believe in the unity of Allâhu 'adhîm-ush-shân and not to attribute a partner to Him.

Islam (Ahkâm-i-islâmiyya) means the commandments and prohibitions of Allâhu 'adhîm-ush-shân.

Dîn wa millat means resolution in the tenets of belief until death.

And also, îmân is protected within five fortifications:

1– Yaqîn

2– Ikhlâs

3– Performing the acts of farz and avoiding the harâms.

4– Adherence to the Sunnat.

5– Steadfastness in adab and being watchful at it.[1]

Any person who is steady in these five fortifications will be steady also in their îmân. Negligence in any one of these fortifications will precipitate enemy ascendancy. Man has four enemies: Evil company on the right hand side; indulgences [desires] of man's own nafs on man's left; fondness for the world in front of man; and the satan close behind; these four enemies vie for taking away îmân. Evil company does not only consist of people who cheat one out of one's property, money, and worldlies. The worst and the most harmful evil company are those who strive to spoil one's faith, îmân, adab, hayâ (sense of shame), and moral conduct, and who thereby, attack one's happiness in this world and everlasting felicity in the Hereafter. May Allâhu ta'âlâ secure our îmân against the evils of such enemies and against the misguidance organized by Islam's enemies.

The blessed meaning of the **Kalima-i-Tawhîd**, i.e. of saying, **"Lâ ilâha il-l-Allah,"** is: There is no person other than Allâhu 'adhîm-ush-shân who is worthy of being worshipped. Allâhu 'adhîm-ush-shân, alone, is so. He always exists and is One. He does not have a sherîk [partner] or a nadhîr [likeness, match]. He is without time and without place.

"Muhammadun Rasûlullah" means Hadrat Muhammad

---

[1] The sixth chapter of the sixth fascicle of **Endless Bliss** provides information about the âdâb (pl. of adab) in eating and drinking.

Mustafâ 'sall-Allâhu ta'âlâ 'alaihi wa sallam' is the born slave and the true Messenger of Allâhu 'adhîm-ush-shân. We are his Ummat, al-hamd-u-lillah.

And also Kalima-i-Tawhîd has eight names:

1– Kalima-i-Shehâdat.

2– Kalima-i-Tawhîd.

3– Kalima-i-Ikhlâs.

4– Kalima-i-Taqwâ.

5– Kalima-i-Tayyiba.

6– Da'wat-ul-Haqq.

7– 'Urwa-t-ul-wuthqâ.

8– Kalima-i-themerat-ul-Jannat.

And also, requirements to be fulfilled for (having) ikhlâs[1] are: Making niyyat (intention), knowing its meaning, and reading or reciting it with due respect.

And, a person making dhikr needs four things: Tasdîq, ta'dhîm, halâwat, and hurmat.

A person who abandons tasdîq is a munâfiq; a person who abandons ta'dhîm is a bid'at holder; a person who abandons halâwat is a hypocrite; he makes a show; a person who abandons hurmat is a fâsiq. Denial of it causes disbelief.

And also, there are three kinds of dhikr:

1– Dhikr-i-awâm.

2– Dhikr-i-khawâs.

3– Dhikr-i-akhas.

Dhikr-i-awâm is the dhikr of unlearned people. Dhikr-i-khawâs is the dhikr made by Islamic scholars, and Dhikr-i-akhas is the dhikr of Prophets.

And also, there are three human limbs to make dhikr:

1– Dhikr made with tongue, i.e. to say the Kalima-i-shahâdat.

2– To make tawhîd and tesbîh (or tasbîh), and to read (or recite) the Qur'ân al-kerîm.

3– Dhikr made with heart.

---

[1] Doing something good only because Allâhu ta'âlâ commands or approves of it and avoiding something evil or sinful only because Allâhu ta'âlâ prohibits or disapproves of it.

There are three kinds of dhikr made with heart:

1– To meditate over the evidence and the symptoms that guide to the Attributes of Allâhu 'adhîm-ush-shân.

2– To meditate over the evidence of the Ahkâm-i-islâmiyya.

3– To meditate over the mysteries of creatures.

Scholars of Tafsîr explain the hundred and fifty-second âyat-i-kerîma of Baqara sûra as follows: The Qur'ân al-kerîm declares: **"O My slaves! If you make dhikr of Me by way of tâ'at** (acts of obedinece to Allâhu ta'âlâ)**, I shall in turn make dhikr of you with Rahmat** (Mercy, Compassion)**. If you make dhikr of Me by way of invocations and prayers, I shall in turn make dhikr of you by way of ijâbat,** (i.e. by accepting your invocations.)**) If you make dhikr of Me by way of tâ'at, I shall in turn make dhikr of you with My Na'îm** [Paradise]**. If you make dhikr of Me in seclusions, then I shall make dhikr of you at the Jem'iyyat-i-kubrâ,** [i.e. at the place of Mahsher,] **If you make dhikr of Me at times of poverty, then I shall make dhikr of you with My help. If you make dhikr of Me by way of ijâbat,** (i.e. by responding to My injunctions,) **then I shall make dhikr of you by way of hidâyat** (guidance)**. If you make dhikr of Me by way of sidq and ikhlâs, then I shall make dhikr of you by way of khalâs and nejât** [salvation]**. If you make dhikr of Me with the Fâtiha-i-sherîfa and with the rubûbiyyat in the Fâtiha-i-sherîfa, then I shall make dhikr of you with My Rahmat."**

And also, Islamic scholars stated some hundred of the uses of making dhikr. We will state some of them:

When a Muslim makes dhikr, Allâhu ta'âlâ will be pleased with them. Angels will be pleased with them. Satan will become sad. That person's heart will become tender and soft. They will perform worship willingly and enthusiastically. Dhikr will remove sadness from their heart, make their heart cheerful, and brighten their face with nûr. That person will become brave and attain muhabbatullah (love of Allah). A gate from ma'rifatullah will be opened for them, so that they will receive fayz (or faydh) from the Awliyâ. They will be beautified with some sixty of the akhlâq-i-hamîda (laudable moral qualities).

"Esh-hadu anna Muhammadan 'abduhu wa Rasûluh." The blessed meaning of this statement is this: Hadrat Muhammad Mustafâ 'sall-Allâhu ta'âlâ 'alaihi wa sallam', Prophet of the latest time, is both a born slave and the Rasûl (Messenger) of Allâhu 'adhîm-ush-shân.

He ate and drank and married women. He had sons and daughters. All of them were from Hadrat Khadîja 'radiy-Allâhu 'anhâ'. Only Ibrâhîm was from a jâriya named Mâriya. And then he passed away before having been weaned. All his children, with the exception of Fâtima 'radiy-Allâhu 'anhâ', died before his own death. He married her to Hadrat 'Alî 'kerrem-Allâhu ta'âlâ'. Hadrat Hasan and Hadrat Huseyn are the sons of Hadrat 'Alî and Hadrat Fâtima 'radiy-Allâhu 'anhum'. Of all his daughters, Hadrat Fâtima is the highest. And she is the beloved one of Hadrat Rasûlullah 'sall-Allâhu ta'âlâ 'alaihi wa sallam'.

Rasûl-i-ekrem 'sall-Allâhu ta'âlâ 'alaihi wa sallam' has eleven blessed wives: Hadrat Khadîja, Sawda (or Sevde), 'Âisha, Hafsa, Umm-i-Selema, Umm-i-Habîba, Zeyneb bint-i-Jahsh, Zeyneb bint-i-Huzayma, Meymûna, Juwayriyya, Safiyya 'radiy-Allâhu 'anhunna'.

The **Edilla-i-shar'îyya** are made up of Kitâb, Sunnat, Ijmâ'-i-Ummat, and Qiyâs-i-mujtahid. From these four sources did the Islamic scholars derive their religious knowledge. The Word of Allâhu 'adhîm-ush-shân is called 'Kitâb (the Book)'. 'Sunnat' is the Qawl-i-Rasûl (Utterances of the Messenger of Allah), the Fi'l-i-Rasûl (Deeds Acts, Behaviours of the Messenger of Allah), and the Taqrîr-i-Rasûl (Confirmation, Ratification of the Messenger of Allah). Ijmâ'-i-Ummat is the consensus reached by the mujtahids who lived in the same century, e.g. by the Ashâb-i-kirâm 'radiy-Allâhu ta'âlâ 'anhum', or by the four Madhhabs. Qiyâs is analogy drawn between two different things by mujtahids.

And also, lexical meaning of madhhab is way. We have two different ways: One of them is our way in i'tiqâd (belief, credo), and the other one is our way in 'amal (practices).

Our imâm, i.e. guide, in the way of i'tiqâd is Abû Mansûr Mâturîdî 'rahima-hullâhu ta'âlâ'. His way is called **Ahl as-Sunnat**. Our guide in the way of 'amal is Imâm a'zam Abû Hanîfa 'rahima-hullâhu ta'âlâ'. His way is called **Hanafî Madhhab**.

Abû Mansûr Mâturîdî's name is Muhammad, his father's name is Muhammad, his grandfather's name is Muhammad, and his teacher's name is Abû Nasr-i-Iyâd 'rahima-humullâhu ta'âlâ'.

Abû Nasr-i-Iyâd's teacher's name is Abû Bakr-i-Jurjânî, whose teacher's name is Abû Suleymân Jurjânî, whose teachers' names are Abû Yûsuf and Imâm-i-Muhammad Sheybânî (or Shaybânî). And the teacher of these two celebrities is Imâm a'zam Abû Hanîfa 'rahima-humullâhu ta'âlâ'. Hence, Imâm a'zam is the chief guide of both our Madhhab in i'tiqâd and our Madhhab in 'amal.

All Muslims have three imâms (guides); it is farz to know them. Our imâm who enjoins the commandments and prohibitions is the Qur'ân al-kerîm. Our imâm who informs us of them, i.e. of Islam, is Hadrat Rasûlullah 'sall-Allâhu ta'âlâ 'alaihi wa sallam'. Our imâm who enforces them, i.e. who sees to that they should be observed, is the Muslim state president on behalf of Rasûlullah.

Imâm a'zam's teacher's name is Hammâd, whose teacher's name is Ibrâhîm Nehâî, whose teacher's name is 'Alqama bin Qays, who is at the same time Hadrat Nehâî's maternal uncle. Hadrat 'Alqama's teacher's name is 'Abdullah ibni Mes'ûd 'rahima-humullâhu ta'âlâ', who in turn received knowledge from Rasûlullah 'sall-Allâhu 'alaihi wa sallam'.

As for Rasûlullah ''alaihis-salâm', he received his knowledge from Jebrâîl ''alaihis-salâm'. And Jebrâîl ''alaihis-salâm', in his turn, was commanded by Hadrat Allâhu subhânahu wa ta'âlâ.

Allâhu 'adhîm-ush-shân has bestowed four jewels upon mankind: 'Aql (mind, wisdom, reason), Îmân, Hayâ, and Fi'l, i.e. 'amal-i-sâlih (pious deeds).

And also, prayers and any pious deed will be accepted, depending on the fulfilment of five conditions and causes: Îmân, 'Ilm, Niyyat, Khulûs, i.e. ikhlâs, not to retain any rights belonging to others, (which are called rights of quls.) First of all, one should hold the belief of Ahl as-Sunnat and know the conditions to be fulfilled for the soundness of the acts of worship to be performed.

[A certain 'amal's being sahîh is different from its having been accepted. Acts of worship have their own conditions and farâid (pl. form of farz or fard) to be fulfilled so that they should be sahîh (valid, sound). If one of them is missing, the act of worship performed will not be sahîh. It will be the same as if that act of worship has not been performed at all, and one will not be absolved from the punishment and torment to be inflicted (for not having performed it). No torment will be inflicted for an act of worship that has been sahîh although it has not been accepted. However, a Muslim will not attain thawâb (special rewards) for his or her worship that has not been accepted. For being accepted, an act of worship has to have been sahîh first of all; that is, the aforesaid five conditions should have been fulfilled. Rights of quls, (which we have already explained,) are included in these conditions.] Imâm Rabbânî 'rahima-hullâhu ta'âlâ' states as follows in the eighty-seventh letter of the second volume (of his masterpiece entitled **Maktûbât**):[1] "If a person performs 'amal identical with the Prophet's 'amal and yet retains a right of qul as much as a danq, [i.e. an iota of it,] he cannot enter Paradise unless he pays it back." [His prayers will not be accepted.]

Ibni Hajar-i-Mekkî 'rahima-hullâhu ta'âlâ' states as follows as he explains the hundred and eighty-seventh sinful act in his book entitled **Zewâjir**: The hundred and eighty-eighth âyat-i-kerîma of Baqara Sûra purports: "**O Believers! Do not consume one another's property in a way that is bâtil!**" What is meant by that way (which is bâtil) is deceit by way of interest, gambling, extortion, theft, cheating, treason, false witness, and perjury. Some hadîth-i-sherîfs read as follows: "**A Muslim who consumes things that are halâl and performs acts that are farz and avoids harâms and does not cause harm to other people will go to Paradise**" and "**A body that is fed on harâms will burn in fire**" and "**If people do not feel secure against a person's malice and harm, that person shall not reap any benefit from his faith or prayers of namâz or zakâts**" and "**If the jilbâb worn by a man has come to him by way of harâm, then the namâz he performs will not be accepted.**" [Jilbâb means an ample head-scarf worn by women. Another piece of clothing that is called 'jilbâb' is a long garment worn by men. According to some people who argue that what is called 'jilbâb' is a two-piece charshaf worn by women, the hadîth-i-sherîf (quoted above) implies that men also wore that charshaf. It is quite obvious that their tenuous argument betrays an ignorant and ludicrous belief.] A hadîth-i-sherîf which he quotes in his treatment of the two hundredth sinful act reads: "**A person who sells adulterated merchandise is not from our community. His destination is Hell.**" It is stated in a hadîth-i-sherîf quoted in the discussion of the two hundred and tenth sinful act: "**Hell is the destination of a person who hurts his neighbours with his tongue although he performs namâz and fasts and gives alms very much.**" Even if one's neighbours are disbelievers, it is necessary not to hurt them, to do them favours, and to be kind to them. It is stated in a hadîth-i-sherîf in the three hundred and thirteenth sinful act: "**A person who unjustly kills a disbeliever during a time of peace shall not enter Paradise.**" Another hadîth-i-sherîf reads: "**When two Muslims fight for worldly interests, both the killed one and the killer shall go to Hell.**" It is stated in a hadîth-i-sherîf in the three

---

[1] This letter occupies the fifteenth chapter of the third fascicle of **Endless Bliss**.

– 36 –

hundred and seventeenth sinful act: "**A person who perpetrates cruelty to people shall be tormented for it on the Rising Day**." So is the case with perpetrating cruelty to non-Muslims. In a hadîth-i-sherîf in the three hundred and fiftieth sinful act: "**There are three people whose invocations shall definitely be accepted: The wronged person, the guest, and parents**." And in another one: "**A wronged person's invocation shall not be refused even if he is a disbeliever**." In a hadîth-i-sherîf in the four hundred and second sinful act: "**A person who kills his friend is not from our community, even if his friend is a disbeliever**." In a hadîth-i-sherîf in the four hundred and ninth sinful act: "**Of all sins, rising against one's government is the one whose torment shall be given most rapidly**." This is the end of our translation from **Zewâjir**. O Muslim! If you wish to attain the grace of Allâhu ta'âlâ and your acts of worship to be accepted, inscribe the hadîth-i-sherîfs quoted above in your heart! Do not attack anyone's property, life, or chastity. Muslims and non-Muslims alike! Do not hurt anyone! Pay people their rights! It is one of the rights of quls for a man to pay 'mahr'[1] to the woman he has divorced. If he does not pay it, he will deserve vehement punishment both in the world and in the Hereafter. The most important one of the rights of quls, (i.e. rights of human beings and other creatures,) which therefore incurs the severest torment (when violated), is to cease teaching Islam to one's kinsfolk, especially if they are under one's care and protection. If a person prevents them and other people from learning Islam and from practising their acts of worship by way of persecution and deceit, it will be concluded that that person is an unbeliever, an enemy of Islam. An example of this irreligious attitude is to attempt to pollute the teachings of Ahl as-Sunnat and thereby to defile the Islamic religion, a strategy pursued by holders of bid'at and by people without a certain Madhhab by making subversive statements and writing seditious articles. Do not stand against the government or against laws. Pay your taxes. That it is a sinful behaviour to revolt against the government, be it a cruel and or fasiq one, is written in the book entitled **Berîqa**, (which was written by Muhammad bin Mustafâ Hâdimî 'rahmatullâhi ta'âlâ 'alaih', d. 1176 [1762 A.D.], Hâdim, Konya, Turkey.) Even if you are in the dâr-ul-harb, i.e. in one of the countries of disbelievers, do not violate their laws and mandates! Do not arouse fitna! Do

---

[1] Please scan the twelfth chapter of the fifth fascicle, and also the fifteenth chapter of the sixth fascicle, of **Endless Bliss**.

not make friends with people who attack Islam, with holders of bid'at, or with people who are not in one of the four Madhhabs! Do not read their books or newspapers! Do not let their radio and television programs enter your homes! Perform **Amr-i-ma'rûf**, (i.e. teach Islam,) to people who will listen to you! In other words, give them advice with a smile and sweet words! With your beautiful moral behaviour, show the grandeur and honour of the Islamic religion to all people around you!

Ibni 'Âbidîn[1] 'rahima-hullâhu ta'âlâ' states as follows in the first volume: "Sev'eteyn (or saw'atayn), i.e. genital and anal areas, is ghalîdh (qaba) awrat in all four Madhhabs.[2] It is farz in all four Madhhabs to cover these private parts. A person who does not attach importance to covering them will become an unbeliever. A man with exposed knees must be (advised, i.e. he must be) made Amr-i-ma'rûf to, so that he should cover his knees. The amr-i-ma'rûf, however, ought to be performed with soft words. And an obstinate reaction on his part must be answered with silence. Obstinacy on the part of a man with exposed thighs, on the other hand, must be reprimanded. If a man with exposed sev'eteyn reacts with obstinacy (to your admonitory remarks), then he must be complained about to the court of justice so that he should be forced [by way of battery or imprisonment] to cover them. The same order of priority applies to the exacerbation of the sinfulness of looking at a man's awrat parts." It is farz in all four Madhhabs for women to cover all their bodies with the exception of their hands and faces to nâ-mahram men and to non-Muslim women, which means that they have to cover their legs, arms, and hair in the presence of such people, (i.e. nâ-mahram men and non-Muslim women.) (Nâ-mahram people for either sex are written in the twelfth chapter of the fifth fascicle of **Endless Bliss**.) In the Shâfi'î Madhhab, also not to show their faces (to aforesaid people) is farz. If they, or their fathers or their husbands, do not attach importance to this injunction, they will become unbelievers. It is a grave sin for

---

[1] A scholar of Fiqh, whose real name is Sayyid Muhammad Emîn bin 'Umar bin 'Abd-ul-'Azîz (1198 [1784 A.D.], Damascus – 1252 [1836], the same place). He wrote the five-volumed book entitled **Radd-ul-muhtâr** as an annotation to the book entitled **Durr-ul-mukhtâr**, which in turn had been written by **'Alâ-ud-dîn Haskafî** 'rahmatullâhi ta'âlâ 'alaih' (1021, Haskaf – 1088 [1677]). Most of the teachings of Fiqh, which occupies a hundred and thirty chapters of the six fascicles of **Endless Bliss**, have been taken from **Radd-ul-muhtâr**.

[2] Please see the eighth chapter of the fourth fascicle of **Endless Bliss**.

boys to dance or play games with their calves and legs exposed and for girls to do so without covering their heads and arms as well, and to watch them doing so. A Muslim should not waste his or her free time by playing games or doing useless things, but they should benefit it by learning and by performing namâz. It is stated in **Kimyâ-i-sa'âdat**: "As it is harâm for women and girls to go out with their heads, hair, arms and legs exposed, it is likewise harâm for them to go out clad as they are in thin, ornamented, tight, and perfumed garments. Their parents, husbands, and brothers who countenance, condone and like their doing so will be their accomplices in the sinful act and will therefore get a share from the torment." In other words, they will burn together in Hell. If they make tawba, they will be forgiven and will not be burned. Allâhu ta'âlâ likes people who make tawba.

ZAWJÂT and GHAZAWÂT-I-PEYGAMBERÎ
The Blessed Wives and the Holy Wars of the Prophet

Rasûlullah 'sall-Allâhu 'alaihi wa sallam' was forty years old, when the angel named Jebrâîl came to him and told him that he was the Prophet. Three years later he declared his Prophethood, in Mekka. That year is called the year of **Bi'that**. He made jihâd (holy war) twenty-seven times. In nine of them he attacked as a private. In eighteen holy wars he was the commander in chief. He had four sons, four daughters, eleven wives, twelve paternal uncles, and six paternal aunts. He was twenty-five years old when he made nikâh with Khadîja-t-ul-kubrâ. One year after the passing of Khadîja-t-ul-kubrâ, when he was fifty-five years old, that is, he made nikâh, as he was commanded by Allâhu ta'âlâ, with 'Âisha, Abû Bakr's 'radiy-Allâhu 'anh' daughter. And he was sixty-three years old when he passed away in her room, which was adjacent to the Masjîd (or Mesjîd, shortened name of Mesjîd-i-Nebî or Masjîd-i-Nabî). He was buried in the same room. Abû Bakr and 'Umar 'radiy-Allâhu 'anhum' also were buried in this room. As the Mesjîd was being widened, the room was included in the Mesjîd. In the seventh year (of the Hegira), he made nikâh with, (i.e. he married,) Umm-i-Habîba, who was the daughter of Abû Sufyân bin Harb, chief of the Qoureish unbelievers in Mekka. Abû Sufyân is the father of Mu'âwiya 'radiy-Allâhu 'anh'. He became a Believer at the conquest of Mekka. He, (i.e. Rasûlullah,) made nikâh with Hafsa, who was 'Umar's 'radiy-Allâhu 'anh' daughter.

In the fifth year of the Hegira (Hijrat), he bought Juwayriyya, who was among the slaves captured from the Benî Mustalaq tribe (in the Holy war of **Mureysî**) and was the daughter of the chief, manumitted her, and then made nikâh with her, (i.e. he married her with a marriage contract prescribed by Islam and which is called 'nikâh', and which is explained in detail in the twelfth chapter of the fifth fascicle of **Endless Bliss**.) For religious incentives he made nikâh with Umm-Salama, Sevda, Zeyneb binti Huzeyma, Meymûna, and Safiyya 'radiy-Allâhu 'anhunna'. As for Zeyneb (or Zaynab), his paternal uncle's daughter; his nikâh with her was made by Allâhu ta'âlâ.

Jebrâîl ''alaihis-salâm' came to him twenty-four thousand times. He was fifty-two years old when he was taken up to (Heaven in an event termed) Mi'râj.[1] At the age of fifty-three he migrated from Mekka to Medîna, (an event which is called Hijrat or Hegira.) He and Abû Bakr stayed in a cave on mount Sawr (or Sevr) for three nights, and left the cave late Monday night. After a week's trudge, they arrived at Kubâ, a village of Medîna, on the twentieth of September; it was Monday then. And it was the following Friday when they entered Medîna.

The Holy War of Bedr (or Badr) was fought in the second year of the Hijrat, on a Monday in the blessed month of Ramadân. Versus the three hundred and thirteen Muslim soldiers, eight of whom were on duties elsewhere, there were a thousand Qoureishis. Thirteen Sahâbîs attained martyrdom. Abû Jahl and seventy other unbelievers were slain.

The Holy War of 'Uhud was fought during the month of Shewwâl in the third year of the Hegira. Seven hundred Muslim soldiers were against a three thousand strong army of unbelievers. Seventy of the Ashâb-i-kirâm became martyrs. Four months after the Holy War of 'Uhud, seventy young Sahâbîs were sent to the inhabitants of Nejd on a mission to invite them to Islam. When they reached at a place called **Bi'ri Me'ûna**, they were ambushed and the entire group, with the exception of two Sahâbîs, were martyred.

The fifth Hegiral year witnessed the Holy War termed Hendek (Trench). Versus the ten thousand unbelievers, there were three

---

[1] There is detailed information about Mi'râj in the sixtieth chapter of the third fascicle of **Endless Bliss**.

thousand Muslims. The unbelievers besieged Medîna. The Muslims had already dug a trench around Medîna. A year before the Holy War of Hayber, which took place in the seventh year, an agreement called **Bî'at-ur-ridwân** was made at a place named Hudeybiya. The Holy War of Mûta is a jihâd made against the Byzantine Caesar Heraclius. There were three thousand Muslims against a hundred thousand strong Byzantine army. Ja'fer Tayyâr 'radiy-Allâhu 'anh' attained martyrdom in this war. The war was won by Khâlid bin Walîd. Mekka was conquered in the eighth year. **Huneyn** is a renowned and grand Holy War. It ended in victory. **Hayber** is a widely known Jewish fortress. Rasûlullah sent Hadrat 'Alî, and the fortress was conquered. It was in that place where Rasûlullah was offered poisoned food, which he refused to eat. As they were on their way back from a Holy War, Hadrat 'Âisha became the target of an ignoble calumny, which saddened the Messenger of Allah very much. Âyat-i-kerîmas came down, whereby it was found out that the calumny was a monstrous lie. Also renowned is the victory of Tâif.

> *If you want happiness, o, young man,*
> *Hold fast to Islam, my child, constantly.*
>
> *Its farz, wâjib, sunnat, and mandûb,*
> *And also amr-i-bi-l-ma'rûf thoroughly.*
>
> *Always perform them, none of them missing,*
> *Grave and venial ones alike, perfectly.*
>
> *It is a must, also, to avoid makrûhs and harâms,*
> *Rights of quls must be shunned, particularly.*
>
> *Learn from the Ahl as-Sunnat, outright!*
> *Practise what you have learned, immediately!*

CONCERNING THE DETAILS of ÎMÂN

There are twelve details of îmân: My Rabb is Allâhu ta'âlâ. My proof-text is the hundred and sixty-third âyat-i-kerîma of Baqara Sûra. My Prophet is Hadrat Muhammad ''alaihi-s-salâm'. My proof texts are the twenty-eighth and the twenty-ninth âyat-i-kerîmas of Fat-h Sûra. My religion is the religion of Islam. My proof-text is Allâhu ta'âlâ's nineteenth âyat-i-kerîma in Âl-i-'Imrân Sûra. My Book is the Qur'ân-i-'adhîm-ush-shân. My proof-text is the second âyat-i-kerîma of Baqara Sûra. My Qibla is the Kâ'ba-i-sherîf. My proof-text is the hundred and forty-fourth âyat-i-kerîma of Baqara Sûra.

My Madhhab in i'tiqâd (îmân) is **Ahl as-Sunnat wa-l-jamâ'at**. My proof-text is the hundred and fifty-third âyat-i-kerîma of An'am Sûra.

My (earliest) ancestor is Hadrat 'Âdam. My proof-text is the hundred and seventy-second âyat-i-kerîma in A'râf Sûra.

My Millat is Millat-i-islâm. My proof-text is the seventy-eighth âyat-i-kerîma of Hajj Sûra.

I am one of the Ummat of Muhammad ''alaihis-salâm'. My proof text is the hundred and tenth âyat-i-kerîma of Âl-i-'Imrân.

I am a Mu'min (Believer), haqqan (by right). My proof-text is the fourth âyat-i-kerîma in Anfâl Sûra. Al-hamdu lillâhi 'ala-t-tawfîqihi wa-s-taghfirullâha min kulli taqsîrin.

'Ilm is higher than 'amal for five reasons: For, 'ilm is depended on whereas 'amal is dependent on it. 'Ilm is necessary whereas 'amal is inseparable from it. 'Ilm can give benefit by itself, whereas 'amal without 'ilm cannot give benefit.

'Ilm is higher than 'aql (mind). For, the former is qadîm (perpetual), whereas the latter is hâdith, (i.e. it came into existence from nothing.)

The zînat (ornament) of man stays with ikhlâs. The zînat of ikhlâs stays with îmân. The zînat of îmân stays with Jannat (Paradise). The zînat of Jannat stays with hûrîs, ghilmâns, and seeing Jemâlullah, (i.e. seeing Allâhu ta'âlâ in a manner that cannot be understood or defined.)

Also, if 'amal were a part from îmân, a menstruating woman would not be absolved from the daily namâz. For, îmân cannot be absolved from.

It is farz to say the Kalima-i-shehâdat (at least) once in one's life time. Its proof-text is the nineteenth âyat-i-kerîma in Muhammad Sûra.

There are four conditions to be fulfilled when saying the Kalima-i-shehâdat: Presence of heart as the tongue utters it. Knowledge of its meaning. Saying it with a sincere heart. Saying it with ta'dhîm (reverence, treating as great).

There are some hundred and thirty benefits in saying the Kalima-i-shehâdat. However, existence of four things will eliminate all its benefits. The four things are: Shirk, shek, teshbîh, and ta'til. Shirk means to attribute a partner to Allâhu ta'âlâ. Shek means meks (to halt, to pause, uncertainty) in the religion. Teshbîh means to liken Allâhu ta'âlâ to an imaginary creature. Ta'til means to (believe and) say that "Allah does not interfere with beings and that everything comes to being on their own when their time comes."

And also, thirty of the hundred and thirty benefits have been listed in this text. Here are the thirty benefits, five of which are in the world, the next five are at the time of death, the next five are in the grave, the next five are at (the place called) Arasât, the next five are in Hell, and the last five are in Paradise. The five benefits in the world are:

1– One's name will be called beautifully.

2– The Ahkâm-i-islâmiyya will be farz (incumbent) on one.

3– One's neck will be safe against the sword.

4– Allâhu 'adhîm-ush-shân will be pleased with one.

5– All Believers will be affectionate towards one.

The five benefits at the time of death are:

1– 'Azrâîl ''alaihis-salâm' (angel of Death) will come onto one in a beautiful guise.

2– The angel will extract one's soul as softly and easily as you would pull a hair out of butterfat.

3– Odours from Jannat (Paradise) will reach there.

4– One's soul will ascend to the 'Illiyyîn (the highest of the eight Gardens of Jannat), and angels carrying good news will come there.

5– A voice will say: "Merhabâ (Hello), o Believer! You are destined for Jannat.

The five benefits in one's grave are:

1– One's grave will be spacious.

2– The (questioning angels named) Munker and the Nekir will come onto one in a beautiful guise.

3– An angel will coach one on what one does not know.

4– Allâhu 'adhîm-ush-shân will inspire into one's memory what one does not know.

5– One will see one's abode in Jannat.

The five benefits at Arasât are:

1– The questioning and calling to account that one is going to experience will be made easy.

2– One's book of deeds, (i.e. a verbatim record of whatsoever one did and said throughout one's lifetime,) will be given to one from one's right-hand side.

3– One's thawâb will weigh heavier on the scales.

4– One will sit in the shade of the 'Arsh-i-Rahmân.

5– One will pass the (bridge called) Sirat as fast as lightning.

The five benefits in Hell are:

1– Should one enter Hell, one's eyes will not be turned gray like those of the other people of Hell.

2– One will not quarrel with one's Satan.

3– One's hands will not be cuffed with cuffs of fire, nor will one be chained (with fetters of fire) around one's neck.

4– One will not be made to drink water called Hamîm (extremely hot water).

5– One will not stay eternally in Hell.

The five benefits in Jannat are:

1– All angels will greet one.

2– One will be befriended by Siddîqs.

3– Jannat will be one's eternal abode.

4– Allâhu ta'âlâ will be pleased with one.

5– One will attain the greatest one of all blessings by seeing Allâhu ta'âlâ.

[Qâdî-zâda Ahmad Efendi (1133–1197 [1783 A.D.]) states as follows in his **sharh of Âmentu** entitled **Farâid-ul-Fawâid**: Hell is made up of seven layers, one below another. The fire of each layer is more fierce than that of the one above it. Muslims with unforgiven sins will be burned in the first layer as long as they deserve on account of their sins; then they will be taken out of Hell and will be taken to Jannat. The other six layers are for various disbelievers to be burned. Munâfiqs will be burned in the seventh layer, the one with the most fierce torment. They are the double-faced unbelievers, who are, in words, admirers of Islam and yet, in heart, abject infidels. When disbelievers are burned to ashes, they will be created anew and burned again, a burning process that will continue forever. Jannat and Jahannam (Hell) exist now.

According to some Islamic scholars, the whereabouts of Hell is not known. According to others, it is below the seven layers of ground. These words of theirs show that it is not within the earth. Since the earth and the sun and all the stars are in the first heaven [sky], wheresoever on the earth we are, there is a heaven below the seven layers of ground. Hence, Hell must be in one of the seven layers of heaven.]

CAUSES of DISBELIEF (KUFR)

There are three kinds of kufr, [i.e. enmity toward Allah:] Kufr-i-inâdî, kufr-i-jehlî (or jahlî), and kufr-i-hukmî.

Kufr-i-inâdî is the stubborn denial of Islam and îmân by a person who does so knowingly, e.g. kufr of people such as Abû Jahl, Fir'awn (Pharaoh), Nemrûd (Nimrod), and Sheddâd (Shaddâd bin Ad). It is permissible to say outright that they are people of Hell.

Kufr-i-jehlî: As the disbelievers among common people know that Islam is the right religion and hear the azân-i-Muhammadî being performed, if you say to them, "Come on, become Muslims," they will reply, "Our way of life is what we learned from our forefathers and families. Likewise shall we carry on."

Kufr-i-hukmî means tahqîr (treating with contempt) instead of ta'dhîm (treating as great) and ta'dhîm instead of tahqîr.

It is also kufr to treat the Awliyâ and the Anbiyâ (Prophets) and the 'Ulamâ (Scholars) of Allâhu 'adhîm-ush-shân and their statements and books of Fiqh and fatwâs with contempt instead of treating them as great. As well, it is kufr to like disbelievers' religious rites and to wear zunnâr (a rope girdle worn by a priest) without darûrat to do so and to wear a priestly hood and other signs of kufr such as a cross.

Kufr causes seven harms: It eliminates faith and nikâh. Edible animals killed by that person cannot be eaten, (even if he has jugulated the animal agreeably with all the rules dictated by Islam.) What he has done with his halâl becomes fornication. It becomes wâjib to kill that person. Jannat gets away from him. Hell becomes close to him. If he dies in that state (of kufr), the namâz of janâza will not be performed for him.

If a person says of his own volition, "So and so has (or does not have) such and such. May I be a kâfir (disbeliever) if I am wrong," he has sworn an oath dragging him into kufr, regardless of whether or not the person named has the specified object. Tejdîd (renewal) of his îmân and nikâh is necessary.

Another act of kufr is to say, for instance, about an act which Islam prohibits, such as fornication, interest, and lying: "I wish it were halâl, so that I could commit it!"

If a person says, for instance: "I believe in Prophets ''alaihim-us-salawât-u-wa-t-teslîmât'. But I don't know if 'Âdam ''alaihis-salâm' is a Prophet," he becomes a kâfir. A person who does not know that Hadrat Muhammad ''alaihis-salâm' is the final Prophet, becomes a kâfir.

As has been stated by Islamic scholars, if a person says: "If what Prophets ''alaihim-us-salawât-u-wa-t-teslîmât' said is true, then we have attained salvation," he becomes a kâfir. Birgivî 'rahmatullâhi 'alaih' says: "If that person says so as an expression of doubt, he becomes a kâfir. He does not become a kâfir if he says so by way of ilzâm (convincing in argument)."

It has been stated (by Islamic scholars) that if a person is invited to perform namâz together and replies that he won't he becomes a kâfir. However, he does not become a kâfir if he means to say: "I will not perform namâz to act on your advice. I will do so because Allâhu ta'âlâ commands to do so."

If people say onto a certain person: "Do not grow your beard shorter than a small handful –or shorten it so as to make it only as long as a small handful, or pare your nails–, for it is a Sunnat of Rasûlullah's 'sall-Allâhu ta'âlâ 'alaihi wa sallam'," and if that person says, "No, I won't (do what you say)," he becomes a kâfir. The same rule applies concerning all other acts of Sunnat, provided that it should be known commonly and by way of tawâtur that the act in question is an act of Sunnat. An example of this is (brushing the teeth with) Miswâk (before or when making an ablution). Hadrat Birgivî[1] adds the following explanation at this point: "It will be kufr if he says so in a way of denying the act of Sunnat. Yet it will not be kufr if he means to say: I shall not do as you say only because you say so. Yet I will do so because it is a Sunnat of Rasûlullah's."

[Yûsuf Qardâwî (or Kardâvî) states as follows in the eighty-first

---

[1] Zeyn-ud-dîn Muhammad Birgivî Efendi 'rahmatullâhi ta'âlâ 'alaih' (928 [1521 A.D.], Balıkesir – 981 [1573], Birgi, d. of plague).

page of the fourth edition of his book entitled **Al-halâl wa-l-harâm fî-l-islâm**: A hadîth-i-sherîf quoted in the book entitled **Bukhârî-i-sherîf** (or **Jâmi-i-sahîh**[1] reads: "**Behave in opposition to mushriks** (polytheists, disbelievers)! **Grow your beard! Pare your moustache!**" This hadîth-i-sherîf prohibits to shave your beard and to make it shorter than a small handful. Fire-worshippers would cut their beard. In fact, some of them shaved their beard. This hadîth-i-sherîf commands us to act contrary to their custom. Some scholars of Fiqh said that this hadîth-i-sherîf shows that it is wâjib to grow a beard and that it is harâm to shave one's beard. One of them, namely Ibni Taymiyya, writes quite vehemently against cutting one's beard. According to some other Islamic scholars, on the other hand, it is a customary act, not an act of worship to grow a beard. The book entitled Fat-h quotes Iyâd as saying that it is makrûh to shave one's beard [without an 'udhr to do so]. That is thruth of the matter. This hadîth-i-sherîf cannot be said to show that it is wâjib to grow a beard. For, it is stated in a hadîth-i-sherîf: "**Jews and Christians do not dye** [their hair and beard]. **Do the opposite of what they do!**" In other words, the hadîth-i-sherîf says to dye (your hair and beard). This hadîth-i-sherîf does not show that it is wâjib to dye one's hair and beard. It shows that it is mustahab to do so. For, some of the Ashâb-i-kirâm dyed their hair and beard. Most of them, however, did not do so. All of them would have done so if it had been an act of wâjib to do so. So is the case with the hadîth-i-sherîf that commands to grow a beard; it shows that it is mustahab to grow a beard, not that it is wâjib to do so. None of the Islamic scholars have been reported to have shaved their beard. For, growing a beard was customary in their time. [It incurs notoriety not to follow Muslims' customary acts. It is makrûh. It will be harâm if it arouses fitna.] Here we end our translation from Qardâwî. In the introduction of his book, Qardâwî writes that he mixes the teachings of Fiqh of the four Madhhabs with one another and that it is not something justifiable to adapt oneself to a single Madhhab. Thereby he deviates from the way guided by the scholars of Ahl as-Sunnat. The scholars of Ahl as-Sunnat 'rahima-humullâhu ta'âlâ' state that each and every Muslim has to imitate one of the four Madhhabs and that a person who commingles the Madhhabs will become a lâ-madhhabî person, a zindiq. However, because Qardâwî's written statements

---

[1] Compiled by Muhammad bin Ismâ'îl Bukhârî 'rahmatullâhi ta'âlâ 'alaih' (194 [810 A.D.], Bukhâra – 256 [870], Samarkand).

concerning beard-growing are in keeping with the teachings of the Hanafî Madhhab in this respect, it has been deemed apropos to refer the readers to them as evidential informants. Hadrat 'Abd-ul-Haqq-i-Dahlawî 'rahmatullâhi ta'âlâ 'alaih' (958 [1551 A.D.] – 1052 [1642], Delhî) states as follows in the third volume of **Eshi'at-ul-leme'ât**: "Islamic scholars followed the local custom of the place they lived in concerning hair and beard-dying. For, it incurs notoriety not to follow the custom of one's locality [in matters that are mubâh, permissible], which, in turn, is makrûh." Muhammad bin Mustafâ Hâdimî 'rahima-hullâhu ta'âlâ' (d. 1176 [1762 A.D.], Hâdim, Konya, Turkey) states in his book entitled **Berîqa**: "It is stated in a hadîth-i-sherîf: '**Grow your moustache short and your beard long**.' Therefore, it has been prohibited to shave one's beard or to grow it shorter than a small handful. It is sunnat to grow one's beard until it becomes as long as a small handful. It is sunnat also to pare it when it becomes longer than a small handful." A small handful is a length equal to the sum of four finger widths, beginning with the lower side of the lower lip. When the Sultân commands something that is sunnat, even if it is something that is mubâh (permissible), it becomes wâjib to do it. Its being done by the Sultân and by all Muslims means a command. At such places it is wâjib to grow one's beard as long as a small handful. To grow it shorter than a small handful or to shave it means to abandon something that is wâjib. It is makrûh tahrîmî. (Please see the next chapter for terms such as wâjib, makrûh, etc.) It is not permissible for a person who does so to be imâm in a mosque (and to conduct namâz in jamâ'at). In the Dâr-ul-harb, however, it is permissible, nay, it is a must to shave your beard lest you should be persecuted or (lose your job, which in effect means to) be unable to make a living and/or so that you can perform amr-i-ma'rûf, serve Muslims and Islam, and protect your faith and chastity. Without an 'udhr, it is makrûh to shorten or shave it. And it is bid'at to (continuously) have a beard shorter than a small handful and to believe that thereby you are performing an act of sunnat. It means to change the sunnat. Committing an act of bid'at is a sin graver than homicide.]

Supposing a girl and a boy reached the age of discretion and puberty, they were married under the contract of nikâh, and yet they failed to answer a question asked concerning the attributes of îmân, that would mean that they were not Muslims. The nikâh between them would be sahîh only after their being taught the tenets of îmân and thereafter their contract of nikâh being renewed. Please see the chapter dealing with the fifty-four fards (or farâid).

If a person pares his moustache and another person, who is with him, says, "It's no good," it is feared that the latter may lose his îmân. For, it is an act of sunnat to shorten one's moustache, and that (latter) person has taken an act of sunnat lightly.

If a person wears silk –which covers his entire body from head to foot– and another person sees him and says, "May you be blessed with it," it is feared that he, (i.e. the latter,) may lose his îmân.

If a person commits an act of makrûh, such as lying with one's feet extended towards the Qibla and spitting or urinating in the direction of Qibla, if thereupon other people try to dissuade him from doing that act of makrûh and the admonished person says, "I wish all our sins were as venial as this," it is feared that he may lose his îmân. For, he has talked about makrûh in such a way as if it were an unimportant matter.

And also, if a person's servant enters his master's room and greets his master (by saying, "Selâmun 'alaikum, sir," and if a third person, who happens to be with his master in the room, chides the servant by saying, "Be quiet, you ill-mannered person! One simply does not greet one's master like that," that (third) person becomes a kâfir. However, if his purpose is to teach rules of decorum to the servant and means to say that the servant might as well do the greeting (silently) in his heart, then, evidently, his statement is not an act of kufr.

If a person backbites another and then replies others' dissuasive remarks, "I haven't done something important at all, have I," he has become a kâfir, according to scholars. For, he has commended an act of harâm, instead of denouncing it.

If a person says, "If Allâhu ta'âlâ gives me Paradise, I won't enter Paradise without you," or "If I am ordered to enter Paradise with so and so, I won't," or "If Allâhu ta'âlâ gives me Paradise, I will not want it, but I will prefer to see His dîdâr (beautiful countenance)," statements of this sort are acts of kufr, according to scholars. Another statement that is said (by scholars) to be an act of kufr is to say that îmân will increase or decrease. According to Birgivî, it is kufr to say that it will increase or decrease with respect to **mu'minun bih**, yet it is not kufr to say so with respect to yaqîn and quwwat-i-sidq. For, many mujtahids spoke on the abundance and paucity of îmân.

Scholars said that it is kufr to say, "There are two Qiblas. One of them is the Kâ'ba and the other one is Jerusalem." According to Birgivî, it is kufr to say that there are two Qiblas now, and yet it is not kufr to say, "Bayt-i-muqaddes was the Qibla. Afterwards Kâ'ba became the Qibla."

If a person hates or swears at an Islamic scholar, it is feared that he may become a kâfir, if he does so without any reason.

It is kufr to say or to believe that kâfirs' acts of worship and rites disagreeable with Islam are lovely.

Scholars have said that if a person says that not to talk when eating is one of the good customs of magians or that it is one of the good deeds of magians not to go to bed with one's wife during menstruation or lochia, he becomes a kâfir.

If a person ask another person if he is a Believer and the latter replies, "Inshâ-Allah ...," it causes kufr if he is incapable of explaining it.

Scholars have said that if a person says to a person bereaved of his son, "Your son is a must for Allâhu ta'âlâ," he becomes a kâfir.

If a woman who wears a black girdle around her waist says that it is a zunnâr when she is asked what it is, she becomes a kâfir and becomes harâm for her husband.

They have said that a person who says, "Bismillah ...," when eating food that is harâm becomes a kâfir. Hadrat Birgivî says: "As far as this faqîr understands, that person will become a kâfir if what he eats is harâm li-'aynihî, [e.g. wine, unclean meat or fat such as that of an animal that died of itself.] However, this rule applies only when that person knows that what he eats is harâm li-'aynihî, (i.e. food which Islam prohibits to eat.) By doing so he will have taken the Name of Allâhu ta'âlâ lightly. For, things of that sort are harâm themselves. As has been reported by our Imâms (Islamic Guides), If a person says, "Bismillah," as he eats the food which he has obtained by extortion. For, the food itself is not harâm. It is the extortion that is harâm."[1] If a person utters a curse against another by saying, "May Allâhu ta'âlâ take away your soul in a state of kufr," Islamic scholars have not been unanimous on whether that person, (i.e. the one who utters the curse,) will

---

[1] To avoid misunderstanding on this subtle subject, please read the first chapter of the sixth fascicle of **Endless Bliss**, which is available from Hakîkat Kitâbevi, Fâtih, Istanbul, Turkey.

become a kâfir. As a matter of fact, it is kufr for a person to approve of his own kufr –Islamic scholars are unanimous on that. As for approval of someone else's kufr; it is still kufr according to some Islamic scholars, while other Islamic scholars say that it will be kufr if the approval is of kufr itself. But it is not kufr if the approval is on account of wickedness and fisq (sinfulness)– so that the torment to be inflicted should be perpetual and fierce. Birgivî 'rahima-hullâhu ta'âlâ' states: "We understand this qawl (scholarly judgement) as essential. For, the true story of Hadrat Mûsâ ''alaihis-salâm' in the Qur'ân al-kerîm is a proof-text for it."

If a person says, "Allâhu ta'âlâ knows that I did not do such and such an act," although he himself knows that he did it, he becomes a kâfir. For, (by saying so) he has imputed ignorance in guise of wisdom to Hadrat Haqq ta'âlâ.

If a person marries a woman by making a nikâh [without any witnesses] and then both the man and the woman say that Allâhu ta'âlâ and the Prophet are their witnesses, both of them become kâfirs. For, our Prophet 'sall-Allâhu ta'âlâ 'alaihi wa sallam' did not know the ghayb (unknown) when he was alive. It is kufr to say that he knows the ghayb.

If a person says that he knows stolen and lost property, he himself and also those who believe him become kâfirs. If he says that genies are informing him, he becomes a kâfir again. Prophets and genies do not know the ghayb, either. Allâhu ta'âlâ, alone, knows the ghayb, and so do those who are informed by Him.

As is stated by scholars, if a person wants to swear an oath by Allâhu ta'âlâ and yet another person dissuades him by saying, "I do not want you to swear an oath on Allâhu ta'âlâ. I want an oath sworn on things such as divorce, emancipation of a slave, honour, and chastity," the latter becomes a kâfir.

If a person says to another, "Your countenance reminds me of the Angel of Death," he becomes a kâfir. For, the Angel of Death is a grand angel.

A person who says, "How nice it is not to perform namâz," becomes a kâfir. As is stated by Islamic scholars, if a person says to another, "Come on and perform namâz," and the latter replies, "It is difficult for me to perform namâz," the latter becomes a kâfir.

If a person says, "Allâhu ta'âlâ is my witness in heaven," he becomes a kâfir, because he has ascribed a place for Allâhu ta'âlâ. Allâhu ta'âlâ is free from having a place. [Also, a person who calls

Allâhu ta'âlâ 'father' becomes a kâfir.]

If a person says, "Rasûlullah 'sall-Allâhu ta'âlâ 'alaihi wa sallam' would lick his blessed finger after eating," and another person says that it is ill-mannered behaviour to do so, the latter becomes a kâfir.

If a person says, "Rizq (food) comes from Allâhu ta'âlâ, yet the qul's (i.e. born slave's) motion is necessary, too," his statement is an act of polytheism. For, man's movements also are created by Allâhu ta'âlâ.

If a person says that it is better to be a Nasrânî than being a Jew, [or that being an American kâfir is better than being a communist,] he becomes a kâfir. One should rather say, for instance, that a Jew is worse than a Nasrânî or [that a communist is more wicked] than a Christian.

If a person says that being a kâfir is preferable to treachery, he becomes a kâfir.

If a person says, "What is my business in an assembly of 'ilm (knowledge)," or "Who could ever do what 'ulama (Islamic scholars) say," or throws a (written) fatwâ down to the ground or says, "Words of religious people are no good," he becomes a kâfir.

If a person says to someone with whom he has a dispute, "Let's apply to the Shar' (Islamic court)," and the latter replies, "I won't go there unless the police take me," or "How do I know Islam," the latter becomes a kâfir.

If a person says something that causes kufr, (he) and also anyone who laughs at it become kâfirs. The latter's laugh will not be kufr if it has been darûrî (inevitable, involuntary, ineluctable).

If a person says, "There is no [empty] space unoccupied by Allah," or "Allâhu ta'âlâ is in heaven," he becomes a kâfir, according to Islamic scholars.

A person who says that souls of the meshâikh are always present and they know, becomes a kâfir. It will not be kufr to say that they will be present.

A person who says, "I do not know (or want) Islam," becomes a kâfir.

If a person says, "If 'Âdam ''alaihis-salâm' had not eaten wheat, we would not have become shaqîs (sinners, evil-doers)," he becomes a kâfir. However, Islamic scholars are not unanimous on his kufr if he says, "... we would not be on the earth now."

If a person says that 'Âdam ''alaihis-salâm' would weave cloth and another person says, "Then we are sons of a weaver," the latter becomes a kâfir.

If a person commits a venial sin and says to a person who tells him to make tawba, "What sin have I committed to make a tawba for," he becomes a kâfir.

If a person says to another, "Come along, let's go to an Islamic scholar," or "Let's read books of Fiqh and 'Ilm-i-hâl and learn," and the latter replies, "What is my business with 'ilm (knowledge)," the latter becomes a kâfir. For, (in effect) it means contempt for 'ilm. A person who insults, despises, or discredits books of Tafsîr and/or Fiqh, becomes a kâfir. Implacable kâfirs who attack these valuable books written by scholars of one of the four Madhhabs, are called 'sham scientists' or 'zindiqs'.

If a person does not know how to answer questions such as, "Whose progeny are you?", "Whose millat do you belong to?", "Who is the Imâm of your Madhhab in i'tiqâd?" and "Who is the Imâm of your Madhhab in 'amal (acts of worship)?", he becomes a kâfir.

As has been stated by Islamic scholars, if a person says, "Halâl," about a harâm-i-qat'iyya (something that is definitely harâm) –such as wine and pork–, or says, "harâm," about a halâl-i-qat'iyya (something that is definitely halâl), he becomes a kâfir. [It is dangerous to say that tobacco is harâm.][1]

It is kufr to wish that a certain harâm act were made halâl if that act has been made harâm (prohibited) in all religions (dispensations) and if it would have been contradictory to hikmat to make that thing halâl. Examples of this are fornication, sodomy, eating after having been satiated with food, and taking and giving interest. It is not kufr to wish that wine were made halâl. For, wine was not harâm in all (the past) dispensations. It is kufr to make use of the Qur'ân al-kerîm amidst words and jokes. If a person says to someone named Yahyâ, "Yâ Yahyâ! Huz-il-kitâba," he becomes a kâfir. For, he has made fun of the Qur'ân al-kerîm. The same rule applies to reading (or reciting) the Qur'ân al-kerîm to the accompaniment musical instruments or amidst dances or songs.

It is âfet[2] to say, "I have just arrived, Bismillâhi." If a person

---

[1] The fourth chapter of the sixth fascicle of **Endless Bliss** enlarges on tobacco and tobacco-smoking.

[2] Âfât is the plural form of âfet, whose lexical meaning is disaster, catastrophe, perdition.

says, "**Mâ khalaqallah**," upon seeing something that he deems too much, he becomes a kâfir if he does not know its meaning.

It is âfât to say, "I will not swear at you now, for they have named swearing 'a sin'."

It is âfât to say, "You have become stark naked like Jebrâîl's calf." For, it means to make fun of the Archangel.

It is harâm to swear an oath on anything other than Allâhu tebâraka wa ta'âlâ. A person will not become a murtadd or kâfir by committing a harâm act. Yet he will be a kâfir by saying halâl about a harâm that is mansûsun 'alaih, (i.e. that which has been declared to be harâm in the Nâss, which in turn means âyat-i-kerîmas and hadîth-i-sherîfs with clear meanings.)

And also, if a person swears on his son's head or on his own head by using the name of Allâhu ta'âlâ, e.g. if he says, "Wallahî by my son's head, it is feared that it may cause kufr".

THE AHKÂM-I-ISLÂMIYYA

Commandments and prohibitions of the Islamic religion are called the **Ahkâm-i-islâmiyya** or **Islam**, in the aggregate. The Ahkâm-i-islâmiyya is made up of eight components: **Farz** (or fard), **wâjib**, **sunnat**, **mustahab**, **mubâh**, **harâm**, **makrûh**, and **mufsid**.

Farz is a command of Allâhu 'adhîm-ush-shân. And that it is His command has been clarified by way of indubitable proof-texts. In other words, it has been clearly stated in âyat-i-kerîmas. A person who denies it or who does not attach due importance to it becomes a kâfir. Examples (of Allâhu ta'âlâ's commandments that are called farz) are: Îmân, the Qur'ân, to make ablution, to perform namâz, to pay zakât, to perform Hajj, to make ghusl from the state of junub, [i.e. to wash the entire body (in a manner taught by Islam).]

There are three kinds of farz: Fârz-i-dâim, farz-i-muwaqqat, and farz-i-'ala-l-kifâya. Farz-i-dâim is to memorize the entire (six-tenet credo which begins with) **Âmantu billâhi ...**, to know and believe its meaning, and to hold this belief perpetually. Farz-i-muwaqqat is any one of the commanded acts of worship which we perform when its prescribed time comes. Examples of it are to perform namâz five times daily, to fast in the blessed month of Ramadân, and to learn the technicalities of one's branch of art or trade. Farz-i-'ala-l-kifâya is a command of Allâhu from which an entire group of people, be there fifty, a hundred, and so forth of them, will be absolved when it is performed by one of them. An example of it is acknowledgement of a greeting.[1] Some other examples are to perform namâz of janâza, to wash the dead Muslim, to learn (the Arabic grammar called) sarf and nahw, to become a hâfidh, to learn (the branch of knowledge called) wujûb, and to learn religious and scientific knowledge more than one would need in one's branch of art or trade.

And also, there are five other farzes within a farz. These farzes are: 'Ilm-i-farz, 'amal-i-farz, miqdâr-i-farz, i'tiqâd-i-farz, ikhlâs-i-farz, and inkâr-i-farz. Inkâr-i-farz is kufr.

Wâjib is a command of Allâhu 'adhîm-ush-shân. However, that it is His command has been understood by way of ambiguous proof-texts. A person who denies that a certain act (which is stated to be wâjib) is wâjib, will not become a kâfir. However, not to perform it incurs torment in Hell. Examples of it are: To recite the prayer called Qunût during the performance of namâz of Witr, to perform (the act of wâjib called) Qurbân, (i.e. to kill the animal called Qurbân in a prescribed manner,) during the Hadjis' 'Iyd, to pay (the alms called) Fitra during the 'Iyd of Ramadân-i-sherîf, and to perform (the sajda termed) **Sajda-i-tilâwat** whenever you read or hear an âyat of sajda (prostration). There are four other wâjibs and one farz within a wâjib: 'Ilm-i-wâjib, 'amal-i-wâjib, miqdâr-i-wâjib, i'tiqâd-i-wâjib, and ikhlâs-i-farz. It is harâm to make a show of farz or wâjib.

Sunnat is an act (or worship) which Hadrat Rasûlullah 'sall-Allâhu 'alaihi wa sallam' omitted to do once or twice. A person who omits to do it will not be tormented (in the Hereafter). However, if a person who makes it a habit to omit it without any 'udhr (good reason) for his omission, he deserves 'itâb (reproach in the Hereafter), in addition to being deprived of its thawâb. Examples of it are: To use (the twig called) miswâk (to brush one's tooth), to perform azân (or adhân) and iqâmat, to perform namâz in jamâ'at, to serve a meal in the evening of one's wedding, and to have one's son(s) circumcised. There are three kinds of sunnat: Sunnat-i-muakkada, sunnat-i-ghayr-i-muakkada, and sunnat-i-'ala-l-kifâya.

Examples of sunnat-i-muakkada are: The sunnat of morning

_____

[1] Please see the sixty-second chapter of the third fascicle of **Endless Bliss**, which deals with greetings among Muslims.

prayer, the initial and final sunnats of early afternoon prayer, the sunnat of evening prayer, and the final sunnat of night prayer. These sunnats are sunnat-i-muakkada. There are Islamic scholars who say that the sunnat of morning prayer is wâjib. These sunnats can never be omitted without an 'udhr. A person who despises any one of them becomes a kâfir.

Examples of sunnat-i-ghayr-i-muakkada are: The sunnat of late afternoon prayer and the initial sunnat of night prayer. Omitting them for a number of time will not necessitate anything. However, never to do them will cause one to be reproached and to be deprived of shafâ'at (intercession in the Hereafter).

[As is written in **Halabî** and in **Qudûrî**, there are two categories of acts of worship: **Farâidh** and **Fadâil**. Acts of worship that are not farz or wâjib are called acts of worship that are **fadâil** or **nâfila** (supererogatory). The sunnats of the daily five prayers of namâz are in the category of nâfila worship, and they make up for the defects in the farzes. In other words, they compensate for the flaws in the performance of farz parts of the prayers. This should not lead us to the misunderstanding that a prayer that is sunnat can be substituted for an omitted farz prayer. Nor will performing a sunnat prayer save a person from torment in Hell which he has deserved by omitting a farz prayer. A sunnat prayer performed by a person who has omitted the farz prayer without an 'udhr will not be sahîh. Niyyat (intention) is necessary for a sunnat prayer that is sahîh, [i.e. that which is performed without a defect.] If niyyat is not made, the thawâb for the (performance of a) sunnat prayer will not be attained. Therefore, people who did not perform their daily five prayers of namâz for many years ought to make their niyyat both to make qadâ of the earliest prayers which they did not perform and to perform sunnat as they perform the sunnats of four of the daily prayers of namâz. When they make this niyyat they will both have made qadâ of the farz parts of their debts of namâz and performed the sunnat parts of their current daily namâz. Doing so does not mean to omit the sunnat.][1]

Sunnat-i-'ala-l-kifâya is the kind of sunnat wherefrom an entire group concerned will be absolved when it is performed by (at least) one person in the group. Greeting, (going into retreat that is called) i'tikâf, and saying the Basmala-i-sherîfa, (i.e. saying,

---

[1] Details on how to manage this double-niyyat performance is available from the twenty-third chapter of the fourth fascicle of **Endless Bliss**.

"Bismillâh-ir-Rahmân-ir-Rahîm,") when starting to do something permitted by Islam, are a few examples.

If a person does not say the Basmala-i-sherîfa when starting to eat, he will suffer three losses: 1– Satan will join him in eating. 2– The food he eats will turn into an illness in his body. 3– There will not be barakat in the food he eats.

If he says the Basmala-i-sherîfa, the food will give him three benefits: 1– The Satan will not get a share from the food. 2– The food he eats will become a healer in his body. 3– There will be barakat in the food. [If one forgets to say the Basmala when starting to eat, one should say it whenever one remembers to say it.]

Mustahab means something which Rasûlullah 'sall-Allâhu 'alaihi wa sallam' did once or twice throughout his lifetime. A person who does not perform it will not be tormented or reproached (in the Hereafter). Nor will he be deprived of shafâ'at (intercession in the Hereafter) for not performing it. Examples of it are: Performing nâfila (supererogatory) namâz, nâfila fasting, performing 'Umra, performing nâfila Hajj, and nâfila almsgiving.

Mubâh is an act (which is permissible and) which engenders thawâb when done with goodwill and causes torment (in the Hereafter) when done with ill-will. Omitting it will not incur torment. Walking, sitting, buying a house, eating all sorts of food that is halâl, and wearing all sorts of clothes, provided that they should be halâl ones.

Harâm is something which Allâhu 'adhîm-ush-shân plainly prohibits in the Qur'ân al-kerîm. In other words, it is one of the 'don'ts' that He declares in the Qur'ân al-kerîm. A person who takes a harâm lightly or denies it, becomes a kâfir. A person who commits a harâm although he believes that it is a harâm, does not become a kâfir. He becomes fâsiq. [Ibni 'Âbidîn 'rahima-hullâhu ta'âlâ' states as follows in his treatment of the subject pertaining to being an imâm:[1] "You should not perform namâz (in jamâ'at) being conducted by a fâsiq imâm. Fâsiq means (a Muslim) who commits a grave sin such as drinking wine, fornication, and taking interest. [A venial sin continuously committed worsens into a grave sin.] At places where Friday prayer is being performed in

---

[1] Imâm, in this context, is a Muslim who conducts namâz being performed in jamâ'at, which in turn is explained in detail in the twentieth chapter of the fourth fascicle of **Endless Bliss**.

more than one mosques, you should perform your Friday prayer in a mosque with a sâlih imâm, rather than in one with a fâsiq imâm. It is wâjib to treat a fâsiq person with betrayal and insult. However learned a fâsiq person may be, he should not be made an imâm. To make him an imâm would mean to treat him as if he were a great person and to respect him. If a person is fâsiq, as well as if he does not belong to any one of the (four) Madhhabs, it is makrûh tahrîmî to make him an imâm. It is called **taqwâ** to avoid harâms. It is **wara'** to avoid things which it is doubtful whether are halâls or harâms. And it is called **zuhd** to do without halâls lest you should do something doubtful. If a person becomes a Believer as he lives in the Dâr-ul-harb, it is wâjib for him to migrate to the Dâr-ul-islâm."]

There are two kinds of harâm: One of them is **harâm li-'aynihî**, and the other one is **harâm li-ghayrihî**. The former is harâm in essence; it is always harâm. Examples of it are: Homicide, fornication, sodomy, consumption of wine or other alcoholic beverages, gambling, eating pork, and women's and girls' going out with their heads, arms and legs exposed. If a person says the Basmala-i-sherîfa as he or she commits the aforesaid sins or believes them to be halâl, i.e. if he or she does not attribute importance to the fact that Allâhu ta'âlâ has made them harâm, that person becomes a kâfir. However, if such people commit these sins although they believe that they are harâm acts and therefore fear the torment that Allâhu ta'âlâ will inflict on them, they will not become kâfirs, yet they will deserve torment in Hell.

Harâm li-ghayrihî is something that becomes harâm because it has been obtained by way of harâm although it is not harâm in essence. Examples of it are: To enter someone's orchard, pick fruit, and eat them without the owner's permission, and to steal someone's household property or money and spend it. If a person who does so says the Basmala as he does so or says that it is halâl, he will not become a kâfir. If a person unjustly withholds someone else's property that weighs as heavy as a grain of barley, in the aftermath of life in this world Allâhu ta'âlâ will expropriate from that person the thawâb for seven hundred rak'ats of namâz which have been performed in jamâ'at —and which have been accepted (by Allâhu ta'âlâ). There is much more thawâb (rewards to be given in the Hereafter) in avoiding either kind of harâms than in doing acts of worship.

Makrûh means something which despoils the thawâb earned by way of 'amal (acts of worship, pious and good deeds). There are two kinds of makrûh: Karâhat-i-tahrîmiyya and karâhat-i-tanzîhiyya (or tenzîhiyya), (or makrûh tahrîmî and makrûh tanzîhî.)

Karâhat-i-tahrîmiyya is to omit (something which is) wâjib. It is qarîb (close) to harâm. Karâhat-i-tanzîhiyya is to omit (something which is) sunnat. It is qarîb to halâl. If a person commits a karâhat-i-tahrîmiyya, he becomes disobedient and sinful if he does so deliberately. He deserves Hell fire. If he has done so during a namâz, he will have to reperform that namâz. If he has done so as a sahw, (i.e. by mistake,) he will have to make the sajda-i-sahw (at the end of the namâz).[1] Thereby it will not be necessary to reperform the namâz. A person who commits (something which is) karâhat-i-tanzîhiyya will not be subjected to torment (in the Hereafter). However, he will deserve being reproached and being deprived of shafâ'at (in the Hereafter) if he commits it habitually. Examples of this are: Eating meat from a horse, eating remnants of food eaten by a cat or mice, and selling grapes to a wine-maker.

Mufsid is something which exterminates 'amals, (i.e. good deeds and acts of worship being performed.) Examples of this are: Spoiling one's îmân or namâz or nikâh or hajj or zakât being performed or buying and/or selling being performed.

[A Muslim who performs acts of farz, wâjib, and sunnat and who avoids acts that are harâm and makrûh will be rewarded with **ejr** or **thawâb**, i.e. recompense, in the Hereafter. If a person commits harâms and makrûhs or neglects farzes and wâjibs, he will be recorded as a **sinful** person. Thawâb for avoiding a harâm is much more than thawâb for performing a farz. Thawâb for a farz is much more than thawâb for avoiding a makrûh, which in turn is much more than thawâb for a sunnat. Among mubâhs (things and acts permitted), the ones that Allâhu ta'âlâ likes are called **khayrât** and **hasanât** (good and pious deeds). Although thawâb will be given to a person who does them, that thawâb is less than thawâb for a sunnat. It is called **qurbat** to do something consciously of the fact that one will be given rewards for it.

Allâhu ta'âlâ, being very compassionate for His slaves, sent them religions, which are sources of comfort and happiness. The final religion is the religion (dispensation) of Muhammad ''alaihis-salâm'. The other religions were changed by wicked people. If any

---

[1] The sajda-i-sahw is explained in the sixteenth chapter of the fourth fascicle of **Endless Bliss**.

person, whether it be a Muslim or a non-Muslim, leads a life in accordance with this religion, regardless of whether he does so knowingly or unknowingly, he will not suffer any trouble in this world. Examples of this maxim are European and American disbelievers working in a manner agreeable with this religion. However, disbelievers will not be given any thawâb or reward in the Hereafter. If a person who works likewise is a Muslim and intends to obey Islam, he shall attain endless bliss in the Hereafter as well.]

ISLAM'S BUILDING

Islam's building has five component parts, In other words, Islam has been built on five essentials. The first one is to say the Kalima-i-shahâdat, and to learn and believe the meaning it carries. The second one is to perform (the prayer termed) namâz (or salât) five times daily within their prescribed times. The third one is to fast every day throughout the blessed month of Ramadân. The fourth one is to pay zakât and 'ushr annually, after it becomes farz to do so. The fifth one is to perform Hajj once in a lifetime, if doing so is within one's means.[1] [Doing these five commandments of Allâhu ta'âlâ, along with avoiding (His prohibitions termed) harâm, is called **doing worship**. It is nâfila (supererogatory) worship for a Muslim who does not fulfil its conditions in the categories called wujûb and adâ to perform Hajj, and so is it for a person who has already performed Hajj to reperform it. It is not jâiz (permissible) to perform a supererogatory act of worship that will entail committing a bid'at or harâm. Hadrat Imâm Rabbânî 'quddisa sirruh', in his twenty-ninth, hundred and twenty-third, and hundred and twenty-fourth letters, and ('Abdullah Dahlawî 'quddisa sirruh',) in the twenty-sixth letter of **Maqâmât-i-Mazhariyya**, do not give permission for nâfila Hajj or 'Umra. ('Afîf-ud-dîn 'Abdullah bin Es'ad Yâfi'î 'rahmatullâhi ta'âlâ 'alaih', 698 [1298 A.D.], Yemen – 768 [1367], Mekka, states as follows in his discourse on the grade of 'zuhd', one of the grades called maqâmât-i-'ashara [ten grades], in his book entitled) **Nashr-ul-mahâsin-il-ghâliyya**: "When Imâm Nevevî (or Nawawî), a great Islamic scholar and a Walî, was

---

[1] The second one of these five essentials and also the third, fourth and the fifth ones are explained in detail in the fourth and fifth fascicles, respectively, of **Endless Bliss**.

asked: 'You observe all kinds of sunnat. But you omit one act of sunnat, and a grand sunnat, too: It is nikâh,' he replied, 'I am afraid that I may commit lots of acts of harâm as I perform one act of sunnat.' " Imâm Yahyâ Nevevî passed away in Damascus in 676 [1277 A.D.]. Prof. Habîb-ur-Rahmân, Dean of Pâkistân's **Jâmi'a-i-habîbiyya**, went on a hajj in 1401 [1981 A.D.]. When he saw that the wahhâbî imâm was conducting the namâz (in jamâ'at) by using a loud-speaker, he performed his namâz individually. Thereupon he was handcuffed, sent to prison, and questioned (on why he had not joined the jamâ'at). When he said that it was not permissible for an imâm to conduct public prayers with a loud-speaker, he was prevented from performing a hajj and was extradited.

The first thing incumbent on a person, no matter in what place of the world, is to learn their faith and îmân. Of old, it was quite easy to learn religion from Islamic scholars. As we live in the latest time today, there are no Islamic scholars left anywhere. Ignorant people and idiots sold to British plotters have spread far and near in the name of religious people. The one and only way of learning faith and îmân properly now is by reading books written by scholars of Ahl as-Sunnat. Finding these books is a great favour granted by Allâhu ta'âlâ. Enemies of Islam are spreading false religious books for the purpose of misguiding young people, so that it has become rather difficult to find true religious books. Youngsters are being enthralled by the mesmerizing inanity of various silly games and thereby being deprived of finding and reading true books. It is being witnessed in dismal helplessness that many youngsters are thinking of nothing but games. This disease is spreading among young people. It is absolutely necessary that Muslim parents should protect their children against this pandemic. For doing so, they ought to inform their children about their faith and accustom them to reading religious books. And this, in turn, should be made possible by protecting their children against fondness for harmful pastimes. We see that some of our acquaintances' children are so deeply engrossed in playing harmful games that they forget to eat their meals. It is impossible for such children even to read their school books and pass their courses. Parents have to somehow steer their children towards book-reading. **Ethics of Islam**, for instance should be read. A person who reads that book will not only learn their faith and îmân but also penetrate the disguises assumed by Islam's enemies and know how they work. If parents neglect this duty of theirs, an irreligious and atheistic younger generation will appear and inflict irreparable damage and harm on our country and nation.

Another matter whereon parents ought to focus their attention is the matter of 'satr-i-awrat', (which is explained in minute detail in the eighth chapter of the fourth fascicle of **Endless Bliss**.) We see youngsters with exposed limbs from knees to groins among people playing harmful games. It is an important act of farz to cover one's awrat parts. People who do not attribute due importance to this may lose their îmân. Muslims go to mosques for the purpose of earning much thawâb for their namâz and/or listening to preachings. Even without these purposes, there is still much thawâb in the sheer act of going to mosques. A place visited by people with exposed awrat parts cannot be a mosque; it is a gathering of fisq (sinning). It is written in all (Islamic) books that it is harâm to go to a gathering of fisq. People who go to such mosques will have gone to gatherings of fisq; they will be sinful. A person who goes to such mosques for the purpose of earning thawâb and listening to religious sermons earn sins instead of thawâb. When people with exposed awrat parts enter mosques they cause Muslims to become sinful. As it is a gravely sinful act to expose one's awrat parts (among other people), likewise it is a grave sin to look at others' exposed limbs of awrat. Therefore, Muslims who go to such mosques earn sinfulness and thereby incur the Ghâdâb-i-ilâhî (Wrath of Allâhu ta'âlâ) instead of earning thawâb.]

CHAPTER ON NAMÂZ

Namâz has twelve farzes: Seven of them are outside (of) it, and five are inside (of) it.

Farzes that are outside (of) namâz are: Tahârat (purification, cleanliness) from hadeth; tahârat from najâsat; satr-i-awrat; istiqbâl-i-qibla; waqt; niyyat; takbîr-i-iftitâh. Farzes that are inside (of) it are: Qiyâm; qirâat; rukû' once in every rak'at; sajda twice (in every rak'at); to sit as long as (to say a certain prayer termed) teshehhud (or tashahhud) at the qa'da-i-âkhira (final sitting posture). Farzes within namâz are called **rukn**s. It is farz to put the forehead and the (big) toes on the ground (or floor, as the case may be) during the sajda.

Tahârat from hadeth means to make an ablution if one is without an ablution, to make a ghusl if one is in a state of junub, and to make a tayammum in want of water when one needs an ablution and/or a ghusl. There are three requirements to be fulfilled for the realization of a tahârat from hadeth:

Meticulous observance of istinjâ and istibrâ, (which will be explained later in the text;) when doing the washings and when making masah on the head, not to leave any spaces undone of the areas that are farz.

There are three requirements to be fulfilled for the realization of tahârat from najâsat: To purify the clothes to be worn during namâz from najâsat. To clean one's body when performing namâz. To clean the place where one is to perform namâz. [Please see the end of the chapter dealing with the fifty-four farzes!]

There are three requirements to be fulfilled for the realization of satr-i-awrat: In the Hanafî Madhhab, for men to cover parts of their bodies from immediately below their navels to immediately below their knees. It is sunnat for men to cover their feet when performing namâz.

For free women to cover, i.e. not to expose parts of their bodies other than their faces and hands. According to a scholarly report (riwâyat), their feet are included in the exception.

For women who are (in the category termed) jâriyas to cover parts of their bodies from upper parts of their backs and breasts to below their knees. [Women who go around with their heads, arms and legs exposed or who wear tight and thin clothes and men who look at them are sinful because they commit harâm by doing so. A person who turns a deaf ear to the fact that it is harâm becomes a kâfir, a murtadd.]

There are three requirements to be fulfilled for the realization of istiqbâl-i-qibla: To turn towards the Qibla.

Not to let one's chest deviate from the direction of Qibla till the end of the namâz.

To humble oneself in the dîwân-i-ma'nawî of Allâhu 'adhîm-ush-shân.

There are three requirements to be fulfilled for the realization of waqt (time of namâz): To know when the time of namâz begins and the time when it ends. Not to postpone the namâz till the time wherein it is makrûh to perform it begins.

Niyyat is realized by knowing and passing through your heart whether the namâz you are to perform is farz or wâjib or sunnat or mustahab, and to expel worldly interests from your heart. It is wâjib, according to Imâm A'zam, and sunnat according to the two imâms, (i.e. the Imâmeyn, who are Imâm Abû Yûsuf and Imâm Muhammad,) and also according to the Mâlikî and Shâfi'î Madhhabs, to perform the (namâz termed) Witr. [It is permissible for a person imitating the Mâlikî Madhhab to omit the Witr when there is haraj (difficulty defined by Islam).]

Takbîr-i-iftitâh is realized by men's raising their hands to their ears and by the heart's being awake and vigilant.

There are three requirements to be fulfilled for the realization of Qiyâm: To stand in the direction of Qibla, to look at the place of sajda, (i.e. the place where you put your forehead and the point of your nose during prostration,) and not to sway from side to side during the Qiyâm.

There are three requirements to be fulfilled for the realization of Qirâat: To do the recitals loudly when they must be done loudly, and as loudly as to hear your own voice when they must be done silently, and to pronounce the sounds correctly. To think of the meanings of the (âyats of the) Qur'ân al-kerîm (that you are reciting. To observe the rules of tajwîd (or tejvîd) as you recite the âyats. [The takbîr that is to be said when beginning to perform namâz and everything recited within the namâz and the azân (or adhân) have to be in the Arabic language. How to recite them in a proper Arabic diction must be learned from a hâfid who knows Islam and who obeys the rules stated in the ilmihâl books of his Madhhab. Âyats of the Qur'ân al-kerîm written in Latin alphabet cannot be read correctly. Reading thereby done will be defective and erroneous. Tafsîr (explanation) of the Qur'ân al-kerîm is possible. Its translation, however, is out of the question. Books brought forward in the name of Turkish versions of the Qur'ân by irreligious and lâ-madhhabî people are not correct. They are incorrect and flawed. Every Muslim must attend courses of Qur'ân al-kerîm, learn Islamic letters, and thereby read (and recite) the Qur'ân al-kerîm and prayers correctly. Namâz performed by reciting the âyat-i-kerîmas and prayers correctly will be accepted. It is stated as follows in the book **Terghîb-us-salât**: "If the âyat-i-kerîmas and prayers recited in namâz by a certain person are incorrect according to nine Islamic scholars and correct according to one Islamic scholar, we should not look on the namâz he has performed as a fâsid one."] (An act of worship that is fâsid is one that has not been accepted.)

There are three requirements to be fulfilled for the realization of rukû': To make the rukû' towards the Qibla, bending down perfectly, (so as to represent a capital letter 'L' túrned upside down.) To keep the waist and the head on a level. To stay so for a while in what we call tumânînat, [i.e. till your heart has become convinced.]

There are three requirements to be fulfilled for the realization of sajda: To prostrate oneself for the sajda in a manner prescribed by the sunnat. To make the sajda in the direction of Qible, with the forehead and the nose on the floor (or on the ground) and in line. To stay at sajda for a while so as to observe tumânînat. [It is permissible for a healthy person to make sajda on something up to twenty-five centimetres higher than the level (whereon they are performing the namâz), yet it is makrûh to do so. For, our Prophet never made sajda on something higher than level, nor did any of the Ashâb-i-kirâm. Making sajda on something even higher will make the namâz fâsid.]

There are three requirements to be fulfilled for the realization of qa'da-i-âkhira: 1– For men to sit on the left foot with the right foot kept erect, and for women to sit in a manner termed tawarruk (or tewerruk), which means to sit on the buttocks with the feet jutting out from the right hand side. 2– To recite (the prayer termed) Tehiyyât (or Tahiyyât) with reverence. 3– At the qa'da-i-âkhira (final sitting posture), to say the Salawât and the other (prescribed) prayers. Prayers to be said after namâz will be taught later in the text.

CHAPTER on GHUSL

There are three farzes to be observed when making a ghusl in the Hanafî Madhhab, five farzes in the Mâlikî Madhhab, two in the Shâfi'î Madhhab, and one farz in the Hanbalî Madhhab. In the Hanafî Madhhab:

1– To wash inside the mouth once with water. It is farz to wet between the teeth and inside the tooth sockets. [A Muslim who is in the Hanafî Madhhab cannot have their teeth filled or crowned unless there is a darûrat to do so. They can have a prosthesis made, so that they can remove it and wash under it whenever they have to make a ghusl. A Muslim who has had his teeth filled or crowned without a darûrat will be a Muslim with an 'udhr on account of the haraj (difficulty) he has thereby encountered; he will have to imitate one of the Shâfi'î and Mâlikî Madhhabs when making a ghusl. In that case, however, they will have to add, "I am imitating the Shâfi'î (or Mâlikî) Madhhab," to their niyyat whenever they are to make a ghusl or an ablution and when performing namâz.]

2– To apply water into the nostrils once.

3– To wash the entire body once. It is farz to wash those parts of the body which do not cause haraj (difficulty) for washing. If a part of the body cannot be washed on account of a darûrat, i.e. a cause that exists in creation and which is not one's own making, it will be forgiven (by Allâhu ta'âlâ) and the ghusl made will be sahîh (valid, sound).

As is stated in the book entitled **Durr-ul-mukhtâr**, food remains between the teeth and/or in the tooth sockets will not prevent the ghusl made from being sahîh. This is the case according to the fatwâ.[1] For, water will penetrate them and wet the place under them. If the remains are solid, the scholars said that they would prevent water's penetration. And that is the truth of the matter. **Ibni 'Âbidîn** 'rahima-hullâhu ta'âlâ' explains the matter as follows: It is written in the book entitled **Khulâsa-t-ul-fatâwâ**, as well, that they will not prevent (water's penetration because water, a liquid, will pass through the food (so as to wet the place under it). If it is found out that water is not passing through the food remains, the ghusl made will not be sahîh, a fact which is acknowledged by all scholars unanimously. The same is stated also in the book entitled **Hilya-t-ul-mujallî**, (written by Ibni Emîr Hâjj) Halabî 'rahmatullâhi ta'âlâ 'alaih', d. 879 [1474 A.D.].) If the remains have solidified under constant pressure, they will not let water pass through, and so the ghusl made will not be sahîh. For, there is not a darûrat in this. [In other words, it is not something that has happened by itself.] Nor is there any haraj [in cleaning these parts (or the body).]

It is written in the book entitled **Halabî-i-saghîr**: If a person makes a ghusl with remains of bread or food or other things between his teeth, his ghusl will be sahîh, according to fatwâs, even if he thinks that the water (used in the ghusl) has not passed through the remains. That the fatwâ given agrees with this is written in **Khulâsa-t-ul-fatâwâ**. According to some scholars, the

_____

[1] Fatwâ is a conclusive explanation wherein an authorized Islamic scholar answers Muslims' questions on a religious matter. Sources and documents on which the fatwâ is based are appended to the fatwâ.

ghusl made will not be sahîh if the remains are solid. This final judgment is written also in the book entitled **Zahîra-t-ul-fatâwâ**, (written by Burhân-ad-dîn Mahmûd bin Tâj-ud-dîn Ahmad bin 'Abd-ul-'Azîz Bukhârî 'rahmatullâhi ta'âlâ 'alaih', 551 [1156 A.D.]–martyred in 616 [1219].) It is the valid judgment concerning the matter. For, the water used will not reach below them. And there is not a darûrat or haraj, either.

It is stated as follows in the book entitled **Durr-ul-Muntaqâ**:[1] Concerning the ghusl made when there are food remains in your tooth sockets, there are Islamic scholars who argue that the ghusl will be sahîh as well as those who believe the other way round. For safety's sake, the food remains ought to be removed beforehand. As is stated in **Tahtâwî**'s commentary to **Marâq-il-falâh**, if there are food remains in the tooth sockets or between the teeth, ghusl will be sahîh. For water is a fluid and will seep through them easily. If the food remains have been hardened by chewing, they will prevent ghusl. So is written in the book entitled **Fat-h-ul-qadîr**.

It is stated in the book entitled **Bahr-ur-râiq** that ghusl will be sahîh if there are food remains in the tooth sockets or between the teeth. For, water is a fine substance which will seep through anything. The same is written in the book entitled **Tejnîs** (or Tajnîs). Sadr-ush-shehîd Husâmaddîn said that ghusl made in that state will not be sahîh and that therefore the remains must be removed and the water must be made to flow through the tooth interiors. It will be safer to remove the remains and wash under them.

It is stated in the book entitled **Fatâwâ-i-Hindiyya**: The argument closer to the truth is the one that holds that ghusl made by a person with food remains in their tooth sockets or between their teeth will be sahîh. The same argument is written in **Zâhidî**. However, it is advisable to remove the remains and make water flow into the sockets. As is stated in the book entitled **Qâdikhân**, it is written in the book entitled **Nâtifî** that ghusl made while there are food remains around the teeth will not have been made adequately and that it is necessary to remove them and wash the places under them.

It is written in the book entitled **al-Mejmû'at-uz-zuhdiyya**: If the food remains between the teeth become like solid dough and

---

[1] Written by 'Alâ-ud-dîn Haskafî 'rahmatullâhi ta'âlâ 'alaih' (1021, Haskaf – 1088 [1677 A.D.]).

prevent the penetration of water, regardless of their amount, they will prevent ghusl as well. The same is written in **Halabî**. It cannot be argued that "there is no haraj, difficulty in removing the food remains, but fillings and crownings cannot be removed; so there is haraj in removing them." Yes, there is haraj. Yet when something done by man causes haraj, it becomes an 'udhr for him to imitate another Madhhab. It does not become an 'udhr to omit a farz. A person's being absolved from a farz requires impossibility of imitating another Madhhab, which in turn means coexistence of a darûrat and a haraj. If it should be asked, "Having one's teeth filled or crowned is intended to prevent toothaches and to protect one from loss of teeth. Then isn't there a darûrat for doing so, (i.e. for being absolved from the farz and thereby doing without washing the tooth sockets,)" then our answer will be, "There being a darûrat requires there not being a (prescribed) way out by imitating another Madhhab."

The argument, "The mandate of having to wash the teeth when making a ghusl shifts to the outer surfaces of the fillings or crownings," is not appropriate in Islam. Tahtâwî (Ahmad bin Muhammad bin Ismâ'îl) states in his annotation to (Shernblâlî's) book entitled **Imdâd-ul-Fattâh**: "When the ablution of a person who put on his mests after having made an ablution breaks, the breaking of the ablution affects the mests instead of the feet."[1] This statement in books of Fiqh appertains exclusively to ablution–making and mest–wearing. To tailor it so as to fit into situations pertaining to tooth crowning, and even to ghusl–making, means to have a shot at issuing personal fatwâs. Nor would it be apposite to compare a filled or crowned tooth to thick beard. For, whereas it is not compulsory to wash the skin under thich beard when making an ablution, it is farz, (and so it is compulsory,) to wash the skin under it when making a ghusl. A person who argues that it is not farz "to wash the skin under thick beard when making a ghusl since it is not farz to wash the skin under thick beard when making an ablution," will not wash the skin under his thick beard. Thereby, the ghusl made by that person and by people who believe him, and ergo the prayers of namâz performed by them, will not be sahîh.

Nor would it be something consistent with books of Fiqh to

---

[1] Please see the third chapter of the fourth fascicle of **Endless Bliss** for expressions such as 'mests' and 'having an 'udhr (excuse)'.

draw a comparison of crownings and fillings with ointments applied to fissures on feet or with wooden splints fastened to wounded or broken limbs or with plaster casts and bandages. For, when there is haraj or a possible damage in removing them from wounds and broken limbs, it is not possible to imitate another Madhhab. On account of these three reasons, one will be absolved from having to wash under them.

Since you have the freedom of choice to have a rotten and aching tooth filled or crowned because you do not want to have it extracted and replaced with a removable false tooth or a set of false teeth furnished with a half or complete palate, to have your teeth filled or crowned or to have a fixed bridge of teeth made will not engender a darûrat. To say that there is a darûrat will not, on its own, constitute a cause to absolve you from the obligation of washing the areas under them. For, it is possible to imitate another Madhhab. No one has the right to exploit the groundless argument that there is a darûrat as a tool for castigating other people, who obey books of Fiqh and imitate the Shâfi'î or Mâlikî Madhhab.

Darûrat means a supernatural cause that compels one to do something (or not to do something), i.e. a cause that cannot be helped. Examples of a darûrat are an Islamic commandment and prohibition, a vehement pain, danger of losing one of one's limbs or one's life, and to have no other option. **Haraj**, on the other hand, means difficulty or hardship to prevent something you have done from preventing you from performing an act that is farz or from causing you to commit an act that is harâm. Commandments and prohibitions of Allâhu ta'âlâ, as an ensemble, are called **Ahkâm-i-islâmiyya**. When observing one of the rules of the Ahkâm-i-islâmiyya, i.e. when performing one of the commandments or avoiding one of the prohibitions, you follow the widely-known and chosen one of the statements made by the scholars of your own Madhhab concerning the matter. If a haraj (difficulty) in following that chosen scholarly statement arises on account of something you have done, you follow a less preferable and weaker one of the scholarly statements (made by other scholars who, too, are in your own Madhhab). If there is a haraj in following that statement as well, then you imitate another Madhhab and follow that Madhhab concerning that matter. If there is haraj in following that other Madhhab as well, then you look into the matter to see whether or not there is a darûrat in doing the thing which causes haraj:

1– When there is a darûrat in doing something that (is farz and which) causes haraj, you will be absolved from having to do that farz.

2– When there is not a darûrat in doing something that causes haraj, [e.g. fingernail polish,] or there is a darûrat and also a few ways of doing that thing and you choose the way that entails haraj, the act of worship that you do (in the way that entails haraj) will not be sahîh. You have to perform that farz by utilizing the way without haraj. That another Madhhab should be imitated in case of haraj, hardship, (i.e. if you choose the way that entails haraj,) regardless of whether or not there is a darûrat, is written in books entitled **Fatâwa-l-hadîthiyya** (written by Ibn-i-Hajar-i-Mekkî 'rahmatullâhi 'alaih', 899 [1494 A.D.] – 974 [1566], Mekka,) and **Khulâsa-t-ut-tahqîq** (by 'Abd-ul-Ghanî Nablusî 'rahmatullâhi 'alaih', 1050 [1640 A.D.], Damuscus – 1143 [1731],) in Tahtâwî's 'rahima-hullâhu ta'âlâ' annotation to Sherblâlî's 'rahimuhullâhu ta'âlâ' book entitled **Merâq-il-felâh**, and in the book entitled **Ma'fuwât** by Halîl Es'irdî 'rahima-hullâhu ta'âlâ'. Molla Halîl (Es'irdî) passed away in 1259 [1843 A.D.]. A Hanafî Muslim who wants to have his aching or rotten tooth filled or crowned instead of having it extracted and replaced with a removable prosthesis or a set of teeth furnished with a palate will have to imitate the Shâfi'î or Mâlikî Madhhab as he makes a ghusl. For, it is not farz in these two Madhhabs to wash one's mouth and nostrils when making a ghusl. And it is quite easy to imitate the Shâfi'î or Mâlikî Madhhab. You will have to make niyyat, i.e. pass through your heart, that you are imitating the Shâfi'î or Mâlikî Madhhab when making a ghusl or an ablution and when beginning to perform namâz or, if you forget, after performing namâz or when you remember to do so. In that case, the ablution and the ghusl that you make and the namâz that you perform will have to be sahîh (valîd, sound) according to the Shâfi'î or Mâlikî Madhhab. For them to be sahîh according to the Shâfi'î Madhhab, you will have to renew your ablution when your skin touches the skin of a woman other than the eighteen women who are eternally harâm for you to make nikâh with[1] and when the palm of your hand touches your own qaba awrat, (i.e. the pubic or anal area of your own body,) and recite the Fâtiha Sûra inwardly when you perform namâz (in jamâ'at) conducted by an imâm. Please scan the sixth chapter of the fourth fascicle of **Endless Bliss** to learn what should

---

[1] Please see the twelfth chapter of the fifth fascicle of **Endless Bliss** for women with whom nikâh is not permissible.

be done when imitating the Mâlikî Madhhab! To imitate another Madhhab does not mean to change your Madhhab. A Hanafî Muslim who imitates another Madhhab has not gone out of the Hanafî Madhhab. He adapts himself to that Madhhab only in farzes and mufsids. He observes the rules of his own Madhhab in wâjibs, makrûhs, and sunnats.

With the statements made by scholars of Fiqh concerning ghusl are still there, attempts are being heard to solve the question of teeth with the writings of incompetent people who do not even belong to a certain Madhhab. They say that it has been stated in a fatwâ written in the 1332 [1913 A.D.] issue of the periodical entitled Sebîl-ur-rashâd that it is permissible to have a tooth filled. We would like to say first of all that the so-called periodical is beset with articles written by reformers and other people without a certain Madhhab. One of its writers, namely Ismâ'îl Hakki of Manastir (Bitola), is an insidious freemason. Another one, Ismâ'îl Hakki of Izmir, is ahead of all those idiots who were misguided by Mehmet Abduh, the masonic mufti of Cairo and a reformer of Islam. He received high school education in Izmir and finished teachers' training school in Istanbul. He has a weak religious education and little religious knowledge. Ingratiating himself with members of Union Party, he became a madrasa teacher and tried to spread Abduh's reformist and subversive ideas. The eulogy that Ismâ'îl Hakki wrote for the book entitled **Telfîq-i-madhâhib**, a translation from Rashîd Ridâ of Egypt and rendered by Ahmed Hamdi Akseki, one of his disciples victimized by his venomous subterfuges, betrays his inner malice.

This very Ismâ'îl Hakki in the aforesaid periodical enlarged on the conflicting arguments among the scholars of Fiqh concerning whether it is permissible to tie the teeth with a gold wire and, putting forth the books, e.g. the commentary to (Muhammad Sheybânî's book entitled) **Siyar-i-kebîr**, which inform about the consensus of scholars on that there is a darûrat in tying the teeth with a gold wire instead of a silver one, concluded that the matter concerning the teeth is a darûrat. However, the question he had been asked was whether ghusl made by a person with a filled or crowned tooth would be sahîh, rather than whether teeth should be tied with gold or silver. Writing a long and detailed discourse on something not asked about and which was commonly known, Ismâ'îl Hakki of Izmir wrote his conclusion as an answer to the real question. What he did is sheer falsification in knowledge. It is an attempt to write one's own opinion in disguise of a fatwâ given by Islamic scholars. His attempt is even worse than that. Quoting the Fiqh scholars' written statements on ghusl, he dubs them into his personal opinions. For instance, he says, "As is stated in Bahr, it is not obligatory to make water touch places where it is difficult to make it reach." On the other hand, the statement written in the book entitled **Bahr** reads: "... parts of the body where it is difficult to make water reach." Thereby he likens something which one does indispensably to something which one experiences indispensably. Nor is he righteous in his using the statement, "If it would harm a woman to wash her head, then she does not wash her head," which is written in **Durr-ul-mukhtâr**, as a proof to show that ghusl made by a person with a filled tooth will be jâiz (permissible, acceptable). The head's being harmed by contact with water is something on account of a physical illness. The crowning or filling of a tooth is one's own choice. It is for this reason that the question of whether ghusl made by people with food remains in their tooth sockets will be jâiz is separately dealt with in the book entitled **Durr-ul-mukhtâr**.

The tricks and misdeeds mentioned so far would fall short of describing the wickedness of Ismâ'îl Hakki of Izmir. He was, for instance, unprincipled enough to attempt to misemploy Islamic scholars as false witnesses for himself by saying, "It is not a requirement (of ghusl) to make water reach below gold and silver crownings and fillings or to wash places under them. Scholars of Fiqh unanimously state that there is a darûrat in the concerned teeth and that it is not obligatory to make water reach parts (of the body) with a darûrat." None of the scholars of Fiqh in the Hanafî Madhhab said that it is a darûrat to have your teeth crowned or filled. In fact, tooth crowning or filling does not date as far back as the times wherein scholars of Fiqh lived. In the sixty-fourth page of the commentary to the book entitled **Siyar-i-kebîr**, which he adduces as a proof, Imâm Muhammad Sheybânî 'rahima-hullâhu ta'âlâ' is quoted to have said that it would be jâiz (permissible) for a person to replace his fallen tooth with a gold tooth or to fasten his teeth with a gold wire. The book does not make any mention of tooth crowning. It is a trumped-up addendum forged by Ismâ'îl Hakki of Izmir. Masonic men of religion, people without a certain Madhhab and heretics, who appeared later, had recourse to all sorts of trickery to deceive Muslims and to preach sedition among them. They wrote wrong and subversive articles.

Imâm Muhammad Sheybânî 'rahima-hullâhu ta'âlâ' stated that a tottering tooth could be tied with a gold, as well as a silver, wire. He did not say that it would be jâiz to crown or fill it with gold. Such things have been implanted by Ismâ'îl Hakki and the like.

Muftis and other valuable men of religion contemporary with Ismâ'îl Hakki of Izmir provided answers so as to reveal the truth versus the untrue and beguiling article of which we have presented samples in the previous paragraphs. One of those estimable scholars is Yûnus-zâde Ahmed Vehbî Efendi of Bolvadin, (Turkey,) 'rahima-hullâhi ta'âlâ'. This deeply learned person with extensive religious knowledge proved that Islamic scholars had been unanimous on that ghusl made by a person with filled tooth socket would not be sahîh.

Administration of the periodical entitled **Sebîl-ur-rashâd** must have been wise to the meagre ruse employed in the jerry-made article written by the Izmirer, so that they deemed it necessary to support the article with further proof by adding to it the fatwâ with the conclusive remark that reads, "... the ghusl will be sahîh," in the second edition, dated 1329 [1911 A.D.], of the book of fatwâs entitled **Majmû'a-i-Jedîda**. However, the so-called fatwâ does not exist in the first edition, dated 1299 A.H., of the book. The misleading remark was inserted into the second edition by Mûsâ Kâzim, a shaikh-ul-islâm brought to office by the notorious Party of Union. Hence, the periodical entitled Sebîl-ur-Rashâd attempted to adduce a statement concocted by a freemason as support for an article written by a reformer of Islam. Not a single scholar of Fiqh said 'darûrat' about tooth crowning or filling. People who say or write so are either masonic men of religion or Islam's reformers or people without a certain Madhhab or Islamically ignorant people suborned or deceived by wahhabite heretics, and none other than them.

Ahmad (bin Muhammad bin Ismâ'îl) Tahtâwî 'rahima-hullâhu ta'âlâ' states as follows in his annotation to (Shernblâlî's book entitled) **Merâq-il-falâh**: "When you (join a jamâ'at and) follow an imâm (conducting the namâz in jamâ'at and) who is in one of the other three Madhhabs, the namâz you perform (behind that imâm) will be sahîh with the proviso that something that nullifies namâz according to your own Madhhab should not exist on the imâm (even if it is something that will not nullify namâz according to his own Madhhab) or, if one of such nullifiers exists on him, you should not know about it as you follow him. This is the more dependable qawl (statement, report). According to another qawl, if the imâm's namâz is sahîh according to his own Madhhab, it will be sahîh to follow him even if it is seen that his namâz is not sahîh according to your own Madhhab." The same rule is written in Ibni 'Âbidîn. As it is understood from this statement which is written both in Tahtâwî's annotation and in Tahtâwî 'rahima-hullâhu ta'âlâ', there are two differring scholarly qawls concerning whether the namâz performed by a Hanafî Muslim without a crowned or filled tooth will be sahîh when he performs it in a jamâ'at conducted by an imâm who has crowned or filled teeth: According to the former qawl, it is not sahîh for a Hanafî Muslim without any crowned or filled teeth to follow an imâm with crowned or filled teeth. For, the imâm's namâz is not sahîh according to the Hanafî Madhhab. According to the latter qawl, if the imâm is imitating one of the Shâfi'î and Mâlikî Madhhabs, it will be sahîh for the Hanafî Muslim without any crowned or filled teeth to follow him, (i.e. to perform the namâz behind him, or to join the namâz in jamâ'at conducted by him.) This is the ijtihâd of Imâm Hindûwânî 'rahmatullâhi 'alaih'. The same rule applies in the Shâfi'î Madhhab as well. Unless it is known that a sâlih imâm with crowned or filled teeth is not imitating the Mâlikî or Shâfi'î Madhhab, Hanafî Muslims who have no crowned or filled teeth ought to join the namâz in jamâ'at conducted by that imâm. It is not permissible to ask him whether he is imitating the Mâlikî or Shâfi'î Madhhab in a prying manner. The latter qawl is a weak one. However, as we stated earlier in the text, when there is haraj (difficulty), it is necessary to act on a weak (da'îf) qawl. That a weak qawl should be acted on to prevent a fitna is written in **Hadîqa** as well. If a person despises the (four) Madhhabs and does not perform his acts of worship in a manner compatible with the teachings written in books of Fiqh, it will be concluded that he is not Sunnî. And a person who is not Sunnî is either a bid'at holder and a heretic, or he has lost his îmân and become a murtadd (renegade, apostate). We are not saying that you should not have your teeth filled or crowned. We are showing our brothers and sisters who have had them filled or crowned ways of performing their acts of worship in an acceptable way. We are showing them easy ways.

There are fifteen kinds of gusl: Five of them are farz, five of them are wâjib, four of them are sunnat, and one of them is mustahab. Ghusls that are farz: When a woman's (or a girl's) menstrual or puerperal period is over, after coitus, i.e. sexual intercourse, after lustful seminal ejaculation, after a nocturnal emission and seeing semen in one's bed or underpants, it is farz to make a ghusl before the prescribed time of an unperformed namâz is over.

Ghusls that are wâjib: It is wâjib to wash a dead Muslim and for a child to make a ghusl as soon as it reaches the age of puberty. When husband and wife sleeping together wake up and see some seminal fluid between them and do not know which party it belongs to, it is wâjib for both of them to make ghusl. When you see on yourself some seminal remains and cannot estimate the time when it was ejaculated, then it will be wâjib for you to make a ghusl. And, when a woman bears a child, it is wâjib for her to make a ghusl even if no bleeding has taken place. (It is farz to make a ghusl in case of bleeding.)

Ghusls that are sunnat: To make a ghusl for Friday and 'Iyd days and at the time of Ihrâm –regardless of your niyya (intention)– and before climbing Arafât (hill).[1] Ghusl that is mustahab: When a disbeliever becomes a Believer, it is –farz for him (or her) to make a ghusl if he (or she) was junub before becoming a Believer, which means a state which necessitates a ghusl. Otherwise, it is– mustahab for him (or her) to make a ghusl.

There are three harâms in ghusl:

1– For both sexes to expose parts of their body between immediately below the navel and between the knees in the presence of other people of their sex when making ghusl; (in other words, it is harâm for men to show their body limbs between below the navel and below the knees to other men, and for women to show their same body areas to other women, as they make a ghusl.)

2– According to a qawl, it is harâm for Muslim women to show themselves to non-Muslim women when making a ghusl. (This rule must be observed at other times as well.)

3– Waste of water; (in other words, it is harâm to use more than necessary water when making a ghusl.)

In the Hanafî Madhhab, there are thirteen sunnats to be observed when making a ghusl:

1– To make istinjâ with water. In other words, to wash the anus and the genitals.

2– To wash the hands below the wrists.

3– If there is any real najâsat on the body, to remove it.

---

[1] Please see the fourth chapter of the fourth fascicle of **Endless Bliss** for 'ghusl', and the seventh chapter of its fifth fascicle for details on 'Hajj'.

4– To be over-attentive in making mazmaza and istinshâq. (Masmaza means to rinse the mouth with water, and istinshâq means to snuff up water through the nostrils.) Ghusl will not be sahîh if there is a space as wide as the point of a needle unmoistened within the mouth or inside the nostrils. To make an ablution for namâz when beginning to make a ghusl.

5– To make niyya(t) for making a ghusl.

6– To rub each limb being poured water on, with hands.

7– To pour water first on the head, and next on the right and left shoulders, three times each.

8– To make khilâl between fingers and toes. In other words, to moisten between fingers and toes.

9– Not to turn your front or back towards the Qibla.

10– Not to talk on worldly matters when making o ghusl.

11– To make mazmaza and istinshâq three times each.

12– To begin washing each limb from the right.

13– Not to urinate at the place where you are making a ghusl if it is a place where the water (being used for the ghusl) is making up pools. There are other sunnats in addition to these sunnats which we have listed.

PRAYER of TAWHÎD

Yâ Allah, yâ Allah. Lâ ilâha il-l-Allah Muhammadun Rasûlullah. Yâ Rahmân, yâ Rahîm, yâ 'afuwwu yâ Kerîm, fa'fu 'annî wa-r-hamnî yâ erham-er-râhimîn! Tawaffanî musliman wa al-hiqnî bi-s-sâlihîn. Allâhummaghfilî wa li-âbâî wa ummahâtî wa li âbâ-i wa ummahât-i-zawjâti wa li-ajdâdî wa jaddâtî wa li-ebnâî wa benâtî wa li-ihwatî wa ahawâtî wa li-a'mâmî wa ammâtî wa li-ahwâlî wa hâlâtî wa li-ustâzî 'Abd-ul-Hakîm-i-Arwâsî wa li-kâffa-t-il-mu'minîna wa-l-mu'minât. 'Rahmatullâhi ta'âlâ 'alaihim ajma'în'.

THE CHAPTER on HAID wa NIFÂS
(Menstrual and Puerperal Periods)

Menstrual period is three days minimum and ten days maximum. There is not a fewest-days limit for puerperal period. As soon as the bleeding comes to an end it is necessary to make a ghusl and to perform namâz and to fast. It is forty days maximum. If the menstrual bleeding stops before the (minimum) three-days limit is over, the woman concerned makes qadâ of the prayers of namâz that she did not perform because she thought she was undergoing menstruation.[1] A ghusl is not necessary in this case. If the bleeding stops after the three-day period is over, then she makes a ghusl and performs the namâz within the prescribed time of which the bleeding stopped. After the (maximum) ten-days limit is over, she makes a ghusl and performs the time's namâz, regardless of whether or not the bleeding has stopped. When the (maximum) forty-days period is over and therefore she has made a ghusl, she performs her namâz regardless of whether or not the bleeding has come to an end. All sorts of discharge during menstrual or puerperal days must be judged to be bleeding, (yellowish and turbid discharge alike.)

If bleeding discontinues for one or two days within the ten days of menstruation or the forty days of lochia and she makes a ghusl and fasts because she thinks that bleeding has come to an end and then bleeding recurs within the period, she will have to make qadâ of the fasts (that she has performed as if she had not performed them at all). And she will have to make a ghusl again when the bleeding is over. If the bleeding stops before her 'âdat and yet after the third day (of bleeding), then she makes a ghusl and performs her namâz. However, she does not have sexual intercourse with her husband before her 'âdat is over. The same rule applies in lochia. If the bleeding comes to an end after her 'âdat[2] is over and yet on the tenth day of bleeding or earlier, the entire period experienced is haid. If bleeding does not come to an end but continues after the tenth day is over, the bleeding after her 'âdat is not haid, and she will have to make qadâ of prayers belonging to those extra days, (i.e. the days after her 'âdat.) Forty puerperal days are identical with ten menstrual days.

When haid (menstrual bleeding) or nifâs (puerperal bleeding)

---

[1] To make qadâ of an act of farz worship means to perform it after its prescribed time is over.

[2] The period between the day when bleeding is seen to start and the day when it is seen to stop is called 'âdat. It is three days minimum and ten days maximum in the Hanafî Madhhab, one day minimum and fifteen days maximum in Shâfi'î and Hanbalî Madhhabs. Please see the fiftieth page of the 2008 – fourteenth edition of the fourth fascicle of **Endless Bliss** for details.

ceases after a day dawns in Ramadân, she does not eat or drink, as if she were fasting, that day. However, it will not stand for a fast. She will have to make qadâ of that day, (i.e. she will have to fast for one day after the blessed month of Ramadân.) And if bleeding starts after dawn, be it seen after late afternoon, she eats and drinks in private. Generally speaking, if a woman sees that she is bleeding, she stops performing namâz and fasting. And if it ceases before the third day is over, she waits patiently until the time of namâz verges on being over and, if bleeding is seen to recur, she does not perform namâz, and yet if the bleeding does not recur, she makes an ablution and performs namâz, and if bleeding recurs again, she ceases from namâz again. If bleeding ceases again, she waits until the time of namâz is nearly over and makes an ablution and performs her namâz in case the bleeding does not recur. She continues likewise until the third day is over, and a ghusl is not necessary in the meantime. Making an ablution only will be sufficient. If the bleeding ceases after the third day, she waits again until the time of the namâz is well-nigh over and makes a ghusl and performs her namâz if the bleeding does not recur, and if it recurs, she ceases from namâz. If it goes on likewise for ten days, then she makes a ghusl and performs her namâz, even in case of bleeding. This rule applies in nifâs (lochia) as well. However, a ghusl will be necessary at each time the bleeding ceases, even if it ceases on the first day. In Ramadân, if it ceases before dawn, she performs her fasting. If bleeding recurs at the time of kushluk, (which is during forenoon,) or after late afternoon, her fasting has not been fasting. So she will have to make qadâ of it (after the blessed month of Ramadân).

In case of a miscarriage, it will be as if she has given birth to a faultless child if its hair or mouth or nose has been formed. If none of its limbs has been formed, then it is not a case of nifâs (childbirth). However, if she bleeds for three or more days, it is a case of haid (menstruation). Yet it is not a case of haid, either, if the miscarriage took place fifteen or more days after the cessation of the previous menstrual bleeding and this new bleeding ceases before the end of three days, or if fifteen days have not elapsed after the cessation of the (previous) menstrual bleeding. It is a mere case of bleeding no different from a bloody nose. She has to perform her namâz. And she has to fast. A ghusl is not necessary before going to bed with her husband.

[Great Islamic scholar (Zeyn-ud-dîn) Muhammad Birgivî (bin 'Alî) 'rahmatullâhi 'alaih' (928 [1521 A.D.], Balıkesir – of plague in 981 [1573], Birgi, Aydın, Turkey,) wrote an extremely valuable book entitled **Zuhr-ul-mutaahhilîn** and explaining women's menstrual and puerperal states. The book is in the Arabic language. 'Allâma Shâmî Sayyid Muhammad Emîn (or Amîn) bin 'Umar bin 'Abd-ul-'Azîz Ibni 'Âbidîn 'rahima-hullâhu ta'âlâ' (1198 [1784 A.D.], Damascus – 1252 [1836], the same place) enlarged that book and entitled it **Menhel-ul-wâridîn**. Here is (a summary of) what is written in **Menhel**(-ul-wâridîn): It has been stated unanimously by scholars of Fiqh that it is farz for every Muslim, man and woman alike, to learn (Islam's teachings called) 'ilm-i-hâl. For that matter, women and their husbands should learn the teachings concerning haid and nifâs. Men should teach them to their wives or, if they do not know them, let them learn them from other women who know them. A woman whose husband will not let her learn them should go out and learn them without her husband's permission. These teachings, which concern women, appears to have sunk into oblivion, as next to no man of religion knows about them. Contemporary men of religion are not learned enough to tell apart the kinds of bleeding called haid (menorrhoea), nifâs (lochial discharge), and istihâda (menorrhagia). They do not possess books enlarging on these subjects. And the ones who have books containing the information cannot read and understand them. For, these teachings are difficult to understand. On the other hand, religious matters such as ablution, namâz, (reading or reciting) the Qur'ân al-kerîm, fasting, i'tikâf, hajj (pilgrimage), reaching (the age of) puberty, marriage, divorce, a (divorced) woman's period of 'iddat, istibrâ, etc. require learning the information pertaining to (the so-called kinds of) bleeding. It took me half of my lifetime to understand these teachings well. I shall try to explain briefly and clearly what I have learned for the benefit of my Muslim sisters:

Haid is the blood that starts to flow from the genitals of a healthy girl (at least) immediately over her eighth year of age, or of a woman after a period of full purity directly succeeding the last minute of her previous menstrual period, and which continues for at least three days. This bleeding is also called **sahîh bleeding**, (or sahîh catamenia.) If no bleeding is observed throughout the period of fifteen or more days following a period of 'âdat and which is between two menstrual periods, this period of purity is called **sahîh purity**. If there exist days of fâsid bleeding before or after a period of fifteen or more days of purity or between two periods of sahîh purity, all these days (interrupted by the so-called days of fâsid

– 79 –

bleeding) are called **hukmî purity** or **fâsid purity**. Periods without any bleeding observed and yet which are shorter than fifteen days are called fâsid purity. Sahîh purity and hukmî purity are called **full purity**. Bleedings that are observed before and after a period of full purity and which continue for (at least) three days each are two separate periods of haid.

Any colour of blood with the exception of white, and yet including a cloudy colour, is blood of haid.

When a girl starts to menstruate she becomes **bâligha**, (that is, she has reached the age of puberty.) In other words, she becomes a woman. The number of the days between the moment when bleeding is observed and the day when the bleeding ceases is period of **'âdat**. Period of 'âdat is ten days maximum. It is three days minimum. In the Shâfi'î and Hanbalî Madhhabs, it is fifteen days maximum and one day minimum.

Haid is not necessarily a non-stop bleeding. If a bleeding observed to have started ceases and then is observed to recur one or two days later, the time of purity that takes place in between and which continues for shorter than three days, must be added to the period as if blood flowed continuously, according to a consensus of Islamic scholars. If that purity continues for three or more days and yet comes to an end before the tenth day of haid, it should be concluded that the bleeding has continued incessantly for ten days, according to a report that Imâm Muhammad 'rahima-hullâhu ta'âlâ' conveys from Imâm A'zam Abû Hanîfa 'rahima-hullâhu ta'âlâ'. There is yet another scholarly report conveyed by Imâm Muhammad. On the other hand, according to Imâm Abû Yûsuf 'rahima-hullâhu ta'âlâ', all the days of purity that are over before the fifteenth day are to be added to the period as if the blood flowed incessantly. If a girl observes bleeding for one day and then experiences purity for the following fourteen days and thereafter bleeds for one day again; or if a woman undergoes a one day of bleeding and thereafter ten days of purity directly followed by one day of bleeding, or observes bleeding for three days and thereafter undergoes five days of purity and thereafter bleeds again for one day; the first ten days of the girl make up her menstrual period called 'âdat, according to Imâm Abû Yûsuf. As for the former woman, the number of days equalling her 'âdat are menstrual, all the days directly thereafter being istihâda (menorrhagia). All nine days of the latter woman are menstrual. According to Imâm Muhammad's 'rahima-hullâhu ta'âlâ' first riwâya(t), (i.e. scholarly report,) only nine days of the former women are menstrual (haid). According to the second riwâyat of Imâm Muhammad, only the first three days of the latter woman are menstrual, and none of the others is menstrual. Translating from the book entitled **Multeqâ** (or Multaqâ)[1] for our current book, we have written all the following information in the light of Imâm Muhammad's first riwâyat. One day, (in this context,) means exactly twenty-four hours. It is mustahab, for unmarried (virginal) women only during menses, and for married women always, to place a piece of cloth or cotton called kursuf (pad, sanitary towel, tampon) on the mouth of their genitalia, and to use perfume on it. It is makrûh for them to insert the entire kursuf into the vagina. A girl who observes blood stains on the kursuf every day for months on end must be accepted to be menstruating for the first ten days and undergoing istihâda for the following twenty days (of each month). This rule applies until this incessant bleeding, which is termed **istimrâr**, ceases. If a girl observes bleeding for three days running and then does not observe it for one day and then observes it again for one day and then does not observe it for two days running and then observes it again for one day and then does not observe it for one day and then observes it again for one day, all ten days are menstrual. If she sees blood one day and yet does not see it the following day, and if this every-other-day process continues for ten days monthly, she ceases from namâz and fasting every other day whereon she sees bleeding, and makes a ghusl and performs her daily namâz every other day whereon no bleeding takes place [Mesâil-i-sharh-i-wikâya].[2] Bleeding that continues for a period shorter than three days, which equals seventy-two hours, be it shorter by five minutes or, for a newly pubescent girl, which is still being undergone after the tenth day when it continues for more than ten days, or, for a woman who is not new, which she undergoes after her 'âdat when it exceeds not only her 'âdat but the ten-day maximum, or which is undergone by a pregnant or âisa [old] woman or by a small girl under the age of nine, is not menstrual. It is called **istihâda** (menorrhagia), or fâsid bleeding. A woman becomes **âisa** around the age of fifty-five. If a woman whose 'âdat is five days observes bleeding when half of the

---

[1] Written by Ibrâhîm bin Muhammad Halabî 'rahmatullâhi ta'âlâ 'alaih' (866, Aleppo – 956 [1549 A.D.]), Istanbul. There is also a French version of the book.

[2] That book, in the Fârisî language, was written by 'Abd-ul-Haqq Sujâdil Serhendî 'rahmatullâhi ta'âlâ 'alaih'.

sun has risen and her bleeding ceases as two-thirds of the sun rises in the eleventh morning, bleeding that she has undergone in excess of her 'âdat of five days isistihâda (menorrhagia). For, her bleeding has exceeded (the maximum limit of) ten days plus ten nights by one-sixth of sunrise. When ten days are over, she must make a ghusl and make qadâ of the namâzes which she did not perform on the days following her 'âdat.

A woman undergoing days of istihâda is a person with an 'udhr, like one who suffers from enuresis or continuous nose-bleeding. She has to perform namâz and fast, and waty (sexual intercourse) is permissible.

According to qawl of Imâm Muhammad, if a girl experiences a bleeding for the first time in her life, and if it continues for one day and pauses for eight days and recurs on the tenth day, all ten days are menstrual. However, if she bleeds for one day and the bleeding pauses for the following nine days and recurs the eleventh day, none of them is menstrual. The two days' bleeding is istihâda. For, as it has been stated earlier, the days, of purity previous to the bleeding that is observed after the tenth day are not counted as menstrual. If she observes blood on the tenth and eleventh days, the days of purity in between will be counted as menstrual as well, and thereby the first ten days will be menstrual and the eleventh day will be istihâda.

Bleeding called istihâda (menorrhagia) is a sign of illness. Flow that is too long may be dangerous. It is necessary to consult a doctor. Red gum called dragon's blood will stop the bleeding if it is rolled into small balls and swallowed with some water twice daily, one gram in the morning and one in the evening. The recommended daily amount is five grams maximum. A woman's period of menstruation, as well as that of purity, is the same number of days every month. One month, in this context, is a length of time between the beginning of one haid and that of the next one. Every woman must learn by heart the number of days and hours during which she menstruates and her days and hours of purity, i.e. her 'âdat. A woman's 'âdat does not change for long years. If it changes, she will have to memorize her new days of haid and purity.

The book entitled **Menhel** (ul-wâridîn) renders the following account on the changing of an 'âdat: If a woman menstruates in keeping with the time and days of her previous 'âdat, it should be concluded that her 'âdat has not changed. If it is out of keeping, then her 'âdat has changed, and the kinds of this change will be explained in the following pages. If it is out of keeping only once, then the 'âdat is accepted to have changed. This rule is confirmed by the fatwâ as well. If a woman with an 'âdat of five days observes blood for six days after a period of sahîh purity, these six days will be her new haid, new 'âdat. Number of the days of purity as well will change at a single event. When it changes, so does the time of 'âdat. Supposing a woman's 'âdat is five days of bleeding followed by twenty-five days of purity; if her new 'âdet becomes three days of bleeding followed by twenty-five days of purity or five days of bleeding followed by twenty-three days of purity, then the days of bleeding or those of purity, respectively, have changed in number. Likewise, if bleeding exceeds the limit of ten days, so that fâsid bleeding takes place and the last three or more days of that fâsid bleeding concur with the days of her previous 'âdat and the remaining last days of her previous 'âdat concur with the new purity, the days concurring with the days of her (previous) 'âdat are her new 'âdat. Her 'âdat has changed now. If her 'âdat is five days and bleeding starts seven days before her days of purity are over and that bleeding continues for eleven days, that bleeding is fâsid bleeding because it exceeds ten days. More than three days of that bleeding, i.e. its four days, are within her previous 'âdat, and one day of her previous 'âdat falls within the new sahîh purity. Her period of 'âdat has become four days, although the period of time within which it takes place has not changed. Let us provide some more clarification for this type of change in 'âdat:

If new days of bleeding that are in number different from those previous to them continue for more than ten days and three or more days of them do not take place within the days of the previous 'âdat, the period of time within which the 'âdat takes place changes. No change in the number of the days (of 'âdat) takes place, and it begins the day when blood is observed. If a woman whose 'âdat is five days does not observe any bleeding within these five days in the following month, or if she does not observe any bleeding on its first three days, and thereafter she observes bleeding for eleven days, her menstrual period is five days, beginning with the day when bleeding is first observed; yet the time of her 'âdat has changed. If three or more days of the (new) bleeding fall within the days of her previous 'âdat, only these (three or more) days are menstrual, the remaining days being istihâda (menorrhagia). If she observes bleeding five days before her (previous) 'âdat and does not observe any bleeding within her (previous) 'âdat and observes bleeding for one day directly after her (previous) 'âdat, the five days of purity in between are, according to Imâm Abû Yûsuf, menstrual, and her 'âdat has not changed. If she observes bleeding for the last three days of her (previous 'âdat) and also for eight more days directly thereafter, its first three days are menstrual, and the number has changed. If the extra days of bleeding are few enough so that the addition will not exceed ten days and there follows a sahîh purity, the entire sum, (i.e. three plus fewer than eight days,) is menstrual. If the purity that followed were fâsid purity, then her 'âdat would not change. If her 'âdat is five days and yet observes bleeding for six days and thereafter undergoes purity for fourteen days and thereafter bleeding for one day, her 'âdat has not changed. Let us give eleven examples based on a hypothetical woman whose 'âdat consists of five days of haid and fifty-five days of purity to add elucidation to what has been said so far:

1– If this woman goes through a period of five days of menstruation and fifteen days of purity and thereafter eleven days of bleeding, no bleeding takes place within her (usual and also previous) 'âdat, which would have taken place fifty-five days later (than the end of her 'âdat of five days). So, the time of the 'âdat has changed but the number of its days has not changed. The first five days of the (final) eleven days are menstrual.

2– If she undergoes five days of bleeding followed by forty-six days of purity and eleven days of bleeding, in that case the last two days of the (final) eleven days fall within the period of 'âdat. However, since they are fewer than three days, the number of the days of 'âdat does not change although its time changes. Then, the first five of the eleven days are menstrual.

3– If she experiences five days of menstruation and forty-eight days of purity and then twelve days of bleeding, five of the twelve days are days of (the usual fifty-five days of) purity, and five days are menstrual. So, no change has taken place.

4– If she goes through five days of bleeding and fifty-four days of purity and one day of bleeding and fourteen days of purity and then one day of bleeding, the one day in between, (the earlier one day, that is,) is the last day of (her usual) purity. Since the fourteen days are nâqis (imperfect) purity, (in other words, because they are five days fewer than the accepted full purity,) they are days of bleeding, and the first five of them are menstrual. The time of 'âdat and the number of its days have not changed.

5– In a succession of five days of bleeding followed by fifty-seven days of purity followed by three days of bleeding followed by fourteen days of purity followed by one day of bleeding, the three days of bleeding are within the time of the 'âdat. The fourteen days which follow them are counted as days of bleeding. However, since the number exceeds eleven days, the 'âdat has changed only in its number of days.

6– If five days of bleeding and fifty-five days of purity and then nine days of bleeding which is followed by a sahîh purity, have been experienced, the (final) nine days of bleeding are menstrual. Only the number (of days of 'âdat) has changed. There are more than three days both in the time of 'âdat and thereafter.

7– In case of five days of bleeding followed by fifty days of purity followed by ten days of bleeding, the ten days are haid (menstrual). The 'âdat of days of purity has changed to fifty days. Days of bleeding are in the time of 'âdat, and so is their number.

8– In case of five days of bleeding and fifty-four days of purity and eight days of bleeding, the eight days are menstrual, and more than three days of it are in the 'âdat. Numbers of menstrual and purity days have changed by one day.

9– In case of five days of bleeding and fifty days of purity and seven days of bleeding, the seven days are menstrual, days as many as the number of nisâb are before the 'âdat and fewer than three days are in the nisâb. So, the haid has changed both in its time and in its number of days, whereas days of purity have changed only in number.

10– In case of five days of bleeding and fifty-eight days of purity and three days of bleeding, the three days are haid, two days of them being in the time of 'âdat and one day being after it. The 'âdat of haid has changed both in its time and in its number of days, and purity has changed only in its number of days.

11– In case of five days of bleeding and sixty-four days of purity and seven or eleven days of bleeding, in the former sub-case the seven days are menstrual, wherein change has taken place in the 'âdat and in time. In the latter sub-case, the earliest five of the eleven days are menstrual, the remaining six days being istihâda. The 'âdat changes only in its time. Since the bleeding continues for more than ten days, the number does not change. Purity changes in its number of days.

It is stated as follows by Imâm Fakhr-ud-dîn 'Uthmân Zeylâ'î 'rahim-hullâhu ta'âlâ' (d. 743 [1343 A.D.], Egypt), in his book

Tebyîn-ul-haqâiq, and by Ahmad bin Muhammad Shelbî 'rahima-hullâhu ta'âlâ' (d. 1031 [1621 A.D.], Egypt), in his annotation to the book: "If she undergoes bleeding one day before the 'âdat and ten days of purity and then one day of bleeding, her haid, according to Imâm Abû Yûsuf 'rahima-hullâhu ta'âlâ', begins with the ten days during which she has not observed any bleeding and continues as long as her 'âdat. The first and last days of her new haid are bloodless. For, bleeding has been observed before the 'âdat and after the tenth day, which means that the fâsid purity in between is to be counted as days of bleeding. According to Imâm Muhammad 'rahima-hullâhu ta'âlâ', the entire period is non-menstrual. Supposing a woman's 'âdat is five days of bleeding followed by twenty-five days of purity:

"1– In case she undergoes bleeding one day earlier and one day of purity directly after that one day of bleeding and thereafter bleeding starts again and continues in a manner called 'istimrâr' (uninterrupted continuation) that carries it beyond the tenth day, five days of it, as long as her 'âdat, are menstrual, according to Imâm Abû Yûsuf. The days before and after it are menorrhagial bleeding (istihâda). According to Imâm Muhammad, three of the days of bleeding, i.e. the ones which concur with her 'âdat, are menstrual. Those three days are the second and third and fourth days of her 'âdat. For, she did not observe any bleeding on the first day of her 'âdat. The fifth one of the days whereon she observed bleeding, on the other hand, is outside of her 'âdat.

"2– If she observes bleeding on the first day of her 'âdat and thereafter undergoes one day of purity which is followed by a continuous bleeding called 'istimrâr' that carries it to beyond the tenth day, five days, i.e. as long as her 'âdat, are menstrual, as is unanimously stated by Islamic scholars. For, its first and final days are bloody.

"3– If she observes bleeding for three days of her 'âdat and thereafter undergoes purity for the other two days and then an istimrâr which carries it to beyond the tenth day, her 'âdat of five days are menstrual, according to Imâm Abû Yûsuf. According to Imâm Muhammad, the first three days of her 'âdat are menstrual. For, in Imâm Muhammad's ijtihâd, the first and last days of menstruation must be bloody."

It is stated as follows in books entitled **Bahr** and **Durr-ul-munteqâ**: "If bleeding exceeds the period of 'âdat and ceases before ten days are over and never recurs during the fifteen days following its cessation, that the bleeding on the exceeding days is menstrual is stated unanimously (by Islamic scholars). In that case, days of 'âdat will have changed. If blood comes out (ot least) once during the fifteen days and nights, the days in excess of her 'âdat will not be menstrual; they will be menorrhagial (istihâda). And when those days are known to have been menorrhagial, she makes qadâ of the namâzes that she did not perform on those days." It is mustahab for her to wait until almost the end of the time of the namâz during which the bleeding ceases, if the cessation takes place after the 'âdat is over and yet before ten days. Then she makes a ghusl and performs that time's namâz. Waty becomes permissible thereafter. If she misses the ghusl and the namâz as she waits, then, when the time of that namâz is over, waty without a ghusl will be permissible.

When a girl observes bleeding on herself for the first time in her life and a woman observes bleeding fifteen days after the end of her 'âdat, if (in both the people sampled) the bleeding ceases before three days, these two people (will have to) wait until it is nearly the end of the prayer time (wherein the cessation took place). Then, making only an ablution without having to make a ghusl, they perform the time's namâz and make qadâ of the namâzes that they did not perform (during the bleeding that continued short of three days). If bleeding recurs after they have performed that namâz, they do not perform namâz. If it ceases again, they make an ablution towards the end of the prayer time and perform the time's namâz and make qadâ of the unperformed namâzes, if there should be any. They keep on doing so until three days are completed. However, waty is not halâl even if a ghusl has been made.

If (in either example) the bleeding continues in excess of three days and yet ceases before the (end of) 'âdat, waty is not halâl until the period of 'âdat is over even if she makes a ghusl. However, if she does not observe a stain of blood until the end of the prayer time, she makes a ghusl and performs that namâz. She does not (have to) make qadâ of the ones that she did not perform (in the meantime). She fasts. If no blood comes out for fifteen days after the day when bleeding ceased, the day when it ceased is the end of her new 'âdat. However, if bleeding recurs, she ceases from namâz. As for the fast that she has performed, she makes qadâ of it after Ramadân. If bleeding ceases, again she makes a ghusl close to the end of prayer time and performs her namâz. She fasts. She goes on doing likewise until an elapse of ten days. After the tenth day she performs namâz again without making a ghusl even if she observes bleeding, and waty (conjugal relationship) before a ghusl is halâl. It is mustahab, however, to make a ghusl before waty. If bleeding ceases before the day dawns and if there is time enough only to make a ghusl and get dresessed and yet not also to say, "Allâhu ekber," before the day dawns, she performs the beginning day's fasting. Yet she does not have to make qadâ of the (previous day's) night prayer. If she has time enough also to say, ("Allâhu ekber," i.e. to say) the Tekbîr, she will have to make qadâ of the night prayer. If menstruation starts before iftâr, (i.e. shar'î sunset, time for breaking fast,)[1] her fast breaks (outright). She makes qadâ of it after Ramadân. If menstruation starts during namâz, her namâz breaks. When she becomes clean, (i.e. after she makes a ghusl at the end of her menstruation,) she does not (have to) make qadâ of it if it was a farz namâz. If it was a nâfila (supererogatory) namâz, however, she makes qadâ of it. After dawn, if she observes blood on her sanity towel (kursuf) when she wakes up, her menstruation starts the moment she observes it. If she sees that her sanity towel is clean when she wakes up, she went out of menstruation in her sleep. In both cases it is farz to perform (the previous) night prayer. For, a namâz's being farz depends on being clean, (i.e. not menstruating,) at the last minute of the time of that namâz. A woman who observes that she is menstruating before she has performed the time's namâz does not (have to) make qadâ of that namâz.

There has to be a period of **full purity** between two periods of menstruation. If that period of full purity is (one which is termed) **sahîh purity**, that the bleedings directly before and after it are two separate haids is stated unanimously (by Islamic scholars). Days of purity amidst the days of bleeding throughout the ten days of haid are accepted as menstrual, while the days of istihâda after the ten days are accepted as days of purity. If a girl undergoes three days of bleeding followed by fifteen days without any bleeding followed by one day of bleeding followed by one day of purity followed by three days of bleeding, the first and last three days during which she observes bleeding are two separate periods of haid. For, because her 'âdat will be of three days, the second haid cannot begin with the one day of bleeding in between. That one day (of bleeding) makes the full purity previous to it a fâsid one. Molla

---

[1] Please see the tenth chapter of the fourth fascicle of **Endless Bliss** for details on kinds of prayer times.

Husraw 'rahima-hullâhu ta'âlâ (d. 885 [1480 A.D.]) is quoted to have stated as follows in Shernblâlî's commentary to his **Ghurer**: "If a girl undergoes one day of bleeding followed by fourteen days of purity followed by one day of bleeding followed by eight days of purity followed by one day of bleeding followed by seven days of purity followed by two days of bleeding followed by three days of purity followed by one day of bleeding followed by three days of purity followed by one day of bleeding followed by two days of purity followed by one day of bleeding; of these forty-five days, only the ten days following the fourteen days are menstrual, and the other days are menorrhagial (istihâda), according to Imâm Muhammad 'rahima-hullâhu ta'âlâ'." For, a new menstrual period does not begin after these ten days, since no full purity takes place. Days of purity that follow thereafter are not accepted as days whereon bleeding took place continuously, since they are not within a period of haid. "According to Imâm Abû Yûsuf 'rahima-hullâhu ta'âlâ', on the other hand, the first ten days and the fourth ten days with a period of purity on each side of it are menstrual." For, according to Imâm Abû Yûsuf, the days of fâsid purity that followed them are days whereon bleeding is accepted to have taken place continuosly. According to the following first case, after the ten menstrual days, twenty days are days of purity and the last ten days, [i.e. the fourth ten days,] are menstrual.

If bleeding continues for fifteen days without any days of purity in the meantime, i.e. in a way of flowing called **istimrâr**, the calculation is based on her 'âdat. That is, beginning after her 'âdat, a period of purity equal in its number of days to the previous month's purity and thereafter menstruation as long as her 'âdat, will be essential.

If istimrâr happens on a girl, it is stated in the booklet entitled **Menhel-ul-wâridîn** that one of the following four situations may be the case:

1– If the bleeding observed abides, the first ten days will be accepted as menstrual, twenty days thereafter being days of purity.

2– If a girl experiences istimrâr after undergoing a period of sahîh bleeding followed by a period of sahîh purity, this girl has become a woman with a certain 'âdat. For instance, if she underwent five days of bleeding followed by forty days of purity, the first five days of the istimrâr will be accepted as menstrual, the following forty days being days of purity. This rule applies until the bleeding ceases.

3– If she undergoes a period of fâsid bleeding followed by a period of fâsid purity, none of the periods will be accepted as menstrual. If the purity was fâsid because it was shorter than fifteen days, bleeding that has been observed for the first time will be accepted to have (abided; i.e. it has) turned into istimrâr. In case of eleven days of bleeding followed by fourteen days of purity and thereafter (a continuous period of bleeding termed) istimrâr, the first period of bleeding is fâsid because it has exceeded ten days. The eleventh day (of bleeding) and the first five days of the istimrâr will be added to the period of purity, and from the additional fifth day on it will become a cycle of ten menstrual days followed by twenty days of purity, and so on. If the purity is a full one and yet it is fâsid because there are days of bleeding mixed with it, then, again, the first bleeding will be accepted to have turned into istimrâr, if the total sum of such days of fâsid purity and days of bleeding does not exceed thirty. So is the case when eleven days of bleeding are followed by fifteen days of purity and thereafter istimrâr follows. The period of sixteen days is a period of fâsid purity since its first day is a bloody one. The first four days of the istimrâr are days of purity. If their total sum exceeds thirty days, the first ten days are accepted as menstrual and all the days till the istimrâr are accepted as days of purity, whereafter a cycle of ten menstrual days followed by twenty days of purity will become established. This rule applies to a situation wherein eleven days of bleeding are followed by twenty days of purity and thereafter there begins istimrâr.

4– If she undergoes sahîh bleeding and thereafter fâsid purity, the days of sahîh bleeding are menstrual, whereafter comes a period up to thirty days of which will be accepted as purity. For instance, if istimrâr takes place after five days of bleeding followed by fourteen days of purity, the first five days are menstrual and the twenty-five days thereafter are days of purity. The first eleven days of istimrâr are accepted as days of purity so as to complement the number to twenty-five. From then on, five days of menstruation plus twenty-five days of purity will follow in turn. Likewise, if istimrâr takes place after three days of bleeding followed by fifteen days of purity followed by one day of bleeding followed by fifteen days of purity, the first three days of sahîh bleeding (being menstrual days), all the days until the istimrâr will be accepted as days of fâsid purity; thereby, her cycle will be three days of haid and thirty-one days of purity. During the istimrâr, however, three days of haid and twenty-seven days of purity will follow in turn. If the second period of purity were fourteen days, bleeding would be accepted to be continuous according to Imâm Abû Yûsuf, in which case the first two days (of those fourteen days) would be added to the one day (before those fourteen days) so as to make the sum menstrual and followed by fifteen days of purity, and so on. For, the first three days of bleeding followed by fifteen days of purity being sahîh periods, they would be accepted as an 'âdat.

A woman who forgets the time of her 'âdat is called **muhayyira** or **dâlla**.

Nifâs means lochia. Blood that comes out after a foetal miscarriage is nifâs (lochial, puerperal) if the hands, feet, and head of the foetus have been formed. There is not a minimum length of time for nifâs. Whenever bleeding ceases, she makes a ghusl and resumes her daily namâzes. However, she cannot resume her conjugal relationship before the number of days equal to her 'âdat elapse. Its maximum length is forty days. Once the fortieth day is over, she makes a ghusl and begins to perform her namâzes even if the bleeding has not ceased yet. Blood that comes out after the fortieth day is istihâda (menorrhagia). If a woman became clean in twenty-five days after her first childbirth, her 'âdat is twenty-five days. If that woman bleeds for forty-five days after her second child, her nifâs will be counted as twenty-five days, the remaining twenty days being istihâda. She makes qadâ of her namâzes which she did not perform during those twenty days. Hence, days of nifâs also should be memorized. If bleeding ceases, for instance, in thirty-five days instead of forty-five days, all forty-five days are nifâs, and her nifâs has changed from twenty-five to thirty-five days.

If, in Ramadân, a woman's menstrual or puerperal bleeding ceases after the time of sahûr [dawn], she does not eat or drink during that day. But (after Ramadân) she makes qadâ of that day's fast. If her haid or nifâs starts after the time of sahûr, be it after late afternoon, she eats and drinks that day.

During the days of haid or nifâs, it is harâm in all four Madhhabs to perform namâz, to fast, to enter a mosque, to read or hold the Qur'ân al-kerîm, to make tawâf (circumambulation around the Kâ'ba-i-mu'azzama within the Mesjîd-i-harâm), and coitus. She makes qadâ of her fasts, but not her namâzes. Her namâzes are forgiven. If, at each time of namâz, she makes an ablution, sits on her prayer-rug as long as she would if she performed namâz, and makes dhikr and says tasbîhs, she will earn as much thawâb as she earned when she performed her best namâz.

It is stated as follows in the book entitled **Jawhara-t-un-neyyira**:[1] "A woman should let her husband know that her haid has started. When her husband asks, it will be a grave sin for her not to tell him. She will be gravely sinful also if she says that her haid is over if her purity is still continuing. Our Prophet 'sall-Allâhu 'alaihi wa sallam' stated: '**A woman who conceals the beginning and the end of her haid from her husband is an accursed one**.' It is harâm to have anal intercourse with one's wife, during her menstrual period or as she is clean. It is a grave sin." A person who commits this sin with his wife is an accursed one. Pederasty is an even worse sin. It is called **livâta**, and is said to be a **habîth** (extremely dirty) **act** in Anbiyâ Sûra. As is stated in the commentary to **Birgivî**, our Prophet 'sall-Allâhu 'alaihi wa sallam' said: '**If you catch two people practising pederasty like people of Lot in the act, kill both of them**!' According to some Islamic scholars, both of them must be burned. Both the partners become junub after this abominable act. Having an enema will not make one junub, although it will break one's fast (Feyziyya).

If a woman observes that her haid is beginning within the time of a namâz that she has not performed yet, she will not have to make qadâ of the namâz of that namâz. [Please read the fourth chapter of the fourth fascicle of **Endless Bliss**!]

CONCERNING THE ABLUTION

An ablution has four farzes (or fards) in the Hanafî Madhhab, seven farzes in the Mâlikî Madhhab, and six farzes in the Shâfi'î and Hanbalî Madhhabs. In the Hanafî Madhhab, they are:

1– To wash one's face.

2– To wash one's forearms, including the elbows.

3– To make masah on one-fourth of one's head.

---

[1] Abridged version of the three-volumed book entitled **Sirâj-ul-wahhâj**, which Abû Bakr bin 'Alî Haddâd-i-Yemenî 'rahmatullâhi ta'âlâ 'alaih' (d. 800 [1397 A.D.]) wrote as a commentary to **Mukhtasar-i-Qudûrî**, which had been written by Abul-Huseyn Ahmad bin Muhammad Bâghdâdî 'rahmatullâhi ta'âlâ 'alaih' (362 [973 A.D.] – 428 [1037], Baghdâd).

4– To wash one's feet, including to heel bones.

There are four kinds of ablution: One of its kinds is farz, the second kind is wâjib, the third kind is sunnat, and the fourth kind is mandûb.

There are four instances of an ablution that is farz: To make an ablution in order to hold the Qur'ân al-kerîm or to perform one of the daily five prayers called namâz or to perform a namâz of janâza –explained in detail in the fifteenth chapter of the fifth fascicle of **Endless Bliss**– or to make a sajda of tilâwat –explained in the sixteenth chapter of the fourth fascicle of **Endless Bliss**.

An ablution that is wâjib is the one which is made for the tawâf-i-ziyârat –explained in the seventh chapter of the fifth fascicle of **Endless Bliss**.

An ablution that is sunnat is the one which is made for reciting the Qur'ân al-kerîm (without holding it) or for visiting Muslims' cemetery, or making an ablution before a ghusl.

An ablution that is mandûb is the one which you make before going to bed and/or after getting up. If you tell a lie or gossip about someone or listen to music arousing lust, it is mandûb to make a tawba and istighfâr for the sin involved and then make an ablution.

It is mandûb as well to have an ablution when going out for a gathering of 'ilm (knowledge) or to renew your ablution although you made an ablution which you still have but after which you have done something which would not be permissible to do without an ablution, [for instance if you have performed namâz.] If you have not performed that act of worship (with the ablution you made), it is makrûh to make an ablution although you have an ablution.

CONCERNING WATER

There are four kinds of water: Mâ-i-mutlaq; mâ-i-muqayyad; mâ-i-meshkuk; mâ-i-musta'mal.[1]

1– Examples of mâ-i-mutlaq are rain water, sea water, running spring water, and water from a well. This kind of water possesses the property to make dirty things clean. It can be used for any purpose.

2– Examples of mâ-i-muqayyad are melon juice, water-melon

_____
[1] 'Mâ' means 'water'.

juice, grape juice, flower juice, and the like.

This kind of water also possesses the property to make dirty things clean, although it is not practicable for an ablution or ghusl.

3– Leftover water from a donkey's drink or from the drink of a mule whose mother is a donkey is called mâ-i-meshkuk.

Both an ablution and a ghusl is permissible to make with this water. One has the choice to make either one before the other.

4– Whether water becomes mâ-i-musta'mal when it falls down onto the floor or when it leaves the body, (i.e. the limb being washed,) is a question at issue (among Islamic scholars). Essentially, it becomes so when it leaves the body, (i.e. the fatwâ is agreeable with this ijtihâd.) Based on this, there are three different qawls, (i.e. statements wherein mujtahids express their ijtihâds.)[1] According to Imâm A'zam (Abû Hanîfa) 'rahima-hullâhu ta'âlâ', it is najâsat-i-ghalîza (qaba najâsat).[2] According to Imâm Abû Yûsuf 'rahima-hullâhu ta'âlâ', it is najâsat-i-khafîfa. And according to Imâm Muhammad 'rahima-hullâhu ta'âlâ', it is clean. This last qawl is the established one (according to the conclusive fatwâ).

There are nine conditions to be fulfilled for the wujûb of ablution, (i.e. so that ablution should be incumbent:)

1– To be a Muslim.

2– To have reached the age of puberty.

3– To be discreet.

4– To be without an ablution.

5– For the water (to be used) for ablution to be clean.

6– Ability to make an ablution.

7– (For a woman) not to be menstruating.

8– (For a woman) not to be in a puerperal period.

9– For each and every one of the daily (five) prayers of namâz, the time of namâz to have come. [This ninth condition applies to a

---

[1] The word 'ijtihâd' is defined at various places throughout the six fascicles of **Endless Bliss**, e.g. in the twenty-fifth, twenty-sixth, twenty-seventh chapters of the first fascicle and in the tenth and twenty-ninth chapters of the third fascicle.

[2] Najâsat, along with its kinds, is explained in the sixth chapter of the fourth fascicle of **Endless Bliss**.

person with an 'udhr, (which is explained in the last six paragraphs of the third chapter of the fourth fascicle of **Endless Bliss**.)

SUNNATS OF AN ABLUTION: Twenty-five of them have been stated.

1– To say, "A'ûdhu... ." (Its complete form is: "A'ûdhu bllâh-imin-esh-shaytân-ir-rajîm.")

2– To say the Basmala. (That is, to say, "Bismillâh-ir-Rahmân-ir-Rahîm.")

3– To wash the hands.

4– To make khilâl between the fingers, (i.e. to wash between them by using the fingers of one of your hands like the teeth of a comb between the fingers of your other hand.)

5– To apply water into your mouth.

6– To apply water into your nose.

7– To make a niyyat (intention). In the Hanafî Madhhab, it is sunnat, not farz, to make a niyyat when washing the mouth. It is farz in the Shâfi'î Madhhab. In the Mâlikî Madhhab, it is farz to make a niyyat when washing the hands.

8– To face in the direction of Qibla.

9– To make khilâl of your beard (by using your fingers like a comb) [if it is thick].

10– To make masah on your beard.

11– To begin with your right hand side.

12– To make khilâl between the toes with the small finger of the left hand, beginning from under the small toe of the right foot.

13– To make masah on the head–by covering the (entire) head.

14– To make masah of the ears and the back of the head, using the water remaining from the head.

15– To observe tertîb, (i.e. to wash the limbs of ablution in prescribed order.)

16– Not to pause in beween, i.e. to wash the limbs of ablution one directly after another.

17– When making masah on the head, to begin with the front part.

18– To use a miswâk.

19– To make water reach the sides of the eyes and the eyebrows.

20– Delk, i.e. to rub the limbs being washed, gently with the hands.

21– To make one's ablution standing on a somewhat raised platform.

22– To wash the limbs of ablution three times each.

23– To refill the ewer with which you have made an ablution.

24– Not to talk on worldly matters when making an ablution.

25– To maintain your niyyat.

USING A MISWÂK

There are fifteen benefits in using a miswâk. These benefits, borrowed from the book entitled **Sirâj-ul-wahhâj** (a three–volumed commentary rendered by Abû Bakr bin 'Alî Haddâd Yemenî 'rahmatullâhi ta'âlâ 'alaih', d. 800 [1397 A.D.], to the book entitled **Mukhasar-i-Qudûrî**, which in turn had been written by Abul Hueyn Ahmad bin Muhammad Baghdâdî 'rahmatullâhi ta'âlâ 'alaih', 362 [973 A.D.] – 428 [1037], Baghdâd), are as follows:

1– It causes you to say the Kalima-i-shehâdat when dying.

2– It hardens the gums.

3– It helps to loosen the phlegm in your chest. (It is a perfect expectorant.)

4– It stops an excessive secretion of bile.

5– It diminishes oral aches.

6– It eliminates bad breath.

7– Allâhu ta'âlâ is pleased with a person who uses a miswâk.

8– It strengthes the cranial veins.

9– The devil becomes sad (when you use a miswâk).

10– Your eyes become bright with nûr (when you use a miswâk).

11– There is an icrease in your pious deeds (khayr and hasanât).

12– You have practised an act of sunnat (by using a miswâk).

13– Your mouth becomes clean.

14– Your speech becomes eloquent.

15– Two rak'ats of namâz performed with (an ablution made

after using) a miswâk yield more thawâb than seventy rak'ats of namâz without (having used) a miswâk.

MUSTAHABS OF AN ABLUTION

There are six of them, as follows:

1– Not to utter with your tongue the niyyat which you make with your heart.

2– To make masah on the back of your neck with the water remaining from your ears.

3– Not to wash your feet in the direction of Qibla.

4– To drink, if possible, the water remaining from the ablution, standing in the direction of Qibla.

5– To sprinkle some water on your clothes after the ablution.

6– To dry your limbs washed by means of a clean towel.

Ibni 'Âbidîn states as follows in his treatment of nullifiers of an ablution: "If something which is not makrûh in your own Madhhab is farz in another Madhhab, (in one of the other three Madhhabs, that is,) it is mustahab for you to do it." Imâm Rabbânî states in his two hundred and eighty-sixth (286) letter: "Because it is farz in the Mâlikî Madhhab to rub the limbs being washed during an ablution gently with the hand, we, (in the Hanafî Madhhab as we are,) should certainly do the rubbing." Ibni 'Âbidîn states as follows as he explains the talâq-i-rij'î.[1] "It is commendable for a Muslim in the Hanafî Madhhab to imitate the Mâlikî Madhhab. For, Imâm Mâlik, (leader of the Mâlikî Madhhab,) is like a disciple of Imâm A'zam Abû Hanîfa, (leader of the Hanafî Madhhab.) When the scholars in the Hanafî Madhhab were unable to find a qawl in the Hanafî Madhhab (for the solution of a certain matter), they gave their conclusive fatwâ in accordance with the Mâlikî Madhhab. Of all the (other three) Madhhabs, the Mâlikî Madhhab is the closest to the Hanafî Madhhab."

MAKRÛHS OF AN ABLUTION

There are eighteen of them, as follows:

1– To splash–water–hard on your face.

---

[1] A kind of divorce, which is dealt with in the fifteenth chapter of the sixth fascicle of **Endless Bliss**.

2– To breathe onto the water being used in the ablution.

3– To wash the limbs (that should be washed three times) fewer than three times.

4– To wash them more than three times.

5– To spit into the water being used for making an ablution.

6– To blow your nose into the water being used in the ablution.

7– To let water get down your throat when gargling.

8– To turn your back towards the Qibla (when making an ablution).

9– To shut your eyes tightly.

10– To open your eyes wide.

11– To begin the washing with the left hand side.

12– To blow your nose by using your right hand.

13– To use your left hand when applying water into your mouth.

14– To use your left hand when applying water into your nose.

15– To stamp your foot on the ground (or floor).

16– To make an ablution with water heated in the sun.

17– Not to avoid (using) mâ-i-musta'mal water. (Please see kinds of water earlier in the text.)

18– To talk on worldly matters.

NULLIFIERS OF AN ABLUTION

Twenty-four of them are stated:

1– Things issuing from one's back.

2– Things issuing from one's front.

3– Worms, stones or the like issuing from one's front or back.

4– To have an enema.

5– For a medicine which a woman has injected into her womb to come back out.

6– If a medicine which you have poured into your ear comes back out through your mouth, it will nullify your ablution. [If it exudes through your ear or nose it will not nullify your ablution (**Fatâwâ-i-Hindiyya**).]

7– For a cotton wick that a man has inserted into his urinary canal to become wet and fall. [If the wick is partly outside of the urinary canal and the part that is outside is dry, it will not nullify your ablution so long as it does not fall out.]

8– For the cotton wick to fall down, its part left outside having been wet.

9– A mouthful vomit. It will not nullify one's ablution to vomit phlegm, regardless of its amount. Liquid issuing from a sleeping person's mouth is clean, be it yellowish.

10– Shedding tears on account of an illness will nullify one's ablution. It will not nullify one's ablution if it happens as a result of weeping or with the effect of lachrymose agents such as onions.

11– Blood, pus, or yellowish liquid issuing from one's nose will nullify one's ablution even if it does go out of one's nostrils. Nasal mucus is not something najs. It will not nullify one's ablution when it goes out of the nose.

12– For the saliva that one has just spit out to contain much blood.

13– When you see blood on something you have just bitten, it will nullify your ablution if your mouth or teeth are smeared with the blood. It will not, if otherwise.

14– If you see that blood has exuded from any part of your body and spread over that part, be it only a little, your ablution will be nullified if you are in the Hanafî Madhhab, and it will not be nullified if you are in one of the Mâlikî and Shâfi'î Madhhabs.

15– Supposing you are riding on a horse not saddled; dozing off as it goes downhill will nullify your ablution.

16– If you are dubious about whether or not you have made an ablution, your dhann-i-ghâlib (prevailing opinion) should be that you are without an ablution.

17– If a man hugs his wife in the nude, (their ablution will be nullified.)

18– If you have forgotten to wash one of your limbs of ablution and you do not know which one, (your ablution becomes nullified.)

19– If pus or blood or yellowish liquid comes out from a blister on one of your limbs, by itself or when you squeeze it, (your ablution will become nullified.)

20– Supposing you have had a sore, with some najs liquid such as yellowish liquid or blood or pus in the middle of it, on your body, your ablution will be nullified when a healthy part of your body or the cotton or bandage on it has been smeared with that najs matter. There is a scholarly statement that colourless liquid exuding from a sore or abscess will not nullify one's ablution. It is permissible for people suffering from diseases such as itch, smallpox and eczema to follow this statement.

21– Supposing you doze off as you are leaning against something; (your ablution will be nullified) if your slumber is so deep as you would fall if the object you have been leaning against were taken away.

22– During a namâz with rukû's and sajdas, to laugh as loudly as to be heard by oneself and by someone beside one. If you laugh only loudly enough so that no one besides you will hear, your ablution will not be nullified, although the namâz you are performing will be fâsid. (In other words, laughing so loud that only you yourself will hear will nullify your namâz, and not your ablution.)

23– An epileptic fit or fainting will nullify one's ablution.

24– If pus or yellowish liquid or blood exudes from your ear and it reaches the part of your body that you have to wash as you make a ghusl, (your ablution will become nullified.)

From us did Europe learn how to wash oneself in a public bath.
Before then their homes would stench so bad they would smell in one's breath.
It was Muslims who spread cleanliness the whole world over,
Thereby saving humanity from an enemy so bitter.

PRAYERS TO BE SAID WHEN MAKING AN ABLUTION

When starting to make an ablution you say: "**Bismillâh-il-'adhîm wa-l-hamd-u-li-l-lâhi 'alâ dîn-il-islâmi wa 'alâ tawfîq-il-îmâni al-hamd-u-li-l-lâh-il-ledhî ja'al-al-mâa tahûran wa ja'al-al-islâma nûran.**"

As you apply water into your mouth you say: "**Allâhummesqinî min hawdi nabiyy-ika ke'sen lâ 'azmau ba'dehu abadan.**"

As you apply water into your nose you say: "**Allâhumma erihnî râyiha-t-al Jannati wa-r-zuqnî min naîmihâ wa lâ turihnî râyihat-an-nârî.**"

As you wash your face you say: "**Allâhumma bayyid wejhî**

binûrika yawma tebyaddu wujûhu awliyâika walâ tusewwid wejhî bizunûbî yawma tesweddu wujûhu a'dâika."

As you wash your right forearm (including the elbow) you say: **"Allâhumma a'tinî kitâbî bi-yemîni wa hâsibnî hisâban yesîran."**

As you wash your left forearm (including the elbow) you say: **"Allâhumma lâ tu'tinî kitâbî bishimâlî wa lâ min warâî zahrî walâ tuhâsibnî hisâban shedîdan."**

As you make masah on your head you say: **"Allâhumma harrim sha'rî wa besherî 'alannârî wa azillenî tahta dhillî 'Arshika yawma lâ dhilla illâ dhilluka."**

As you make masah on your ears you say: **"Allâhumma-j'alnî minalla-dhîna yestemi'ûna-l-qawla fa yettebi'ûna ahseneh."**

As you make masah on (the back of) your neck you say: **"Allâhumma a'tik reqâbatî min-an-nâri wahfaz min-es-selâsili wa-l-aghlâl."**

As you wash your right foot you say: **"Allâhumma thebbit qadamayya 'ala-s-sirâti yawma tezillu fîhil-aqdâm."**

As you wash your left foot you say: **"Allâhumma lâ-tatrud qadamayya 'ala-s-sirâti yawma tatrudu kullu aqdâmi a'daika. Allâhumma-j'al sa'yî meshkûran wa zenbî maghfûran wa 'amalî maqbûlan wa tijâratî len'tebûra."**

When you are through with your ablution you say: **"Allâhumma-j'alnî min-at-tewwâbîna wa-j'alnî min-al-mutetahhirîna wa-j'alnî min 'ibâdika-s-sâlihîna wa-j'alnî min-al-ledhîna lâ khawfun 'alaihim walâ hum yahzenûn."**

Thereafter, looking at the sky, you say: **"Subhânakallâhumma wa bihamdika esh-hadu an lâ ilâha illâ Anta wahdaka lâ sherîka laka wa anna Muhammadan 'abduka wa rasûluka."**

Thereafter you say the Sûra of **Innâ anzelnâ** once or twice or three times, beginning the Sûra by saying, "Bism-illâh-ir-Rahmân ir-Rahîm," before saying it.

It is necessary to learn the religious teachings that your family and children need to learn and to teach them these teachings. On the Rising Day men will be questioned about their wives.

CONCERNING THE TAYAMMUM

In the Hanafî Madhhab tayammum will be sahîh also before a prayer time begins. It will not be sahîh in the other three

Madhhabs. There are three fards (farzes) in a tayammum: A tayammum that is required for making an ablution is the same as a tayammum required for making a ghusl. They differ only in their niyyats (intentions). Therefore, the two tayammums cannot be used for each other's place.

1– To make a niyyat, which is compulsory.

2– To touch soil with both hands and thereafter to make masah on the entire face, covering the face with the hands.

3– To strike the soil with both palms once again and then first make masah on your entire right forearm with your left hand and then your entire left forearm with your right hand, (including the elbows.) These acts are all rukns, (i.e. they are fards within the tayammum. If any one of them are omitted, the tayammum will become null and void.)

The proof-texts showing that the tayammum is farz are the forty-third âyat-i-kerîma of Nisâ Sûra and the sixth âyat-i-kerîma of Mâida Sûra. In the Mâlikî and Shâfi'î Madhhabs, it is not permissible to make a tayammum (which you are to use instead of an ablution to perform a certain namâz) before the beginning of (that) namâz, and more than one namâzes cannot be performed with one tayammum. (In other words, you will have to make a new tayammum for every individual namâz, waiting until its prescribed time begins.)

There are six things with which it is not permissible to make a tayammum, except when there is soil dust on them. The six things are: Iron, copper, bronze, tin, gold, silver, and all other metals. Tayammum is permissible with anything other than these metals, which melt when they are heated; glass, which softens when it is heated; and glazed porcelain. However, its substance has to be earthen.

Earthen ground whereon someone has urinated can be used for performing namâz on it when it dries up. But a tayammum cannot be made from it.

For it being permissible to make a tayammum, it is required that you look for water, fail to find it, and ask an 'âdil and sâlih Muslim. (An 'âdil Muslim is one who never commits a grave sin and who does not commit a venial sin habitually. A sâlih Muslim is one who avoids not only harâms but also doubtful acts lest he should commit a sin inadvertently. Please see the first chapter of the sixth fascicle of **Endless Bliss** for the doubtful.)

There are five obligatory essentials to be fulfilled when making a tayammum:

1– To make a niyyat. 2– To make a masah. 3– For the object to be used for making a tayammum to be of earthen matter. If it is not something made of earth, there will have to be earth dust on it. 4– The earthen object or the dust on it to be used for a tayammum has to be clean. 5– To be actually or virtually unable to use water (for making an ablution). [Weakness after a certain illness is an 'udhr as well, (in which case you may make a tayammum instead of making an ablution by using water.) So is the case with weakness on account of old age. Another convenience to be utilized by such people is that they may perform their namâz sitting.]

There are seven sunnats to be performed when making a tayammum:

1– To say the Basmala, (which means to say, "Bismillâh-ir-Rahmân ir-Rahîm," when beginning to make a tayammum.) 2– To strike the (palms of the) hands (gently) against clean soil. 3– To rub the object against which you strike your hands (gently) by moving your hands forward and backward on it once. 4– To open the fingers. 5– To shake off the dust on the hands by striking them against each other. 6– To make masah on the face first. 7– To make masah on the entire forearms including the elbows.

There are four conditions to be fulfilled for looking for water.

1– For your location to be inhabited.

2– If you are informed of the existence of water.

3– If you are firmly convinced that there is water.

4– If you are not at a frightful place.

If a person has found water and yet the place of the water is farther than a mile away, then it will be permissible (for that person) to make a tayammum (instead of going there to make an ablution). If the distance is shorter than a mile and it is early enough so that the prayer time will not be over, it will not be permissible to make a tayammum. [One mile is a distance of four thousand zrâ', i.e. 0.48x4000=1920 metres in the Hanafî Madhhab.]

On the other hand, if he looks for water, fails to find it, makes a tayammum and performs the namâz, and thereafter sees water, will he have to reperform his namâz? This is a question at issue (among Islamic scholars). The conclusive solution is that he will not have to reperform the namâz that he has performed.

If a person becomes wet and yet cannot find water to use for an ablution and cannot find something to use for a tayammum either, he dries a piece of mud and makes a tayammum with it. Supposing a few people have made a tayammum each; if only one of them sees water, the tayammums made by all of them will become null and void.

If a person brings some water (for a group of people) and says that one of the group is to use the water for making an ablution, the tayammums made by all the group will become fâsid, (i.e. null and void.) However, if he says that the water is for the entire group to make an ablution each and yet the water provided is enough for only one person's ablution, the tayammums made by all of them will be sahîh (valid and sound).

Supposing a person has become junub[1] and cannot find water anywhere but in a mosque; first he makes a tayammum for a ghusl and thereafter enters the mosque to get the water. However, if he cannot find water in the mosque, he will have to make another tayammum for performing namâz.

Supposing a person sitting in a mosque experiences a nocturnal emission; he makes a tayammum and leaves the mosque.

Supposing a person does not have hands; he may make a tayammum. However, that person will not be absolved from having to make an istinjâ if they have someone to help them do so.[2] If they do not have anyone to help them, they will be absolved from it.

If a person does not have hands and feet, they will be absolved from having to perform namâz, according to the Tarafeyn, (i.e. Imâm A'zam Abû Hanîfa and his disciple Imâm Muhammad Sheybânî.) According to Imâm Abû Yûsuf, however, that person still has to perform namâz.

On the other hand, it is not permissible to make a tayammum for Friday prayer. In other words, if a person does not have time long enough to make an ablution (for Friday prayer), it will not be permissible for him to make a tayammum in a hurry lest he should

---

[1] Junub means (one) who needs to make a ghusl for reasons such as sexual relationship and nocturnal emission. Please review the chapter dealing with ghusl.

[2] Istinjâ means to clean one's front or back after urination or defecation. Please see the final part of the sixth chapter of the fourth fascicle of **Endless Bliss** for detail.

miss the Friday prayer. [For, there is the early afternoon prayer (for people who have missed the Friday prayer. They will have to perform the day's early afternoon prayer).] It is written in the book entitled **Durr-ul-mukhtâr** as well that it is not permissible to make an ablution with treacle of dates termed 'nebîdh'. (Please see the eleventh paragraph of the third chapter of the sixth fascicle of **Endless Bliss** for 'nebîdh'.)

If a person experiences a nocturnal emission during a journey, he makes a tayammum and performs his morning prayer. Thereafter he continues with his journey until noon. When there is little time left before late afternoon prayer, so that the prescribed time for early afternoon prayer is about to come to an end, he makes a tayammum and performs the early afternoon prayer. Supposing this person finds water after late afternoon, will he have to reperform his morning and early afternoon prayers? Islamic scholars have not reached a consensus on this question. According to one qawl, he will have to do so, and according to another qawl, he will not have to do so. Probably, this matter should be made to take after the matter termed 'tertîb', (and which is explained in the seventh paragraph of the twenty-third chapter of the fourth fascicle of **Endless Bliss**.)

Supposing a person has a donkey carrying some water on it and loses his donkey; this person, (when it is prayer time and he needs an ablution,) makes a tayammum and performs his namâz. As he performs, the moment he hears his donkey's braying he loses his ablution.

Supposing a person is travelling on a horse and his companions will not wait for him if he dismounts from his horse; he makes a tayammum on his horse and performs his namâz (in a manner termed) îmâ, (i.e. simulation, signs.)

If a person is making a perilous journey in a cold weather, so that making a ghusl may cause him to become ill, then he performs his namâz with a tayammum.

A person who is setting out for a journey must have a tile or a brick among his personal belongings. For, if he has to make a tayammum at a place where things around him are all wet, then he makes a tayammum with the (tile or the) brick and performs his namâz.

Supposing a person starts to perform the namâz of 'Iyd and somehow loses his ablution (during the namâz); he makes a tayammum and resumes his namâz if he knows that he will be too late to catch up with the remaining part of the namâz of 'Iyd, or fears that he may be stranded in the crowd, he makes a tayammum and resumes his performance of the namaz. This qawl is according to Imâm A'zam (Abû Hanîfa). According to the qawl of the Imâmeyn,[1] however, he should make an ablution.

[It is stated as follows in (Ahmad bin Muhammad bin Ismâ'îl) Tahtâwî's annotation to (Abul-Ikhlâs Hasan bin Ammâr) Shernblâlî's (commentary book entitled) **Merâq-il-felâh**: "Illness is an 'udhr, (i.e. a good reason justified by Islam,) to (make it permissible to) make a tayammum (instead of making an ablution). It is not an 'udhr for a healthy person to fear that he may become ill should he make an ablution. Scholars who said that it is permissible for a healthy person to leave his fast to qadâ, (i.e. to postpone fasting until a later date,) if he fears that he may become ill should he fast (in the blessed month of Ramadân), said (also) that it is permissible for a person who fears that he may become ill to make a tayammum (instead of an ablution). Four things are meant by 'becoming ill': Water may be harmful (to one's health). Movement may be harmful. One may be unable to use water. One may not be able to make a tayammum, either. Harm will be judged either by one's strongly sensing it or by a warning on the part of an 'âdil Muslim doctor and a specialist. If an 'âdil Muslim doctor cannot be found, decision made by a doctor whose sinfulness is not known openly and publicly will be admitted. A person who is unable to use water on his own makes a tayammum if he cannot find someone to help him to make an ablution. If he has children or servants or someone to help him to make an ablution for friendship's sake, one of these people will help him with an ablution. If none of these people is available, then he makes a tayammum. According to Imâm A'zam, he does not have to hire someone to help him in return for a payment. A person who cannot make a tayammum, either, leaves the namâz to qadâ, (i.e. postpones the namâz until he recovers.) Although husband and wife de not have to help each oher to make an ablution or to perform namâz, the husband ought to ask his wife for help. Supposing a person is outside of town and village and therefore cannot find hot water; he makes a tayammum if he is afraid of becoming ill should he make a ghusl with cold water. A fatwâ has been given that this rule applies within urban areas as well. If more

---

[1] Imâm Abû Yûsuf and Imâm Muhammad Sheybânî, two greatest disciples of Imâm A'zam Abû Hanîfa.

than half of a person's limbs of ablution and/or ghusl is sore, he makes a tayammum (instead of an ablution and/or ghusl). If the parts that are sore covers an area half of the limbs (of ablution and/or ghusl), then he washes the healthy parts and makes masah on the sore parts; if the masah will cause harm to the sore parts, then he makes masah on the bandages. If this also will cause harm, then he does not make masah, either. If there is a sore on his head, so that masah will cause harm, he will be absolved from (having to make) masah. Supposing there are cuts on the places that are farz to wash (when making an ablution) of both hands of a person whose face is sore, too; then that person will not be able to make a tayammum; so he performs namâz without an ablution, and will not have to reperform the namâz performed. If his face is healthy, he has his face washed. If he does not have a helper he rubs his face (gently) on soil. If one of the hands of a healthy person is apoplectic or wounded or cut or crippled, he makes an ablution with his other hand. If his both hands are so, he rubs his face on soil. If the bandage or piece of wood or ointment or plaster cast applied perforce on a sore or abscessed or broken limb for treatment and protection cannot be removed and so that part of the limb cannot be washed or made masah on, masah is made on the major part of its surface and on the healthy skin in between. If possible, it is necessary to remove the bandage or the piece of wood or the ointment or the plaster cast, make masah on the problematic area, and wash the healthy area of the skin. These things do not necessarily have to be applied after making an ablution; nor is there a deadline for their usage. It is permissible to wash the healthy foot and make masah on the bandage on the other one. If the thing put on it falls off before the injury heals, the ablution will not become nullified. Nor will it become nullified if the bandage is changed after masah has been made on it. If the ointment applied on a broken or injured nail or on a cut on one's foot should not be removed because it will be harmful to remove it, one has been involved in an impasse called 'quandary', in which case one washes the outer part of the ointment. In case washing may be harmful, one makes masah on it. If masah may be harmful, too, then one does not make masah, either. [Since the same rule applies in the other three Madhhabs as well, it is out of the question to imitate another Madhhab.] That this ointment is like a splint is written in the book entitled Ibni 'Âbidîn. However, having one's teeth filled or crowned is quite a different matter. For, it is possible to imitate Mâlikî or Shâfi'î Madhhab. If a person loses his mind or faints without he himself causing it and stays in that state throughout six prayer times, he will not have to make qadâ of the namâzes which he did not perform (during those six prayer times. In other words, he will not have to perform them afterwards). Regardless of the number of the namâzes which an invalid failed to perform by way of îmâ (signs, simulation), he does not (have to) add to his will that an isqat of them should be performed. He makes qadâ of them all if he recovers." (Please see the twenty-first chapter of the fifth fascicle of **Endless Bliss** for 'isqat' and dawr.)

Ibni 'Âbidîn 'rahmatullâhi 'alaih' states: "It is makrûh for a healthy person to have his limbs of ablution washed or made masah on by someone else. It is permissible for a second person to bring him water for an ablution or to pour water as he himself washes (his limbs of ablution). If an invalid dirties his clothes or his bed all the time, or if it is burdensome to change them, he performs his namâzes with his najs clothes on. If the flat pieces of wood splints, plasters, ointments fall off after the injury under them heals, the (invalid's) ablution becomes nullified. If the injury heals and the things on it do not fall off, the (invalid's) ablution and/or ghusl will become nullified again if they could be removed harmlessly.

Allâhu ta'âlâ inflicts pains and illnesses on His beloved slaves in order to forgive their sins or increase the blessings they will be given in Paradise. Their worship is troublesome and laborious. In return for that, He gives them ease and succour in their worldly activities and barakat in their rizq (food, drink, and vital needs which Allâhu ta'âlâ foreordained in the eternal past for each and every one of His slaves. There is plenty of information about rizq throughout the six fascicles of **Endless Bliss**). He does not give the same ease and barakat to people who neglect their worship. Such people earn much by way of arduous toil, trickery, and treason and lead a life of pleasures, debauchery, which do not last long. Shortly thereafter they wind up in hospitals and prisons, grovelling in misery for the rest of their lives. The torment they will suffer in the Hereafter will be incomparably more severe.]

ISTINJÂ, ISTIBRÂ, and ISTINQÂ

Istinjâ means to wash the known parts with water, and istibrâ means, after urination, to wait by walking around or doing something else until urinary bladder is no longer wet (before making an ablution). Istinqâ means the heart's becoming assured about physical cleanliness.

There are four kinds of istinjâ:

The one that is farz; if there is najâsat heavier than one dirham on one's clothes or body or on the place where one is to perform namâz, it is farz to remove that najâsat with water. Istinjâ is farz also when making a ghusl. [One dirham in this context is a weight equal to one mithqâl, which in turn is equal to four grams and eighty centigrams.]

The one that is wâjib; if there is najâsat as heavy as one dirham on one's clothes or on the place where one is to perform namâz, it is wâjib to remove it.

If it is lighter than one dirham it is sunnat to remove it.

The one that is mustahab; if there is very little najâsat it is mustahab to remove it. The one that is mandûb; if one breaks wind when one's bottom is wet it is mandûb to wash it.

If one breaks wind when one's bottom is dry it is bid'at to wash it.

Sunnats of istinjâ: It is sunnat to clean oneself with a piece of stone or soil and thereafter to wash the cleaned part with water.

If the najâsat cannot be completely removed and the remainder exceeds one dirham, if more than one dirham of it has smeared areas around the anus, it becomes farz to wash them with water. Thereafter the areas must be dried with a clean piece of cloth, or with the hand if a piece of cloth is not available.

There is only one act that is mustahab to do when making istinjâ: To hold an odd number of stones. In other words, the number of stones (you hold in your hand) had better be three or five or seven.

[A person suffering from enuresis must get a 12x12 cm. square piece of cloth and tie a half metre long piece of string onto one corner of it. The point of the penis is wrapped up in the cloth and the string is wound around the ends of the cloth, i.e. around the penis once. Its part close to the wrapper is doubled, the doubled end is passed under the wrapper and pulled so as to make the wrapper tight. Its loose end is tied into a loop, which is then attached to the underpants with a safety pin. In need of urination the safety pin is opened, the loop is taken off, and the cloth is undone by simply pulling the string. If it turns out to be difficult to take the loop of the string off the safety pin, then the loop is attached to a paper clip wire, which in turn will be attached to the safety pin. With some old men, the penis tapers, so that it becomes no longer possible to wrap a piece of cloth around it. Such men should place their penis and scrotum in a small nylon bag and fasten the mouth of the bag. A person in the Hanafî Madhhab and who suffers from involuntary urination and yet who does not have an 'udhr makes his niyyat to imitate the Mâlikî Madhhab as he begins to make an ablution and/or ghusl and to perform namâz. It is stated as follows in the book entitled **Kitâb-ul-fiqh 'ala-l-madhâhib-il-erba'a** and which is prepared by Egyptian Islamic scholars presided over by 'Abd-ur-Rahmân Jezîrî 'rahmatullâhi 'alaih' (d. 1384 A.H.), one of the professors of Jâmi'ul-azhar: "According to a second qawl in the Mâlikî Madhhab, when an invalid or old person encounters a situation wherein their ablution becomes nullified, they become a person with an 'udhr outright, which in turn will absolve them from losing their ablution. Hanafî and Shâfi'î Muslims undergoing a (tough situation termed) haraj should imitate this qawl (ijtihâd)." [A Hanafî Muslim who involuntarily lets urine out during namâz imitates this qawl of the Mâlikî Madhhab when conditions are inconvenient. Making his niyyat, he continues with his namâz as a person with an 'udhr.]

HOW TO PERFORM NAMÂZ

There are four things whereby we enter namâz: By (way of) farz; by wâjib; by sunnat; by mustahab. In the Hanafî Madhhab, it is sunnat to raise your hands to a height level with your ears. It is sunnat to turn their palms to the direction of Qibla. It is mustahab, for men, to touch their earlobes with their thumbs, and for women to raise their hands to a height level with their shoulders; and it is farz to say, "**Allâhu ekber.**" It is sunnat to clasp your hands after making the Tekbîr, i.e. after saying, "Allâhu ekber." It is sunnat to put your right hand on your left hand. It is sunnat for men to put their hands below their navel, and for women to put them on their bosoms. It is mustahab for men to clasp the wrists of their left hands with their right hands, like with a claw.

In namâz, it is sunnat for the imâm as well as for the person who follows him, and also for a person performing namâz individually, to say the prayer termed 'Subhânaka'.[1] (After the

---

[1] 'Subhânaka' is said as follows: "Subhânaka Allâhumma wa bi hamdik wa tebâraka-s-muk wa ta'âlâ jed-duk wa lâ ilâha ghayruk."

Subhânaka) it is sunnat to say, "A'udhu billâh-im-in-esh-sheytân-ir-rajîm," which is said by the imâm conducting the namâz (in a namâz in jamâ'at), and by a person performing a namâz individually, (and not by a person following the imâm in a namâz in jamâ'at.) It is sunnat to say the Basmala (after the "A'ûdhu ...). It is wâjib to say the Fâtiha-i-sherîfa (the first Sûra of the Qur'ân al-kerîm); it is farz to say three âyats or a long âyat as long as three âyats after the Fâtiha; it is farz to say an âyat from the Qur'ân al-kerîm when standing in all the rak'ats of namâzes that are sunnat and in all those of the namâz of Witr and, when performing namâz individually, in the (final) two rak'ats of namâzes that are farz (and which consist of four rak'ats).

It is farz to bow down (by bending the body) by the waist for the rukû'; it is wâjib to stay in that bowing position as long as a duration of time within which you could say, "**Subhân-Allah**," three times. It is sunnat to say, "**Subhâna Rabb-iy-al 'adhîm**." three times (as you are in that position). It is mustahab to say that prayer five or seven times. When you rise from the position of rukû', and between the two sajdas, to remain motionless as long as a length of time within which you would be able to say, "**Subhân-Allah**," once, is farz according to Imâm Abû Yûsuf; and wâjib according to the Tarafeyn, (i.e. Imâm A'zam Abû Hanîfa and his blessed disciple Imâm Muhammad.) Although it is sunnat according to some scholars, that it is wâjib is the dominant qawl.

For the sajda, it is farz to put the head on the ground (or floor). It is wâjib to stay put for a length of time wherein you would be able to say, "**Subhân-Allah**," three times. It is sunnat to say, "**Subhâna Rabb-iy-al-a'lâ**," three times, and it is mustahab to say it five or seven times.

Ibni 'Âbidîn 'rahima-hullâhu ta'âlâ' states: "When making the sajda, first the two knees, next the two hands, next the nose, and finally the forehead are put onto the floor. The thumbs and the ears must be in one line. In the Shâfi'î Madhhab the hands must be in a line with the shoulders. It is farz for at least one of the toes to be in contact with the ground (or floor). The ground (or floor) has to be hard enough for the head not to sink into it. A carpet or matting laid or wheat or barley spread on the ground will serve this purpose. A table, a sofa, or a carriage placed on the ground is a substitute for the ground. Swings, or cloths, rugs or mattings tied to trees or masts and hanging taut in the air are not substitutes for the ground. Sajda made on glassy things such as rice and millet or flax seeds will not be sahîh. It will be sahîh if they are in a sack. If the level of the place of sajda is half a zrâ', i.e. sum of the widths of twelve fingers [twenty-five centimetres] higher than that of the place where you put your knees, your namâz will be sahîh; yet it is makrûh. During the sajda your elbows should be kept apart from your body, and your ventral region should be clear of your thighs. Your toes should be pointing in the direction of Qibla. As it is sunnat to make the heal bones touch each other when bending the body for the rukû', they should be touching each other during the sajda as well.

As a woman starts to perform namâz she raises her hands to a height level with her shoulders. Her hands should not be outside of her sleeves. She puts her hands on her breast, her right palm being on her left hand. She bends her body slightly for the rukû'. Her waist should not be level with her head. She does not open her fingers when making the rukû' and the two sajdas. They should be in contact with one another. She puts her hands on her knees, which in turn must be bent. She does not clasp her knees. As she makes the sajda she lays her forearms flat on the floor, with her elbows quite close to her abdomen. Her abdomen should be in touch with her thighs. At the teshehhud (sitting posture) she sits on the floor with her feet jutting out towards her right hand side. Her fingertips should be pointing towards her knees. [Men do not clasp their knees, either, (as they sit for the teshehhud.)] Her fingers should be closed, touching one another. It is makrûh for women to perform namâz in jamâ'at among themselves or to join men when the latter are performing namâz in jamâ'at. It is not farz for them to perform Friday Prayer or the Namâz of 'Iyd. (In other words, Allâhu ta'âlâ has not commanded them to perform these two prayers. Detailed information about these two prayers is provided in the twenty-first and twenty-second chapters, respectively, of the fourth fascicle of **Endless Bliss**.) They say the **Takbîr-i-teshrîq** silently after the farz namâzes throughout the 'Iyd of Qurbân. It is not mustahab for them to perform morning prayer at its latest time. They do not say loudly the prayers to be said during namâz." Here we end our translation from Ibni 'Âbidîn. Sayyid Ahmad Hamawî bin Muhammad Mekkî 'rahmatullâhi ta'âlâ 'alaih' (d. 1098 [1686 A.D.]) states as follows in his book entitled **Uyun-ul-besâir**, which is a commentary to the book entitled **Eshbâh** (and which had been written by Zey-al-'âbidîn bin Ibrâhîm ibni Nujaym-i-Misrî 'rahmatullâhi ta'âlâ 'alaih', 926 A.D. – 970 [1562 A.D.], Egypt:) It is makrûh tahrîmî for women to remove the hair on their head by shaving or cutting it or by using a chemical. [Hence, it is permissible for them to shorten their hair so as to make it level with ears, provided that they should not look like men.] It is makrûh for a woman to say the azân or the iqâmat, (which are dealt with in the eleventh chapter of the fourth fascicle of **Endless Bliss**.) She cannot set out for a (long distance journey called) safar without her husband or any one of his (male) mahram relatives to accompany her.[1] She must not expose her head during a hajj. She performs the (act of worship termed) Sa'y between the hills Safâ and Merva (during hajj), even if she is undergoing her monthly period. She performs the Tawâf at a distance from the Kâ'ba. She must not perform the Khutba. For, it is sahîh that her voice is awrat. She wears mests during the hajj. A woman must not (join the people) carry(ing) the janâza. She will not be killed if she becomes a murtadd (apostate, renegade). She will not be accepted as a witness in lawsuits pertaining to (punishments termed) hadd and/or qisâs, (which are dealt with in chapters ten through fifteen of the sixth fascicle of **Endless Bliss**.) She must not perform i'tikâf in a mosque.[2] It is permissible for her to dye her hands and feet with henna. [She must not use fingernail polish.] She is half a man in matters like inheritance, testimony, and providing nafaqa[3] for poor kinsfolk. A muhsina woman is not summoned to the lawcourt. The judge or his deputy goes to her residence. (A muhsina, or muhsana, woman is one who is married and chaste. Please scan the fifth and sixth paragraphs of the tenth chapter, and also the paragraph under the heading 'HADD FOR QAZF' in the same chapter, of the sixth fascicle, of **Endless Bliss**.) A young woman does not greet a man nâ-mahram to her or offer condolences to a bereaved (nâ-mahram) man or say anything to one who sneezes (and then says, "Al-hamd-u-lillâh,") or acknowledge a nâ-mahram man's saying so to her. She does not sit in a room privately with a nâ-mahram man. Here we end our translation from Hamawî.

It is wâjib to sit for the qa'da-i-ûlâ (first sitting posture in the performance of namâz), and it is farz to sit for the qa'da-i-âkhira

---

[1] Please see the fifteenth chapter of the fourth fascicle of **Endless Bliss** for long distance journeys.

[2] Please scan the final section of the nineteenth chapter of the fourth fascicle of **Endless Bliss** for 'i'tikâf'.

[3] Please see the eighth chapter of the sixth fascicle of **Endless Bliss**.

(last sitting posture). It is wâjib to say the (prayer termed) Tehiyyât during the last sitting posture.

It is sunnat to say the prayers termed Salawât only during the last sitting postures of namâzes that are farz and of those which are wâjib and of the first sunnat of early afternoon prayer and of the first and last sunnats of Friday prayer, and during both sitting postures of other namâzes [such as the four-rak'at sunnats of late afternoon and night prayers]. It is wâjib to say the word of salâm, (i.e. to say, "Es-salâmu 'alaikum wa rahmatullah,) (when making the salâm by turning the head to both sides). It is sunnat to look at both shoulders when making the salâm. And it is mustahab to look attentively.

A namâz's acceptability to perfection is conditional on [your avoiding harâms and] khushû' and taqwâ and ceasing from mâlâya'nî and terk-i-kesel and 'ibdâd. Khushû' means to fear Allâhu 'adhîm-ush-shân; taqwâ means to protect one's nine limbs against harâms and makrûhs; to cease from mâlâya'nî means to avoid talks that will produce no benefits in this world or in the Hereafter; terk-i-kesel means to avoid reluctance in the observance of the acts within namâz; and 'ibdâd means to stop doing whatsoever you have been doing and hurry for the jamâ'at at the moment you hear the azân-i-Muhammadî being called, and to be consistent with that.

There are six procedures whose observance during namâz is essential: ikhlâs; tefekkur; khawf; rejâ; ru'yat-i-taqsîr, and mujâhada.

Ikhlâs means there to be khulûs (sincerity) in the performance, [which means to be performing (namâz) only for the grace Allâh]; tefekkur means to be thinking over matters within namâz; khawf means to fear Allâhu 'adhîm-ush-shân; rejâ means to be hopeful of attaining compassion of Allâhu 'adhîm-ush-shân; ru'yat-i-taqsîr means to know oneself to be imperfect; mujâhada means to be contending with one's nafs and with Satan.

As the Azân-i-Muhammad is called, you must envisage Isrâfîl ''alaihis-salâm' blowing the Sûr (Trumpet for the Day of Judgment); as you stand up for the purpose of making an ablution you must envisage yourself rising from your grave; as you go to the mosque you must envisage yourself going to the place of Mahsher (Assemblage for Judgment); as the muazzin calls the Iqâmat and the jamâ'at stand in lines you must envisage the lines of Muslims as the hundred and twenty immense lines of people at the place of

Mahsher, eighty of the lines made up by the Ummat of our Prophet and forty of them by the Ummats of other Prophets; after you have adapted yourself to the Imâm and the Imâm has started to say the Fâtiha-i-sherîfa you must envisage yourself in an environment with Paradise on your right hand side and Hell on your left and Azrâîl "alaihis-salâm' close behind you and the Beytullah against you and your grave before you and the Sirat Bridge under your feet. You must be wondering if your interrogation (at the place of Mahsher) will be easy, if your worship will be made into a crown on your head, a comrade in your trek to the Hereafter, and a light in your grave, or whether it will be cast in your teeth like an old rag.

Unfaithful are all your benefits, o, you, world, and you are so lowly! Storms of death destroy all you offer in the name of glory.

AZÂN-I-MUHAMMADÎ

The following excerpt has been translated from the book entitled **Durr-ul-mukhtâr** and from its commentary entitled **Ibni 'Âbidîn**:

A discreet Muslim's recitation of certain words coached in books teaching Islam's practices and performed by a discreet Muslim is called **Azân-i-Muhammadî**. In other words, the person to perform the Azân (or Adhân) should climb the minaret and recite the Arabic words standing. It will not be Azân to say its versions in other languages even if their meanings are known. Azân is called for the purpose of announcing the times of the daily five prayers (called namâz). It is sunnat muakkad for men to mount a raised platform outside of the mosque and call it. It is makrûh for women to perform the Azân or the Iqâmat. It is harâm for them to let (nâ-mahram) men hear their voice.

The muazzin, (i.e. person to perform the azân,) has to mount a raised platform outside (of) the mosque and call the Azân loud enough for the neighbours to hear him. It is not permissible for him to shout too loud. As he says, "**Ekber** (or Akbar)," he either pauses at the end of it in a manner called jezm (or jazm) or continues by pronouncing the (Arabic script vowel indicating an 'a' and called) ustun. He does not pronounce the (Arabic script vowel indicating an 'u' and called) oetra. It is not halâl to add vowel points or sounds so as to extend or prolong its established phonetic value or defile it into a musical performance, or to listen

to such desecrated applications. It is sunnat to turn the head
rightward and leftward as the words 'salât' and 'felâh',
respectively, are being uttered. The feet and/or the chest are not
turned away from the direction of Qibla. Or it is called from the
minaret; and meanwhile the (caller termed) muazzin makes a turn
on the gallery surrounding the minaret. The earliest minaret was
made at the behest of Hadrat Mu'âwiya 'radiy-Allâhu 'anh' (19
B.H. – 60 [680 A.D.]). There was a raised platform made on
Rasûlullah's Mesjîd (Mosque). Bilâl Habashî 'radiy-Allâhu 'anh'
(d. 20 A.H. Damascus) would mount it to call the Azân.
Rasûlullah 'sall-Allâhu 'alaihi wa sallam' ordered Bilâl to put his
fingers on his ears (during the performance of the Azân). Talking
during the performance will necessitate to repeat the performance.
It is permissible for more than one people to call the Azân
together. The Azân, however, will not be sahîh if the words said by
one of them are not said by the others. It is makrûh tahrîmî to
perform the Azân sitting. It is sunnat for the muazzin to be a sâlih
Muslim, to know the acts of sunnat within the Azân and the times
of the Azân, to perform the Azân every day in stability and
continuity, and to perform it only for the grace of Allah and not for
payment. However, it is permissible (to pay him a stipend for his
performance and) for him to accept being paid. Azân performed
by a child below the age of discretion will not be sahîh. For, its
voice is tantamount to a bird's singing or a sound produced by a
musical instrument. [For that matter, Azân or Iqâmat performed
by using a loudspeaker will not be sahîh. Azân performed by a
fâsiq person is untenable, and so are the takbîrs made by the imâm
conducting a namâz in jamâ'at and yet conveyed by that person. It
is makrûh for him to call the Azân. It is essential that the muazzin
should know that he performs the Azân after the commencement
of its prescribed time and for other Muslims to know that they
perform the namâz within its prescribed time. If a person starts to
perform a namâz uncertain as he is as to whether its time has
commenced, the namâz he performs will not be sahîh, even if it is
found out afterwards that he performed it within its time. Namâz
performed in accordance to a calendar prepared by disbelievers or
by fâsiq people is not sahîh. Concerning the correctness of a
calendar being used in (one of the countries termed) Dâr-ul-harb,
one must ask a Muslim who one believes is sâlih and learned and
learn the truth from him.] Supposing Azân is being performed in
keeping with the (genuine manner called) sunnat simultaneously
at various places and you hear them all; you should repeat after

only the first one you hear and, if it is from the mosque you have been attending for your daily prayers, you should go there for the jamâ'at. You should repeat after it even if you are reading (or reciting) the Qur'ân al-kerîm. You do not have to repeat after it if you are performing namâz in jamâ'at or in toilet or eating or in mosque or teaching or learning religious knowledge. An azân being performed in a language other than Arabic or in a manner that sounds much the same as music is in violation of the Sunnat. It is mustahab for a person who hears an azân being called to stand up if he is sitting and to stop walking if he is walking. It is stated as follows as vows are being dealt with in the subject of oaths: "It is wâjib for the (Muslim) government to build a mosque in every quarter. Mosques are built with money from the Beyt-ul-mâl. It is wâjib for Muslims to build a mosque for themselves if the government does not build one.

[As is seen, if Islam is obeyed and a mosque is built in every quarter of a town, Azân will be performed in every town and everybody will hear the azân being called in their own quarter. There will be no need for the muazzin to shout too loud or to use a loudspeaker. The loudspeaker is a bid'at that causes violation of the sunnats of Azân. It causes these sunnats to lose their beauty. It is for this reason that the fifteenth article of the seven hundred and thirty-seventh resolution adopted by a commission assigned with the deliberation and study of religious works at the behest of the directorate of religious matters (in Turkey) and dated 1.12.1954 reads as follows: "Installment of loudspeakers over minbars (in mosques) is definitely prohibited. If the jamâ'at (congregation of Muslims performing namâz in jamâ'at) is too great for the imâm's tekbîrs and recitations to be heard, then one of the muazzins and/or another one farther away can assume the duty of conveying his voice." It is explained at great length in the chapter dealing with the sajda-i-tilâwat of the book entitled **al-Fiqh-u-'alal madhâhib-ul-arba'a** and also in the latter half of the sixteenth chapter of the fourth fascicle of **Endless Bliss** that the Qur'an al-kerîm read (or recited) or the azân called on the radio or put on a tape or performed by way of a loudspeaker is not human voice, that it is an instrumental sound produced by magnetic and electrical appliances activated by the performer, and that it is supposed to be the performer's voice although it is not the original human voice that causes its production. The **Azân-i-Muhammadî** commanded by Islam has to be the voice of a sâlih Muslim. The sound coming out of a pipe is not Azân. Hamdi Efendi of Elmalı 'rahima-hullâhu ta'âlâ', one of the contemporary religious scholars, states as follows in the twenty-three hundred and sixty-first page of the third volume of his book of Tafsîr: [As is seen, the commandments pertaining to 'listening and silence' have been made incumbent as regards *qirâat*, which in turn is an optional linguistic activity and is performed by observing the prescribed places of articulation and voicing in association with intention and comprehension. As a matter of fact, even the act performed by Jibrîl, (i.e. the Archangel Gabriel,) (during the revelation of the Qur'ân al-kerîm to Muhammad ''alaihis-salâm',) was an act of making (the blessed Prophet) perform *qirâat*, rather than performing the *qirâat* himself. The divine act (performed by Allâhu ta'âlâ), on the other hand, was an act of tenzîl (revelation) and the creation of (the act of) *qirâat*. Therefore, voices issuing from brainless beings cannot be called *qirâat*; nor should we call a sound reflected off a surface *qirâat*. It was for that matter that the Fuqahâ, (i.e. the Islamic scholars who had majored in the Islamic branch of science termed **Fiqh**,) have stated that the echo of a qirâat being performed should not be called *qirâat* and that it would not necessitate a performance, such as performing the sajda termed 'tilâwat',[1] which is incumbent on a Muslim who (reads or recites or) hears an âyat of sajda. As quiet study of a certain book is not an activity of *qirâat*, likewise, listening to the echo of a sound ringing or being produced by something (such as a musical instrument) being played is not actually listening to an activity of *qirâat*. Hence, sound or voice issuing from a record player or a radio (or a television set or a DVD player) reflecting the voice of a man reading or reciting the Qur'ân al-kerîm, is the echo and reproduction of *qirâat*, rather than *qirâat* itself, and therefore it does not make listening and silence incumbent (upon a Muslim who hears it or listens to it). In other words, the (verses of the) Qur'ân al-kerîm that is wâjib (compulsory) to quietly listen to is the verses that are being read or recited in the act of *qirâat*, rather than the (sounds of the) verses that are being played. Still, the fact that listening to it is not an act of wâjib or mustahab should not bring one to the conclusion that it is not permissible to listen to it or that it is wâjib not to listen to it. For, playing (âyats from) the Qur'ân al-kerîm (on the radio, etc.) and listening to (âyats from) the Qur'ân al-kerîm being thus played are two different activities. It is obvious that it is not something justifiable to play (âyats from) the Qur'ân

---

[1] Please see the latter part of the sixteenth chapter of the fourth fascicle of **Endless Bliss**.

al-kerîm (on the radio, etc.) or to convey it through instrumentation. As a matter of fact, an act of qurbat[1] as it is to read (or recite the Qur'ân al-kerîm, it is a guilty act to do so at places detrimental to the veneration that should go with the performance. However, should this guilty act be committed (by some people), not listening to it, rather than listening to it, will be another guilty act. For instance, it is a guilty act to perform qirâat, (i.e. read or recite the Qur'ân al-kerîm,) in a public bath. Yet, should it be performed (by others), it will not yield any thawâb (reward in the Hereafter) not to listen to it, either. By the same token, the already precarious supposition that it is not a duty to listen to an echo of a qirâat of the Qur'ân al-kerîm being performed or its much the same reproduction being played on (something like) a record player or being broadcast on the radio, should not be stretched into a forged duty of not listening to it. For, it is something resembling a qirâat, although it is not a qirâat itself. For, it is something indicative of the Kelâm-i-nafsî, (i.e. Word of Allâhu ta'âlâ.) Therefore, although it is not wâjib or mustahab like listening to the qirâat itself, it is not only permissible, but also commendable; in fact, irreverence towards it is by no means justifiable. A situation of that sort is akin to one wherein a Muslim saw a page of the Qur'ân al-kerîm left at a place sacrilegious to its high honour and in which case it would be his religious duty to pick it up and put it somewhere worthy of its holiness, instead of just passing by indifferently."]

It is written in most books of Fiqh, e.g. in **Qâdikhân**: "It is an act of sunnat to perform the Azân (or Adhân). Because it is one of the characteristics, symbols of the Islamic religion, if the inhabitants of a certain city or quarter of a city cease from performing the Azân, the government should use force to make them resume the practice. A muazzin, (i.e. Muslim whose duty is to perform the azân,) has to know the direction of Qibla and the times of the daily five prayers. For, it is sunnat to perform, (i.e. to call,) the Azân standing with your face towards the Qibla from the beginning till the end. The Azân is called for the purpose of letting the people know the times of the daily five prayers of namâz and the time of iftâr, (i.e. time when Muslims are to break fast.) It causes fitna for a person who does not know prayer times or a fâsiq one to perform the Azân. It is makrûh for an indiscreet child or a drunkard or a

---

[1] See the thirteenth paragraph of the first chapter of the first fascicle of **Endless Bliss**.

mentally disordered person or a junub person or a woman to call the Azân. In such a case, the Azân will have to be reperformed by the muazzin. [It yields plenty of thawâb to perform the Mawlid, to have it performed, and to go to a place to listen to the Mawlid being performed there. However, it is harâm for a woman to let nâ-mahram men hear her voice by performing the Mawlid or the Azân or by singing or by talking more loudly than needed, and for (nâ-mahram) men to listen to her. A woman (who is to perform such acts of worship) should do so only among other women, and then she mustn't tape or record her voice or let it be broadcast through radio or television programs.] Although it is makrûh also for a man sitting or without an ablution, or for one riding an animal (such as a horse) within an urban area, to call the Azân, an Azân performed by one of them will not have to be reperformed. The Azân is performed on a minaret or (anywhere directly) outside (of) the mosque. It is not performed inside the mosque. It is makrûh to perform it in a manner called 'telhîn', i.e. by chanting melodiously and prolonging the syllables so as to distort the words. The Azân is not performed in any language other than Arabic." It is stated in the book entitled **Fatâwâ-i-Hindiyya**: "It is makrûh for a muazzin to shout so loud as to exhaust himself (as he performs the Azân). **Ibni 'Âbidîn** 'rahima-hullâhu ta'âlâ' states: "It is sunnat for the muazzin to mount an elevated place to perform the Azân so that it should be heard at distant places. It is permissible for more than one muazzins to perform the Azân together." As is understood from these scholarly passages, it is bid'at to perform the Azân or the Iqâmat or to conduct a namâz (in jamâ'at) by using a loud-speaker. And it is gravely sinful to commit a bid'at. A hadîth-i-sherîf reads: **"If a person commits a bid'at, none of his acts of worship will be acceptable."** Although a voice heard from a loud-speaker is quite similar to the human voice, it is not the human voice itself. It is a sound produced by pieces moved by magnetism. It is not the voice of a person standing on an elevated platform. The sin becomes doubled when they place the loud-speaker on the right or left or back side of the minaret or roof, so that the voice does not come out in the direction of Qibla. It is not necessary, on the other hand, for the voice to reach distant places or for us to stand the shrill metallic screaming of the loud-speaker. For, it is wâjib to build a mosque in every quarter. Thereby the Azân will be performed in every quarter and a quarter's Azân will be heard from all its residences. Moreover, the **Azân-i-jawq** is something permissible. More than one muazzins' calling the same azân together is called **Azân-i-jawq**. A touching human voice will be heard from afar, move hearts and souls, and freshen people's îmân. [The muazzin performs the Azân and the imâm performs the qirâat with their natural voices loud enough only to be heard by the Muslims around the mosque and by the jamâ'at inside the mosque, respectively. It is makrûh for them to exert themselves so that their voices should be heard from afar. That also shows the frivolity of using a loud-speaker.] In short, the sound issuing from the horn called a loud-speaker is not the Azân. The **Azân-i-Muhammadî** is the voice coming out from the muazzin's mouth. A hadîth-i-sherîf quoted in the book entitled **Hilya-t-ul-Awliyâ** and written by the great Islamic scholar named Abû Nuaym Isfahânî (Ahmad bin 'Abdullah) 'rahmatullâhi 'alaih' (336 [948 A.D.] – 430 [1039]) reads as follows: "**Voice of azân that comes out of a musical instrument is the Satan's voice. People who** (use a loud-speaker to) **perform it are the Satan's muazzins.**"

It is stated as follows in hadîth-i-sherîfs: "**As Doomsday draws near the Qur'ân al-kerîm will be read** (and recited) **through mizmârs. It will be read** (and recited) **not for the grace of Allah, but for pleasure.**" "**There are many people who read** (and recite) **the Qur'ân al-kerîm, but the Qur'ân al-kerîm condemns them.**" "**A time will come when muazzins will be the meanest ones of Muslims.**" "**A time will come when the Qur'ân al-kerîm will be read** (or recited) **through mizmârs. Allâhu ta'âlâ will condemn those people** (who do so)." Mizmâr means all sorts of musical instruments and pipes. The loud speaker is a mizmâr, too. Muazzins should fear these hadîth-i-sherîfs and avoid performing (their acts of worship) through loud-speakers. Some religiously unlearned people claim that the loud-speaker is useful because it carries voices to distant places. Our Prophet stated: "**Perform acts of worship as you see me and my Sahâba perform them! People who make changes in acts of worship are called 'ahl-i-bid'at'** (people of bid'at, bid'at holders). **Holders of bid'at shall definitely go to Hell. None of their acts of worship shall be accepted.**" It is not right to say, "We are adding useful things to acts of worship." Statements of this sort are lies fibbed by enemies of religion. Islamic scholars, alone, know whether a change will be useful. These profound scholars are called **mujtahid**s. Mujtahids do not make a change on their own. They know whether a certain addition or change will be a bid'at. There is a consensus that it is a bid'at to call the Azân by using a 'mizmar'. It is a person's heart that will make them attain grace and love of Allâhu ta'âlâ. The heart is congenitally like a pure mirror. Acts of worship increase the heart's purity and polish it. Bid'ats and sins darken the heart, so that it can no longer receive the fayzes and nûrs coming to it by way of love. Salih Muslims sense this moribund state and become worried. They do not want to commit sins. They want to perform more acts of worship. In addition to performing five prayers of namâz daily, they wish they could perform more. The human nafs relishes committing sins; it feels as if it is something useful. All bid'ats and sins nourish and strengthen the human nafs, which is an enemy of Allâhu ta'âlâ. An example of this is calling the Azân through a loud-speaker. Rauf Ahmad, one of the successors of 'Abdullah Dahlawî, states as follows in his foreword to **Durr-ul-ma'ârif**: "It is harâm to read or recite the Qur'ân al-kerîm or perform other duties by using musical instruments called 'mizmârs'." An example is to call the Azân through a loud-speaker.

[It is stated as follows in the Shâfi'î books entitled **al-Muqaddima-t-ul-hadramiyya** (by 'Abdullah bin 'Abd-ur-Rahmân) and **al-Anwâr li-a'mâl-il-ebrâr** (by Yûsuf Erdebîlî, d. 799 A.H.): "For being sahîh in the Shâfi'î Madhhab, the act of following an imâm (conducting a namâz in jamâ'at) in a certain mosque (to be performed) by a Muslim outside (of) that mosque, there are three conditions to be fulfilled: 1) He has to (be in a position enabling him to) see the imâm; 2) He has to hear the imâm; 3) There should not be a distance of three hundred dhrâ' (300x0.42=126 metres) between him and the hindmost line (of the jamâ'at)." Neither in the Hanafî Madhhab nor in the Shâfi'î Madhhab is a namâz sahîh (valid) which is performed by following a far-off imâm who is seen and heard on television. It is an act of **bid'at** to vitiate the acts of worship by adding to them such practices as they did not contain during the times of the Salaf-i-sâlihîn. As is understood from the hundred and fourth âyat of Nisâ Sûra, people who practise the bid'at of attenuating the performances such as azân (adhân) and namâz with radios, televisions and loud-speakers, will go to Hell. The voice heard from a loud-speaker or from the radio is not the azân itself, but it is something very similar to it. By the same token, a person's vision in a mirror or a photograph is not the person him or herself, but it is something quite similar, despite the exactitude in appearance.]

WÂJIBS of NAMÂZ: Wâjibs of namâz in the Hanafî Madhhab are as follows: Not to recite anything after (reciting) the "Subhânaka..." (when you are performing namâz in jamâ'at) behind the imâm. For the imâm (when conducting namâz in jamâ'at) and for a Muslim who is performing namâz on his own, to say the Sûra called Fâtiha sherîfa once at each of (any) two rak'ats of a namâz that is farz and at every rak'at of any other kind of namâz. To say (an additional Sûra called) the Dhamm-i-Sûra once at each of the first two rak'ats of a namâz that is farz and which contains four or three rak'ats and at each and every rak'at of any other kind of namâz. To apportion the Fâtiha-i-sherîfa to the first two rak'ats in a namâz of three or four rak'ats. To pass from one farz to another farz. To recite the Fâtiha before (reciting) the dhamm-i-sûra. To sit for the Qa'da-i-ûlâ (first sitting posture). To make the (two) sajdas one after the other. To say the (prayer termed) Tehiyyât during the Qa'da-i-âkhira (last sitting posture). To exit the namâz saying the Salâm, (i.e. to say, "Es-salâm-u-'alaikum wa rahmatullah.") To say the prayers called Qunût during the Salât-i-witr. During the performance of the namâz of 'Iyd, to say the additional takbîrs. To say the prayers (to be said during namâz) with ikhfâ', (i.e. in a whisper,) whereat they are to be said with ikhfâ', and with jehr, (i.e. audibly,) whereat they are to be said with jehr. To observe the Ta'dîl-i-erkân as you perform namâz, [which means, as was explained earlier in the text, to stay motionless for a length of time that would allow you to say, "Subhânallah," during the rukû' and during the qawma, –which means the standing position after straightening up from the position of rukû'–, and during the two sajdas and during the jalsa, –which means the sitting posture betwen the two sajdas–.) These motionless stances during namâz are called 'tumâninat'.] To make the sajda of Tilâwat if you say an âyat of Tilâwat during namâz or if you hear the imâm say one (during namâz in jamâ'at). Tho make the sajda-i-sahw (when necessary). (The sajda-i-tilâwat and the sajda-i-sahw are explained in the sixteenth chapter of the fourth fascicle of **Endless Bliss**.) In namâzes that are farz and which contain four rak'ats, to stand up immediately after saying the (prayer called) Tehiyyât, without lingering, at the Qa'da-i-ûlâ. To adapt yourself to the imâm in all cases. According to a qawl, to perform the farz namâzes in jamâ'at unless you have an 'udhr, (i.e. a good reason dictated by Islam,) to hinder you from doing so. After each of the twenty-three farz namâzes that you perform from the morning prayer of the 'Arafa Day (which is the day previous to the first day) of the 'Iyd of Qurbân till late afternoon prayer on the fourth day of the 'Iyd of Qurbân, (that last prayer included,) to say the **takbîr-i-teshrîq**, (which is explained in the twenty-second chapter of the fourth fascicle of **Endless Bliss**.)

SUNNATS of NAMÂZ: Sunnats of namâz in the Hanafî Madhhab are as follows:

At the takbîr of iftitâh, (i.e. takbîr which is said when starting to perform namâz,) and also at the takbîr of Qunût, (i.e. as you say, "Allâhu ekber," before starting to say the prayers called Qunût during the final standing position,) in the Salât-i-Witr, for men to raise their hands to their ear-lobes and for women to raise their hands to a height level with their shoulders, and (for both sexes) to turn their palms so as to keep them in the direction of Qibla (momentarily). During the Qiyâm, (i.e. standing position in namâz,) the wrist of the left hand should be clasped by using the thumb and the small finger of the right hand. Women, however, put their right hands atop their left hands. Men clasp their hands below their navels, and women place them on their bosoms. To say the prayer that reads, "**Subhânaka...**,' during the first rak'at of every namâz –for the imâm and the jamâ'at and the single– handed performer alike. For the imâm and for the individual performer, to say the A'ûdhu and the Basmala after the Subhânaka in the first rak'at. Likewise, for the imâm and for the individual performer, to say the Basmala-i-sherîfa before (saying) the Fâtiha-i-sherîfa at each rak'at. To say, "Âmîn –silently–," (at the end of the Fâtiha-i-sherîfa,) which is incumbent both upon the imâm (conducting a namâz in jamâ'at) and upon (the congregation of Muslims called) the jamâ'at as soon as the imâm says, "**... wa la-d-dâllîn**," (which are the last two words of the first Sûra of the Qur'ân al-kerîm and called) the Fâtiha, and upon the individual performer[1] when they finish (reciting) the Fâtiha. To make the Takbîr, (i.e. to say, "Allâhu akbar,") when bending down for the Rukû' from the Qiyâm (standing position). To put your hands, with fingers wide apart, on your knees, at Rukû'. To say, "**Subhâna Rabb-iy-al 'adhîm**," three times at Rukû'. At Rukû', your head and your waist should be level with each other.[2] For the imâm (conducting a namâz in jamâ'at) and for the individual performer, to say, "**Semi'-Allâhu liman hamideh**," when straightening up from the Rukû'. For a Muslim performing a namâz in jamâ'at or on his own, to say,

---

[1] By the 'individual performer' we mean a Muslim performing namâz on his own.

[2] It goes without saying that some of these rules apply for men only. We recommend that women read the last paragraph of the fourteenth chapter of the fourth fascicle of **Endless Bliss** for details on women's performing namâz.

"**Rabbanâ laka-l-hamd**," after straightening up from the Rukû'. To say, "**Allâhu ekber**," when going down for the Sajda from the (standing position termed) Qiyâm. To say, "Subhâna Rabb-iy-al-a'lâ," during the Sajda. To say, "**Allâhu ekber**," when (raising your head and) sitting up from the first sajda. To say, "**Allâhu ekber**," when going down (for the second sajda). To bring the fingers together at the sajda. At the sajda, men (should) put their knees on the floor (or on the ground) and separate their thighs from their abdomens, whereas women (should) bring their thighs into contact with their abdomens. To say, "**Allâhu ekber**," when rising from the second sajda. Men (should) sit on their left foot, with their right foot erect. To say the prayer of salawât at the Qa'da-i-âkhira (last sitting posture). To turn your head (right and left) as you make the salâm to your right and left. During the (sitting posture whereat you say the prayer called) Tehiyyât, to put your hands on your laps with your finger tips in line with the points of your knees and the fingers themselves left to themselves. To turn your hands and toes to the direction of Qibla, at the Sajda, and in the meantime your hands should be in line with your ears. To make the Sajda with seven of your limbs on the floor (or ground) simultaneously. To say only the (Sûra called) Fâtiha-i-sherîfa during the (standing positions of the) last two rak'ats of namâzes that are farz and which centain four rak'ats. To say the Azân-i-Muhammadî in a manner dictated by the Sunnat-i-sherîfa. For men to perform the Iqâmat (or Qâmat) (before beginning to perform) the farz namâzes, no matter whether they are being performed in jamâ'at or by individual performers.

MUSTAHABS of NAMÂZ: Mustahabs of namâz in the Hanafî Madhhab are as follows:

For the jamâ'at not to remain seated and to stand up as soon as the muazzin pronounces the expression, "Hay-ya-'ala-s-salâh," as he performs the Iqâmat, (which calls the Believers to perform namâz in jamâ'at.) For men to touch their ear-lobes with their thumbs as they say the Takbîr of Iftitâh and the Takbîr for the prayers of Qunût in the namâz of Witr. As they clasp their hands during the Qiyâm, to clench the wrist (of left hand) rather tightly. To look at the place of sajda during the Qiyâm. At the Rukû' and at the sajda, to say the tasbîh, (i.e. to say, "**Rabb-iy-al 'adhîm**," and, "**Rabb-iy-al-a'lâ**," respectively,) five or seven times. To look onto your feet as you make the Rukû'. To bring your feet together as you are bending down for the Rukû'. To detach your left foot from your right foot as you straighten up back to the (position) of

Qiyâm. To put your nose on the floor or ground before (putting) your forehead (on the floor or ground). To look at both sides of your nose during the Sajda. To look at your shoulder as you make the Salâm. For the person on the left hand side of the imâm (conducting the namâz in jamâ'at), to make his niyya(t) that he is greeting the imâm, the angels of Hafazâ,[1] and (the Muslims making up) the jamâ'at. For the person on the right hand side of the imâm, to make his niyya that he is greeting the angels of Hafaza and the jamâ'at. For a person with no one on his right and left, to make his niyya that he is greeting only the angels of Hafaza. Not to wipe the sweat off your face in namâz. To avoid coughing. To avoid yawning. To look down onto your thighs as you are seated for the Tahiyyât. For the imâm, to turn his face towards the jamâ'at after the namâz.

ÂDÂB (ADABS) of NAMÂZ

1– For an individual performer as well as for on who has (joined the jamâ'at and) followed the imâm, to say the following prayer after the Salâm: "**Allâhumma anta-s-salâm-u-wa minka-s-salâm tebârakta yâ dhel-jelâli wa-l-ikrâm.**" Thereafter to say as follows, three times: "**Es taghfirullah-al 'adhîm al-ledhî lâ ilâha illâ Huw-al-hayyel-Qayyûma wa etûbu ilaih.**" This prayer is called the **Istighfâr**. It is jâiz (permissible) as well to say it without an ablution.

2– Thereafter to say the (âyat-i-kerîma termed) **Âyat-al-kursî**.

3– To say, "**Subhânallah,**" thirty-three times.

4– To say, "**Al-hamd-u-li-llâh,**" thirty-three times.

5– To say, "**Allâhu ekber,**" thirty-three times.

6– To say the following prayer once: "**Lâ ilâha il-l-Allâhu wahdehû lâ sherîkaleh lehul mulku wa lehul hamdu wa Huwa 'alâ kulli shey'in qadîr.**"

7– To hold out your arms forwards and open your hands in the direction of the 'Arsh, which is the Qibla for benedictions, and offer your benedictions with earnest and heartfelt sincerity.

---

[1] Please see the twenty-first paragraph of the chapter entitled. 'Fundamentals of Îmân' of the book **Belief and Islam**, one of the publications of Hakîkat Kitâbevi, Fâtih, Istanbul, for the angels of **Hafaza**, also called **Kirâman Kâtibîn**.

8– If you are with the jamâ'at, (i.e. if you have performed the namâz in jamâ'at,) to wait for the benedictions (that will be made altogether).

9– To say, "Âmîn," at the end of the benedictions.

10– To rub your hands gently on your face.

11– Thereafter, to say the (Sûra called) **Ikhlâs-i-sherîf** eleven times, saying the Basmala before each time you say the Sûra, which is an act commanded in a hadîth-i-sherîf quoted in the last page of the first volume of (the book entitled) **Berîqa**. Thereafter to say the (two) âyat-i-kerîmas beginning as, "**Qul-a'ûdhu...,**" once each, and thereafter to say, "estaghfirullah," sixty-seven times, complementing the number to seventy by saying the full form of this prayer of Istighfâr three times, and thereafter to say, "**Subhânallâhi wa bihamdihi subhânallâh-il 'adhîm**," ten times. Thereafter to say the (full form of the) âyat-i-kerîma that reads: "**Subhâna Rabbika... .**" These adabs are written in the book entitled **Merâq-il-felâh**. It is stated as follows in a hadîth-i-sherîf: "**Benedictions offered after performing** (any of the daily) **five** (prayers termed) **namâzes will be accepted** (by Allâhu ta'âlâ)." However, benedictions offered (and any other prayers sent) should be performed with a heart that is on the alert and in whispers. It is makrûh to offer benedictions (or to say other prayers) only after the daily five prayers or at other established times or to recite poetry memorized in the name of benedictions (or prayers). When the benedictions (or prayers) are finished, it is sunnat to gently rub your hands on your face. Rasûlullah 'sall-Allâhu 'alaihi wa sallam' would say his prayers also after the Tawâf, after meals, and before going to bed. During prayers of this sort, he would not hold out his blessed arms, and he would not rub his blessed hands on his blessed face. Prayers said, benedictions offered, and any other kinds of dhikr should rather be performed in whispers. (Please scan the forty-sixth and the forty-eighth chapters of the first fascicle, the twentieth, the twenty-third, the thirty-seventh and the forty-sixth chapters of the second fascicle, the fifty-seventh chapter of the third fascicle, and the twenty-fifth chapter of the sixth fascicle, of **Endless Bliss**, for 'dhikr'.) It is mustahab to be with an ablution as you offer benedictions or say other prayers such as Istighfâr. It is harâm to dance, to whirl, to clap hands, to play musical instruments such as tambourines, drums, reed flutes, or any string instruments; such practices have been rife among (false) men of Tasawwuf; that they are harâm has been declared unanimously (by Islamic scholars). As is seen, it is commendable for the (Muslims in the) jamâ'at and the imâm to say their prayers (or to offer their benedictions) in whispers. It is also permissible for each and every one of them to say their prayers singly or to stand up and leave without having said their prayers. It is stated as follows in the book entitled **Fatâwâ-i-Hindiyya** (prepared by a group of scholars presided over by Shaikh Nizâm Mu'în-ud-dîn Naqshibandî): "In a namâz that contains a final sunnat, (e.g. early afternoon and evening and night prayers,) it is makrûh for the imâm (who has conducted the farz part of the namâz in jamâ'at) to remain seated after making the salâm. He should immediately perform the final sunnat after moving rightwards or leftwards or backwards a little. Or, he may as well leave, go home, and perform the final sunnat at home. The (Muslims making up the) jamâ'at, as well as a Muslim who has been performing the namâz on his own, may remain seated and say their prayers. It is also permissible for them to stand up and perform the final sunnat at the place where they have been sitting or somewhat moving rightwards or leftwards or backwards. In namâzes that do not have a final sunnat, it is makrûh for the imâm to remain seated in the direction of Qibla; in fact, it is an act of bid'at. He ought to get up and leave or turn towards the jamâ'at or turn right or left and then sit down again."

PRAYERS TO BE SAID (or benedictions to be offered) AFTER NAMÂZ

"Al-hamd-u-li-l-lâhi Rabb-il-'âlamîn. Es-salâtu wa-s-salâmu 'alâ Rasûlinâ Muhammadin wa 'alâ Âlihî wa Sahbihî ajma'în. Yâ Rabbî (o my Rabb, Allah)! Please do accept the namâz that I have performed! Please do bless me with khayr (goodness) in my âkhir (latter life) and in my 'âqibat (end). Bless me with the fortune of saying the Kalima-i-Tawhîd in my last breath, (i.e. when dying.) Bless my dead kinsfolk with Thine 'afw and maghfirat (forgiveness and compassion). Allâhum-maghfir warham wa anta khayr-ur-rahimîn. Teveffenî Musliman wa-al-hiqnî bi-s-sâlihîn. Allâhummaghfirlî wa-li-wâlidayya wa-li-ustâziyya wa-li-l-mu'minîna wa-l-mu'minât yawma yaqûm-ul-hisâb. Yâ Rabbî! protect me against the evils of the Satan and against the evils of the enemy and against the evils of my own nafs-i-ammâra! Please do bless our home with goodness and halâl and good sustenance (food, etc.). Please do bless the ahl-i-islâm, (i.e. Muslims,) with salâmat (salvation, safety)! Please annihilate and destroy the a'dâ-yi-muslimîn, (i.e. Muslims' enemies!) Please help the Muslims who have been making jihâd against unbelievers, and bless them with Thine imdâd-i-ilâhî! Allâhumma innaka 'afuwwun kerîmun tuhib-b-ul-'afwa fa'fu 'annî. Yâ Rabbî! Bless our invalids with good health and the wretched ones among us with relief! Allâhumma innî es'eluka sihhata wa-l-âfiyata wa-l-amânata wa husn-al-khulqi wa-r-ridâa bi-l-qadari bi-rahmatika yâ erham-er-râhimîn. Please bless my parents and my children and my kinsfolk and my friends and all my Muslim brothers with a life embellished with khayr and with husn-i-khulq and with good health and with rushd-u-hidâyat and istiqâmat, yâ Rabbî! Âmîn. Wa-l-hamd-u-li-l-lâhi Rabb-il-'âlemîn. Allâhumma salli 'alâ seyyidinâ Muhammadin wa 'alâ Âl-i-Muhammad kamâ sall-ey-ta 'alâ Ibrâhîma wa 'alâ Âl-i-Ibrâhîm innaka Hamîd-un-Mejîd. Allâhumma bârik 'alâ Muhammadin wa 'alâ Âl-i-Muhammad kamâ bârakta 'alâ Ibrâhîma wa 'alâ Âl-i-Ibrâhîm innaka hamîd-un-mejîd. Allâhumma Rabbanâ âtinâ fi-d-dünyâ hasanatan ve fil âhirati hasanatan wa qinâ 'adhâb-an-nâr birahmatika yâ-Erham-er-rahimîn. Wa-l-hamd-u-li-l-lâhi Rabb-il-'âlamîn. Estaghfirullah, estaghfirullah, estaghfirullah, estaghfirullah-al-'adhîm al-kerîm al-ledhî lâ ilâha illâ Huw-al-Hayya-al-Qayyûma wa etûbu ilaih."

MAKRÛHS of NAMÂZ

1– To look at both sides, with the neck bent.

2– To play with something on yourself.

3– Without an 'udhr, (i.e. a good reason to do so,) to sweep the place of sajda with your hand (during namâz).

4– For men to keep their hands on their chest when standing (in namâz) and to keep them in line with their chest when making the sajda.

5– To snap your fingers, (or to make your fingers crackle.)

6– To sit cross-legged without any 'udhr to do so.

7– To raise one of your legs during the Sajda.

8– As you perform namâz, to wear something which you would not wear in the presence of your superiors (or seniors).

9– To perform namâz against someone's face.

10– To perform namâz against fire.

11– To have a picture –photograph– on your body or clothes.

12– To yawn without any 'udhr to do so.

13– To perform namâz with your hands inside your sleeves.

14– To sit with your shins erect, like dogs.

15– To close your eyes.

16– To turn your hands away from the direction of Qibla.

17– When performing namâz in jamâ'at, to perform it in a rear line while there is room enough (at least for one person) in a line before it. It is tanzîhî (or tenzîhî) kerâhat (makrûh) if there is (at least) one person with you in that rear line, and tahrîmî kerâhat when there is no one else doing the same thing. In the latter case, you will have omitted something which is wâjib; that error can be repaired only by reperforming the namâz.

18– To perform namâz against a grave without (something like) a barrier between you and the grave.

19– To perform namâz against najâsat. (Najâsat is explained in detail in the sixth chapter of the fourth fascicle of **Endless Bliss**.)

20– For a man and a woman to perform different namâzes side by side.

21– To perform namâz while you feel an urge for going to the toilet.

22– After straightening up from the Rukû', to go down for the Sajda by putting your hands on the floor before (putting your knees on the floor), without an 'udhr compelling you to do so.

23– To relieve an itch on any part of your body twice within one rukn, (which begins with the beginning of one standing position and ends with the beginning of another. Your namâz will be fâsid if you raise your hand three times and do the scratching three times, and in that case you will have to reperform the namâz.)

24– To bend down for the Rukû' before the imâm does so, (if you are performing namâz in jamâ'at.)

25– To straighten up from the Rukû' before the imâm does so.

26– To prostrate yourself for the Sajda before the imâm does so.

27– To rise from the Sajda before the imâm does so.

28– To get up in support of something around you, unless you have an 'udhr making it inevitable.

29– As you rise from the Sajda, to detach your knees before

your hands from the floor (or prayer rug).

30– To wipe dust off your face and eyes.

31– In any later rak'at, to skip the sûra that is (immediately) after the sûra which you have recited during the previous rak'at.

32– To recite the same sûra in both the two suras in continuous succession, or to recite a sûra twice in one rak'at. (It is permissible in nâfila [supererogatory] namâz.)

33– In any later rak'at, to recite the sûra that is before the sûra which you recited in the previous rak'at.

34– In any later rak'at, to recite three âyats more than the âyats contained in the dhamm-i-sûra which you recited in the previous rak'at.

35– To bend down and/or straighten up in support of something around you, unless you have an 'udhr, (i.e. a good reason dictated by Islam,) that compels you to do so.

36– To wave away flies.

37– To perform namâz with your sleeves rolled up or with your shoulders or feet exposed.

38– To neglect covering yourself when you are outdoors.

39– To perform namâz on a passageway.

40– When making the Rukû' or the Sajda, to count the tasbîhs with your fingers.

41– For the imâm to be so deeply in the mihrâb as he would be thoroughly inside of it if a curtain were drawn down.

42– For the imâm to be at a level more than one dhrâ' higher or lower than that of the jamâ'at, if he is alone (at that level). (One dhrâ' is approximately equal to half a metre.)

43– For the imâm to conduct the namâz from somewhere other than the mihrâb.

44– To say the Âmîn within the namâz loudly.

45– Whatever is to be said during the Qiyâm, to complete it, (i.e. the Sûra Fâtiha or the dhamm-i-sûra,) after having bent down for the Rukû'.

46, Whatever is to be said during the Rukû', (i.e. "Subhâna Rabb-iy-al 'adhîm",) to complete it after having straightened up back to the (standing position called) Qiyâm.

47– To stand on one foot without (any good reason called) 'udhr.

48– To sway from side to side during namâz.

49– To kill lice and the like that do not bite.

50– To smell something during namâz.

51– To perform namâz bare-headed. Hadjis perform it bare-headed as they wear the Ihrâm. (Please scan the seventh chapter of the fifth fascicle of **Endless Bliss** for 'Ihrâm'.)

52– To start performing namâz with arms exposed.

53– To start performing namâz bare-footed. (According to one qawl, it is makrûh for a woman to perform namâz bare-footed. According to another qawl, it nullifies her namâz.) It is written in the four hundred and thirty-ninth page of Ibni 'Âbidîn that when you enter a mosque it is makrûh to leave your shoes, etc. somewhere behind you. It is written in the final part of **Berîqa** that it is sunnat to put them somewhere on your left, instead of somewhere before you or on your right.

It is written in **Terghîb-us-salât** that it is makrûh to say prayers, such as prayers called 'evrâd', between the farz and the sunnat parts of namâz.

NULLIFIERS of NAMÂZ: In the Hanafî Madhhab, some fifty-five nullifiers have been stated, which will make your namâz null and void, regardless of whether they have been done wittingly or inadvertently:

1– To utter something worldly.

2– To laugh as loudly as it will be heard by the laugher him or herself.

3– To do something that can be said to be an 'amal-i-kethîr.

4– To skip one of the farzes (of namâz) without an 'udhr to do so.

5– To skip one of the farzes involuntarily.

6– To cry loudly for something worldly.

7– To clear your throat or to cough without an 'udhr.

8– To chew gum.

9– To relieve an itch on one of your limbs three times with one hand, or to raise your hands and clap them, within one rukn.

10– To shake hands (with someone).

11– Not to say the takbîr of iftitâh as loudly as you can hear it.

12– Not to say (the sûras and prayers in namâz) as loudly as you can hear them.

13– To say, "**Lâ hawla walâ quwwata il-lâ billâh-il-'aliy-yil 'adhîm**," or "**Subhânallah**," or "**Lâ ilâha il-l-Allah**," when someone calls you. Your namâz will not become fâsid (null and void) if your purpose is to let them know that you are performing namâz. However, it will nullify your namâz if it has been intended to answer that person.

14– To intentionally acknowledge a greeting. (Please see the sixty-second chapter of the third fascicle of **Endless Bliss.**)

15– To taste something sugary in your mouth, and for its juice to seep down your throat.

16– As you perform namâz outdoors, to open your mouth toward the sky, and for rain or hail or the like to pour down your throat.

17– To pull on the halter of the animal (you are riding) three times.

18– To raise your hand three times or to kill lice, fleas or the like by pressing them.

19– To pull out three hairs within one rukn.

20– To pronounce a word of three phonemic sounds such as damn, puff, etc.

21– When performing namâz on horseback in a manner agreeable with Islam, to spur three times with one foot.

22– To spur once with both feet.

23– (When performing namâz in jamâ'at), to stand ahead of the imâm.

24– To walk a distance between two lines without an 'udhr, (i.e. something which compels you to do so and which Islam accepts as a good reason.)

25– To comb your hair or beard.

26– For a man and a woman to perform namâz side by side in the same line behind an imâm – in a namâz in jamâ'at which the imâm is conducting with the intention of being imâm for (a congregation of) men and women. (It is permissible if theiy are not in the same line or side by side or if there is a curtain between them. It is harâm for women and young girls to go out without properly covering their heads or arms, i.e. with any of their awrat parts exposed, whatsoever the purpose, going to a mosque or else. Acts of worship that they perform this wise will earn them sinfulness, rather than thawâb, [i.e. rewards in the Hereafter.])

27– To solve the difficulty of an imâm other than your own imâm, (i.e. to help an imâm who is conducting namâz in another jamâ'at and who falters as he recites the prescribed âyats.)

28– Supposing a woman stands at an unoccupied place and starts to follow the imâm and thereafter other men arrive and the new lines of jamâ'at they have made spread out so as to cover the place where she is performing the (same) namâz; the namâz of three men, one of them (immediately) on her right, the second one on her left, and the third one behind her, will become fâsid (nullified).

29– To hug one's child.

30– To eat or drink something.

31– To swallow something as big as a chickpea and which has remained between your teeth.

32– To bring both ends of your collar together with your both hands, or to take off your headgear with one hand or to take it off and put it on again.

33– To say, "**Innâ lillâh wa innâ ilaihi râji'ûn,**" upon hearing some sad news.

34– To say, "**Al-hamd-u-lillâh,**" upon hearing some good news.

35– According to a qawl, to sneeze and thereupon say, "**Al-hamd-u-lillâh.**"

36– To say, "**Yerhamukallah,**" to a person who sneezes near you.

37– To say, "**Yehdîkumullah,**" upon another person's sneezing.

38– For a man to come and kiss the woman performing namâz.

39– When saying prayers during namâz, to ask for something worldly, such and gold and silver.

40– To turn your chest away from the (direction of) Qibla. There are two ways for finding the direction of Qibla. 1– By way of the angle of Qibla. 2– By way of the hour of Qibla. 1– If a straight line is drawn between a city and Mekka on a map, that line is (the direction of Qibla from that city and is called) **line of Qibla**. Its difference from south is the **angle of Qibla**. 2– Any person who turns towards the sun at the time of Qibla written as the **hour of Qibla** (or time of Qibla) on a calendar will have turned to the direction of Qibla. Kadûsî provides the following explanation in his annotation (to Rub'–i-dâira): "When the cursor of the rub'-i-dâira set (for the date) is moved to the arc of Qibla, the complement of the angle indicated by the (string called) khayt on the arc of altitude is the Fadl-i-dâir (H) of Istanbul's time of Qibla." When a time machine (clock) is held with its face towards the sky and its hour hand pointing towards the sun, the bisector of the angle between the hour hand and the number twelve points to the south. Please scan the ninth chapter of the fourth fascicle of **Endless Bliss**!

41– To raise both feet from the ground (or floor) during the Sajda.

42– To recite the (âyats of) Qur'ân al-kerîm with such inaccuracy as will change the meaning.

43– For a woman to suckle her baby.

44– To change one's place at somebody's bidding.

45– To whip the animal (you are riding) three times.

46– To open a closed door.

47– To write something with at least three letters.

48– To put on your caftan.

49– To remember your qadâ namâzes, (i.e. daily prayers that you did not perform in their dictated times,) if they are fewer than six.

50– When performing a farz namâz –with an 'udhr– on [a ship or train] or on the back of an animal (such as a horse), to turn to a direction other than the Qibla.

51– To load the animal as you are on its back.

52– To become a murtadd (renegade, apostate) with your heart.

53– To become junub or for a woman to start menstruating.

54– For the imâm (who is conducting namâz in jamâ'at) to make someone substitute for him because he thinks his own ablution has broken.

55– To recite (âyats of) the Qur'ân al-kerîm with such alterations in letters as will spoil their meanings. [Ibni 'Âbidîn 'rahimahullâhu ta'âlâ' states as follows as he embarks on his discourse on the sunnats of namâz: "A namâz performed following someone outside of namâz will not be sahîh. It is makrûh for the imâm or the muazzin to raise their voice louder than for the jamâ'at to hear them. As the imâm and the muazzin say the takbîr of iftitâh when starting to perform namâz (in jamâ'at), they should make their niyyat to start performing namâz. Their namâz will not be sahîh if they make their niyyat (intention) only to get their voice heard by the jamâ'at. And the namâz of the people following will not be sahîh, either. It is makrûh for the muazzin to repeat the takbîrs within the namâz loudly if the imâm's voice is audible enough. It is a hideous bid'at to do so. It is mustahab for them to do so when needed, but then a muazzin's namâz will be fâsid if he does so for the purpose of singing a melody." Hence, the imâm's and the muazzin's making their voices heard by using a loud-speaker not only makes the jamâ'at's namâz fâsid but also prevents their own namâz from being sahîh. It is a hideous bid'at into the bargain. And it is gravely sinful to commit a bid'at. That it is not sahîh to follow an imâm who is conducting a namâz in jamâ'at at some other place and whom you see and hear by way of television, is written by documentation with proof-texts in an article in the twelfth issue, dated Rabî'ul-awwal, 1406, and December, 1985, of the periodical entitled **al-Mu'allim**, published by Indian scholars in Malappulam.]

And What Will Not Nullify Your Namâz: If there is an unoccupied line before you and you walk there by taking one or two steps or if you say, "Âmin," not in reply to someone or if you acknowledge someone's greeting, (i.e. someone's saying, "Salâmun 'alaikum,")[1] by making a sign with your eye-brows or eyes or if someone asks you how many rak'ats you have performed and you make a sign with your fingers; in none of these cases will your namâz break.

Lexical meaning of 'salât' is 'compassion on the part of Allâhu 'adhîm-ush-shân and istighfâr on the part of angels and prayers on the part of Believers'. Its technical meaning is 'ef'âl-i-ma'lûma and erkân-i-mahsûsa', i.e. 'namâz' in Turkish, and 'prayer' in English. Ef'âl-i-ma'lûma means 'acts which we perform outside of namâz', and erkân-i-mahsûsa means 'rukns (dictated standing positions, sitting postures, genuflections, and prayers) within namâz, and all these acts in the aggregate, are proper to namâz.

One day, Rasûlullah 'sall-Allâhu 'alaihi wa sallam', in the beatitude special to his most blessed person, stated to Hadrat 'Alî

---

[1] Please see the sixty-second chapter of the third fascicle of **Endless Bliss** for salutations and greetings.

'kerrem-Allâhu wajhahu wa radiy-Allâhu 'anh': "**Yâ 'Alî! You must observe the farzes, the wâjibs, the sunnats, and the mustahabs of namâz.**" Thereupon a blessed Sahâbî among the Ansâr[1] remarked: Yâ Rasûlallah (O the Blessed Messenger of Allah)! Hadrat 'Alî already knows all these things. Tell us about the virtues of observing the farzes, wâjibs, sunnats and mustahabs of a namâz, so that we will act accordingly." Hadrat Rasûlullah 'sall-Allâhu 'alaihi wa sallam' stated: "**O my Ummat and my Sahâba! Namâz is what Allâhu 'adhîm-ush-shân is pleased with. It is what Ferishtehs (angels) like. It is the sunnat of Prophets. It is the nûr of ma'rifat. It is the best of a'mâl** (Islamic practices). **It is energy for the body. It is berekât for the rizq. It is nûr for the soul. It is acceptance for prayers. It is intercessor with the Angel of death. It is the lamp of the grave. It is an answer to** (the questioning angels called) **Hadrat Munkar and Nakîr. It is a canopy over you on the Rising Day. It is a curtain between Hell and you. It will make you pass the Sirât like lightning. It is a crown on your head in Paradise. It is a key to Paradise.**"

VIRTUE of NAMÂZ in JAMÂ'AT

Supposing someone performed a namâz of two rak'ats in jamâ'at and a namâz of twenty-seven rak'ats on his own, the namâz of two rak'ats that he performed in jamâ'at would still yield more thawâb.

According to another riwâyat (scholarly tradition), even if the namâz he performed consisted of a thousand rak'ats, two rak'ats of namâz performed in jamâ'at would still earn him more thawâb. There is plenty of thawâb in performing namâz in jamâ'at. Here are a few of its benefits:

1– When Believers come together, they will love one another.

2– Ignorant ones will learn about matters concerning namâz from learned ones.

3– If the namâz performed by some of them is acceptable while

---

[1] When the Best of Mankind, Rasûlullah 'sall-Allâhu 'alaihi wa sallam' migrated to Medina (from Mekka) in 622 A.D., Muslims living in Medina met him with greatest happiness and accommodated the most blessed Prophet and the other Sahâbîs who migrated later with great hospitality. The emigrants have been called 'Muhâjir' (pl. Muhâjirîn) and the Muslims of Medina who helped them have been called 'Ansâr'.

others' namâz is not, the unacceptable namâz of the latter group will be accepted for the grace of the acceptable namâz of the former.

A hadîth-i-sherîf reads: **"O my Ummat and my Sahâba! I have put forth two paths for you: One of them is the Qur'ân al-'adhîm ush-shân, and the other one is my Sunnat. A person who follows a path other than these two is not my Ummat!"** ['Abd-ul-Ghânî Nablusî 'rahima-hullâhu ta'âlâ' (1050 [1640 A.D.], Damascus – 1143 [1731]) states as follows in the ninety-ninth page of his book entitled **Hadîqa** (and which is a commentary to the book entitled **Tarîqat-i-Muhammadiyya** and written by Imâm Birgivî): While Allâhu ta'âlâ announced a part of Islam by way of the Qur'ân al-kerîm, He announced its other part throught the Sunnat of His blessed Prophet 'sall-Allâhu 'alaihi wa sallam'. The Sunnat of Rasûlullah consists of his beliefs, utterances, practices, moral behaviour, and his tacit admission of someone's act or statement, [which was construed as his accepting (what had been done or said).]" This hadîth-i-sherîf indicates the second one of the (four Islamic sources called) **Edilla-i-shar'iyya.**]

IMÂMAT in NAMÂZ (in jamâ'at)

There are four kinds of people following the imâm (who is conducting namâz in jamâ'at): Mudrik, Muqtedî, Mesbûq, and Lâhiq.

1– Mudrik is a Muslim who makes the takbîr iftitâh together with the imâm. (In other words, he says, "Allâhu ekber," (almost) at the same time as the imâm does so, which in turn means that he has started to perform the namâz in jamâ'at together with the imâm conducting the namâz in jamâ'at.)

2– A Muslim who fails to catch up with the takbîr iftitâh is called muqtedî.

3– Mesbûq is a Muslim who (joins the jamâ'at and) starts to follow the imâm after the imâm has performed one or two rak'ats of the namâz.

4– Lâhiq is a Muslim who made the takbîr iftitâh together with the imâm; however, he has undergone a state of hadas, (he has somehow lost his ablution;)[1] he makes an ablution and resumes his namâz behind the imâm. This Muslim performs the namâz

---

[1] Please see the second chapter of the fourth fascicle of **Endless Bliss** for 'hadas'.

exactly as he did when he was behind the imâm, (i.e. he does not make qirâat, but he makes the Rukû, the Sajda and the tasbîhs during them.) If he has not uttered any words pertaining to worldly matters (as he leaves the mosque to renew his ablution), it is the same as if he performed the entire namâz behind the imâm and together with the imâm. However, after leaving the mosque (for the purpose of renewing his ablution), he ought to make an ablution at a place nearest the mosque. There are Islamic scholars who state that his namâz will become fâsid if he goes too far away.

If a person finds the imâm making the Rukû' as he enters the mosque and, in the hurry of catching up with the imâm, makes the takbîr iftitâh as he bends down for the Rukû', he has not followed the imâm, (i.e. he has not joined the jamâ'at.) If he, when he finds the imâm making the Rukû', makes his niyyat to follow the imâm, makes the takbîr (iftitâh) completely within the standing position, then bends down for the Rukû' and says the tasbîh as the imâm is still in the position of Rukû', he has caught up with the imâm (and joined the jamâ'at) within that rak'at. Yet, if the imâm straightens up as this Muslim bends down for the Rukû', he has not caught up with that rak'at.

TA'DÎL-I-ARKÂN in NAMÂZ

If a person skips (observing) the ta'dîl-i-arkân at five places of namâz, not forgetfully but deliberately, his namâz becomes fâsid (null and void) according to Imâm Abû Yûsuf 'rahima-hullâhu ta'âlâ'. According to the Tarafeyn (Imâm A'zam Abû Hanîfa and Imâm Muhammad), it does not become fâsid, but then it will be necessary for him to reperform the namâz for the purpose of making up for an imperfection arising from the negligence of an act that is wâjib. **Sajda-i-sahw** will be necessary when you fail to observe it forgetfully. [Please review the section of the current book dealing with the causes of losing one's îmân!]

Skipping the ta'dîl-i-arkân engenders some twenty-six harms:

1– It causes poverty.

2– 'Ulamâ (savants) of the Hereafter hate you.

3– You fall from 'adâlat, so that you will no longer be acceptable as a witness.

4– The place where you perform that (imperfect) namâz will bear witness against you on the Rising Day.

5– A person will be sinful for not (kindly and with due tact and finesse) warning another person whom he sees to perform namâz without the ta'dîl-i-arkân.

6– You have to reperform the namâz (which you performed without observing the ta'dîl-i-arkân).

7– It causes dying without îmân.

8– It makes you a thief who steals from namâz.

9– The namâz you have performed will be flung like an old rag to your teeth on the Day of Judgment.

10– You will be deprived of the Mercy of Allâhu ta'âlâ.

11– You will have behaved improperly in your supplication to Allâhu ta'âlâ.

12– You will be deprived of the plenty of thawâb inherent in namâz.

13– It causes the thawâbs that you are to be given for your other acts of worship to be withheld.

14– It causes you to deserve Hell.

15– It causes ignorant people who see you to (follow your bad example and) disignore the ta'dîl-i-arkân. It is for the same matter that sinning on the part of a man of religion will incur more torment.

16– You will have opposed your imâm.

17– You will have omitted the sunnats at the intiqâlât (transitions).

18– You will incur Wrath of Allâhu 'adhîm-ush-shân.

19– You will have pleased the Satan.

20– You will be far from Paradise.

21– You will be close to Hell.

22– You will have been cruel to your own nafs.

23– You will have made your own nafs dirty.

24– You will have hurt the angels on your right and left.

25– You will have saddened Rasûlullah 'sall-Allâhu 'alaihi wa sallam'.

26– You will have caused harm to the entire creation. For, on account of your sin, there will be no rains and crops, or there will be unseasonable rains, which will cause harm to crops, instead of nourishing them.

NAMÂZ DURING LONG-DISTANCE JOURNEYS

It is written as follows in the book entitled **Ni'mat-i-islâm** (and written by Hâdji Muhammad Zihnî 'rahmatullâhi ta'âlâ 'alaih', 1262–1332 [1914 A.D.], Küplüce-Beğlerbeği, Istanbul:) It is permissible, always and everywhere, to perform nâfila (supererogatory) namâz sitting even when it is possible to perform it standing. As you perform namâz sitting, you bend down your body for the Rukû'. For the Sajda you put your head on the ground (or floor, or on the prayer rug). However, if a person performs namâz sitting without any 'udhr (a good reason justified by Islam) to do so, he will be given half the thawâb that he would earn if he performed it standing. The sunnats of the daily five prayers (namâzes) and the namâz of Tarâwîh are among the nâfila namâzes. (Please see the nineteenth chapter of the fourth fascicle of **Endless Bliss** for 'tarâwîh'.) On a journey, i.e. outside of urban areas, it is permissible to perform nâfila namâzes on the back of an animal, (e.g. a horse.) It is not obligatory to turn towards the Qibla or to make Rukû' or Sajda. You perform it with îmâ, (i.e. with signs.) In other words, you bend down a little with your body. For the Sajda, you bend down somewhat more. Existence of plenty of najâsat on the animal will not have a detrimental effect on the namâz. It is permissible for a person who becomes tired as he performs namâz on the ground to perform it leaning against a walking stick or another person or a wall. It is not sahîh to perform namâz as you yourself are walking. (In other words, namâz performed thereby will not be valid.) As for namâzes that are farz or wâjib; it is only when there is an 'udhr can they be performed on an animal outside (of) urban areas. An 'udhr (in this matter) is one of the following cases: To fear that your fellow travellers will leave you alone in case you dismount from your animal; to fear that there may be highwaymen around, so that you may lose your life, your property, or your animal; muddy ground; inability to mount your animal; other similar situations. If possible, you make your animal stand in the direction of Qibla and perform your namâz. If it is not possible you perform it in the direction wherein your animal is walking. The same rule applies in performing it in a box-like litter placed on the animal. If the animal is made to stop and a mast is placed under the litter, it changes into a **serîr**, i.e. a table or couch, so that performing namâz on it is like doing so on the ground. In that case you will have to perform your namâz standing in the direction of Qibla.

Performing namâz on board a ship is as Rasûlullah taught it to Hadrat Ja'fer Tayyâr[1] as the latter was to leave for Abyssinia (Ethiopia), as follows: Even a namâz that is farz or wâjib can be performed aboard a sailing ship, and there is no need for the existence of an 'udhr for doing so. Namâz in jamâ'at can be performed aboard a ship. On a sailing ship it is not permissible to perform namâz with îmâ, (i.e. by making signs;) the Rukû' and the Sajda must be made. As well, it is obligatory to perform it in the direction of Qibla. As you start to perform the namâz, you stand towards the Qibla. As the ship changes its direction, you must turn toward the Qibla. As well, tahârat from najâsat is obligatory on board a ship. (Please see the sixth chapter of the fourth fascicle of **Endless Bliss** for 'tahârat from najâsat'.) In the Hanafî Madhhab, it is permissible to perform even a namâz that is farz sitting on the floor aboard a sailing ship with no need for the existence of an 'udhr for doing so.

A ship at anchor out in the sea is like a sailing ship if it is rolling and pitching violently. If it is rolling slightly, it is like a ship lying moored near the shore. Namâz that is farz cannot be performed sitting on a ship lying moored near the shore. It is not sahîh to perform it standing, either, if it is possible to go ashore. It is necessary to go ashore and perform it on land. In case of risks such as losing your property or life or the ship's sailing off, it becomes permissible to perform your namâz standing on board the ship. Here we end our citation from **Ni'mat-i-islâm**.

It is stated in Ibni 'Âbidîn: "Performing namâz on a two-wheeled horse-drawn cart that cannot stand flat on the ground without being tied to the animal, in motion or motionless alike, is like performing it on the back of an animal. A four-wheeled carriage, when motionless, is like a serîr (table, couch). When it moves, namâz that is farz can be performed in it on account of the

---

[1] Ja'fer Tayyâr 'radiy-Allâhu 'anh' was one of the four sons of Rasûlullah's paternal uncle Abû Tâlib. He was ten years older than Hadrat 'Alî and ten years younger the Hadrat 'Uqayl. He migrated to Abyssinia and returned on the day of Hayber. In the eighth [8] year of the Hijrat (Hegira), he was making war against the Byzantines with a three thousand strong army at a place called Mu'ta in the vicinity of Damascus, when he attained martyrdom after making many attacks and receiving more than seventy wounds in one day. He was forty-one years old. He was one of the seven people most closely resembling Rasûlullah.

same 'udhrs as the aforesaid ones concerning namâz on an animal; you stop the carriage and perform it in the direction of Qibla. If you fail to stop it, then you perform it like doing so aboard a sailing ship." If a person who is (on a long-distance journey and who is therefore called) safarî cannot sit on the floor or turn towards the Qibla on the means of transport, he imitates one of the Shâfi'î and Mâlikî Madhhabs and makes jem' of two successive prayers of namâz when he gets off the vehicle.[1] It is not permissible for a person who is able to sit on the ground (or floor) to sit on a chair or in an armchair and perform namâz with îmâ. Performing namâz on a bus or on an aeroplane is like performing it on a carriage. A person who sets out for a long-distance journey and who makes his niyyat (intention) to travel a distance of three days, i.e. eighteen fersâh (parasang) = 54 miles [54 x 0.48 x 4 = 104 kilometres] from the outskirts of the city or village, becomes (a person who is) safarî by the time he leaves the outskirts of the city. According to Ibni 'Âbidîn, a mile is equal to 4000 dhrâ', and a dhrâ' is equal to twenty-four [24] fingerwidths. [A fingerwidth is a length equal to two centimetres. In the Shâfi'î and Mâlikî Madhhabs, 16 fersah = 48 miles = 48 x 0.42 x 4000 = 80 km.]

Come on, let's perform namâz, and wipe rust off our heart,
You cannot be close to Allah, unless you perform namâz!

Wherever namâz is performed, all your sins are dumped,
You can never reach perfection, unless you perform namâz!

In Qur'ân al-kerîm Haqq praises namâz a lot,
He says, "I shall never love you, unless you perform namâz!"

A hadîth-i-sherîf: Îmân won't be manifest
At all on your outer person, unless you perform namâz!

Not to perform namâz, of all sins, is the gravest,
Penitence won't do, unless you perform omitted namâz!

He who disdains namâz will lose his îmân outright,
He will not regain his Islam, unless he performs namâz!

Namâz purifies the heart, and bars it from guilt,
You can never be enlightened, unless you perform namâz!

---

[1] Please see the fifteenth chapter of the fourth fascicle of **Endless Bliss**.

VIRTUES of the TAKBÎR IFTITÂH

When a person makes the takbîr iftitâh together with the imâm, his sins will fall like leaves falling with autumnal winds.

One morning, Rasûlullah 'sall-Allâhu 'alaihi wa sallam' was performing namâz, when someone arrived, but he was too late for the takbîr iftitâh of morning prayer, (that is, he failed to make the takbîr iftitâh with the imâm.) He manumitted a slave. Afterwards, he asked Rasûlullah 'sall-Allâhu 'alaihi wa sallam': "Yâ Rasûlallah (O Messenger of Allah!) Today I was unable to catch up with the takbîr iftitâh of morning prayer. I manumitted a slave. I wonder if I was able to attain the thawâb inherent in the takbîr iftitâh?" Rasûlullah 'sall-Allâhu ta'âlâ 'alaihi wa sallam' asked Hadra Abû Bakr 'radiy-Allâhu ta'âlâ 'anh': "**What would you say concerning this takbîr iftitâh?**" Abû Bakr Siddîq 'radiy-Allâhu 'anh' replied: "Yâ Rasûlallah 'sall-Allâhu ta'âlâ 'alaihi wa sallam'! If I had forty camels all forty of which laden with jewelry and I gave all of them as alms to the poor, I would still not attain the thawâb to be earned by making the takbîr iftitâh with the imâm." Thereafter, when the cause of the entire creation asked: "**Yâ 'Umar! What would you say about this takbîr iftitâh?**" Hadrat 'Umar 'radiy-Allâhu 'anh' stated: "Yâ Rasûlallah 'sall-Allâhu ta'âlâ 'alaihi wa sallam'! If I had as many camels as to cover the distance between Mekka and Medîna and all those camels were laden with jewelry, and if I gave them all to the poor in the name of alms, I would still not be able to attain the thawâb earned by making the takbîr iftitâh with the imâm." Thereupon, when the most blessed Prophet asked: "**Yâ 'Uthmân, what would you say about this takbîr iftitâh?**" Hadrat 'Uthmân zin-nûreyn 'radiy-Allâhu 'anh' said: "Yâ Rasûlallah 'sall-Allâhu ta'âlâ 'alaihi wa sallam'! If I performed a namâz of two rak'ats at night and recited the entire Qur'ân al-'adhîm-ush-shân at each rak'at, I would still fail to attain the thawâb that would be earned by making the takbîr iftitâh with the imâm." Thereafter, Hadrat 'Alî 'kerrem-Allâhu wejheh' was asked: "**Yâ 'Alî! What do you say about this takbîr iftitâh?**" He replied as follows: "Yâ Rasûlallah 'sall-Allâhu 'alaihi wa sallam'! If all the unbelievers between the west and the east attacked for the purpose of annihilating the Muslims and Allâhu ta'âlâ gave me power and I made jihâd against the unbelievers and slew them all, I still would not attain the same thawâb as that to be given for making the takbîr iftitâh made together with the imâm."

Thereafter Rasûlullah 'sallAllâhu ta'âlâ 'alaihi wa sallam'

stated: "**O my Ummat and Sahâba! If seven layers of earth and seven layers of heaven were paper and if all oceans were ink and if all trees were pens and if all angels were scribes and if they wrote** (continuously) **until Doomsday, they would still fail to write the thawâb for making the takbîr iftitâh with the imâm.**"

If you should say, "Are the angels created by Allâhu 'adhîm-ush-shân that many?" (here is the answer): On the night of Mi'râj,[1] when Rasûlullah 'sall-Allâhu ta'âlâ 'alaihi wa sallam' ascended to Heaven, angels were visiting Paradise and Hell and the Bayt-i-ma'mûr (Kâ'ba) and going (away). Rasûlullah 'sall-Allâhu 'alaihi wa sallam' asked: "**O my sibling Jebrâîl! Angels visiting this Bayt-i-ma'mûr are not going back. Where do they go?**" Jebrâîl 'alaihis-salâm' stated: "Yâ Habîballah (o the Beloved One of Allah)! Since the day I was created, I have never seen any angels return after visiting this Bayt-i-ma'mûr and leaving. Once an angel makes tawâf of the Bayt-i-ma'mûr and leaves, their turn never comes again-until Doomsday."

When a person says the A'ûdhu and the Basmala during namâz, Allâhu 'adhîm-ush-shân gives that slave of His as many thawâbs as the number of hairs on his body. When that slave recites the Fâtiha-i-sherîfa, Hadrat Allâhu ta'âlâ gives him the same amount of thawâb that He would give for a hajj that has been accepted. When that slave bends down for the Rukû' Allâhu 'adhîm-ush-shân gives him the same thawâb that He would give him for having dispensed thousands of gold coins as alms, and when he makes the Tasbîh, (i.e. when says, "Subhâna Rabbiy-al-'adhîm,") three times, as is taught in the Sunnat, Allâhu 'adhîm-ush-shân gives that slave as much thawâb as if he had read the four books revealed from heaven and also the hundred heavenly suhûf (small heavenly booklets). When he says, "**Semi' Allâhu liman hamideh,**" (as he straightens up from the Rukû',) Allâhu 'adhîm-ush-shân covers that slave with oceans of His Rahmat (Mercy, Compassion). When he goes down for the Sajda Allâhu ta'âlâ gives that slave as many thawâbs as the sum of the number of humans plus that of genies. When he says the Tasbîh, (that is, when he says, "Subhâna Rabbiy-al-a'lâ,") three times, as is commanded in the Sunnat, there is many a virtue that Allâhu 'adhîm-ush-shân gives that slave of His. A few of them stated (by Islamic savants) are as follows:

---

[1] Please see the sixtieth chapter of the third fascicle of **Endless Bliss** for 'Mi'râj'.

The first virtue is that He shall give him thawâb as heavy as the sum of the weights of the 'Arsh and the Kursî.[1] Second, Allâhu 'adhîm-ush-shân shall treat that slave of His with maghfirat (forgiveness). The third virtue is, when that slave dies, Mikâîl ''alaihis-salâm' shall visit his grave (frequently) till Doomsday. Fourth, on the Day of Rising, Mikâîl ''alaihis-salâm' shall take that slave on his blessed wing, intercede for him, and carry him to Jannat-i-a'lâ (Paradise).[2]

When that person sits down for the Qa'da-i-âkhira (the final sitting posture), Allâhu 'adhîm-ush-shân shall give that person the same thawâb as He gives to the fuqarây-i-sâbirîn (Muslims who are both poor and patient).

The fuqarây-i-sâbirîn shall enter Paradise five hundred years before the aghniyây-i-shâkirîn (Rich and grateful Muslims.) When the aghniyây-i-shâkirîn see the former, they will say: "How we wish we had been among the fuqarây-i-sâbirîn in the world!"

In grave, questioning angels will come to you;
"Did you perform namâz properly," they shall say.
"Do you reckon death has come to your rescue?
Bitter torment is ready for you," they shall say.

ABOUT the JANNÂT-I-ÂLIYYÂT
(The Sublime Gardens of Paradise)

There are eight gates and eight keys for the eight Gardens of Paradise. The first one is the îmân (belief) held by the Believers who perform (the daily five prayers called) namâz. The second one is the Basmala-i-sherîfa, (i.e. to say, "Bismillâh-ir-Rahmân-ir-Rahîm.") The (next) six are within the (first Sûra of the Qur'ân al-kerîm called) Fâtiha-i-sherîfa. The eight Jannats (Gardens of Paradise) are:

1– The Dâr-i-jelâl. 2– The Dâr-i-qarâr. 3– The Dâr-i-salâm. 4– The Jannat-ul-khuld. 5– The Jannat-ul-Me'wâ. 6– The Jannat-ul-'adn. 7– The Jannat-ul-firdevs. 8– The Jannat-ul-na'îm.

---

[1] Please see the twenty-first chapter of the sixth fascicle of **Endless Bliss** for the 'Arsh and the Kursî.

[2] All the good news that has been given so far include all Muslims, regardless of their sex.

1– The Dâr-i-jelâl is of white nûr.

2– The Dâr-i-qarâr is of red ruby.

3– The Dâr-i-salâm is of green chrysolite.

4– The Jannat-ul-khuld is of coral.

5– The Jannat-ul-Me'wâ is of silver.

6– The Jannat-ul-'adn (Eden) is of gold.

7– The Jannat-ul-firdevs is both of gold and of silver.

8– The Jannat-ul-na'îm is of red ruby.

Believers who enter will stay there eternally; they will never go out. The houris being there do not undergo menstrual or lochial periods; nor do they have any whims or caprices. Any kind of food or drink they desire will come before them, ready and at their disposal. They will be far from troubles such as cooking and picking. Fowls will be flying over their heads. Believers will see them as they sit in their villas. "If we were in the world and you came so close to me I would roast you." No sooner will this desire have come to their heart than they will be eating the newly roasted fowl in the dish made of nûr before them. (After eating the fowl) the Believer will heap the bones somewhere and wish through his heart that the bones became a fowl again. The moment the wish comes to his heart the bones will become a fowl as before, and the new fowl will fly away.

The soil of Paradise is made of musk and its buildings are made of adobes, one made of silver alternating with another made of gold.

Each and every man in Paradise will be given the power of a hundred men. Each of them will be given at least seventy houris and two worldly women.

There will be four streams in Paradise. Springing from a common source, they differ both in flowing and in flavour. One of them is sheer water, the second one is pure milk, the third one is Paradise beverage, and the fourth one is unmixed honey.

There are tall villas in Paradise. They bend down, Believers mount them and are caried to whereever they wish. (Their semblance in the world are moving stairs and aeroplanes, as of today.)

There is a tree called 'Tûbâ' in Paradise. The roots of this tree are on top, and its branches and shoots hang down. Its semblance in the world is the moon and the sun.

People of Paradise enjoy eating and drinking and relish what they eat and drink; but they do not feel any need to urinate or defecate; they are far from such human needs and anguishes.

Allâhu ta'âlâ will address His slaves, Believers in Paradise: "**O My slaves! What more do you want Me to give you? Go ahead and enjoy the pleasures and comfort!**" The slaves will reply: "Yâ Rabbî! You have freed us from Hell and made us enter Your Paradise, and given us so many houris and ghilmâns and wildâns. It would be embarrassing for us to ask for more." Thereupon Rabb-ul-'âlamîn will address them once again, saying: "**O My slaves! There is something you are to ask from Me and which is other than these things**." When the slaves reply, "Yâ Rabbî! We do not have the face to ask for more. Besides, we don't know what to ask for," Rabb-ul 'âlamîn will ask them: "**O My slaves! What did you use to do when you encountered a matter in the world**?" When they reply that they used ask the 'ulamâ (Islamic scholars) and their problem would be solved when they learned the matter, Hadrat Haqq subhânahu wa ta'âlâ will say: "**Do the same thing now and become acquainted by consulting with the 'ulamâ.**" So the 'ulamâ will say to the Believers: "Have you forgotten about Jemâlullah? When you were in the world you used to yearn (to see Allâhu ta'âlâ) and say: 'In the Hereafter our Rabb, who is far from place, will make us see His Jemâl (Beauty).' That is what you should ask for now." Thereupon they will ask for the ru'yet-i-jemâlullah (seeing the Beauty of Allah), and Allâhu 'adhîm-ush-shân, free and far as He is from place, will show them His jemâl-i-bâkemâl. When they see Haqq ta'âlâ's jemâl-i-pâk, their admiration will last many a thousand years.

As a Believer sits in his villa, there will be fruits around him and before his windows. When he thinks, "Let me reach out my hand, pull that branch, pick the fruit, and eat it," he will not need to get up from his seat to pull the branch. Presently the branch he wants will be where he is sitting, he will pick the fruit and put it in his mouth, and before its flavour reaches his throat another fruit will appear where he picked the first one. When he puts the fruit in his mouth it will be ripe and delicious. Thus, Rabb-ul-'izza will create another fresh one.

If you are wise, perform namâz, for it is a crown of happiness. Your knowledge of namâz should be that it is Mi'râj for Believers.

PRAYERS NOT PERFORMED
WITHIN THEIR TIME
(Qadâ Namâzes)

A namâz that has been performed within its dictated time yields very many virtues. Some of them have been stated (by Islamic savants):

1– Its first virtue is that the performer's face will become nûr all over.

2– The performer's life will have barakât.

3– Benedictions pronounced by the performer will be accepted (by Allâhu ta'âlâ).

4– The performer will become a person with khayr.

5– The performer will be beloved to all Believers.

Omitting a namâz without any 'udhr, i.e. performing it after its dictated time without any excuse sanctioned by Islam to do so, causes fifteen harms. Five of these harms are in the world; three of them are at the time of death; three of them are in grave; and four of them are at the place of Arasât.

Its five harms in the world are:

1– There will be no nûr on that person's face.

2– There will be no barakât in his life.

3– His prayers and benedictions will not be accepted.

4– Blessings that he invokes on a Muslim brother will not be accepted (by Allâhu ta'âlâ).

5– He will not receive any thawâb for his other acts of worship.

Its three harms during the sekerât-i-mawt (agonies of death) are:

1– He will die hungry.

2– He will die thirsty.

3– He will die in a despicable manner. No amount of food will gratify his hunger or water, no matter how much, will slake his thirst.

Its three harms in grave are:

1– His grave will squeeze him, so that his bones will intertwine.

2– His grave will be fire all over.

3– A dragon will fall upon him. The dragon's name is Aqra. It will hold a whip in one hand. One stroke with the whip will send that person down to the depths of the earth. He will rise back, only to be whipped again. The whipping will continue until Doomsday. So that person will be tormented until Day of Rising.

Its four harms at the place of Arasât are:

1– He will undergo a severe trial.

2– He will have incurred the Wrath of Allâhu 'adhîm-ush-shân.

3– He will enter Hell.

4– There will be three different written statements on his forehead:

The first one will read: This person deserves Allah's Wrath.

The second statement will be: This person has wasted the right of Allâhu ta'âlâ.

The third one will say: As you have wasted the right of Allâhu 'adhîm-ush-shân, you are far from the Compassion of Allâhu ta'âlâ.

Namâz is the mainmast of Islam. If a person performs his (daily five prayers of) namâz, he will have erected the mainmast of his faith. Thereby he will have made a bower to shelter under.

If a person omits a single namâz wittingly and does not make qadâ of it, (i.e. if he does not perform it later, either,) in all three Madhhabs a fatwâ will be given that he is to be killed. According to the Hanafî Madhhab, it will not be necessary to kill him. However, he will have committed one of the grave sins termed 'akbar-i-kebâir'. It will be necessary (to imprison him and) to keep him in prison until he begins to perform (his daily prayers of) namâz. A person who neglects namâz because he does not attribute due importance to namâz and because he does not believe the fact that namâz is (a Believer's) primary duty, will become an unbeliever.

If a person omits any one (of the daily five prayers of) namâz wittingly and thereafter makes qadâ of it, (i.e. even if he pays his debt by performing it afterwards,) he shall be kept burning in Hell for a length of time called 'huqba', i.e. eighty years. To be absolved from that torment, he will have to make tawba and beg and supplicate for forgiveness.

(One day in the Hereafter is equal to a thousand worldly years. Years in the Hereafter should be reckoned accordingly.)

[Muhammad Amîn Ibni 'Âbidîn 'rahmatullâhi 'alaih' states in his book entitled **Radd-ul-muhtâr**: As has been stated (by Islamic savants), namâz has been a religious commandment in all heavenly religions. 'Âdam ''alaihis-salâm' performed namâz (daily) at the time of late afternoon, Ya'qûb ''alaihis-salâm' performed it (daily) in the (early) evening (after sunset), and Yûnus ''alaihis-salâm' performed it (daily) at night. As it is one of the tenets of îmân to believe acts that are farz and those which are harâm, likewise it is a tenet of îmân to believe that it is a duty, a debt to perform (the daily five prayers of) namâz. However, it is not a tenet of îmân to perform (these prayers of) namâz.

It is farz for every discreet and pubert Muslim, male and female alike, to perform namâz five times daily, unless they have an 'udhr, (i.e. something to absolve them from responsibility.) Daily five prayers of namâz became farz (an Islamic commandment) on the night of Mi'râj. Hadîth-i-sherîfs quoted in the books entitled **Muqaddima-us-salât** and **Tafsîr-i-Mazharî** and **Halabiy-i-kebîr** read as follows: "**Jebrâîl ''alaihis-salâm'** (and I performed namâz together, and Jebrâîl ''alaihis-salâm) **conducted the namâz as imâm for two of us, by the side of the door of Ka'ba, for two days running. We two performed the morning prayer as the fajr dawned; the early afternoon prayer as the Sun departed from meridian; the late afternoon prayer when the shadow of an object equalled its midday shadow increased by the length of the object; the evening prayer after sunset,** [i.e. when its upper limb disappeared;] **and the night prayer when the evening twilight darkened. The second day, we performed the morning prayer when the morning twilight matured; the early afternoon prayer when the shadow of an object increased again by the length of the object; the late afternoon prayer immediately thereafter; the evening prayer at the prescribed time of breaking fast; and the night prayer at the end of the first third of the night. Then he said: 'O Muhammad, these are the times of** (the daily five prayers of) **namâz for you and the Prophets before you. Let your Ummat perform each of these five prayers between the two times at which we have performed each.'** " We are commanded to perform namâz five times daily. It is incumbent upon parents to command their seven year-old child to perform namâz, and to make it perform namâz by beating it with hand if it still does not perform when it is ten years old. It is not permissible to beat one's disciple with more than three strokes or to beat him with a stick. The same beating is applied to a child to make it fast (in the blessed month of

Ramadân) or to prevent it from consuming alcoholic beverages. A person who denies the fact that it is farz to perform namâz and that it is a Muslim's primary duty, becomes an unbeliever (kâfir). If he does not perform namâz because of sloth although he believes that it is farz, he becomes a **fâsiq** Muslim. He is imprisoned until he begins to perform namâz. This should be done without any forbearance or forgiveness. If he does not begin to perform (the daily five prayers of) namâz, he is detained in prison until he dies. There are other scholars who say that he is beaten until he bleeds. In the Shâfi'î and Mâlikî Madhhabs, a person who omits one namâz will not become an unbeliever, but then he will be killed as a punishment. It is stated (by savants) in the Hanbalî Madhhab that he both becomes an unbeliever and is killed. There are scholars with the same ijtihâd in the Shâfi'î Madhhab as well. If a person performs a namâz in jamâ'at, it must be judged that he is a Muslim. For, other (previous) dispensations did not contain namâz in jamâ'at; believers would perform namâz on their own. Another act of worship that they also performed was hajj (pilgrimage). Because namâz is an act of worship that is performed only physically, a Believer cannot perform namâz on behalf of another Believer. Because zakât is an act of worship that is performed only with property, a person, without any 'udhr on his part, may depute another person to pay zakât on his behalf and by using his, (i.e. the former's,) property. Because hajj (pilgrimage) is an act of worship which is performed both phyiscally and financially, a person who has an 'udhr, (i.e. something which prevents him from making hajj,) may depute another person to go on a hajj by spending his, (i.e. the former's) money. A very old person unable to fast throughout his life may pay poor Muslims property called fidya for each day's fast (which he has failed to perform). It is not permissible to pay fidya in lieu of namâz. If a person unable to perform namâz expresses in his last will, it is good, after his death, to pay fidya for his debts pertaining to namâz from the property he has left behind him. If the property he has left is not sufficient for the isqât, it will be permissible to perform **dawr**. As for fast, it is wâjib to perform isqât for it. (Please see the twenty-first chapter of the fifth fascicle of **Endless Bliss** for details.)

In the Summer in northern countries, at locations where fajr (dawn) breaks before evening dusk develops into complete darkness, which means times of night and morning prayers never begin, it is not necessary to perform these two prayers, according to the Hanafî Madhhab. The great mujtahid Imâm Shâfi'î 'rahima-hullâhu ta'âlâ' ferreted out the ijtihâd that the two prayers must be performed. However, according to most of the Islamic savants, they, (i.e. people experiencing the aforesaid situation,) do not have to perform morning and night prayers. Nor do they have to make qadâ of them. (In other words, they do not have to perform the two prayers later, either.) For, the prescribed time of either prayer has not commenced. It is not farz to perform a namâz whose time has not commenced. Not so with fasting. When the new moon is seen in one country, Ramadân commences in all countries.

If a **haraj** arises as you perform an act that is farz or avoid an act which is harâm, you ought to imitate another Madhhab, (i.e. one of the other three Madhhabs,) wherein that haraj does not exist. Haraj means to do something with difficulty or not to be able to do it at all. If none of the other three Madhhabs is free from that haraj, either, and if the cause of the haraj exists on account of a darûrat,[1] you will be absolved from having to perform that farz or avoid that harâm, respectively. If its existence is not on account of a darûrat, then you have to rid that haraj by somehow doing without its cause. Please see the fourth chapter of the fourth fascicle of **Endless Bliss**!

A Muslim who is late for (the sunnat of) morning prayer should omit the sunnat lest he should miss the (farz part of the morning prayer being performed in) jamâ'at. It is *afortiori* necessary for him to omit the sunnat (part of the morning prayer) lest he should miss the time (within which the morning prayer should be completed). If he (estimates that he) will be able to catch up with the jamâ'at, he performs the sunnat outside (of) the mosque or behind one of the pillars (within the mosque). In case there is not a convenient place (for performing the sunnat), he should rather omit the sunnat than perform it near (the Muslims making up) the jamâ'at. For, an act of sunnat should be ommitted for the purpose of avoiding an act of makrûh.

Farz namâzes missed on account of an 'udhr are called **fawâit**, which means (farz) namâzes which you have failed to perform (within their prescribed times). Namâzes omitted because of sloth and without an 'udhr are called **metrûkât**, which means those which have been omitted without an 'udhr. Scholars of Fiqh have termed namâzes (missed on account of 'udhrs and) left to qadâ

---

[1] A darûrat is a samâvî (involuntary) reason that forces you to do something or which makes it impossible for you to avoid something, i.e. a situation which arises beyond your will.

'fâitas (fawâit)', instead of calling them 'omitted namâzes'. For, it is a grave sin not to perform a namâz within its prescribed time without an 'udhr. This sin will not be pardoned (only) by making qadâ of it, (i.e. by performing it later and thereby paying the debt.) In addition, it is necessary to make tawba and to make a hajj-i-mebrûr. When the qadâ is made, (i.e. when, later, the omitted namâz is performed and the debt is paid,) the only sin pardoned is that which has been incurred for omitting the namâz and not performing it (within its prescribed time). Tawba made without making qadâ, (i.e. without paying the debt,) will not be sahîh, (i.e. it will not be a valid tawba.) For, tawba (to be made for a certain sin) is conditional on ceasing from the sin involved.

There are five 'udhrs (good reasons sanctioned by Islam) for postponing a namâz till its prescribed time is over: If, confronted by the enemy, a person cannot perform namâz, even sitting or turning to a direction away from Qibla or riding on a animal; if a musâfir, (i.e. a person making a long-distance journey termed 'safar',) is at the risk of being caught by thieves, highwaymen or predators on the way; if a midwife is at the risk of causing the mother or her bady to die; it is an 'udhr for these (three) people to postpone their namâz. The fourth 'udhr is to forget, and the fifth one is to be asleep. It is **adâ** (or edâ),[1] in the Hanafî Madhhab, to manage to make the takbîr iftitâh, and in the Shâfi'î Madhhab, to have performed one rak'at (of the namâz), before its prescribed time expires.

It is farz to make qadâ of namâzes that are farz, wâjib to make qadâ of those which are wâjib. If a person makes qadâ of a namâz that is sunnat, he will earn thawâb for a (a namâz that is) sunnat. It is necessary to observe the order of precedence when making adâ of the farz parts and the witr of the daily five prayers of namâz as well as when making qadâ of them. This rule does not apply when the prayer time narrows down. In other words, the current time's namâz should not be left to qadâ, (i.e. omitted,) for the purpose of making qadâ of the previous namâz, (i.e. performing the namâz that belongs to the previous prayer time and which you omitted.) Another event that invalidates this rule is for you to forget that you have fâita namâzes, (i.e. namâzes that you have missed (or omitted), or for the number of the fâita namâzes to

---

[1] To make **adâ** of a certain namâz means to perform it within the time prescribed for it. To make **qadâ** of it means to perform it after that time is over.

become six. The tertîb, (i.e. the five-namâzes rule,) will not return if their number falls down to below six. Although farz namâzes performed without observing the tertîb will become fâsid, (which means that they will not be valid,) if their number becomes six all of them will become sahîh (valid) when the time of the fifth one is over. For instance, supposing a person who did not perform morning prayer performs early and late afternoon and evening and night and witr prayers (without performing morning prayer) although he remembers that he did not perform morning prayer, none of them will be sahîh; yet all of them will become sahîh when the sun rises (the following morning).

Fâita namâzes should be made qadâ of, the soonest. Only, it is permissible to postpone them till after you have earned means of subsistence for your family and performed the sunnat part of the daily five namâzes and the namâzes termed duhâ and tasbîh (or tesbîh) and tehiyyat-ul-masjîd.[1] Ibni 'Âbidîn states as follows in the section where he deals with the sunnats of ablution: " 'Permissible' means 'not interdicted'. An act that is makrûh tanzîhî is said (by Islamic savants) to be 'permissible'." Hence, it is necessary not to do things that are said to be 'permissible (jâiz)', and yet qadâ namâzes should not be delayed for the purpose of performing such sunnat namâzes. Qadâ of days that you have failed to fast during Ramadân is not something for doing which you have to make haste.

A person who embraces Islam in (a country of disbelievers termed) Dâr-ul-harb does not have to make qadâ of (acts of farz worship such as) namâz, fast and zakât which he did not perform within their prescribed times because he did not know about them. However, not knowing about acts that are farz and those which are harâm is not an 'udhr for people who live in (a country of Muslims termed) Dâr-ul-islâm. If a murtadd, (i.e. a renegade who has abandoned Islam,) becomes a Believer again, he will not have to make qadâ of namâzes which he did not perform during his apostasy. For, Islam does not address itself to unbelievers. If a sabî, (a child under the age of puberty and who therefore is not liable for Islam's commandments,) performs night prayer and (then goes to bed and) then experiences a nocturnal emission and then wakes up after fajr (dawn) the following morning, he will have to make qadâ of the (previous night's) namâz, (i.e. the night prayer that he

[1] All these terms are defined at various places of the six fascicles of **Endless Bliss**.

performed.) For, the namâz which he performed (the previous night) was nâfila (supererogatory). It became farz for him as he was asleep. If there are namâzes that you did not perform as you were healthy, it is permissible to make qadâ of them with a tayammum[1] and with îmâ[2] when you are ill. A namâz of four rak'ats that has been left to qadâ must be made qadâ of by performing all four rak'ats even during a (long distance journey termed) safar. The four-rak'at farz part of an early afternoon prayer that has been left to qadâ during a (long-distance journey called) safar must be made qadâ of by performing two rak'ats even when you are muqîm (settled). As you (start to) perform the farz of an early afternoon prayer you make your niyya(t) to perform the farz of "today's early afternoon prayer, or only", "to perform the farz of early afternoon prayer." If there are more than one fâita namâzes (to be made qadâ of one by one), you make your niyya(t) to perform, say, "the farz of the earliest early afternoon prayer left to qadâ, (i.e. not performed within its dictated time,)" or "the farz of the latest early afternoon prayer left to qadâ," as you (begin to) make qadâ of each; on the other hand, as you make qadâ of a few days' fast of Ramadân one by one, it is not necessary to observe the order of time among them.

As you make qadâ of namâzes (that you did not perform within their prescribed time without any justifiable reason called 'udhr and which are) called metrûk (abandoned, omitted) namâzes, you should not let others know. For, it is a grave sin not to perorm a namâz within its prescribed time. It is yet another sin to let others know about your sin. Another sinful act is to tell others during the day about a sin that you committed the previous night. Here we end our translation from Ibni 'Âbidîn.

As is seen, fâita namâzes must be made qadâ of as soon as possible, in the Hanafî Madhhab. This rule applies in the Shâfi'î Madhhab as well. Shems-ud-dîn Muhammad Remlî 'rahmatullâhi 'alaih', an Islamic scholar in the Shâfi'î Madhhab, states as follows in his book of fatwâs: "If a person has namâzes not performed on account of an 'udhr, it will not be sinful for him to perform the namâz called Terâwih during Ramadân and to make qadâ of his fâita namâzes after Ramadân. However, it will be sinful for a person who has namâzes omitted without an 'udhr to do the same

---

[1] There is detailed information about tayammum in the fifth chapter of the fourth fascicle of **Endless Bliss**.

[2] It means to perform namâz by making signs.

thing. For, omitted namâzes must be made qadâ of promptly."
Islamic scholars in the Shâfi'î Madhhab state openly that it is sinful
to perform sunnat namâzes such as the terâwih instead of first
performing namâzes omitted without an 'udhr. The same rule
applies in the Hanafî Madhhab as well. The Hanafî Madhhab's
ruling that it is permissible to delay the qadâ of the fâita namâzes
that you failed to perform (within their prescribed times) on
account of an 'udhr, is an indication of the fact that it will be better
not to delay making qadâ of them. For, permissible (jâiz) means
(that) which has not been banned. Ibni 'Âbidîn 'rahima-hullâhu
ta'âlâ' explains the expression, "... permissible (jâiz) to use flowing
water wastefully," as, "it is makrûh tenzîhî (or tanzîhî)... ." When
it is better to make haste in making qadâ of namâzes that you
missed on account of an 'udhr, it must be obligatory to perform
namâzes omitted without an 'udhr in lieu of the sunnats (of the
daily five prayers). Ibni 'Âbidîn 'rahima-hullâhu ta'âlâ' states:
"When making an ablution, it is sunnat-i-muakkada to wash (each
limb to be washed in ablution) three times. It is not makrûh to omit
this sunnat on account of an 'udhr such as costly water, cold water,
and water needed." This is another indication of the fact that, for
getting over the gravely sinful situation by making qadâ of omitted
namâzes, it is necessary to perform also the qadâ of those namâzes
in lieu of the sunnats (of the daily five prayers) with the exception
of that of morning prayer. How to perform qadâ namâzes in lieu
of the sunnats is explained towards the end of the chapter dealing
with importance of namâz.]

ISQÂT of NAMÂZ for the DECEASED

['Isqât of namâz' means 'to deliver the deceased from his debts
pertaining to namâz'. For doing this, kaffârat[1] for his (missed or
omitted) namâzes is paid. For the payment of kaffârat, it is wâjib
for the deceased to have commanded in his will that it should be
done and to have handed down a legacy rich enough to finance it.
In other words, one-third of the property he has left behind him
should not be below the amount needed for the kaffârat. The
kaffârat is paid by the deceased's walî, who in turn is the person
entrusted by the deceased with the care of the legacy, or one of the
inheritors. There are four kinds of walîs (guardians) in Islam. The

---

[1] Please scan the thirteenth chapter of the sixth fascicle of **Endless Bliss**
for details on 'kaffârat'.

deceased's (meyyit's) walî; a yetîm's (orphan's) walî; the walî of a
woman whose (marriage contract termed) nikâh, (and which is
enlarged on in the twelfth chapter of the fifth fascicle of **Endless
Bliss**,) is to be made; and the walî of a slave or jâriya. The last
(fourth) kind of walî is also called **mawlâ**. There are walîs other
than these four kinds of walîs: Allâhu ta'âlâ's Walîs, who are also
called **Awliyâ**. They are people whom Allâhu ta'âlâ loves very
much. Attaining this profound love requires being possessed of all
the qualifications pertaining to words, actions, and ethics and
taught by Muhammad ''alaihis-salâm'. These teachings can be
acquired easily from a true Islamic savant. A person who is unable
to find an Islamic savant should learn them from books written by
savants of Ahl-as-sunnat. **Ibni 'Âbidîn** 'rahima-hullâhu ta'âlâ'
states: "If a person with fâitas, i.e. namâzes that he did not perform
on account of an 'udhr, commands (in his last will) that their
kaffârats should be performed, half a sâ' [2.1 litres], or 520 dirham
[1750 gr] of wheat or wheat flour must be paid to the poor for each
namâz that is farz or wâjib. All of it might as well be given to one
poor person. It is better to pay its value [in gold or silver]. If the
testator has not left any property behind or if one-third of the
property he left is short of meeting the requirements of the
kaffârat, or if he has died intestate and his walî (guardian) will
perform his kaffârat by donating a small amount of money, –and
since the amount required per day is: 1750 x 6 = 10500 gr. or ten
and a half [10.5] kg. of wheat,– he borrows a year's amount = 3780
kg. of wheat [or, –since the value of ten and a half kg. of wheat is
always about one gram of gold–, gold coins equal to it in value, i.e.
52.5 gold coins, or 60 gold coins, to be prudent, or other gold
articles with equal weight [432 gr] such as bracelets, rings, and the
like.] Considering also that the namâzes performed (by the
deceased) may have been flawed, he subtracts the years of
childhood,– twelve years for a man and nine years for a woman,–
and thereby finds the number of years throughout which the
deceased was mukallaf, (i.e. liable for performing namâz.) Because
the daily number of namâzes for which kaffârat is necessary is six,
he borrows [3780 kg.] of wheat, or sixty gold coins, –which is a
better choice,– which is needed for the kaffârat of a solar year's
namâzes. He gives this to a poor Muslim as he makes his niyyat to
perform the isqât of the kaffârat of (the meyyit's) namâzes. The
poor person must be a discreet, pubescent, sâlih (pious), and male
Muslim. This poor person says, "I accept it," and takes it. Then he
gives it to the heir as a present. The heir takes it and then gives it

to the same poor person or to another poor one. The same procedure is repeated as many times as the years during which the meyyit was mukallaf (liable for performing namâz). If the gold borrowed is more (than the exemplified amount), the number of dawrs (cycles) to be performed will change at an inverse ratio. In case gold coins are not available, the walî borrows gold jewellery such as bracelets and rings from a lady, weighs it, separates (years during which namâz was not performed x 7.2 grams) and puts the separated amount in a handkerchief, so that it contains gold coins as many as the number of the years during which the deceased did not perform namâz. This number multiplied by sixty [60] and the product divided by the number of the poor people partaking in the dawr will yield the number of dawrs (circulations) to be performed. If the gold available is little, half the gold in the former case is weighed. The number of dawrs will be twice number performed in the former. For a man who the died at the age of sixty [60], 60x48x7.2=20736 gr. of gold is given to one poor person. For, one year's isqât of namâz costs sixty [60] gold coins. Thirty [30] dawrs will be made with 100 gr. of gold and seven poor people. Or 43 dawrs will be made with 70 gr. of gold and seven poor people. When the dawrs are finished the last poor person gives the gold as a present to the walî (guardian), who, in his turn, pays his debt. Thereafter dawrs will be made for fasts, qurbâns, and oaths. However, at least ten poor people are needed for a dawr for an oath, and one person cannot be given more than half a sâ' per day, whereas one person can be paid kaffârats of a number of namâzes in one day, nay, at one time. Isqât for zakât cannot be performed if the deceased did not command it in his will. The deceased should have commanded it in his will. However, since this stipulation does not apply in fasting, the walî had better see to the dawrs of zakât also, by donating from his own property. After all the dawrs have been finished, the heir gives some property or money as a gift to the poor people (who partook in the dawrs).

"In case one-third of the property left by the deceased who commanded kaffârat in his will is not sufficient for the performance of all his kaffârats, the walî (guardian) cannot perform kaffârats by spending more than one-third (of the property left by the deceased) without the inheritors' permission. In case one-third is sufficient for the kaffârats and yet the deceased has a debt, payment of the debt takes precedence over the kaffârat even if the creditor gives it for the isqât. After the creditor is paid his due, he cannot give it (back) as a gift so that kaffârat should be managed. For, (completion of) kaffârat will be valid only with the property donated by the heir. If a deceased commanded kaffârat for all his namâzes throughout his life, in his will, and yet if it is not known how long he lived, (that part of) his will becomes bâtil (null and void). However, if the one-third is less than the amount estimated to be enough for all his namâzes throughout his lifetime, he will have commanded that all the one-third should be given, in which case (that part of) his will have been made for a certain amount, wherefore (that part of) his will becomes sahîh (valid).

"[Even if the deceased commanded in his will (that kaffârat should be made), it is not wâjib for the walî, [i.e. for the heir or the wasî (executor),] to donate so that kaffârat be made. It is wâjib for the deceased to leave behind him the amount of property one-third of which will suffice for his kaffârats and to command in his will that his kaffârats should be made with that one-third. If he commands that kaffârat should be done with a part of the one-third and the remainder should be donated to his inheritors or to other people, he will have overstepped the wâjib, which is a sinful act. For that matter, it is not sahîh to command that a part of the one-third be spent making dawr and the remainder be spent making khatms of Qur'ân al-kerîm and tehlîls. Moreover, it is not permissible to read (or recite) the Qur'ân al-kerîm in return for a payment. Both the person who pays and the one who accepts it will be sinful. Although it has been stated (by some scholars) that it is permissible to teach the Qur'ân al-kerîm in return for payment, no one, (i.e. no scholar,) has said that it is permissible to read (or recite) it (for payment).

"If a deceased person commanded in his will that his namâzes, (i.e. those which he had not performed,) should be performed by his heir, it is not sahîh (valid) for the heir to make qadâ of his, (i.e. the deceased's) namâzes. However, it is sahîh for a person to perform namâz or to fast and donate the thawâb that he earns as a gift to the deceased. It is not permissible for a person on his deathbed to pay fidya for his own namâzes." Here we end our rendition from Ibni 'Âbidîn.

Ahmad Tahtâwî 'rahmatullâhi 'alaih' states in his annotation to the (the book entitled) **Merâq-il-felâh**: It is stated in the Nass, (i.e. âyat-i-kerîmas and hadîth-i-sherîfs with clear meanings,) to perform isqât of fasts failed to perform (within their prescribed times) by paying fidya for them. "Since namâz is more important than fasting, the same rule applies for namâz," is a statement unanimously made by Islamic savants. Therefore, the statement, "Isqat for namâz is something without foundation," on the part of (a person who passes for) a man of religion is an acknowledgement of ignorance. It is a statement contradicting a scholarly consensus.

If an invalid is unable to perform namâz even by making signs with his head as he lies, he does not have to command them in his will even if the namâzes that he cannot perform are fewer than the (daily) five namâzes. Likewise, if a person unable to fast on account of a (long-distance journey termed) safar or illness cannot find a time of iqâmat, (i.e. being settled at a place,) or good health long enough to make qadâ of debts of fast, he does not (have to) command their isqât in his will. Wasiyyat, (i.e. command in one's will,) is viable also for (failures pertaining to) sadaqa-i-fitr,[1] wife's means of subsistence,[2] felonies committed after having assumed ihrâm for hajj,[3] alms pertaining to votive offerings.[4] If a person died intestate, it is, inshâ-Allah, permissible for his heir or any other person to donate for him. If a (deceased) person commanded hajj in his will, his wakîl (deputy) goes on hajj from the deceased's city or from a place one-third of the property that he left will afford, whereas the donator has the option to choose the place from where he will set off for hajj. It is not sahîh for anybody to fast or to perform namâz on behalf of a deceased person, whether for a fee or gratis. The hadîth-i-sherîf concerning this matter is mansûkh.[5] On account of the alms paid as a kaffârat, Allâhu ta'âlâ will forgive the debts of the deceased (pertaining to acts of worship). It is stated in the Shâfi'î book entitled **Anwâr**: "It is not wâjib for the deceased to pay fidya for the namâzes that he did not perform. If it is paid, it will not be isqât." Muslims in the Mâlikî or Shâfi'î Madhhab perform dawr by imitating the Hanafî Madhhab.

If the amount of the property which the deceased commanded in his will does not suffice for the kaffârat or if one-third of the property he left is not sufficient or if he died intestate, dawr is made so that isqât of all his debts can be accomplished with a little

[1] See third chapter of fifth fascicle of **Endless Bliss**.
[2] See eighth chapter of sixth fascicle of **Endless Bliss**.
[3] See seventh chapter of fifth fascicle of **Endless Bliss**.
[4] See fifth chapter of fifth fascicle of **Endless Bliss**.
[5] The fifteenth kind of hadîth-i-sherîf in the sixth chapter of the second fascicle of **Endless Bliss**.

property donated by someone. This little amount is handed to a poor person with the intention of isqât. That poor person, after taking it, gifts it to the walî or to another poor person, who, in his turn, has to get hold of it, i.e. take it in his hand; then he hands it to another poor person by way of donation and with the intention of the isqât of the deceased's debt (of acts of worship such as namâz and fast). Here we end our rendition from Tahtâwî's annotation.]

CONCERNING FRIDAY

Friday prayer's being sahîh requires seven conditions to be fulfilled:

1– The location where Friday prayer (namâz) is to be performed to be large enough to be called a city.

2– To make the (dictated speech called) khutba.

3– To make the khutba before the namâz.

4– For the Friday prayer to be performed within the time prescribed for early afternoon prayer.

5– For the jamâ'at to exist. (That is, there should be a certain number of people to make up a jamâ'at [congregation of Muslims], for, Friday prayer has to be performed in jamâ'at.) According to Imâm A'zam and Imâm Muhammad 'rahima-humallâhu ta'âlâ', in addition to the imâm, who has to be a man who has reached the ages of puberty and discretion, there have to be (at least) three men; and this minimum number is two men plus the imâm, according to Imâm Abû Yûsuf 'rahima-hullâhu ta'âlâ'. The Tarafeyn's qawl is essential. (Imâm A'zam Abû Hanîfa and his blessed disciple Imâm Muhammad are called 'Tarafeyn'.)

6– There to be freedom for the public to go and join the assembly for Friday prayer.

It is stated as follows in the book of fatwâ entitled **Hindiyya**: "It is farz-i-'ayn for men who are free and healthy and who are not safarî to perform Friday prayer. It is not farz for a person making a (long-distance journey called) safar or for an invalid or for women to perform Friday prayer. It is not farz, either, for men who cannot go out for fear of getting caught in torrential rain or being wronged by government officials. Superiors or commanders or employers can not prevent people under their command from performing Friday prayer. They can deduct the undeserved amount from their wages. If the imâm conducting the Friday prayer is fâsiq[1] and you are unable to prevent him, the scholarly advice is that you should perform the prayer behind him rather than ceasing from Friday prayer. At other times, (e.g. daily five prayers,) you should go to a mosque where a sâlih imâm conducts the namâzes in jamâ'at instead of performing namâz behind a fâsiq imâm. It is makrûh for a woman to go to a mosque for the purpose of performing namâz in jamâ'at, regardless of who the woman concerned is and what the namâz to be performed is."

If a person catches up with the imâm at the rukû' of the second rak'at of Friday prayers, he performs (the day's) early afternoon prayer, according to Imâm Muhammad 'rahima-hullâhu ta'âlâ'. According to Imâm A'zam and Imâm Abû Yûsuf 'rahima-humallâhu ta'âlâ', he should perform the Friday prayer even if he catches up with (the imâm as late as during) the teshehhud (sitting posture). If a person is performing a nâfila (supererogatory) namâz as the khatîb performs (reads or recites) the khutba, he performs (only) two rak'ats of it, and no more than that. If the namâz he is performing is the (initial) sunnat of Friday prayer, there is not a scholarly consensus on whether he should perform two rak'ats of it and thereafter make the salâm or perform all four rak'ats of it. It is essential, however, that he should perform all four rak'ats.

There are five wâjibs that should be observed on Friday:

1– To stop all sorts of activity at the time of azân (for early afternoon prayer).

2– To go to the mosque on a walk that is called 'sa'i', (i.e. exerting yourself as you do when walking between the hills called Safâ and Merva during hajj, which is enlarged on in the seventh chapter of the fifth fascicle of **Endless Bliss**.)

3– Not to perform a nâfila namâz as the imâm, (i.e. the khatîb,) makes the khutba.

4– To avoid worldly talks.

5– To be silent.

There are six mustahabs to be observed on Friday:

1– Râyiha-i-tayyiba, (which means to dab or spray on perfume.)

---

[1] A person who frankly commits one of the harâm acts such as consuming alcoholic beverages, fornication, etc., is called 'fâsiq'.

2– To use miswâk, (which is a twig from a tree called erâq.)[1]

3– To wear clean clothes.

4– Tebkîr, [which means to go to the mosque early for Friday prayer. During the (era called) Zamân-i-Se'âdet, (i.e. the blessed time of felicity during which the Best of Mankind, Rasûlullah 'sall-Allâhu 'alaihi wa sallam', and his earliest four Khalîfas, Hadrat Abû Bakr and Hadrat 'Umar and Hadrat 'Uthmân and Hadrat 'Alî 'radiy-Allâhu 'anhum ajma'în' lived,) the Sahâba 'radiy-Allâhu ta'âlâ 'anhum ajma'în' would not disperse after morning prayer (on Friday); they would disperse after Friday prayer. What this Ummat, (i.e. Muslims,) neglected first, was the behaviour that is sunnat and which is termed tebkîr.]

5– To make a ghusl, (which is explained in the fourth chapter of the fourth fascicle of **Endless Bliss**.)

6– To pronounce the benediction called Salawât, (which is pronounced over the blessed soul of our Prophet 'sall-Allâhu ta'âlâ 'alaihi wa sallam' and which reads as follows: "**Allâhumma salli 'alâ sayyidinâ Muhammadin wa 'alâ [âlihi wa sahbihi] ajma'în.**")

The are five makrûhs to be avoided on Friday:

1– To make salâm, (i.e. to greet as prescribed by Islam,) as the khatîb makes the khutba. (Greetings prescribed by Islam are explained in detail in the sixty-second chapter of the third fascicle of **Endless Bliss**.)

2– To read (or recite) the Qur'ân al-kerîm (as the imâm makes the khutba).

3– To say, "**Yerhamukallah**," to a person who sneezes (and then says, "Al-hamd-u-li-llah,") (as the imâm makes the khutba.)

4– To eat and drink (during Friday prayer and its khutba).

5– To commit an act that is makrûh. [An act of makrûh, for instance, is the khatîb's making a rather long speech in the name of khutba.]

After the first azân of Friday, which is performed (called) on

---

[1] Please see the thirteenth paragraph under the heading, 'Adabs of ablution' in the second chapter of the fourth fascicle of **Endless Bliss**, or enter Google and type the word 'miswâk' to see how Islam taught us, more than fourteen hundred years ago, how to take care of our teeth, mouth, and alimentary canal.

the minaret, (which in turn is outside [of] the mosque,) the khatîb performs the initial sunnat of the Friday prayer near the minbar. Thereafter he comes before the minbar, says a short prayer, standing in the Qibla direction, mounts the minbar, sits with his face towards the jamâ'at, and listens to the second azân. Thereafter he stands up and begins to perform the khutba.

[People called Wahhâbîs are not in the Madhhab of Ahl as-sunna. They are without a certain madhhab. They are called **Wahhâbîs** or **Nejdîs**. Wahhâbîsm was founded by British conspirators. They established it by using an ignoble and ignorant man of religion from Nejd and named Muhammad the son of 'Abd-ul-wahhâb. They call non-wahhâbî Muslims disbelievers in their books. They write that it is permissible to kill those non-wahhabite people and to seize their wives, daughters and possessions as ghanîmat. Lavishly bribing ignorant and lâ-madhhabî men of religion to collusion, they mould them into wahhâbîs and send them to wahhâbî centers called **Râbita-t-ul 'âlam-il-islâmî** and which they established in countries the world over. Dubbing their anti-Islamic publications 'Fatwâs issued by universal unity of Islamic scholars', they spread them over all Muslim countries. During the yearly season of pilgrimage they hand them out gratis to hadjis (Muslim pilgrims). In one of their writings it says: "It is farz for women to perform Friday prayer." They use force to send women out for Friday prayer. They perform namâz in mixed groups where men and women perform the same namâz in jamâ'at. It says in another one of their publications: "Khutbas of Friday and 'Iyd should be read in a language intelligible to (the Muslims making up) the jamâ'at. It should not be read in the Arabic language." True Islamic scholars in Muslim countries disprove such fatwâs of theirs by adducing proof-texts. Some of these true confutations are the fatwâs issued by the scholars of Ahl as-Sunnat in various parts of India. For instance, 'Allâma hibr-un-nihrir wa-l-fehhâma sâhib-ut-taqrîr wa-t-tahrîr Mawlânâ Muhammad Temîmî bin Muhammad Madrasî 'nevver-Allâhu merqadehu', Muftî of Madras, states as follows:

It is makrûh to perform, (i.e. to read, recite or say,) the khutba in a language other than Arabic or to perform it both in Arabic or in its translation in another language. It is wâjib to perform the entire khutba in the Arabic language. For, Rasûlullah 'sall-Allâhu 'alaihi wa sallam' performed all his khutbas in the Arabic language. It is stated in the chapter dealing with namâzes of 'Iyd of the book entitled **Bahr-ur-râsiq**: "Nâfila (supererogatory namâzes, with the exception of namâzes termed Terâwih (or Tarâwih) and Kusûf, are not performed in jamâ'at. Since namâzes of 'Iyd are performed always in jamâ'at, they must be wâjib, not nâfila." As is seen, an act of worship which Rasûlullah 'sall-Allâhu 'alaihi wa sallam' performed steadily is wâjib. 'Allâma Zebîdî 'rahima-hullâhu ta'âlâ' states as follows in his commentary to **Ihyâ-ul-'ulûm**: "An act of worship which Rasûlullah 'sall-Allâhu 'alaihi wa sallam' performed regularly is wâjib. It is not necessarily an act that is farz. 'Allâma Muftî Abu-s-su'ûd Efendi 'rahima-hullâhu ta'âlâ' states in his book entitled **Fet-h-ullah-il-mu'în**: "Rasûlullah's 'sall-Allâhu 'alaihi wa sallam' having performed it regularly shows that it is an act of worship that is wâjib." Ibni 'Âbidîn 'rahima-hullâhu ta'âlâ' states as follows in his treatise on the sunnats of ablution: "An act of worship which Rasûlullah 'sall-Allâhu 'alaihi wa sallam' performed regularly is sunnat-i-muakkada if he never omitted it. If he not only did not neglect it but also dissuaded any person whom he saw to omit it, then it is wâjib. For, not to dissuade (a person from omitting it) would have been construed as (his) approval to omit it. For that matter, Abu-s-su'ûd Efendi said that an act of worship which the blessed Prophet performed regularly without omission is wâjib." It is stated at the end of the section where makrûhs of namâz are being explained that it is makrûh tahrîmî to omit either one.] Rasûlullah's 'sall-Allâhu 'alaihi wa sallam' performing his khutbas always in the Arabic language is an indication of the fact that it is wâjib to perform khutba in the Arabic language. Hence, it is makrûh tahrîmî to perform khutbas in any language other than Arabic or to perform them both in Arabic and in their translated versions. For, in the former case, the rule that they must be performed in Arabic will have been violated; and in the latter case the rule that it must be performed only in Arabic will have been violated. In both cases, something which Rasûlullah 'sall-Allâhu ta'âlâ 'alaihi wa sallam' performed continuously will have been neglected. Likewise, saying the takbîr (of iftitâh, i.e. saying "Allâhu ekber,") in the Arabic language when beginning to perform namâz and saying, "Allâhu ekber," in between are two different things. It is makrûh tahrîmî to omit either one. For, it became wâjib to do so because Rasûlullah 'sall-Allâhu 'alaihi wa sallam' always said, "Allâhu ekber," and, for the same matter, it became makrûh tahrîmî not to do so. Ibni 'Âbidîn 'rahima-hullâhu ta'âlâ' states as follows in **Radd-ul-muhtâr**: "Makrûh means something, (e.g. an act or behaviour,) by doing or not doing which something which is wâjib or sunnat is violated. The former, (i.e. to violate something which is wâjib,) is makrûh tahrîmî; and the latter, (i.e. to violate something sunnat,) is (makrûh) tanzîhî (or tenzîhî)." It is written as follows in the book entitled **Halabî-i-kebîr** (by Ibrâhîm bin Muhammad Halabî (866, Haleb [Aleppo] – 956 [1549 A.D.]): "It is makrûh tenzîhî to omit (or violate) something that is sunnat. It is makrûh tahrîmî to omit something which is wâjib." It is written in the book entitled **Fatâwâ-i-Sirâjiyya** (written by 'Alî 'Ûshî bin 'Uthmân 'rahmatullâhi ta'âlâ 'alaih' (d. 575 [1180 A.D.]) that it is "permissible to perform the khutba in the Fârisî (Persian) language." It would be bâtil (null and void) to adduce this statement as a proof and give a fatwâ arguing that it is permissible to make the khutba in a language other than Arabic and that it is not makrûh, neither tahrîmî nor tenzîhî. For, the statement in Sirâjiyya means that it is "sahîh (valid)", which it turn does not mean that it is "not makrûh". Ibni 'Âbidîn 'rahima-hullâhu ta'âlâ' states in **Radd-ul-muhtâr**: "His, (i.e. 'Alî 'Ûshî's,) saying that it is sahîh does not show that it is not makrûh." Muhammad 'Abd-ul-Hayy Luqnevî 'rahima-hullâhu ta'âlâ' states in his book entitled **'Umdet-ur-riâya**: "The statement that 'making the khutba in the Arabic language is not a condition to be fulfilled (for the validity of Friday prayer); it is permissible to make it in Persian or in any other language,' shows that the (Friday) prayer thereby performed will be permissible. In other words, the condition of making a khutba for the validity (being sahîh) of Friday prayer will have been fulfilled. It does not show that the khutba performed will be without kerâhat, (i.e. something which makes it makrûh. For, Rasûlullah 'sall-Allâhu 'alaihi wa sallam' and all the Sahâba 'radiy-Allâhu 'anhum' always and everywhere made the khutba only in the Arabic language. It is makrûh tahrîmî to go contrary to them." As well, the Tâbi'în and the Taba'i tâbi'în 'rahima-humullâhu ta'âlâ' performed the khutba in the Arabic language, always and everywhere. Not only did they not perform it in a language other than Arabic, also none of them performed it both in the Arabic language and in its translation (in another language). [That was the case also in countries like Asia and Africa, where people listening to their khutbas did not understand what was being said in the khutbas because they did not know Arabic. Although it was necessary for them to say also the translations of the khutbas and thereby to teach Islam to new Muslims, they did not deem it permissible to use languages other than Arabic in their khutbas. They told them about Islam on occasions other than khutbas. They advised them to learn Arabic for the purpose of understanding the khutbas as well and learning Islam well. We should imitate those savants in this respect as well.]

It is **bid'at** to go contrary to them by performing khutbas in languages other than Arabic. It is makrûh tahrîmî to do so. It is bâtil to call the former case 'tahrîmî' and the latter case 'tenzîhî'. For, makrûh tenzîhî means to omit an act that is sunnat. Because Rasûlullah 'sall-Allâhu 'alaihi wa sallam' always performed all his khutbas only in the Arabic language, it is wâjib to perform the entire khutba only in the Arabic language. How can it ever be tenzîhî to omit this act which is wâjib? It is wâjib to avoid doing something which is makrûh tahrîmî. Mawlânâ Bahr-ul-'ulûm 'rahima-hullâhu ta'âlâ' states as follows in **Erkân-ul-arba'â**: "It is wâjib not to do something that is makrûh tahrîmî. To do that act of makrûh means to disobey a (commandment called) wâjib."

A person who always commits an act that is makrûh tahrîmî is not an 'âdil Muslim. Ibni 'Âbidîn 'rahima-hullâhu ta'âlâ' states as follows on the authority of Ibni Nujaym 'rahima-hullâhu ta'âlâ' as he begins his discourse on the wâjibs of an ablution in his book entitled **Radd-ul-muhtâr**: "It is a venial sin to commit something that is makrûh tahrîmî. Persistence in committing venial sins divests a Muslim of his 'adâlat.[1] (In other words, several venial sins committed or a certain venial sin committed several times add up to a grave sin. And a grave sin committed frankly causes a Muslim to lose his 'adâlat, so that he is no longer an 'âdil Muslim.)" For that matter, khatîbs who perform khutbas in their translations lose their 'adâlat and become fâsiq Muslims. (Incidentally a fâsiq Muslim is a Muslim who commits one of the grave sins openly. Examples of grave sins are: Not to perform, without an 'udhr, one of the open commandments of Islam or to commit one of its prohibitions (harâms) frankly.) It is makrûh tahrîmî to perform namâz behind such people, (i.e. to join a namâz in jamâ'at conducted by one of them.) It is written in the book entitled **Nûr-ul-îdhâh**, (by Abûl-Ikhlâs Hasan bin 'Ammâr Shernblâlî 'rahmatullâhi ta'âlâ 'alaih', 994 – 1069 [1658 A.D.], Egypt,) and in **Ibni 'Âbidîn**: "It is makrûh for a slave or a villager or an illegitimate boy, if they are unlearned, and for a bid'at holder, even if he is a learned person, to act as imâm (and conduct a namâz in jamâ'at). It is sinful to let them act as imâm (and conduct a namâz that you are to perform in jamâ'at)." 'Allâma Ibrâhîm Halabî

---

[1] Please scan the second chapter of the fifth fascicle of **Endless Bliss**.

'rahima-hullâhu ta'âlâ' states in **Halabî-i-kebîr**: "Muslims who let fâsiq people be imâm (and conduct the namâzes that they perform in jamâ'at) will have committed a sin (by doing so). For, it is makrûh tahrîmî to let fâsiq people be imâm." It is written in **Merâq-il-felâh**: "It is makrûh to let a fâsiq person be imâm (and conduct a namâz in jamâ'at) even if he is learned (in Islam). For, he is slack in adapting himself to Islam. It is wâjib to treat him with contempt. To let him be imâm means to respect him. If you cannot prevent him from conducting namâz in jamâ'at, then you must perform Friday namâz and all other namâzes in another mosque." As 'Allâma Tahtâwî 'rahima-hullâhu ta'âlâ' explains this passage, he says: "It is makrûh tahrîmî (for Muslims) to let a fâsiq person to be imâm (and conduct their namâzes in jamâ'at)."

You should not cause the khatîb to perform the khutbas in a language other than Arabic. It is sinful to cause it. Ibni 'Âbidîn 'rahima-hullâhu ta'âlâ' states in **Radd-ul-muhtâr**: "Namâz (in jamâ'at) should not be performed behind a fâsiq imâm. You should look for an imâm who is not fâsiq. Friday namâz is a different matter. However, even Friday namâz is makrûh to perform behind a fâsiq imâm if it is being performed in various mosques of the city. For, in that case it would be possible to perform it behind another imâm. The book entitled **Fat-h-ul-qadîr**[1] renders the same account." Therefore, you should not perform it behind an imâm who performs the khutba also in its translation in a second language instead of performing it only in Arabic and you should search for an imâm who performs the khutba only in Arabic and perform Friday prayer behind that imâm, (i.e. you should join the namâz in jamâ'at conducted by that imâm.) For details, read the book entitled **Et-tahqîqât-us-seniyya fî-kerâhat-il-khutba-t-i-bi-ghayri-l-'arabiyya wa qirâatiha bi-l-'arabiyyat-i-ma'a terjemetihâ bi-ghayr-il-'arabiyyati**. Here we end our translation from 'Allâma Muhammad Temîmî Madrasî's writing.

The writing above, which was written in Arabic in India in 1349 [1931 A.D.], was endorsed and undersigned by India's highest thirteen Islamic scholars. Alongside this historic fatwâ, Arabic fatwâs of Indian scholars from **Diobend** and **Bâqiyât-us-sâlihât**

---

[1] It was written by Ibni Humâm 'rahmatullâhi ta'âlâ 'alaih' (730 [1388 A.D.] – 861 [1456]) as a commentary to **Hidâya**, which in turn had been written by Burhânaddîn Merghinânî 'rahmatullâhi ta'âlâ 'alaih' (593 [1197 A.D.] – martyred by the hordes of Jenghiz Khân.)

and **Madrâs** and **Haydarâbâd** were printed in Istanbul, Turkey, in 1396 [1976 A.D.]. Thousands of world-famous profound Ottoman Islamic savants and Shaikh-ul-islâms 'rahima-humullâhu ta'âlâ' searched for ways of helping people to understand the khutbas they were listening to. Failing to find any clue to the permissibity of addition of Turkish versions to khutbas, they did not give permission for them. The purpose of enlightening the (Muslims making up the) jamâ'at was achieved by establishing Friday preaches in all mosques after Friday namâzes and people in mosques were informed about the contents of fatwâs for six hundred years, and thereby periphery of Islamic practices was protected against violation.]

'Iyd prayer, (i.e. namâz which is performed in the morning on the first day of each one the two 'Iyds,) has nine (takbîrs that are called) **Takbîrs of Zewâid**: One of them is farz. Another one is sunnat. Seven of them are wâjib. The takbîr-i-iftitâh is farz. The takbîr for the first rukû' is sunnat. The takbîrs of zewâid are wâjib. Takbîr of rukû' in the second rak'at is wâjib on account of its coinciding with another takbîr that is wâjib; (in other words, it is at the same time the last one of the seven takbîrs of zewâid, which are wâjib.)

TO PERFORM NAMÂZ

It is written as follows in **Ni'met-i-islâm**: It is farz for every discreet and pubescent Muslim to perform namâz five times daily. Nobody can perform namâz on behalf of any other person. A person may gift the thawâb for a namâz or any other act of worship that they performed to another person [alive or dead alike. Each and every one of them, (i.e. people to whom the thawâb of the worship performed has been donated,) shall be given the same amount of thawâb as that which has been earned by the donator; and no amount of thawâb shall be deducted from the donator.] It is not permissible to perform namâz and donate the thawâb thereby earned to your adversary or creditor so that they will waive their rights violated. A person who believes that (the daily five prayers of) namâz is farz and yet does not perform it without any 'udhr, will not become a disbeliever. They will become (a) fâsiq (Muslim). [It is stated (in authentic Islamic sources) that punishment for a single omitted namâz is Hell fire for seventy thousand years.] (A person who ceases from performing his daily namâzes) will be sent to prison and will be kept there until he begins to perform his namâzes again. When a child is seven years old, it will be commanded (by its parents) to perform namâz. If it still does not perform namâz at the age of ten, it will be beaten with hand. It should not be patted more than three times. It should not be thwacked with a cane, either. Thwacking with a cane is a punishment applicable to an adult guilty of homicide, and then it requires a court decision. A man cannot beat his wife with a cane [It is not permissible to hit any living being on the head or in the face or on the chest or front or abdomen.] It is farz also for an invalid to perform namâz to the best of their ability and energy. (The fourth fascicle of **Endless Bliss** mostly deals with namâz.)

BEING WITH AN 'UDHR

If something exuding from one's body is continuous, it is called an **'udhr**, (and a person experiencing this inevitable emission is said to be one with 'udhr.) A person suffering from continuous enuresis or diarrhea or anal gas incontinence, nasal bleeding or bleeding from a sore, etc., ichor (from a wound or ulcer), tears shed as a result of swollen or sore eye, and a woman suffering from **istihâda** (menorrhagia) are called **people with an 'udhr**. They have to eliminate the cause of the 'udhr by using methods such as clogging, medication, and performing namâz sitting or making signs. [A man with urinary incontinence inserts a natural cotton wick as big as a grain of barley into his urinary canal. If synthetic cotton is used, its fibers may penetrate the kidneys and cause infection. During urination, the wick is naturally ejected out. In case an excessive amount of urine gushes out from the bladder, the excess will flow through the wick and leak out, causing the person's ablution to break. The urine leaking out should not dirty the underpants, which can be prevented by wrapping a piece of cloth around the urinary organ and it can be made fast with a piece of thread sewn to a corner of the cloth and fastened to the underpants with a safety pin. If the urine leaking is still too much, some cotton may be put in the cloth. If the loop at the end of the thread is difficult to detach from the safety pin, a paper clip may be attached to the safety pin and the loop may be hanged on it. It will be easier to detach the loop from it so that that the cloth can be washed three times at the handbasin. A person with urinary incontinence should carry three to five pieces of cloth in his pocket. To prepare a piece of cloth with thread, one corner of a piece of cloth with dimensions (12x15) cm. is twisted and a 50 cm.

long string is fastened on the twisted corner. With aging people and some invalids, the penis dwindles, so that the cloth wrapped around it comes off. Such people put a piece of cloth as large as a handkerchief in a small synthetic bag, place the penis and the scrotum in the bag, and fasten up the mouth of the bag. If the amount of the urine on the cloth becomes more than one dirham (4.80 gr.), the cloth should be replaced. When the prayer time is over, the ablution of the person with the 'udhr becomes null and void. If, in addition to the already existent 'udhr, another reason for an 'udhr arises before the prayer time is over, their ablution becomes null and void on account of that (new) reason before the end of the prayer time. For instance, supposing you made an ablution during a (continuous) bleeding through one of your nostrils; this ablution becomes void if another bleeding starts in your other nostril. In the Hanafî and Shâfi'î Madhhabs, being a person with an 'udhr requires continuous existence of a nullifier of ablution throughout a prayer time. If, for instance, a person's bleeding stops temporarily and does not start again until that person makes an ablution and performs the farz part of the namâz of that prayer time, then that person is not one with an 'udhr. Once a person has become one with an 'udhr, his being so will continue throughout the following prayer times as long as the cause of his 'udhr recurs during each of those times, e.g. if, say, bleeding takes place only once within each prayer time, be it a single drop of blood observed. If no bleed recurs within a prayer time, that person is no longer one with an 'udhr. If more than one dirham of the najâsat[1] that has caused the 'udhr has smeared the person's clothes, it is necessary to wash the part smeared with the najâsat if it is possible to prevent any more smear. It is stated as follows in the book **al-Fiqh-u-'ala-l-Madhâhib-il-erba'a**: "There are two qawls concerning an invalid's being a person with an 'udhr in accordance with the rules of the Mâlikî Madhhab: According to the first qawl, something which nullifies an ablution must continue for more than half a prayer time and it must not be known when it began and when it ended. According to the second qawl, the invalid becomes a person with an 'udhr when the (inevitable) exudations start even in nonexistence of the two stipulations in the

---

[1] Something, such as blood, urine, alcohol, etc. that has to be washed away from the place where you will perform namâz and/or from your clothes. Please see the sixth chapter of the fourth fascicle of **Endless Bliss** for details.

first qawl. The invalid's ablution does not become void. If the time when the exudation stopped is known, it is mustahab for the invalid to make an ablution before starting to perform namâz. An invalid or elderly person who is in one of the Hanafî and Shâfi'î Madhhabs and who is not a person with an 'udhr (according to those two Madhhabs) had better imitate the second qawl of the Mâlikî Madhhab."]

If a person fears that he may be taken ill or that his illness may become worse or linger in case he makes an ablution, then he makes a tayammum. This fear makes sense in the light of the person's own experiences or a Muslim and 'âdil doctor's advice. A doctor's advice is acceptable so long as he is not notorious as a blatant sinner. Some probable causes of illness are: Cold weather and no place to shelter; failure to find something to heat the water or money to pay a public bath. In the Hanafî Madhhab you can perform as many farz namâzes as you wish with one tayammum you have made. In the Shâfi'î and Mâlikî Madhhabs you have to make a new tayammum for every farz namâz.

If a person has running sores on half of his limbs of ablution, (i.e. on limbs that must be washed when making an ablution,) he makes a tayammum (in lieu of an ablution). If the running sores cover less than half (of the limbs of ablution), then that person washes the ones that are healthy and makes masah on the sore(s). Since the entire body is deemed as a single limb in ghusl, in case half of your body is covered with running sores, you make tayammum. If the part covered with running sores is less than half (of your entire body), than you wash the healthy part(s) and make masah on the sore(s). If masah on the sore(s) will exacerbate the sore(s), then you make masah on the bandage(s). If doing so also will be harmful, then you have been let off masah as well. If, when making an ablution or ghusl, masah on your head will be harmful, then you do not make masah on your head. A person who can not use water with his hand on account of something wrong with it [such as eczema or a running sore] on it, makes tayammum. (For doing so,) he rubs his face and arms gently on the ground [or on a wall covered with lime, stone or soil]. Supposing a person has no hands and feet and has a running sore on his face, then he performs namâz without an ablution. A person who cannot find someone to help him to make an ablution makes a tayammum. His children or his slaves or people whom he has hired have to help him (to make an ablution). As well, he asks others to help him. However, others do not have to help him. Husband and wife do not have to help each other to make an ablution.

Supposing a person uses a bandage [or a plaster applied on a gauze or cotton or ointment] as a result of bleeding or applying leeches or a running sore or a boil or a broken or injured bone; if he is unable to wash that (delicate) part with cold or hot water or even to make masah on it, then, as he makes an ablution or ghusl, he makes masah once on more than half of that part. In case it would be harmful to undo the bandage, the healthy places under it needn't be washed. Masah is made over the healthy parts of the skin seen through the bandage. It is unnecessary to be with an ablution when applying the bandage. If the bandage is replaced after the masah, masah on the new bandage is unnecessary, even after another one is applied on it.

NAMÂZ DURING AN ILLNESS

If an invalid is unable to stand or strongly believes that standing will linger their illness, then they perform their namâz sitting; they bend their body a little for the rukû'; and, after sitting up, they make the sajda on the floor, (i.e. with their nose and forehead on the floor.) Then they sit in a manner that comes easy to them. It is permissible for them to kneel or to sit cross-legged or to squat on their buttocks with their arms around their knees drawn close to their body. A headache and a toothache and an eye sore are deemed as illnesses. Another 'udhr (in this respect) is the fear of being seen by the enemy. As well, a person who will lose his ablution should he stand performs namâz sitting. A person who can stand by leaning against something performs namâz leaning. A person unable to stand long makes the takbîr of iftitâh, (i.e. starts performing namâz by saying, "Allâhu ekber,") standing, and continues (with his namâz) sitting when he (or she) feels pain.

A person unable to make sajda on the floor (or ground) recites (the âyats) standing and then sits down to make the rukû' and the sajda with signs. (To do so,) they bend their body a little for the rukû' and somewhat more for the sajda. People unable to bend their body bend their head. It is unnecessary (for such people) to make sajda on something. Should they make sajda on something, their namâz will be sahîh if their bending for the sajda has been somewhat exaggerated in comparison with their bending for the rukû', yet they will have committed an act that is makrûh, (since it is makrûh to make sajda on something that makes the place of sajda higher than level.) It is not permissible to lie down and perform namâz with signs if it is possible to sit and lean (against something). Our blessed Prophet 'sall-Allâhu 'alaihi wa sallam' saw an invalid making sajda on a pillow placed before him; he picked the pillow and threw it away. Thereupon, that person put something wooden before him. The Best of the entire creation threw it away, too, and stated: "**Perform it on the earth**, [i.e. putting your forehead on the earth,]! **If you are unable to do so, make signs, bending (your body) a little more for the sajda than doing so for the rukû'**!" As is stated in the book entitled **Bahr-ur-râiq** (and written by Zeynel'âbidîn bin Ibrâhîm ibni Nujaym-i-Misrî 'rahmatullâhi ta'âlâ 'alaih', 926 – 970 [1562 A.D.], Egypt, as a commentary to the book entitled **Kenz-ud-deqâiq**, which in turn had been written by Abul-berekât Hâfidh-ud-dîn 'Abdullah bin Ahmad Nesefî (or Nasafî) 'rahmatullâhi ta'âlâ 'alaih', d. 710 [1310 A.D.], Baghdâd), it is purported in the hundred and ninety-first âyat-i-kerîm of Âl-i-'Imrân Sûra that "He who can performs namâz standing. He who cannot do so performs it sitting. And he who cannot do so, either, performs it lying." When 'Imrân bin Husayn 'radiy-Allâhu 'anh' became ill Rasûlullah 'sall-Allâhu 'alaihi wa sallam' said to him: "**Perform** (namâz) **standing! If you cannot do so, either, then perform it lying on your side or back.**" [As is seen, an invalid who cannot stand performs it sitting. One who cannot sit one way or another performs it lying down. It is not permissible for a person who can sit on the ground (or floor) or for one who is travelling on a bus or on an aeroplane to perform namâz sitting in a armchair or on a chair and with their feet hanging down. If a person cannot perform namâz standing in jamâ'at in a mosque, he performs it standing in his home. There are twenty 'udhrs existence of (any one of) which absolves you from having to go out (to the mosque) for jamâ'at, (i.e. for the purpose of performing namâz in jamâ'at.) The following situations are 'udhrs for not leaving your place for Friday prayer: Rain; blistering heat or extreme cold; fear of an enemy who may attack to take away your life or property; fear of your companions' leaving you alone in your journey; pitch darkness; an indebted poor person's fear of being arrested and imprisoned; blindness; being too paralyzed to walk; having (only) one foot (the other being) cut off; being crippled; mud; being unable to walk; being too old to walk; fear of missing a rare class on Fiqh; fear of missing one's favorite food; being about to set off for a journey; being a trained medical attendant who has no one to take over duty; a terribly stormy night; urinary (or excretory) urgency; being an invalid who fears that their illness may become worse or linger or a medical attendant who fears that their invalid may be left with no one to look after them; having difficulty walking with old age. Walking to and from a mosque for Friday prayer is more meritorious than using a vehicle. It is not permissible to perform namâz with signs sitting on a chair or in an armchair in a mosque. It is **bid'at** to perform acts of worship in a manner not prescribed by Islam. And it is written in books of Fiqh that it is gravely sinful to commit an act that is bid'at.]

A person who is too ill to (perform namâz) turn(ing) towards the Qibla performs it in any possible direction. If the invalid is lying flat on their back, something (soft) should be put under their head so that their face will be in the direction of Qibla. The knees had better be drawn up. If a person (is so ill that they) cannot even make signs with their head, it is permissible for them to leave the namâz to qadâ, (which means to postpone it until the prayer time is over.) A person who becomes ill during namâz carries on performing it as well as they can. If an invalid who is performing namâz sitting recovers during the namâz, they carry on performing it standing. A person who loses his or her mind does not perform namâz. If they recover before five prayer times are over, they make qadâ of the five namâzes. If six prayer times have passed, they do not make any qadâ.

It is farz to make haste in making qadâ of a namâz that you failed to perform within its proper time, at least with signs. If a person finds himself on his deathbed before having had time to make qadâ, it will not be wâjib for him to command in his will that an amount of fidya should be paid from the property he leaves behind for the isqât of the namâzes that he did not perform. However, it becomes wâjib for him to do so if he recovers and remains healthy as long as time enough to make qadâ. If he does not command it in his will, it is permissible, according to a scholarly statement, for his walî, or even for an outsider, to perform isqât by spending their own property. Here we end the passage that we borrowed from Ni'met-i-islâm.

It is stated as follows in a hadîth-i-sherîf: **There are twenty-four acts that bring poverty onto a person**:

1– To urinate standing without a darûrat to do so. (A darûrat is a situation that you cannot help and which compels you to do or not to do something.)

2– To eat food while you are (in a state called) **junub**, (i.e. when you need to make a ghusl.)

3– To despise crumbs of bread and step on them.

4– To burn onion and garlic peelings.

5– To walk ahead of seniors.

6– To call one's parents by their names.

7– To pick one's teeth with twigs from trees or brooms.

8– To wash one's hands with mud.

9– To sit on a threshold.

10– To make an ablution at a place where one urinates.

11– To put food in unwashed pots and pans.

12– To sew clothes as one is wearing them.

13– To eat onions when hungry.

14– To dry one's face with one's skirt.

15– To let spiders live in one's house.

16– To hurry out of the mosque after performing the morning prayer (in jamâ'at).

17– To go to the market place early and leave there late.

18– To buy bread from a poor person.

19– To pronounce a malediction over one's parents.

20– To sleep naked.

21– To leave pots and pans without putting a cover on them.

22– To blow out a light such as a candle.

23– To do everything without saying, "Bismillah."

24– To put on one's shalwar standing.

If a person recites the Sûra "**Innâ a'taynâ...,**" before going to bed and then entreats, "Yâ Rabbî (O my Allah)! Please wake me up in time for morning prayer tomorrow," Bi-iznillâhi ta'âlâ, that person will wake up in time for morning prayer.

IMPORTANCE of NAMÂZ

The book entitled **Eshi'at-ul-leme'at** (and written by **'Abd-ul-Haqq bin Seyf-ud-dîn Dahlawî** 'rahmatullâhi ta'âlâ 'alaih', 958 [1551 A.D.] – 1052 [1642], Delhi) contains various hadîth-i-sherîfs stating the importance of namâz. The book is a commentary written in the Persian language to the book of hadîths entitled

Mishkât-ul-Mesâbih (and written by Waliyy-ud-dîn Khatîb-i-Tebrîzî Muhammad bin 'Abdullah 'rahmatullâhi ta'âlâ 'alaih', d. 749 [1348 A.D.]) as a commentary and complementary to the book entitled **Mesâbih** (and written by Imâm Beghâwî Huseyn bin Mes'ûd Muhy-is-sunna 'rahmatullâhi ta'âlâ 'alaih', d. 516 [1122 A.D.]). Eshi'at-ul-leme'at is a book in four volumes. Its ninth edition was published in 1384 [1964 A.D.] in Lucknow, India.

Namâz is called '**salât**' in the Arabic language. And the original meaning of salât is prayer, rahmat (compassion, mercy) and istighfâr (begging Allâhu ta'âlâ for forgiveness). Because namâz contains all three meanings, namâz has been called 'salât'.

1– Abû Hurayra 'radiy-Allâhu 'anh' quotes Rasûlullah 'sall-Allâhu 'alaihi wa sallam' as having stated: "**The daily five prayers and the Friday prayer are expiations for the sins to be committed until next Friday; and fasting** (for thirty days) **in Ramadân is an expiation for the sins to be committed until next Ramadân. They cause forgiveness for the venial sins committed by Muslims who avoid committing grave sins**." They annihilate the venial sins that are committed in the meantime and which do not involve human rights. With Muslims whose venial sins have all been forgiven and there are no more of them left, they, (i.e. Friday prayer and fasting in Ramadân,) cause alleviation of the torment for their grave sins. Forgiveness of grave sins requires, in addition, making tawba for them, (which in turn means to repent for the sins committed, to beg Allâhu ta'âlâ, to be firmly resolved not to commit them again, and to promise Allâhu ta'âlâ not to commit them again.) If a Muslim has not committed any grave sins, then they cause his spiritual promotion. This hadîth-i-sherîf is written in the book entitled **Sahîh-i-Muslim**. Friday prayers cause forgiveness of Muslims whose five daily prayers are defective. If their Friday prayers also are defective, then their fasting in Ramadân causes them to be forgiven.

2– Abû Hurayra 'radiy-Allâhu 'anh', again, narrates: Rasûlullah 'sall-Allâhu 'alaihi wa sallam' stated: "**Supposing there is a stream running before the door of a person's house and he bathes five times daily in that stream. Will there be any dirt left on him**?" "No, there won't be any dirt left, o the blessed Messenger of Allah," replied the Sahâba. Thereupon Rasûlullah said: "**So is the case with the daily five prayers. Allâhu ta'âlâ forgives the venial sins of Muslims who perform namâz five times daily**." This hadîth-i-sherîf is written in **Sahîh-i-Bukhârî** as well as in **Sahîh-i-Muslim**.

3– 'Abdullah ibni Mes'ûd 'radiy-Allâhu 'anh' relates: Someone kissed a woman who was nâ-mahram to him. Or, in detail, one of the Ansâr was selling dates. A woman came up to buy dates. He felt a strong bestial attraction to the woman. "I have better ones at home. Come along and let me give you better dates," he said. When they went to his place he hugged the woman and kissed her. "What are you doing? Fear Allah," remonstrated the woman. He repented. He came up to Rasûlullah and told him what he had done. Rasûlullah 'sall-Allâhu 'alaihi wa sallam' did not answer him, and waited for wahy from Allâhu ta'âlâ. Thereafter that person performed a namâz. Allâhu ta'âlâ sent the hundred and fourteenth âyat of Hûd Sûra (to His blessed Messenger). The âyat-i-kerîma purports: "**And perform namâz regularly at the two sides of the day and at the approaches of the night! For, things that are good remove those which are evil; ... .**" The two sides of the day are forenoon and afternoon. So, the namâzes meant are morning prayer and early and late afternoon prayers. And namâzes at the approaches of the night are evening and night prayers. This âyat-i-kerîma declares that the daily five prayers cause forgiveness of sins. The blessed person asked: "Yâ Rasûlallah (O Messenger of Allah)! Is that good news for me only?" "**It is for all my Ummat** (Muslims)," said the blessed Prophet. This hadîth-i-sherîf is written in both the books entitled 'Sahîh', (i.e. in Sahîh-i-Bukhârî and in Sahîh-i-Muslim.)[1]

4– Eness bin Mâlik 'radiy-Allâhu 'anh' relates: Someone came up to Rasûlullah 'sall-Allâhu 'alaihi wa sallam' and said: "I have committed a crime that deserves punishment of hadd.[2] Have me flogged for hadd." Rasûlullah did not ask him what sin he had committed. When it was prayer time we performed namâz together. When Rasûlullah 'sall-Allâhu 'alaihi wa sallam' completed the namâz, that blessed person stood up and said: "Yâ Rasûlallah 'sall-Allâhu 'alaihi wa sallam'! I have commited a sin to be punished with the penalty of hadd. Inflict on me the punishment commanded in the book of Allâhu ta'âlâ!" "**Haven't you performed namâz with us**," asked the Best of Prophets. The latter said: "Yes, I have." "**Don't be sad. Allâhu ta'âlâ has forgiven your sin**," came the good news from the beloved one of Allâhu ta'âlâ. This hadîth-i-sherîf is in the two basic books of hadîths. That

---

[1] Please see the sixth chapter of the second fascicle of **Endless Bliss**.
[2] Please see the tenth chapter of the sixth fascicle of **Endless Bliss**.

blessed person believed that he had committed a grave sin that incurred hadd. Its being pardoned owing to the namâz performed shows that it was a venial sin. Or, by saying, "hadd," he meant 'ta'zîr', which is inflicted as a requital for venial sins. That must have been the case, since he did not say, "Inflict hadd on me," in his second inquiry.

5– 'Abdullah ibni Mes'ûd 'radiy-Allâhu 'anh' relates: I asked Rasûlullah 'sall-Allâhu ta'âlâ 'alaihi wa sallam' what deed Allâhu ta'âlâ liked best. "**Namâz performed in its right time**," replied the most beloved creature. In fact, it is stated in some hadîth-i-sherîfs that Allâhu ta'âlâ "**likes very much a namâz that is performed in its early time**." I asked what deed Allâhu ta'âlâ liked second best. "**Being good to parents**," he said. I asked what deed He liked third best, and the blessed Darling of Allâhu ta'âlâ replied: "**Making jihâd in the way of Allah**." This hadîth-i-sherîf also is written in the two books of Sahîh. It is stated in another hadîth-i-sherîf: "**The best of deeds is to give a dinner**." In another one: "**The best deed is to spread the manner wherein Muslims greet one another**." (Please see the sixty-second chapter of the third fascicle of **Endless Bliss**.) In another one: "**The best deed is to perform namâz at midnight, when all people are asleep**." In another hadîth-i-sherîf: "**The most valuable deed is (to behave in such a way) that noone will be hurt by your hands**, (i.e. manners) **and tongue**, (i.e. words)." In another hadîth-i-sherîf: "**Jihâd is the most valuable deed**." In another hadîth-i-sherîf it is stated: "**The most valuable deed is the hajj-i-mebrûr**." Hajj-i-mebrûr means a hajj that is accomplished without committing any sins. Another hadîth-i-sherîf states that the most valuable deed is "**To make dhikr of Allâhu ta'âlâ**." And another one states that it is "**A deed which is performed (regularly and) steadily**." Variability of the answer was on account of the variation of the people who asked the question and the various states they were in. Or, different times called for different answers. For instance, jihâd was the most meritorious deed in the early, fledgling days of Islam. [In our time, the most meritorious deed is to refute unbelievers and people who deny the Madhhabs by way of publication and broadcasting, and to spread the creed taught by the (scholars of) Ahl as-sunnat. People who support such champions of jihâd, financially and/or by donation and/or physically, will have a share in the thawâb earned by them. Âyat-i-kerîmas and hadîth-i-sherîfs show that namâz is more valuable than zakât or any other kind of alms. What is even more valuable than performing namâz, however, is to give something to someone about to die and thereby to save them from death.]

6– Jâbir bin 'Abdullah 'radiy-Allâhu 'anh' narrates: Rasûlullah 'sall-Allâhu 'alaihi wa sallam' stated: "**The borderline between man and kufr** (unbelief) **is to cease from namâz**." For, namâz is a curtain protecting man from contacting kufr. Once this curtain disappears from between, the slave (man) slithers down into kufr. This hadîth-i-sherîf is written in **Sahîh-i-Muslim**. This hadîth-i-sherîf shows how disastrous it is to neglect namâz. Most of the Sahâba-i-kirâm stated that a person who omits namâz without an 'udhr to do so becomes an unbeliever (kâfir). That person does not become a kâfir according to the Shâfi'î and Mâlikî Madhhabs, but then it becomes wâjib to put him to death. In the Hanafî Madhhab he is imprisoned and beaten and kept in prison until he begins to perform his namâzes again.

Ubâda bin Thâbit 'radiy-Allâhu 'anh' narrates: Rasûlullah 'sall-Allâhu 'alaihi wa sallam' stated: "**Allâhu ta'âlâ commanded (us) to perform namâz five times (daily). If a person makes an ablution beautifully and performs them in time and in perfect mindfulness of their rukû's and khushû's, Allâhu ta'âlâ promises that He shall forgive that person. He does not make the same promise for those who do not do these things. He shall either forgive them or torment them, depending on His Will.**" This hadîth-i-sherîf is quoted by Imâm Ahmad, by Abû Dâwûd, and by Nesâ'î. As is seen, it is a must to be mindful of the essentials of namâz, such as its rukû's and sajdas. Allâhu ta'âlâ never breaks His Word. He shall definitely forgive Muslims who perform namâz properly.

8– Abû Emâma-i-Bâhilî 'radiy-Allâhu 'anh' narrates: Rasûlullah 'sall-Allâhu 'alaihi wa sallam' stated: "**Perform your namâz five times (daily)! Fast for one month (in Ramadân)! Pay zakât for your property! Obey your commanders. Enter your Rabb's Garden.**" As is seen, a Muslim who performs namâz five times daily and fasts in Ramadân and pays zakât for his property and obeys the Islamically suitable commandments of commanders, who are Allâhu ta'âlâ's khalîfas on the earth, shall enter Paradise. This hadîth-i-sherîf is quoted by Imâm Ahmad and by Tirmuzî.

9– Burayda-i-Eslemî 'radiy-Allâhu 'anh', one of the eminent Sahâbîs, narrates: Rasûlullah 'sall-Allâhu 'alaihi wa sallam' stated: "**Namâz is one of the covenants between you and us. He who ceases from namâz becomes a kâfir.**" As is seen, a person who performs namâz is judged to be a Muslim. If a person does not attach importance to namâz and does not perform namâz because he does not admit that it is one's primary duty, he becomes a kâfir (unbeliever). This hadîth-i-sherîf is quoted by Imâm Ahmad, by Tirmuzî, by Nesâî, and by Ibni Mâja, (four of the greatest savants of Hadîth.)

10– Abû Zer-i-Ghifârî 'radiy-Allâhu ta'âlâ 'anh' relates: On one of the days of Autumn Rasûlullah 'sall-Allâhu 'alaihi wa sallam' and I went out. Leaves were falling. He picked two twigs from a tree. All their leaves fell at once. "**Yâ Abâ Zer! When a Muslim performs namâz for the grace of Allah, all their sins will fall like the falling leaves of these branches**," he said. This hadîth-i-sherîf is quoted by Imâm Ahmad.

11– Zeyd bin Khâlid Juhemî narrates: Rasûlullah 'sall-Allâhu 'alaihi wa sallam' stated: "**When a Muslim performs a namâz of two rak'ats properly and with khushû', his past sins will be forgiven**." That is, all his venial sins will be forgiven. This hadîth-i-sherîf is quoted by Imâm Ahmad 'rahima-hullâhu ta'âlâ'.

12– 'Abdullah bin 'Amr ibni 'Âs 'radiy-Allâhu ta'âlâ 'anhumâ' narrates: Rasûlullah 'sall-Allâhu 'alaihi wa sallam' stated: "**If a person performs namâz, that namâz will become a nûr** (light) **and a burhân** (voucher) **and cause them to attain salvation. If they do not protect the namâz, it will not become a nûr and a burhân, so that they will not attain salvation. They will be kept together with Qârûn, with Pharaoh, with Hâmân, and with Ubeyy bin Khalef.**" As is seen, if a Muslim performs namâz mindfully of its fards, wâjibs, sunnats, and adabs, that namâz will cause them to be in nûr on the Rising Day. If they do not keep performing namâz in this manner, they will be among the aforesaid unbelievers on the Rising Day. That is, they will be subjected to severe torment in Hell. Ubeyy bin Khalef was one of the implacable Meccan unbelievers. In the Holy War of Uhud, Rasûlullah 'sall-Allâhu 'alaihi wa sallam' dispatched him to Hell with his own blessed hand. This hadîth-i-sherîf is quoted by Imâm Ahmad, by Imâm Beyhekî, and by Dârimî ('Abdullah bin 'Abd-ur-Rahmân Hâfid Abû Muhammad).

13– 'Abdullah bin Shaqîq 'rahima-hullâhu ta'âlâ', one of the greater ones of the Tâbi'în, states: "The Sahâba-i-kirâm 'radiy-Allâhu 'anhum' said that of all acts of worship the namâz is the only one which will cause its neglecter to become a kâfir (enemy of Allah)." This information has been furnished by (Muhammad bin 'Îsâ) Tirmuzî 'rahmatullâhi 'alaih'. 'Abdullah bin Shaqîq narrated hadîth-i-sherîfs on the authority of (Sahâbîs such as)

'Umar, 'Alî, 'Uthmân, and 'Âisha 'radiy-Allâhu 'anhum'. He passed away in the hundred and eighth year of the Hegira.

14– Abu-d-derdâ 'radiy-Allâhu 'anh' states: My very much beloved one said to me: "**Even if you are torn to pieces or burned in fire, never attribute any partner to Allâhu ta'âlâ! Never omit farz namâzes! A person who omits farz namâzes goes out of Islam. Never drink wine. Wine is a key to all evils.**" As is seen, a person who heedlessly omits farz namâzes becomes a kâfir. A person who omits them because of indolence does not become a kâfir; yet it is a grave sin. It is not sinful to fail to perform them on account of one of the five 'udhrs prescribed by Islam. Wine and all the other alcoholic beverages suspend one's mind. A person with suspended mind is prone to do any evil.

15– 'Alî 'radiy-Allâhu 'anh' narrates. Rasûlullah 'sall-Allâhu 'alaihi wa sallam' stated: "**Yâ 'Alî! There are three things which you shouldn't postpone to do: When a prayer time comes, perform that namâz immediately! When a janâza** (a dead Muslim to be buried) **is ready** (for burial)**, perform the namâz of janâza immediately! When you find your daughter's kufw, marry her off immediately!**" This hadîth-i-sherîf is quoted by Tirmuzî 'rahima-hullâhu ta'âlâ'. A namâz of janâza should be performed even within the three times during which it is makrûh to perform namâz. (The three times are called 'Kerâhat' and are explained in detail in the final section of the tenth chapter of the fourth fascicle of **Endless Bliss**.)

[As is seen, a woman or girl must be married off to her kufw, i.e. to a man suitable for her. To be kufw does not mean to be rich or to have a handsome salary. To be kufw means for a man to be a sâlih Muslim, to have the creed of Ahl as-sunnat, to perform namâz five times daily, not to consume alcoholic beverages, i.e. to obey Islam, and to have an income sufficient for nafaqa; (that is, he must be able to raise a family.) Parents whose only criterion for a man to meet is to be rich and have apartment houses will have dragged their daughters to perdition and thrown them into Hell. And the girl must perform namâz (five times daily), must not go out with her head and arms exposed, and must not sit with a nâ-mahram man in private, even if he is one of her kinsfolk.]

16– 'Abdullah ibni 'Umar 'radiy-Allâhu 'anhumâ' narrates: Rasûlullah 'sall-Allâhu 'alaihi wa sallam' stated: "**Allâhu ta'âlâ is pleased with people who perform their namâz as soon as its time comes. And He forgives those who perform it at its latest time.**"

This hadîth-i-sherîf is quoted by Tirmuzî 'rahima-hullâhu ta'âlâ'.

In the Shâfi'î and Hanbalî Madhhabs it is more meritorious to perform every namâz early in its time. The Mâlikî Madhhab also approximates to this. However, in a very hot weather a single performer had better delay the early afternoon prayer. In the Hanafî Madhhab it is more meritorious to perform morning and night prayers rather late, and to perform early afternoon prayer when the weather cools down in months when it is hot. [It is good and precautious, however, to perform early afternoon prayer before late afternoon prayer time starts according to the Tarafeyn's qawl, and to perform late afternoon and night prayers after the times for late afternoon and night prayers start according to Imâm A'zam Abû Hanîfa's qawl. (For details on prayer times please see the tenth chapter of the fourth fascicle of **Endless Bliss**.) People with taqwâ (fear of Allâhu ta'âlâ) are precautious in everything they do.]

17– Umm-i-Ferwa 'radiy-Allâhu 'anhâ' narrates: Rasûlullah 'sall-Allâhu 'alaihi wa sallam' was asked what deed was the most meritorious. He said: "**The most meritorious deed is the namâz that is performed early in its time**." This hadîth-i-sherîf is quoted by Imâm Ahmad, by Tirmuzî and by Abû Dâwûd 'rahima-humullâhu ta'âlâ'. Namâz is the highest act of worship. It becomes even higher when it is performed as soon as its time starts.

18– 'Âisha 'radiy-Allâhu 'anhâ' states: "I did not see Rasûlullah 'sall-Allâhu ta'âlâ 'alaihi wa sallam' perform a namâz at its latest time twice."

19– Umm-i-Habîba 'radiy-Allâhu 'anhâ' narrates: Rasûlullah 'sall-Allâhu 'alaihi wa sallam' stated: "**If a Muslim slave** (of Allâhu ta'âlâ) **performs twelve rak'ats of namâz as an act of tetawwu' in addition to the farz namâzes daily, Allâhu ta'âlâ makes a villa for him in Paradise**." This hadîth-i-sherîf is written in **Sahîh-i-Muslim**. As is seen, Rasûlullah 'sall-Allâhu 'alaihi wa sallam' calls the sunnat namâzes that are performed together with the farz namâzes daily, tetawwu', which means nâfila (supererogatory) namâz.

20– 'Abdullah bin Shaqîq 'rahima-hullâhu ta'âlâ', one of the greater ones of the Tâbi'în: I asked Hadrat 'Âisha 'radiy-Allâhu 'anhâ' about Rasûlullah's 'sall-Allâhu 'alaihi wa sallam' namâzes of tetawwu', that is, nâfila (supererogatory) namâzes. Our blessed mother said: "He used to perform four rak'ats before the farz part of early afternoon prayer and two rak'ats after it, (i.e. after the farz part,) two rak'ats after the farz part of evening prayer, two rak'ats after the farz part of night prayer, and two rak'ats before the farz part of morning prayer. This information has been provided by Muslim and by Abû Dâwûd 'rahima-humallâhu ta'âlâ'.

21– 'Âisha 'radiy-Allâhu 'anhâ' stated: "Of the acts of supererogatory worship, the sunnat of morning prayer was the one which Rasûlullah 'sall-Allâhu 'alaihi wa sallam' performed most steadfastly." This narration is written in (Sahîh-i-)**Bukhârî** and in (Sahîh-i-)**Muslim**. Here, 'Âisha 'radiy-Allâhu 'anhâ' calls the sunnat namâzes performed along with the daily five namâzes 'supererogatory namâz'.

[Imâm Rabbânî mujaddid-i-elf-i-thânî Ahmad bin 'Abd-ul-Ahad Fârûqî Serhendî 'rahmatullâhi 'alaih', a great Islamic savant, the Ahl-i-sunnat's most powerful champion against heretics and la-madhhabî people, a great mujâhid who spread the religion chosen by Allâhu ta'âlâ and who demolished bid'ats, states as follows in the twenty-ninth letter of the first volume of his book entitled **Maktûbât**, the like of which has not been written in the Islamic religion:

Deeds which Allâhu ta'âlâ likes are acts that are farz and those which are supererogatory (nâfila). The supererogatory ones, when compared with the farz ones, have no value. To perform one farz namâz within its dictated time is more valuable than performing acts of supererogatory worship continuously for a thousand years. This maxim applies to all sorts of supererogatory worship, e.g. namâz, zakât, fasting, 'umra, hajj, dhikr, and fikr (meditation). In fact, when performing a namâz that is farz, to do one of its sunnats and adabs is much more valuable than performing other nâfilas. One day, when the Emîr-ul-mu'minîn 'Umar-ul-Fârûq 'radiy-Allâhu 'anh' conducted morning prayer in jamâ'at, he noticed that someone he knew was absent and asked (the Muslims who were present) why that person was not there. "He performs nâfila worship every night. He must have fallen asleep and failed to come here for the jamâ'at," they explained. Thereupon the blessed Khalîfa stated: "It would have been better if he had slept throughout the night and performed his morning prayer in jamâ'at." As is seen, as you perform an act of worship that is farz, (e.g. the farz part of one of the daily five prayers,) to observe one of its adabs (or mendubs) or to avoid one of its makrûhs is a myriad of times as valuable as doing one of the (self-standing supererogatory) acts of worship such as dhikr, fikr, and murâqaba. It is true that the so-called acts of supererogatory acts of worship are certainly very useful if they are done in addition to observing those adabs and avoiding the makrûhs. Yet they are no good when they are without the ones to which they are additional. Likewise, to pay one (Turkish) lira as zakât, (which is farz for Muslims defined in detail in the first chapter of the fifth fascicle of **Endless Bliss**,) is better than dispensing thousands of liras in the name of alms which is supererogatory. Indeed, to observe one of the adabs (of zakât) as you pay that lira, i.e. to pay it to one of your close relatives,[1] is much better than that supererogatory worship. [Hence, people who wish to perform midnight namâz (called tahajjud [or tehejjud]) should perform qadâ namâzes. Commandments of Allâhu ta'âlâ are called **farz** (or **fard**), and His prohibitions are called **harâm**s. Our Prophet's commandments are called **sunnat**s, and his interdictions are called **makrûh**s. All these things, in the aggregate, are called **Ahkâm-i-islâmiyya**. It is farz to acquire beautiful conduct and to do good to people. A person who denies or despises one of the tenets of the Ahkâm-i-islâmiyya becomes an **unbeliever (kâfir)**, a **renegade (murtadd)**. A person who believes all the Ahkâm-i-islâmiyya, in the aggregate, is called a **Muslim**. A Muslim who disobeys the Ahkâm-i-islâmiyya because of sloth is called a **fâsiq** Muslim. A fâsiq Muslim who violates one of the commandments or prohibitions shall go to Hell. None of the good acts and sunnats that a fâsiq Muslim does will be accepted and no thawâb will be given for them. If a person does not pay zakât, be it one (Turkish) lira, none of their acts of donation or charity shall be accepted. They shall not be given any thawâb for any of the mosques and/or schools and/or hospitals built at their expense or for any of their donations to charity organizations. The namâz of Terâwih performed by a person who has not performed night prayer shall not be accepted. Acts of worship other than those which are farz or wâjib are called **nâfila** (supererogatory). Sunnats are supererogatory worship. In light of this definition, a person who performs qadâ namâz will have performed sunnat namâzes as well. The thawâb (to be earned) for performing a farz or for avoiding a harâm is more than the thawâb earned by doing millions of acts of supererogatory worship. A person who omits a farz or commits a harâm shall be subjected to fire in Hell. Their supererogatory worship cannot save them from Hell. Changes made in acts of worship are called **bid'at**s. To commit a bid'at when performing an act of worship is harâm and will spoil that act

---

[1] It goes without saying that that close relative should not be one of those whom you have to support, such as you wife, children, parents.

of worship. [Please review the chapter dealing with the Azân-i-Muhammâdî!] It is stated in a hadîth-i-sherîf: "**None of the acts of worship performed by a person who commits bid'ats shall be accepted**." If a person is fâsiq; for instance, if his wife and daughters are going out without properly covering themselves; or if he is committing a bid'at; for instance, if he is using a loud-speaker in worship; you should not perform namâz behind him; (in other words, you should not join a namâz in jamâ'at conducted by that person;) you should not listen to his perfidious speeches or read his books. However, you should treat everybody with a smile, friend and foe alike, and talk with them suavely; you should not have an altercation with anybody. It is stated in a hadîth-i-sherîf: "**Idiots should not be replied**." Worship enhances heart's purity. Sins darken a heart, so that it does not receive fayz any longer. It is farz for every individual Muslim to learn the essentials of îmân and fards and harâms. Not knowing them is not a valid 'udhr. That is, it is tantamount to not doing them although one knows them.] The book entitled **Maktûbât** is in the Arabic language. Translation from that book ends here. Hadrat Imâm Rabbânî passed away in the Serhend city of India in 1034 [1624 A.D.].

As is understood from what has been written so far, the sunnats of daily five namâzes are among the nâfila (supererogatory) namâzes. Because they are performed together with the farz namâzes and compensate for the deficiencies in the farz parts performed, they are more meritorious than other supererogatory namâzes. A Muslim who has not performed a farz namâz within its prescribed time without (any good reason called) an 'udhr although he values namâz highly and looks on namâz as his primary duty, has committed a grave sin by doing so. He shall be together with Pharaohs and with Hâmân in Hell. Supererogatory namâzes, i.e. the sunnat parts (of the five daily namâzes), cannot save him from that grave sin and from the severe torment it entails. For that matter, it is farz to make qadâ of the omitted farz namâzes. It is gravely sinful to delay their qadâ. This ever increasing and ever breeding sinfulness has to be put an end to. Since it is farz to perform qadâ namâzes, the thawâb it yields thousands of times more thawâb than does performing the sunnats. Therefore, and since it is permissible to omit the sunnats on account of an 'udhr, every Muslim should perform qadâ of the farz namâzes which he omitted without an 'udhr also in lieu of the sunnats of the four of the daily four prayers. Because there are Islamic savants who say that the sunnat of morning prayer is wâjib, qadâ should not be performed in lieu of the sunnat of morning prayer. Thereby they will get rid of the grave sin as soon as possible by always performing their qadâ namâzes. When the qadâs have all been performed, the sunnats of the daily five prayers should be performed continuously. For, it is a venial sin to persist in not performing the sunnats without an 'udhr (to prevent one from performing them). And a person who slights a sunnat becomes a kâfir.

Although it is farz also to make qadâ as early as of (farz) namâzes that you missed, i.e. those which you failed to perform in time on account of an 'udhr, savants of the Hanafî Madhhab said that it is permissible to delay making qadâ of them until you have performed the sunnats (of the daily five prayers), since it is not sinful to fail to perform a farz namâz within its prescribed time because of an 'udhr. However, this (unanimous) statement of theirs does not mean also that it is permissible to delay farz namâz omitted without an 'udhr. Moreover, to say 'permissible' does not mean to say 'wâjib' or 'good'. There is many an act that is said to be 'permissible' and which is said to be 'makrûh' at the same time. For instance, it is permissible to pay **sadaqa-i-fitr** to dhimmî disbelievers, yet it is makrûh to do so. (Please see the third chapter of the fifth fascicle of **Endless Bliss** for sadaqa-i-fitr. Dhimmî means a non-Muslim who lives in a country of Muslims.)

> *Perform namâz, and don't let your hands touch harâm;*
> *Don't expect to live long, or an endless world!*
> *Hold fast to namâz five times, as you are young yet!*
> *What you sow here, you will collect in next world.*

> *Two people will never remember death at all:*
> *One commits harâm, the latter omits prayer!*
> *One day these hands will not be able to hold;*
> *Tongues that don't say, "Allah," will fail to utter!*

TO PAY ZAKÂT

The proof-texts for the fact that (paying) zakât is farz are the forty-third and the hundred and tenth âyat-i-kerîmas of Baqara Sûra.

There are twelve people to whom it is not permissible to pay zakât:

An insane person; for a dead Muslim's kefen (shroud); a kâfir (non Muslim); a rich person; one's usûl (ancestors) and furû' (posterity); one's wife; one's slave; one's mukâtaba [slave who will be manumited on payment of a certain price]; one's mudebbera [slave who will attain freedom upon the owner's death]. As for a woman's paying zakât to her husband; this is a matter of issue (among Islamic savants); essentially, it should not be done.

Supposing you think a certain person is not one of your relatives and yet that person turns out to be one of your children, or he or she turns out to be a disbeliever although you thought that they were a Muslim; these people are not eligible for zakât; but if you have given zakât to one of such people unknowingly, –essentially– repayment is unnecessary.

The following eight people are eligible for being paid zakât:

1– A person who is 'miskîn' in Islamic terminology. (A Muslim who has no more than a day's sustenance is termed 'miskîn';)

2– Poor Muslims whose property is below the amount of nisâb for Qurbân. (Nisâb means border. It means border between richness and poverty in the Islamic terminology. Nisâb for Qurbân and for the special alms called Fitra differs from that for Zakât. Please see chapters 1, 3, and 4 of the fifth fascicle of **Endless Bliss** for particulars;)

3– A Muslim in debt;

4– A Muslim charged with collecting property of zakât and 'udhr (amount of a wage);

5– A Muslim who is poor at his present location, rich as he may be back at home;

6– A Muslim who has become poor en route for jihâd or hajj;

7– A slave who has to pay his owner a certain amount of money in return for emancipation;

8– Non-Muslims called muallafa-í-qulûb, who do not exist today.

A person who possesses property more than a day's sustenance but less than the amount of nisâb is called 'poor' (in Islamic terminology). Every civil servant who has difficulty in earning a living for his family, regardless of the salary he gets, is eligible to receive zakât, and does not have to perform Qurbân or pay Fitra. A Muslim who is teaching or learning Islamic knowledge is eligible to receive zakât even if he possesses property or money enough to sustain him for forty years. Money of zakât cannot be spent for mosque-building, for jihâd, or for buying a shroud for a dead Muslim. You cannot pay zakât to a rich person's small child, or to your own parents or children or wife. It yields more thawâb to pay it to your siblings, daughter-in-law, son-in-law, mother-in-law, father-in-law, paternal aunt, paternal uncle, maternal uncle, and/or maternal aunt. A poor Muslim should be paid less than the amount of nisâb. However, if he has a wife and children, the total amount may be more (than the nisâb) provided that no individual in the family will have been paid more than the amount of nisâb. Zakât should not be paid to a person who squanders his property or spends it in a way that is harâm. Sayyids also can be paid zakât since they can no longer get their rightful shares from ghanîmat. (Please scan the 'Beyt-ul-mâl' in the final part of the first chapter of the fifth fascicle of **Endless Bliss**.)

There are six conditions that a person has to fulfil so that zakât should be farz (for him) to pay:

1– To be a Muslim;

2– To have reached the age of puberty;

3– To have reached the age of discretion;

4– To be free;

5– To have halâl property of zakât the amount of nisâb for zakât;

6– For the property that one possesses to be in excess of one's needs and debts.

So long as a person does not pay his zakât to the poor after zakât has become farz for him, he is identical with a person in debt, and therefore his acts of charity such as donation and alms will, let alone yield thawâb, earn him sinfulness. It is farz for him to pay his zakât or pay his debt, if he has any. As is written in the six hundred and thirty fifth (635) page of the second volume of **Hadîqa** and in the thirteen hundred and sixty ninth (1369) page of **Berîqa**, it is not permissible to [pay zakât and to] give alms to people who spend their money at harâm places or who squander their money. For, it is harâm to support something which is harâm.]

It should not be likely that the person who pays zakât will still benefit from it. If one of the husband and wife pays zakât to the other, its benefit to the party who pays it will not completely discontinue. As in any act of worship, niyyat (intention) is necessary in paying zakât. The property of zakât has to be in excess of one's debt(s) and also in excess of one's **hâjat-i-'asliyya** (vital needs), and (the sum of) that property in excess has to be the **amount of nisâb**. The (amount of) nisâb for gold is 20 mithqals, [which is equal to 96 grams or 13.3 gold coins.] The nisâb for silver is 200 dirhams [672 grams]. For it to be farz for one to pay zakât, the property of zakât, after reaching the amount of nisâb, has to remain in one's position until the end of one hijrî (hegiral) year. According to Imâm Muhammad, it is makrûh to perform a (legal trick termed) hîla-i-shar'iyya before the end of the (hijrî) year lest zakât should be farz. It is not makrûh according to Imâm Abû Yûsuf. The former explained: For, once it becomes farz, it will be sinful to disobey it. And it is **tâ'at** to avoid sinfulness. The Fatwâ agrees with Imâm Muhammad's qawl. (Fatwâ is a conclusive explanation wherein an authorized Islamic scholar answers Muslims' questions. Sources of a fatwâ are appended to it. Conditions to be fulfilled to be an authorized Islamic scholar are explained in our publications, **Belief and Islam**, **The Sunni Path**, and **Endless Bliss** [chapter 33 of second fascicle and chapter 10 of third fascicle].)

Property of zakât means property which increases, multiplies. There are four kinds of property of zakât: Quadruped animals that graze on pastureland for more than half a year in mixed groups, or only females, and which are called **sâima**; property bought and sold for commercial purposes; gold and silver articles; food products obtained from land. Owners of only male animals or donkeys or mules pasturing at liberty do not have to pay zakât for them; i.e. zakât is not farz for them. When youngs of animals such as camels, cattle and sheep are with their adults, they are added in the calculation of zakât. In lieu of property to be paid as zakât, as 'ushr, as kaffârat, (which is defined in the sixth chapter of the fifth fascicle, and also in the thirteenth chapter of the sixth fascicle, of **Endless Bliss**,) and as sadaqa fitr, it is permissible to pay their equivalents in value. In the Shâfi'î Madhhab it is not permissible to do so. If one's property perishes after zakât becomes farz (to pay), it falls from being compulsory; (i.e. it is no longer farz to pay it. It does not fall if its owner dispatches the property; (i.e. it is still farz to pay zakât for the property.)

One (lunar) year after a discreet and pubescent Muslim's property of zakât reaches the amount of nisâb, if it is their full property and they earned it in a way that is halâl, it becomes farz for them to pay a certain amount of that property to one or a few of eight groups of Muslims; this (compulsory) payment is called zakât. The person to whom zakât is to be paid has to be a Muslim. One's full property is property which is possible and permissible for one to use. Property that you buy becomes your property once an agreement has been made; yet it is not your full property before delivery, since it is not possible to use it. Property obtained by extortion, by oppression, by force, by theft, by interest, by bribery, by gambling or earned by playing a musical instrument, by singing or by selling alcoholic beverages, is called **khabîth property**. Zakât is not paid for khabîth property. For, that property is not your (owned property called) mulk; (in other words, it is not your own property.) It has to be returned to its owner, or to its dead owner's inheritor(s), or, in the absence of inheritors, to poor Muslims. If property (which you have obtained by one of the aforesaid harâm ways) is mixed with other harâm property or with your own halâl property, it becomes your mulk, (i.e. your own property;) yet this time it is **mulk-i-habîth** (khabîth property), which is harâm to give someone else or to use anywise, and zakât is not paid for it since it is not your full mulk. After you indemnify the owners by paying them from your own halâl property of zakât the mithl (some kind) of the khabîth property, or its value in case its mithl is not available, it will be halâl for you to use the mulk-i-khabîth and you will have to add it to your calculation of nisâb. If you do not have enough halâl property to pay these debts of yours, you pay them by borrowing (from some of your acquaintances). Although it is harâm to use the mulk-i-habîth or to give it to someone; if you sell it or donate it as a gift, it will not be harâm for the person who buys it or accepts it as a gift. If the owners or the owners' inheritors are not known, or if the harâm goods collected from various people have been mixed with one another and thereby become mulk-i-khabîth, then all the mulk-i-khabîth must be dispensed as alms to poor Muslims.

If a poor Muslim returns as a gift something which he has been given as alms, then it will be permissible for the person who has given it to take it back.

Gold and silver are not used in their pure state. If they are more than fifty per cent pure, their zakât must definitely be paid and their weight must be taken as the basis of calculation. If two kinds of them exist out on the market and are being used as themen, the one with higher purity is called **jeyyid**, and the one with lower purity is called zuyûf. If their purity is below fifty per cent and are being used in trade, their zakât must be given when their value reaches the amount of nisâb for gold or silver, respectively.

Even if produce from land whose water is supplied by rain or streams is little or it is vegetable and fruit, which rot and moulder fast, one-tenth of it should be given to the official charged with collecting 'ushr. Thereafter the official sells the 'ushr he has collected and delivers the money to the treasury department called **Beyt-ul-mâl**. (Please scan the first and the twenty-ninth and the thirty-seventh chapters of the fifth fascicle of **Endless Bliss**.) There are scholarly narrations stating that it is farz to pay 'ushr for fruit when it appears or when it ripens or when it is reaped. One-twentieth of the crop is paid when watering is done by animal power or with a pump or an engine or other machinery. It should be paid before deducting the expenses whatsoever. It is not permissible for the government to donate the 'ushr to the owner of the property or to forgive or cancel it. 'Ushr is paid also for honey obtained from mountains or from land with 'ushr.

Zakât is not paid to dhimmîs. They can be paid sadaqa-i-fitr and/or vowed things or other alms. (Dhimmîs are non-Muslims living in a country of Muslims.) A non-Muslim who is not a dhimmî should not be paid alms that is farz or wâjib or nâfila (supererogatory), regardless of whether he is a muste'min one, (i.e. a non-Muslim who lives temporarily in a country of Muslims,) or a harbî one, (i.e. one who lives in a country of non-Muslims.) (Please scan the forty-sixth chapter of the fifth fascicle of **Endless Bliss**.)" If a poor Muslim is not in debt, it is makrûh to give him zakât as much as or more than the amount of nisâb. If the poor person has a family to support, i.e. wife and children, then it is permissible to give him a sum whose division into the number of the members of the family will be an amount somewhat below nisâb.

It is permissible to sell property in return for fulûs that is current on the market. Fulûs means monetary coins made of metals other than gold and silver, or paper money; because it is customarily used as themen (price), it does not necessarily have to be made ta'yîn of; i.e. it is not necessary to point it out, to show it. If it becomes kâsid, that is, if it is no longer current on the market, the sale (that is made) becomes bâtil (invalid) according to Imâm A'zam Abû Hanîfa 'rahima-hullâhu ta'âlâ'. (On the other hand,) according to the Imâmeyn, i.e. Imâm Abû Yûsuf and Imâm Muhammad 'rahima-humallâhu ta'âlâ', the sale does not become bâtil. Currency with equivalent value is paid. If fulûs, (i.e. metal or paper money,) becomes kâsid, (so that it is no longer currency on the market,) after being borrowed, its mithl, i.e. fulûs as much as the amount borrowed, is repaid, according to Imâm A'zam. According to the Imâmeyn, however, currency, (i.e. gold or silver,) whose value is equal to the amount borrowed is repaid. Buying and selling by using disused fulûs requires making ta'yîn of the fulûs, i.e. showing it. Property that is made ta'yîn of has (the attribute of) ta'ayyun. (Please see the twenty-ninth chapter of the fifth fascicle of **Endless Bliss** to acquire a notion of the terminology being used.) That means to say that once certain property has been made ta'yîn of, (i.e. shown,) that very property has to be given (in the transaction being carried out). Its likeness cannot be given. Supposing a person gives the money changer silver that weighs one dirham and asks the latter to give him fulûs for half a dirham of it and silver that weighs a habba lighter than half a dirham for the remaining half of it, the bey' (sale) will become fâsid. For, it is an act of fâiz (or fâidh) to sell half a dirham of silver in return for silver that weighs less than half a dirham. (Habba is a unit of weight equal to that of a grain of barley.) If he says, "Give me fulûs for half of this and give me silver that weighs a habba lighter than half a dirham for the remaining half of it," the sale of the fulûs will be sahîh (valid). If he says, "Give me fulûs that weighs half a dirham and silver that weighs a habba lighter than half a dirham in return for this one dirham of silver," then both the sales will be sahîh. For, silver that weighs a habba lighter will have been sold in return for silver with equal weight and half a dirham of fulûs will have been sold in return for silver that weighs a habba heavier than half a dirham of silver. Although the fulûs and the silver given in return for it differ in weight, the sale is permissible since they differ in genus as well.

It is stated in the book entitled **Bedâyi'us-sanâyi' fî tertîb-ish-sherâyi'**:[1] "Property to be paid as zakât has to be property of the same genus or property of zakât of a different genus. [It is not

---

[1] Written by Abû Bakr bin Mes'ûd Alâuddîn Shâshî Kâshânî 'rahmatullâhi ta'âlâ 'alaih' (d. 587 [1191 A.D.], Aleppo) as a commentary to the book entitled **Tuhfa-t-ul-fuqahâ**, which in turn had been written by his educator Alâuddin Muhammad bin Ahmad Samarkandî 'rahmatullâhi 'alaih' (d. 540 [1145 A.D.]).

permissible to pay the poor clothes, shoes, wheat, fat, or other similar things in lieu of gold.] Property of zakât is either an 'ayn or a deyn. Property of zakât that is an 'ayn is either measurable, by weight or by volume, or something which is not measured. If it is something not measured, it is either a sâima animal, or commercial 'urûz, (i.e. portable qiyamî property other than animals.) (Please see the seventeenth paragraph of the twenty-ninth chapter of the fifth fascicle of **Endless Bliss** for 'qiyamî'.) If it is a sâima animal; when the animal itself, which is defined in the Nass (âyat-i-kerîmas and hadîth-i-sherîfs with clear meanings) is to be given, a medium one is given. When a meagre one is to be given, its difference from a medium one is offset by also giving gold or silver equal to the difference in value. When the value of the animal is to be given, the value of a medium one, again, is given. When the value of a meagre one is to be given, then the difference is offset by adding gold or silver. In lieu of two medium sheep, it is permissible to give one fleshy sheep equivalent to the sum of their values. For, value is taken into consideration with property susceptible to fâiz (interest). Of the commercial 'urûz, one-fortieth of the property stated in the Nass is paid (as zakât). In case other property of the same genus is to be paid, payment of something of medium or lower quality entails offsetting the difference (in quality or value). For, 'urûz means property that is not measured by weight or by capacity. With urûz, difference of quantity does not cause fâiz. For instance, two suits of clothes of meagre quality can be given in lieu of one suit of good quality. When other property of a different genus is paid, payment of something below the amount that is farz necessitates offsetting the difference. When the property of zakât is something measured by weight or by capacity, one-fortieth of the property itself is paid. If one should pay property of zakât of a different genus, one has to pay an amount equal in value. If one should pay other property of the same genus, one pays the same amount, not an amount of the same value, according to the Shaikhayn, (i.e. Imâm A'zam Abû Hanîfa and his disciple Imâm Abû Yûsuf,) 'rahima-humallâhu ta'âlâ'. For instance, supposing the value of two hundred kilograms of good quality wheat is two hundred dirhams of silver, it is permissible to pay five kilograms of meagre quality wheat as its zakât. Likewise, in lieu of five dirhams of jeyyid (high quality) silver as the zakât of two hundred dirhams of jeyyid silver, five dirhams of zuyûf (low quality) can be paid. This rule applies in matters concerning nazr. (Please see the fifth chapter of the fifth fascicle of **Endless Bliss** for 'nazr'.)

"Gold and silver are absolute **themen**s (prices). They were created as themens. They are not used themselves for the purpose of satisfying people's needs. They are means for buying their vital needs. Other things, on the other hand, have been created both as themens and as things to be used themselves." Here we end our translation from **Bedâyi'**.

Things that man needs so that he may live comfortably and in a manner agreeable with Islam are termed **vital needs**. Please scan the tenth chapter of the book entitled **Ethics of Islam**! Vital needs change, depending on states, situations, and times wherein people live. Superfluous things that are not needed for a comfortable life and which are used for pleasure or as ornaments or to arouse admiration are called ornamental things (zînat, or zînet). Gold and silver are not among vital needs; they are ornamental things. Using ornamental things that are mubâh (permitted) is permissible for men both at home and outdoors, and for women only when they are at home.

As is seen, fulûs that is current is always commercial property. When its value reaches the amount of nisâb on the basis of the least valuable one of the gold coins being used at the market, it becomes farz to pay zakât for them. For, the nisâb amount of commercial property is calculated, according to the Imâmeyn (Imâm Abû Yûsuf and Imâm Muhammad 'rahima-humallâhu ta'âlâ', two most eminent disciples of Imâm A'zam Abû Hanîfa 'rahima-hullâhu ta'âlâ'), with gold or silver, preferably with the one that is more widely used in commercial transactions. And zakât for that property is either paid with the money, (i.e. gold or silver,) on the basis of which its value has been calculated or one-fortieth of the property is given. The poor person uses it for their vital needs. Fulûs means money other than gold and silver. It consists of metal coins minted from copper or bronze or other mixtures, or paper bills. That means to say that paper bills are fulûs. Zakât must be paid for them. However, their value, unlike the values of gold and silver, is not **real value**. It is **nominal value**. It is value attached by governments. They may undo their own making. When the nominal value (of fulûs) is gone, it can no longer be **themen** (price). It has lost its function as property of zakât. Ibni 'Âbidîn states: "Value of commercial property is calculated with gold or silver coins that have been minted as monetary units and which are oft-used for commercial purposes. Supposing the value of certain property is equal to two hundred and forty dirhams of silver when it is calculated with silver and twenty mithqal of gold when it is calculated with gold, its value is the amount of nisâb in both cases; however, that property should be evaluated on the basis of silver. For, the owner of the property will have to give six dirhams of silver or half a mithqal of gold, which is equivalent to the value of five dirhams of silver, and which in turn will be less advantageous to the poor person (to be paid zakât). [For, since twenty mithqals of gold and two hundred dirhams of silver indicate the same (amount of) nisâb, they are the same in value.] A gold coin that weighs one mithqal is called a **dinâr**. [All Turkish gold liras weigh one and a half mithqals, that is, 7.2 grams, each.] It is wâjib to pay zakât for the currency called fulûs [in gold or silver] which has been used to calculate its amount of nisâb." That means to say that nisâb for paper bills must be calculated with the one with the lowest value of the gold liras being used for commercial purposes and their zakât must be paid in gold. For, silver is no longer being used as currency now. Zakât for paper bills is paid in the metal, i.e. gold, which is being used in calculating their (amount of) nisâb. One-fortieth of their value cannot be paid in paper bills. For, paper bills themselves cannot be used for vital needs. It would be prodigality to use paper bills in lieu of scrap paper which is available. And prodigality, in turn, is harâm. Nor is it permissible to pay paper bills as zakât of paper bills so that they can be used as currency. For, there is the gold, the ever-valuable and genuine currency, which should always be preferred in the payment of zakât.

Gold can be paid, not only in coinage but also in any other form. It is available, always and everywhere. Supposing a Muslim cannot find gold in the city where he lives; then he sends paper bills to a friend of his living in a city where gold articles are being sold and writes to him to buy gold with the money and pay zakât on his behalf. It is permissible for him to pay his debt in paper bills afterwards. With this facilitated practicability in paying zakât for paper bills, it is not something justifiable to refuse to pay gold for the sake of paying paper bills with nominal and provisory face values, *afortiori* when the so-called preference is displayed at the cost of disobeying the commandment declared in Islam's books of Fiqh.[1] People who are reluctant to adapt themselves to the Islamic teachings supplied in books of Fiqh and who attempt to practise

---

[1] Please be sure to see the thirty-third chapter of the second fascicle of **Endless Bliss** for detailed information on the branch of Islamic teachings termed 'Fiqh'.

acts of worship in accordance with their own inferences from the Qur'ân's âyat-i-kerîmas, are called **lâ-madhhabî** people, (i.e. people without a certain Madhhab,) or **heretics**. Our reply to such heretics should be: "I perform my acts worship not in accordance with your inferences from the Qur'ân al-kerîm and from hadîth-i-sherîfs, but in agreement with what the Imâms of (the four) Madhhabs understood and explained." Books teaching the undestandings of the Imâms of Madhhabs 'rahima-hullâhu ta'âlâ' are called **books of Fiqh**.

Kitâb-ul-fiqh 'alal-madhâhib-il-erbe'a, prepared by a group of muderrisîn (professors) of the madrasa (university) of **Jâmi'ul edhher** presided over by Prof. 'Abd-ur-Rahmân Jezîrî, supplies all the teachings of Fiqh in four separate sets, each set of the teachings belonging to one of the four Madhhabs. The entire book, in five divisions, was printed in Cairo in 1392 hijri [1972 A.D.]. It states as follows in its chapter entitled 'Zakât for awrâq-i-mâliyya (banknotes)': "Savants of Fiqh stated that it is necessary to pay zakât for awrâq-i-mâliyya, i.e. paper bills. For they are being used in lieu of gold and silver in trade. They can always be exchanged with gold or silver easily. For a person who has plenty of paper bills not to add their value to that of their gold and silver as they calculate the amount of nisâb for zakât, and in effect not to pay zakât for them, is not something acceptable to the human mind. For that matter, savants of Fiqh in three Madhhabs unanimously stated that it is necessary to pay zakât for paper bills. The only Madhhab differring with this consensus is the Hanbalî Madhhab. Savants of the Hanafî Madhhab said that paper bills are **deyn-i-qawî** and that they can be exchanged for gold and silver at will and immediately. (Please scan the first chapter of the fifth fascicle of **Endless Bliss** for 'deyn-i-qawî'.) They added that for that matter zakât for them must be paid without delay. For, to pay zakât for a loan that is due becomes farz when gold or silver is taken possession of. Although zakât becomes farz before they are taken possession of, it does not become farz to pay it." In that case, you have two choices: You may either wait until you are able to collect them and pay zakâ for the passed years as well, or pay zakât for them as well yearly by spending the 'ayn gold an silver in your possession. You cannot pay the promissory notes in your possession as the zakât of the gold coins owed to you; when you collect the gold and silver coins written on the promissory notes from the debtor, it becomes farz for you to separate one-fortieth of them for each of the passed years and dispense them to the poor.

By the same token, paper bills cannot be paid as zakât. What must be done is to buy gold coins with the lowest value from a money changer by spending one-fortieth of them and dispense the coins you have bought, or gold rings and/or bracelets with a total weight equal to the coins, to the poor.

It is not permissible to absolve your debtor from his debt in return for the zakât you are to pay him in a way whereby the zakât and the debt are offset against each other, so that neither he (actually) pays you his debt nor you (actually) pay him zakât. You have to (actually) pay the zakât to the poor person, and thereafter he has to pay his debt by returning what he has been given. For a creditor who cannot believe that his debtor will return what he has been given, there is a technique suggested at the final part of the sixth volume of the book entitled **Fatâwâ-yi-Hindiyya**. It says: "The creditor shows a person whom he trusts to his debtor and says, 'Appoint this person your deputy to take the zakât which I am going to pay you and to pay me your debt.' Thereupon the poor debtor appoints that person his deputy. When that person takes the zakât, the property that he takes (as zakât) becomes the poor person's property. Thereafter he gives that property back to the rich person, and thereby the poor person's debt has been paid. Supposing a poor person owes debts to two different people and one of those people wants to absolve the poor person from his debt to him by paying him zakât as much as the poor person's debt to him; then he donates his due as alms to the poor person. Thereby he absolves the poor person from the debt in a way that is halâl. Thereafter the poor person returns (the gold paid him as) the zakât to the rich person as a gift. Or, the poor person borrows gold equivalent to his debt from someone and donates it as a gift to the rich person, who in his turn returns the gold to the poor person with the intention of paying him zakât, and absolves the poor person from his debt, that is, he forgives his debt. Thereafter the poor person returns the gold he has been paid as zakât (by the rich person) to the lender of the gold. (Property to be paid as) zakât [or property vowed] cannot be spent for pious acts or for charity (in lieu of paying zakât [or paying the property vowed]). For doing so you pay them (as zakât [or thing vowed]) to a poor person you know, and that person carries out the so-called acts of charity." As will be concluded from these examples, to manage to pay zakât in paper bills, you borrow ornamental gold articles the same weight as the gold coins you intend to pay in lieu of the paper bills from your wife or from one of your acquaintances. You give these gold articles with the intention of zakât to one of you poor acquaintances or relatives. Now you have paid zakât for your paper bills (by giving gold articles equal in weight to the gold coins which are equal in value to calculated amount of the paper bills to be paid as zakât). Thereafter the poor person donates the gold coins as a gift to you, and you in turn pay your debt by returning the gold articles to the lender. Since the zakât has been paid, you, the rich person, give some of the paper bills in your possession and which you have reserved for the purpose of paying zakât to the poor person. You can spend the remainder doing all sorts of charity you wish. If the poor person also wishes to attain a share from the thawâb that the charity yields, he sells you the gold coins that he has received as zakât. Thereafter he returns the paper bills to you and appoints you his deputy to dispense charity on his behalf.

Sayyid 'Abd-ul-Hakîm Arwâsî 'rahmatullâhi 'alaih' (1281 [1865 A.D.], Başkale, Van, Turkey–1362 [1943], Ankara), an expert in the teachings of all four Madhhabs, stated: "The value of paper money is a nominative value. When it is demonetized, it loses its value. Therefore, it is not permissible to pay fitra and/or zakât in paper money. The zakâts that you paid in paper money in the past should be made qadâ of, (i.e. reperformed,) by way of dawr with gold. All sorts of monetary acts of worship, with the exception of hajj, can be made qadâ of by way of dawr." (Please see the twenty-first chapter of the fifth fascicle of **Endless Bliss** for 'dawr'.)

It says as follows in Durr-ul-mukhtâr: If Bâghîs, i.e. Muslims who revolted against the government and seized power, and oppressive Muslim rulers collect the zakât of animals and the zakât (called 'ushr) of crops and dispense them (in manners and) at places commanded by Allâhu ta'âlâ, the property thereby collected (from Muslims) becomes zakât (and 'ushr) (of those Muslims). If, however, the so-called property is dispensed (otherwise and) at other places, that property collected will not stand for zakât (and/or 'ushr). Owners of the property will have to pay zakât (and/or 'ushr) again by dispensing it to poor Muslims. If the aforesaid authorities collect the zakât for commercial property and the zakât for money, it will not stand for zakât, according to a vast majority of Islamic savants. The fatwâ given agrees with their ijtihâd. According to other Islamic savants, since those oppressive rulers who collect them are Muslims (at the same time) and the property thereby collected belongs to the people by right, they will be held as poor people, and hence property paid to them with the niyyat (intention) of zakât will stand for zakât." **Ibni 'Âbidîn**'s account of the matter is as follows: "This rule applies also to property and money collected as taxes or duties or in any other nomenclature. The more common scholarly argument that property thereby collected will not stand for zakât despite the intention is the sahîh one. In other words, tyrannical Muslim rulers do not have the right to collect zakât for people's property." That the fatwâ agrees with this ijtihâd is written in **Tahtâwî**'s annotation (to the aforesaid book). As is seen, zakât paid for animals and 'ushr (paid for crops) will be sahîh (valid in Islam) only if the government who collects them is a Muslim government and dispenses them to people who have dues from the four departments of the State Treasury called **Beyt-ul-mâl**. None of the taxes paid to the government, according to most Islamic savants, will stand for zakât for property or money. There is a scholarly report stating that it will be permissible on condition that the government to collect them be known to be a Muslim government and the property and the money be given with the intention of zakât. The source of this report, however, is a da'îf (weak) one. (Please scan the sixth chapter of the second fascicle of **Endless Bliss** for the technical meaning of 'da'îf.)

Come on, o my brother, have reason and get over this obduracy!
Your life is so valuable, do not waste it in superfluity!

Protect your heart against the desires of the nafs!
Let your inside, like your outside, attain purity!

When gold is commingled with copper,
Will the money-changer receive it with jollity?

Do not boast with your diploma from a high school!
Think before you talk, lest you be involved in oddity!

Find a person of ma'ârif and harken to him!
So that from Haqq you attain kindness so plenty!

Go to the ocean of Haqîqat and dive therein,
And come up with something superb in quality!

Do not let an ignorant graduate mislead you!
The early scholars show you the way to purity!

CHAPTER ON FASTING

There are three fards in fasting:

1– To make a niyyat (intention).

2– To make the niyyat between the time of beginning of fasting and that of its end.

3– To avoid the nullifiers of fast during the nehâr-i-shar'î (daytime in Islamic tems), and ends at sunset. The time of imsâk is when the whiteness called fajr-i-sâdiq is sighted immediately over the line of ufq-i-zâhirî (apparent horizon). A person who avoids the nullifiers of fast until evening without having made niyyat (intention) for fasting (within the time dictated by Islam) will not have fasted that day. He will have to make qadâ of only that day's fast.

There are seven conditions to be fulfilled for its being farz for a person to fast:

1– To be a Muslim. 2– To have reached the age of puberty. 3– A child's fasting is sahîh. 4– To have reached the age of discretion. 5– For a Muslim living in the dâr-ul-harb to have heard that it is farz to fast (in Ramadân). 6– To be muqîm (stationary, i.e. not making a long-distance journey. Please see the fifteenth chapter of the fourth fascicle of **Endless Bliss**.) 7– (For a woman or a girl) not to be in a state of haid (menstruation). 8– (For a woman) not to be in a state of nifâs (lochia, puerperium).

There are six nullifiers of fasting: To eat food; to drink something to drink; haid; nifâs; to vomit a mouthful. Lying, backbiting, nemîma, i.e. talebearing among Muslims, and perjury are not among nullifiers of fasting. However, such acts will eliminate the thawâb to be earned by fasting.

Seven people (are entitled to) discontinue fasting:

1– An invalid; 2– A musâfir [the following day]; (A musâfir is a person making a long-distance journey called safar. He is also called a safarî person, versus the aforesaid muqîm person.) 3– (A woman going through her monthly period called) haid; 4– A woman in (her puerperal period called) nifâs; 5– A pregnant woman, if she is too weak to fast; 6– A woman in her period of lactation, if her fasting will be harmful to the baby; 7– A (person called) pîr-i-fânî (and who is too old and too weak to fast).

It is necessary to make niyyat (intention) daily for fasting. It is written in **Fatâwâ-i-Hindiyya**: "Niyyat is made with the heart. To get up for the (late-night meal called) Sahûr means to make niyyat." There are two kinds of niyyat for fasting: The first kind of niyyat is the niyyat that is made daily in the month of Ramadân, or for a fast that is nâfila (supererogatory) or for a fast that is performed for the fulfilment of a certain vow, and which has to be made between the previous day's sunset and the current day's time of **dahwa-i-kubrâ**. Dahwa-i-kubrâ is half the shar'î daytime, i.e. half the daily duration of fasting, which is calculated as follows in terms of azânî time:

$$\text{Fajr} + \frac{24 - \text{Fajr}}{2}, \text{ or Fajr} + 12 - \frac{\text{Fajr}}{2} = 12 + \frac{\text{Fajr}}{2}.$$

That means to say that the time of dahwa-i-kubrâ is half the number indicating the time of fajr in terms of azânî time. It is before zawâl (midday) by as long as the difference between half the shar'î daytime and that of the solar daytime in terms of standard time; that difference is equal to half the hissa-i-fajr, which in turn is the duration of time between sunrise and fajr, or time of imsâk. You fast by making niyyat by as late as the time of Dahwa-i-kubrâ – if you have not eaten or drunk anything (after the time of imsâk). It is not permissible to make niyyat at the time of Dahwa. The niyyat to be made before fajr should be as follows: "I make niyyat to fast tomorrow," whereas the niyyat to be made after fajr should be: "I make niyyat to fast today."

The second kind of niyyat is for qadâ or for kaffârat or for nazr-i-mutlaq. These three kinds of fasting require the same kind of niyyat, i.e. the second kind of niyyat. Its earliest time is the previous day's sunset, and its latest time is immediately before the fajr-i-sâdiq, i.e. before whiteness on the horizon is sighted. Niyyat after dawn –for any one of these three kinds of fasting– is not permissible. It is written in Ibni 'Âbidîn, at the final part of the chapter wherein namâz of qadâ is dealt with, that as you make qadâ of several days' fast that you failed to perform in the month of Ramadân of a certain past year you do not have to state the days with respect to their names or order of precedence. There are three grades of fasting, depending on the people who fast: Unlearned people's fasting; learned people's fasting; and fasting performed by Enbiyâ (Prophets) and by Awliyâ (blessed people who have attained love of Allâhu ta'âlâ). When unlearned people fast, they do not eat or drink or have sexual intercourse. But they commit other wrong acts. Learned people do not commit other wrong acts, either. The Enbiyâ and the Awliyâ avoid all sorts of doubtful acts as they fast.

There are three kinds of 'Iyd, depending on the people who celebrate it after fasting: 'Iyd of unlearned people; 'Iyd of learned people; and 'Iyd of Enbiyâ and Awliyâ. Unlearned people (break their fast and) have (the meal called) iftâr in the evening, eating and drinking whatsoever they like, and say, "This is our 'Iyd." Learned people as well have iftâr in the evening, but they say, "It is our 'Iyd if Allâhu 'adhîm-ush-shân is pleased with our fasting." And they think pensively, "What will become of us if He is not pleased with our performance!" The 'Iyd of Enbiyâ and Awliyâ is ru'yetullah. They have deserved the grace of Allâhu 'adhîm-ush-shân.

There are five kinds of 'Iyd for all Believers:

1st one is when the angel on a Believer's left hand side cannot find anything in the name of evil acts.

2nd one is when, during a Believer's agony of death (sekerât-ul-mevt), angels of glad tidings come onto him and greet him and give him the good news that he is a Believer and bound for Paradise.

3rd one is when a Believer arrives in his grave and finds himself in one of the Gardens of Paradise.

4th one is when a Believer finds himself sitting with Enbiyâ and Awliyâ and 'Ulamâ and Sulehâ in the shade under the 'Arsh-ur-Rahmân on the day of Rising.

5th one is when a Believer has answered all the questions that he shall be asked at seven places throughout his trek along the bridge called 'Sirât', which is thinner than a hair, sharper than a sword, and darker than a night's darkness, and which is a way of a thousand years downhill, a thousand years uphill, and a thousand years level. If he fails to answer the questions, he shall be tormented for a thousand years for each failure. Of the seven questions, the first one shall be on îmân, the second one shall be on namâz, the third one shall be on fasting, the fourth one shall be on hajj, the fifth one shall be on zakât, the sixth one shall be on rights of creatures, and the seventh one shall be one ghusl, on istinjâ, and on ablution. (Istinjâ means cleaning one's front or back after urination or defecation, which is explained in detail in the sixth chapter of the fourth fascicle of **Endless Bliss**.)

If a person intentionally breaks (before sunset) his fast for which he made niyyat before the time of imsâk, he will have to make both kaffârat and qadâ. (Breaking) a supererogatory fast or a fast of qadâ (within the distance) does not necessitate kaffârat.

For making kaffârat, a slave is manumitted. A person who cannot afford it fasts for sixty days running and outside of the days of Ramadân and the five days on which it is harâm to fast. In addition, he fasts with the intention of qadâ for as many days as the number of days whereon he broke his fast (prematurely). [It is harâm to fast on the first day of the 'Iyd of Ramadân or on any of the four days of the 'Iyd of Qurbân.] A person who cannot afford it, either, he feeds sixty poor people twice daily for one day or one poor person twice daily for sixty days. Or he gives each and every one of them property whose amount is equal to that which is paid as fitra.

For making qadâ of one day's fast, you fast for one day.

Five people do not have to make kaffârat. The first one is an ailing person. The second one is a musâfir, (i.e. one who is on a long-distance journey called safar.) The third one is a woman undergoing lactation and who did not fast lest it should be harmful. The fourth one is a pîr-i-fânî. The fifth one is a person who fears dying of hunger or thirst.

When their 'udhrs no longer exist, these people will have to make qadâ only a day for a day.

As for niyyat for a yevm-i-shekk,[1] there are a few kinds of it: For a yevm-i-shekk it is permissible, although with kerâhat, to make niyyat (to fast) for a day in Ramadân or for another fast that is wâjib or to make niyyat to fast for a day in Ramadân, if it is Ramadân, or for a fast that is nâfila (supererogatory) or which is not wâjib, if it is not (a day in) Ramadân. Another kind of niyyat is one that is without kerâhat and which is made for sheer fasting or for (a fast in) Sha'bân, which means to make niyyat for a nâfila fast. (Kerâhat means something, e.g. a manner, a time, wherein it is not liked or advised by our blessed Prophet 'sall-Allâhu 'alaihi wa sallam' to perform a certain act such as an act of worship. If that act is a supererogatory one, it should not be done within a time of kerâhat. If it is an act that is farz and which you have not done it

_____

[1] It means a doubtful day, lexically. In the Islamic terminology, it means a day that is not certainly known to be the first day of Ramadân or the last day of Sha'bân.

although it has to be done before its prescribed time is over, you have to do it even at the cost of having done something with kerâhat. Please see 'times of kerâhat' towards the end of the tenth chapter of the fourth fascicle of **Endless Bliss**.)

A kind of fasting that is never permissible is one which is performed by making niyyat like this: "I make niyyat for fasting if the month (we are in) is Ramadân; if not, I am without a niyyat."

Supposing a person does not make niyyat for fasting till after fajr, i.e. till after whiteness appears on the eastern horizon, in Ramadân, and eats something before noon; this person does not have to make kaffârat, (which means to fast for sixty days running after Ramadân,) according to Imâm A'zam Abû Hanîfa. According to the Imâmeyn, however, this person has to make kaffârat. For, he has eaten while it was possible for him to make niyyat and perform his fasting. If he eats in the afternoon, he does not have to make kaffârat – according to the unanimous ijtihâd.

Supposing a person violated the latest two or three months of Ramadân, breaking his fast prematurely once in each of the blessed months, does he have to make kaffârat for each violation separately, or will it be sufficient to make kaffârat once for all two or three violations? This matter is controversial (among Islamic scholars). It will be prudent to make kaffârat for each violation separately. Supposing a person has debt(s) of fast belonging to Ramadân; according to some scholarly statements, that person becomes sinful if one year elapses and that person still has not paid his debt(s) by fasting for the day(s) owed.

Supposing the time of one of the two yearly 'Iyds, i.e. the 'Iyd of Ramadân-i-sherîf or the 'Iyd of Qurbân, comes as a person makes kaffârat, i.e. as he performs the successive sixty-day fasting for kaffârat, –as is known, it is harâm to fast on the days of 'Iyd, whatsoever the reason for fasting–, he will have to resume his fasting for kaffârat from the beginning. His former fasts will not be added (so as to complement the sixty-day fasting).

If a person breaks his fast without having made his niyyat for a safar (long-distance journey) and thereafter makes his niyyat for a safar and leaves, he will have to make both qadâ and kaffârat, (i.e. he will have to fast for that one day of violated fast and also for sixty successive days for the penalty called kaffârat.) A long-distance journey does not make it mubâh (an allowed act) to break a fast. When a person leaves for a safar, it is wâjib for him not to break his fast during that day. If a musâfir makes his niyyat (for fasting) by night or any time before the time called Dahwa-i-kubrâ, it is not halâl for him to break his fast during that day. If he breaks his fast, he will only have to make qadâ of it, (i.e. he will have to fast for one day after the blessed month of Ramadân.) What a long-distance journey makes mubâh is: 'not to start a (daily) fast'.

If a person loses his mind during Ramadân, so that he cannot fast, and recovers afterwards, he makes qadâ of the days whereon he failed to fast. If he does not recover throughout Ramadân, so that his mental disorder lingers, then he becomes absolved from that Ramadân's fast.

If a person forgets that he is observing fast and breaks his fast, his fast does not become fâsid (nullified). If he remembers that he is observing fast but goes on eating because he thinks that his fast has become fâsid, then he will have to make qadâ of it (after Ramadân). Kaffârat will not be necessary. However, if he goes on eating although he knows that his fast has not become fâsid, then he will have to make both qadâ and kaffârat.

If a fasting person swallows his own sweat or chews a dyed piece of string and then swallows the dye on it or swallows someone else's saliva or swallows his own saliva after having let it leave his mouth or swallows a food remain between his teeth and bigger than a chickpea or injects himself with a hypodermic medicine, his fast becomes nullified and he will only have to make qadâ.

If a person eats a piece of paper or a handful of salt or swallows a grain of raw wheat or rice, his fast becomes nullified. However, he will only have to make qadâ. For, it is not customary to eat a handful of salt, neither as food, nor as medicine. It is like a handful of soil. On the other hand, if the salt eaten is a small amount, then kaffârat also will be necessary. This is written in the book entitled **Eshbâh**. For, a small amount of salt is used both as food and as medicine.

If a worker knows that he will fall ill as he works for a living, it (still) is not permissible for him to break his fast before he becomes ill. If he breaks his fast (before the time of iftâr), he will have to make kaffârat. To avoid (having to make) kaffârat, he should swallow a piece of paper first, (i.e. before eating something.) If a pregnant woman or a breastfeeding woman feels too weak (–with hunger, thirst, etc.– to go the distance with her fasting) eats (or drinks), she will only have to make qadâ. A person who eats and drinks floutingly without an 'udhr to do so on a day of Ramadân becomes a murtadd (renegade, apostate). (Fatâwâ-i-Feyziyya.)

If a person only chews a grain of sesame, his fast does not become fâsid. However, if he swallows it, regardless of whether he chewed it or not, his fast becomes fâsid. It will be necessary to make qadâ of it.

There are fifteen kinds of fast: three of them are farz, three of them are wâjib, five of them are harâm, and four of them are sunnat. Fasts that are farz are: fasting in Ramadân, fasting for making qadâ, and fasting for kaffârat.

Fasts that are wâjib are: fasting for a nazr-i-mu'ayyen, fasting for a nazr-i-mutlaq, and to carry on a nâfila fast until sunset once you have started performing it.

Fasts that are harâm are: fasting on the first day of the 'Iyd of Ramadân and on any of all four days of the 'Iyd of Qurbân. It is harâm to fast on any of these five days.

Fasts that are sunnat are: Fasting on the eyyâm-i-beydhî of every (Arabic) month, on the days called sawm-i-Dâwûd, on Mondays, on Thursdays, on the 'Ashûra day, on the 'Arafa day, and on similar blessed days. The fourteenth and fifteenth and sixteenth days of Arabic months are called **eyyam-i-beydhî**. Fasting every other day, and not fasting on the days in between, yearly, is called **sawm-i-Dâwûd**. (The **'Ashûra day** is the tenth day of Muharram, the first Arabic month. The **'Arafa day** is the ninth day of the Arabic month Du'l-hijja, i.e. the day previous to the first day of the 'Iyd of Qurbân.)

There are eleven benefits in fasting:

1– It shields you against Hell.

2– It causes other acts of worship (which you have performed) to be accepted (by Allâhu ta'âlâ).

3– It is a dhikr performed by one's body.

4– It breaks one's kibr (arrogance, conceit, vanity).

5– It breaks one's 'ujb (egoism, taking pride in one's acts of worship).

6– It enhances khushû' (fear of Allâhu ta'âlâ).

7– The thawâb earned for it will be on the mîzân (balance to weigh one's good deeds in the Hereafter).

8– Allâhu is pleased with His (fasting) slave.

9– If one dies with îmân, it, (i.e. one's fasting,) will cause one to enter Paradise early.

10– One's heart becomes brilliant with nûr.

11– One's mind becomes enlightened with nûr.

When the Sun sets on the twenty-ninth day of Sha'bân, it is wâjib to look for Ramadân's new moon on the western apparent horizon. When a Muslim who is 'âdil, i.e. who does not commit a grave sin, and who is in the Madhhab of Ahl as-sunnat, sees the new moon in an overcast sky, he notifies the law court judge or the governor. Ramadân commences upon a Muslim's sighting the new moon. Information offered by a person who holds a bid'at or who is fâsiq is not taken into account. In clear weather several notifiers are needed (as eye-witnesses in determining the beginning of Ramadân). If the new moon is not sighted, the month of Sha'bân (of the current year) is accepted to consist of thirty days, and the day thereafter is, admittedly, (the first day of the month of) Ramadân. Beginning of Ramadân is not determined with a calendar or by way of astronomical calculations. It is written in the books entitled **Bahr-ur-râiq** and **Fatâwâ-i-Hindiyya** and **Qâdikhân**: "If a slave living in the **Dâr-ul-harb** and unaware about the beginning of Ramadân uses the information on a calendar and fasts for one month, he may have started to fast one day earlier than the first day of Ramadân or on the second day or exactly on the first day of Ramadân. In the first case he has observed fast one day before Ramadân and celebrated the 'Iyd on the last day of Ramadân. In the second case he has not observed fast on the first day of Ramadân, and observed fast on the 'Iyd day with the intention of fasting on the last day of Ramadân. In either case he has observed fast on twenty-eight of the days of Ramadân; therefore he will have to fast for two days with the intention of qadâ after the 'Iyd. In the third case, it is doubtful whether the first and last days of a month wherein he has observed fast coincide with Ramadân. Since fast observed on days doubtful to be within Ramadân will not be sahîh, he will have to make qadâ of fast for two days in this case as well." Hence, people who begin their fasting for Ramadân not after sighting the new moon in the sky but under the guidance of previously prepared calendars will have to fast for two days with the intention of qadâ after the 'Iyd of Ramadân. How to calculate the first day of Ramadân is explained at length in the tenth chapter of the fourth fascicle of **Endless Bliss**.

[Ibni 'Âbidîn 'rahima-hullâhu ta'âlâ' states: "In overcast

weather iftâr should not be made, (i.e. fast should not be broken,) unless one is convinced that the Sun has set, even if the azân (to annouce the time of evening prayer [and that of iftâr]) has been performed, (i.e. called.) As long as one makes iftâr before the (time called) ishtibâk-un-nujûm, i.e. by the time most of the stars appear in the sky, one has carried out the act of mustahab called 'ta'jîl' (and which means 'making haste for the iftâr). When sunset is observed and iftâr is made at a certain location, a person who is at an elevated place, e.g. one who is on a minaret, should not make iftâr unless he knows that the Sun has set. This rule applies also to morning prayer and sahûr." In the tabulated lists of **Tamkin** in books of Astronomy, height is one of the variables of the length of time called tamkin, (which is defined and explained in detail in the tenth chapter of the fourth fascicle of **Endless Bliss**.) As all prayer times are being calculated, a single time of tamkin is used for a certain location, i.e. the time of tamkin commensurate with the highest place of that location. (Please see appendix V of the fourth fascicle of **Endless Bliss** for the table of tamkins.) Calendars prepared without the periods of tamkin being taken into account provide sunset times a few minutes earlier (than times of sunset in the calculation of which the periods of tamkin has been taken into consideration). The Sun does not appear to have set at the time of sunset (written on those calendars). Fast performed by people who make iftâr in keeping with calendars without tamkins becomes fasid.]

THERE ARE THREE CONDITIONS (to be fulfilled) FOR (the performance of) QURBÂN:

1. To be a discreet and pubescent Muslim.

2. To be muqîm (settled, i.e. not to be safarî).

3. To possess property sufficient to fulfil the amount of nisâb.

The rukn (fundamental principle) for (the animal to be killed as the) Qurbân being a sheep or a goat or a camel or a bovine animal (like a bull or a cow or an ox), a camel or a bull (or cow or ox) passes for seven qurbâns, which means that seven people may have an ox (or bull or cow) killed as the qurbân for all seven of them. If another person says, "Let me join you," that eighth person's qurbân becomes fâsid (null and void). The nisâb for Qurbân is the same for the nisâb for Fitra, (which is dealt with in detail in the third chapter of the fifth fascicle of **Endless Bliss**.)

[As is stated by Ibni 'Âbidîn 'rahima-hullâhu ta'âlâ', if the share of any one of them is less than one-seventh, none of the seven people's qurbâns will be permissible. Therefore, it is permissible for fewer than seven people to come together for the common qurbân. It is sahîh (valid) to participate during the purchase. Although it is sahîh to participate after the purchase as well, it is better to participate before the purchase. A person may perform Qurbân in partnership with another person by buying from one-seventh to six-sevenths of the bull (or cow or ox) owned by the latter. They share the meat in direct ratio to the partners' shares. If one of the partners dies, it will be sahîh if his heirs says (to the other partners), "Perform the Qurbân on his behalf and on your own behalves." For, it is (an act of) Qurbat to perform the Qurbân on behalf of a dead Muslim. If the heirs do not say so, the dead partner's qurbân will not be Qurbat and none of the partners' qurbâns will be sahîh. If one of the partners is a disbeliever or if he joined the partnership (only) for the meat, none of the partners' qurbâns will be permissible. For, each partner has to make niyyat for Qurbat. A disbeliever's niyyat is bâtil (null and void). To make one's niyyat for eating, on the other hand, is not (an act of) Qurbat. Likewise, if one of the partners makes niyyat for the current year's Qurbân and the others make niyyat for the next year's Qurbân, the others' niyyat is bâtil (null and void) and the meat that falls to their shares becomes tetawwu' [alms], and they have to dispense it as alms to the poor. The niyyat made by the first one is sahîh (valid), but then he cannot eat the meat. For, the judgment that the meat has to be dispensed as alms has spread throughout the meat. The Qurbat for which niyyat is made does not necessarily have to be a Qurbat that is wâjib. It might as well be a Qurbat that is sunnat or nâfila. It might as well be a Qurbat consisting of various acts of wâjib. It is permissible as well for it to be an 'Aqîqa for a child or an adult. (Please see the final paragraph of the fourth chapter of the fifth fascicle of **Endless Bliss** for 'Aqiqa.) For, 'Aqîqa is a Qurbat performed as a thanksoffering for having been blessed with a newborn baby. As well, a congregate dining where Muslims are entertained to celebrate the performance of a nikâh (marriage contract made in a manner dictated by Islam, and which is explained in detail in the twelfth chapter of the fifth fascicle of **Endless Bliss**), is a kind of thanksoffering and a Qurbat that is sunnat. The most meritorious thing to do is for all the partners to make their niyyat for the Qurbân of 'Iyd. To kill an animal for 'Aqîqa is not an act of sunnat in the Hanafî Madhhab. It is mustahab or mubâh. An act of mustahab is a Qurbat. An act of mubâh also is a Qurbat when it is performed with the niyyat of thanksoffering. There is many another customary act which becomes an act of worship owing to the niyyat made. A mubâh as well becomes an act of tâ'at when one's niyyat is made (for tâ'at). The Arabic books entitled **'Uqûd-ud-durriyya** and **Durr-ul-mukhtâr** provide detailed information about killing (by jugulation) an animal for 'Aqîqa.]

HAJJ HAS THREE RUKNS:

1– To make niyyat for hajj as you assume the (special garb called) ihrâm.

2– To perform (the stand-still called) waqfa on the (hill called) 'Arafât.

3– To perform the Tawâf-i-ziyârat (at the Ka'ba).

The early time for performing waqfa on the 'Arafât is between the time of zawâl (midday) on the ninth day of Dhu'lhijja and the following morning. [If you stand for waqfa one day earlier or one day later the hajj you perform becomes bâtil (null and void). Wahhâbîs celebrate the 'Iyd (of Qurbân) one day earlier, without having seen the new moon (the previous evening). Hajj performed by people who do not stand for waqfa within the prescribed time is not sahîh (valid).]

There are seven kinds of tawâf (circumambulations around the Ka'ba-i-mu'azzama within the Masjîd-i-harâm):

The first one is the tawâf-i-ziyârat.

The second one is the tawâf for 'umra. (These two kinds of tawâf are farz.)

The third one is the tawâf-i-qudum, which is sunnat.

The fourth one is the tawâf for wadâ (farewell).

The fifth one is the tawâf for nazr, which is wâjib.

The sixth one is the tawâf-i-nâfila.

The seventh one is tawâf of tetawwu' (or tatawwu'), which is mustahab.

It is farz to make niyyat to assume the ihrâm for hajj. It is sunna to put on the piece(s) of cloth called ihrâm. It is wâjib to avoid wearing sewn clothes.

There are eight conditions to be fulfilled for it to be farz for a person to perform hajj:

1– To be a Muslim.

2– To have reached the age of puberty.

3– To have reached the age of discretion.

4– To be healthy.

5– No to be a slave.

6– To possess property in excess of a person's essential needs.

7– For it to be time for hajj. Time for hajj is the 'Arafa day and the four days of 'Iyd (of Qurbân). Time to be spent on the way is added to the calculation.

8– For a woman as far (from Mekka) as it will take for a (long-distance journey called) safar –three days' walk, or around a hundred and four kilometres in the Hanafî Madhhab,– to be accompanied either by her husband or by a male and mahram relative with whom she is eternally forbidden to make (an Islamic marriage contract called) nikâh. [It is farz for people who fulfil these eight conditions to perform hajj once in their entire life-time. If they perform hajj more than once, the hajj that they perform in later years is a nâfila hajj. An act of **worship that is nâfila** is one that is performed of one's own volition although it is not farz or sunnat (to perform it). Thawâb for nâfila worship, when compared with thawâb for farz worship, is as less as a drop of water compared with water in an ocean. Islamic scholars have not consented to a second performance of hajj by Muslims living in places far from Mekka. 'Abdullah-i-Dahlawî 'quddisa sirruh' states as follows in the sixty-third letter of his valuable book entitled **Mekâtîb-i-sherîfa**: "On a journey undertaken for making hajj, it is mostly impossible to perform acts of worship properly. For that matter, Imâm Rabbânî 'rahmatullâhi 'alaih' states in his hundred and twenty-third and hundred and twenty-fourth letters (in the first volume of his blessed work entitled Maktûbât) that he does not approve of going (on a journey) for the purpose of making 'Umra or nâfila hajj."[1] Nâfila hajj is harâm if it prevents performance of an act of worship that is harâm or a woman's covering herself properly. To go for a nâfila hajj of this sort incurs sinfulness, rather than yielding thawâb. So is the case with going on a journey for making 'Umra.

---

[1] Both letters were written to Molla Tâhir Bedakhshî. English versions of the letters and a brief biography of Tâhir Bedakhshî have been appended to the current book.

THE FIFTY-FOUR FARZES (or FARDS)

A child becomes a **Muslim** when it reaches the age of puberty, and so does a non-Muslim who utters the **Kalima-i-tawhîd**, i.e. says, "**Lâ ilâha il-l-Allah Muhammadun rasûlullah**," and believes what is meant by this utterance. All the sins committed by the non-Muslim until that time become pardoned then and there (by Allâhu ta'âlâ). However, these two people, like any other Muslim, have to memorize the six fundamentals of îmân, which are called Âmentu in the aggregate, whenever they have time, learn their meanings and believe them, and say, "I believe (the fact) that the entire Islam, i.e. all the commandments and prohibitions (in the aggregate), has been declared by Allâhu ta'âlâ." Later on, whenever they have time and favourable conditions, it is also farz for them to learn the farz ones, i.e. the commandments, and the harâm ones, i.e. the prohibitions among all Islam's teachings pertaining to ethical and behavioral conduct and new situations that they come up against. If they deny or disbelieve or scoff at the fact that it is farz to learn these teachings and that it is farz to perform any one of the farz ones and to avoid any one of the ones which are harâm, they become a **murtadd** (renegade, apostate). In other words, a person who scoffs at any one of these teachings, e.g. women's covering themselves (in a manner dictated by Islam, becomes a murtadd. Unless a murtadd makes tawba for the cause of their apostasy, they will not become a Muslim by saying, "**Lâ ilâha il-l-Allah** or by doing some of Islam's commandments such as performing namâz, fasting, going on hajj or by doing good deeds or acts of charity. Nor will they reap any benefits for these good deeds of theirs in the Hereafter. They have to repent and make tawba for their denial, i.e. for the Islamic tenet they have refused to believe.

Islamic scholars have culled fifty-four of the farzes that every individual Muslim has to believe and observe:

1– To know that Allâhu ta'âlâ is One and never to forget Him.

2– To eat and drink what is halâl.

3– To make an ablution.

4– To perform the daily five namâzes, each when its time comes.

5– When you are to perform namâz, to make a ghusl from haid (if you are a girl or a woman) and from junub.

6– To know for certain and believe that Allâhu ta'âlâ

guarantees a person's rizq (sustenance).

7– To wear clean and halâl clothes.

8– To work and put your tawakkul (trust) in Allâhu ta'âlâ.

9– To be contented.

10– To express gratitude to Allâhu ta'âlâ for His gifts. That is, to use them at places (and in manners) commanded.

11– To welcome the qadâ that comes from Jenâb-i-bârî with resignation.

12– To be patient about dramatic events. That is, not to protest against them.

13– To make tawba for the sins (committed). [To say (the prayer called) istighfâr daily.]

14– To perform acts of worship with ikhlâs. (That is, to worship only for the grace of Allâhu ta'âlâ, for the purpose of pleasing Allâhu ta'âlâ.)

15– To look on human and genie devils as your enemy.

16– To hold the Qur'ân-i-'adhîm-ush-shân as a document, proof-text. To be resigned to its rulings.

17– To know that death is haqq (Allâhu ta'âlâ's Will), and to make preparations for death.

18– To love whatsoever and whosoever is loved by Allâhu ta'âlâ and avoid all which (and whom) he dislikes. [This is called Hubb-i-fillah and bughd-i-fillah.]

19– To be good to one's parents.

20– To encourage doing good and to discourage from doing evil.

21– To visit one's mahram relatives.

22– Not to abuse someone's trust.

23– To fear Allâhu ta'âlâ all the time and avoid committing harâm acts.

24– To obey Allâhu 'adhîm-ush-shân and His Messenger. That is, to perform the farz acts and to avoid the harâm ones.

25– To avoid sinning and to spend one's time doing worship.

26– Not to disobey the ulu-l-emr and not to violate the laws.

27– To look at the entire creation around you with deep admiration.

28– To meditate over the existence of Allâhu ta'âlâ, i.e. over

His Attributes and creatures.

29– To protect one's tongue against harâm and indecent talk.

30– To purify one's heart from mâ-siwâ [love of this world].

31– Not to mock at anybody.

32– Not to look at something harâm (to look at).

33– To keep your promises whatsoever the cost.

34– To protect your ears against listening to sinful things like indecent talks and musical instruments.

35– To learn farzes and harâms.

36– To use balances and tools of measurement with integrity.

37– Not to be complacent about the torment that Allâhu 'adhîm-ush-shân may conflict on you and to always feel fear.

38– To pay zakât to poor Muslims and to help them.

39– Not to give up hope of the mercy of Allâhu 'adhîm-ush-shân.

40– Not to indulge in the harâm desires of your nafs.

41– To feed a hungry person for the grace of Allah.

42– To work and earn sufficient rizq, [i.e. food, clothes, and dwelling.]

43– To pay zakât for your property and 'ushr for your crops.

44– Not to have sexual intercourse with your wife during her menstrual and lochial periods.

45– To keep your heart purified from sins.

46– To avoid being arrogant.

47– To protect the property of an orphan that has not reached the age of puberty.

48– Not to be close to young boys.

49– To perform the daily five namâzes in time and not to leave them to qadâ, (i.e. not to delay them until their prescribed times are over.)

50– Not to extort anyone's property.

[It is a human right to pay the money called mahr to your wife when you divorce her. Not to pay that right incurs a severe penalty in the world and bitter torment in the Hereafter. Of the human rights, the most important one is to do emr-i-ma'rûf to your relatives and to people under your command, (i.e. to teach them

Islam,) and it incurs the severest torment (in the Hereafter) when neglected. Hence, a person who prevents them and all other Muslims from learning their religion and from practising their acts of worship by having recourse to persecution and stratagems is an unbeliever and an enemy of Islam. An example of this is bid'at holders' and lâ-madhhabî people's defiling the belief of Ahl as-sunnat and misguiding Muslims out of Islam and îmân by way of subversive speeches and publications.]

51– Not to attribute partners to Allâhu 'adhîm-ush-shân.

52– To avoid fornication.

53– Not to consume wine and other alcoholic beverages.

54– Not to perjure yourself.

[Wine and Spirit and all other alcoholic beverages are qaba najâsat, (one of the two kinds of najâsat defined and explained in detail in the sixth chapter of the fourth fascicle of **Endless Bliss**.) It is written in the books entitled **Bahr-ur-râiq** and **Ibni 'Âbidîn** that when water and earth are mixed with each other the resultant mud will be clean when one of the two ingredients is clean, that this qawl is a sahîh one, and that the conclusive fatwâ is agreeable with this ijtihâd. Although there are scholars who argue that that fatwâ is a da'îf one, it is written in **'Ibni 'Âbidîn** and in **Hadîqa** that a da'îf qawl may be acted upon when there is haraj (difficulty). Hence, if the substances mixed with alcohol to obtain purposive materials such as eau-de-colgone, varnish, alcoholic medicines and dyes are clean, the mixtures also will be clean. It is written in the commentary made by Suleymhan bin 'Abdullah Shi'rîdî 'rahmatullâhi ta'âlâ 'alaih' to Molla Halîl Shi'rîdî's 'rahmatullâhi ta'âlâ 'alaih book entitled **al-Ma'fuwât** that that rule applies in the Shâfi'î Madhhab as well. They will not prevent namâz (from being sahîh) if there is haraj in cleaning them. Theoretically clean as these liquids are on account of haraj (in cleaning them), it is not permissible to drink them unless there is a darûrat to do so. Alcoholic beverages are never clean. For, the alcohol in these beverages have been mixed with other substances not for the purpose of satisfying a need but for pleasure. Anything smeared with them becomes najs as well. It is always harâm to drink them without a darûrat.]

CONCERNING the GHUNÂH-I-KEBÂIR
(GRAVE SINS)

There are many kinds of grave sins, which are called ghunâh-i-kebâir. Seventy-two of them are as follows:

1– Unjust homicide.

2– To commit fornication.

3– Sodomy is harâm in every religion.

4– To drink wine or any other sort of alcoholic beverages.

5– Thieving.

6– To eat or drink narcotics.

7– To lay hands on someone else's property by using force. That is, to commit extortion.

8– To bear false witness.

9– Without an 'udhr, to eat before other Muslims during the blessed month of Ramadân.

10– Ribâ, i.e. to borrow or lend property or money at an interest.

11– To swear solemnly time and again.

12– To disobey your parents.

13– To cease from making sila-i-rahm to mahram relatives who are sâlih Muslims. (Sila-i-rahm means visiting your close relatives.)

14– In a war, to desert from the battlefield and run away from the enemy.

15– To utilize an orphan's property without the orphan's consent. It is stated as follows towards the end of the two hundred and sixty-sixth page (of the tenth edition) of the fifth fascicle of **Endless Bliss**: "The (orphan's) executor cannot pay the deceased's debts with the orphan's property. Nor can he pay the orphan's fitra or perform the Qurbân for the orphan (out of the orphan's property). But the (orphan's) father can. If the executor becomes needy, he can utilize the orphan's property, but he cannot donate it to someone else."

16– Not to use your scales or measures properly.

17– To perform daily five namâzes before or after their (prescribed) times.

18– To hurt your Believer brother's heart.

19– To make a false statement under the pretense of giving a quotation from Rasûlullah 'sall-Allâhu 'alaihi wa sallam' although in fact the statement does not belong to the Prophet.

20– To take a bribe.

21– To avoid bearing true witness.

22– Not to pay zakât or 'ushr for your property.

23– When you see a person committing a sin, not to try to dissuade him although you could.

24– To burn an animal alive.

25– After learning (how to read) the Qur'ân 'adhîm-ush-shân to forget how to read it.

26– To give up hope of mercy of Allâhu 'adhîm-ush-shân.

27– To betray people's trust; it makes no difference whether they are Muslims or non-Muslims.

28– To eat pork, which is harâm.

29– To hate and curse any one of Rasûlullah's Sahâba 'ridwânullâhi ta'âlâ 'alaihim ajma'în'.

30– To continue eating after being satiated; it is harâm to do so.

31– For a woman to avoid conjugal act with her husband (without any good reason).

32– For a woman to go out to visit an acquaintance without her husband's permission.

33– To accuse a chaste woman of fornication.

34– Nemîma, i.e. to practise talebearing among Muslims.

35– To show one's awrat parts to others. [A man's awrat parts are between their navel and their knees. A woman's hair, arms and legs also are within her awrat parts.] To look at others' awrat parts.

36– To eat flesh of an (edible) animal that died (of itself). Such flesh is called 'lesh'. As well, an (edible) animal that has been killed in a way disagreeable with the way dictated by Islam is called 'lesh', (and it is no longer edible.)

37– To commit a breach of trust.

38– To backbite a Muslim.

39– To be jealous.

40– To attribute a partner to Allâhu 'adhîm-ush-shân. (This evil deed is called shirk [polytheism].)

41– To lie.

42– Arrogance, to think of oneself as superior.

43– For a person in his death bed to disinherit a heir (somehow).

44– To be avaricious and very miserly.

45– To be fond of the world, [harâms, that is.]

46– Not to be afraid of torment to be inflicted by Allâhu ta'âlâ.

47– If a certain thing is harâm, not to believe that it is harâm.

48– If a certain thing is halâl, not to believe that it is halâl.

49– To believe a fortune-teller's words about people's fortunes and about the ghayb (unknown, future).

50– To abandon one's religion, to become a murtadd (renegade).

51– To look at someone else's wife or daughter without an 'udhr to do so.

52– For women to wear men's clothes.

53– For men to wear women's dresses.

54– To commit sins within the harem-i-sherîf.

55– To call the azân or to perform namâz before prayer time comes.

56– To disobey state authorities, to violate laws.

57– To liken your wife's mahram parts to your mother's mahram parts.

58– To swear at one's wife's mother.

59– To aim a gun to each other.

60– To eat or drink a dog's leftovers.

61– To taunt (someone) about the favours you have done (them).

62– For men to wear silk clothes.

63– To persist in remaining ignorant. [To not learn the belief of Ahl as-sunnat, farzes, harâms, and all sorts of necessary learnings.]

64– To swear on names other than the Name of Allâhu ta'âlâ or by mentioning names other than those which are stated by Islam.

65– To run away from knowledge.

66– Not to understand that ignorance is an evil.

67– To persistently carry on with committing venial sins.

68– To laugh with an uproarious laughter without an 'udhr to do so.

69– To remain junub for such a length of time as will cause you to miss one of the daily prayer times.

70– To have sexual intercourse with your wife during her menstrual or lochial period.

71– To make melody. To sing indecent songs. To play musical instruments.

Mirzâ Maz-har-i-Jân-i-Jânân 'rahima-hullâhu ta'âlâ', one of India's greatest Islamic scholars, states as follows in his book entitled **Kalimât-i-tayyibât** and in Persian: "It is a unanimous statement (by Islamic scholars) that it is harâm to play any kind of musical instrument or to listen to them being played. There is a scholarly statement that the flute is the only instrument that is makrûh to play and that it is mubâh (permitted) to play the drum at a wedding. [As the Qur'ân al-kerîm is being read or recited melodiously or the azân is being performed melodiously, it is harâm if the meaning is changed or a phoneme is reiterated (so as to change the meaning). It is stated as follows in the book entitled **al-Fiqh-u-'alal-Madhâhib-ul-erba'a**: "It is harâm to perform the azân melodiously. It is not permissible to listen to such performances." It is called **teghannî** or **simâ'** to read (or recite) a well-proportioned utterance in a well-proportioned voice.

Teghannî means to utter, (read or recite) in a mellifluous voice that is pleasing to hear. There are two kinds of reading (or reciting) the Qur'ân al-kerîm or performing the azân or the mawlid or ilâhîs (eulogies) with teghannî:

1– Teghannî that is sunnat and which therefore yields thawâb, (i.e. rewards in the Hereafter. It is to perform them in keeping with the science that is called 'tejwîd' (and which teaches how to read or recite the Qur'ân al-kerîm properly). Teghannî of this kind invigorates hearts and souls.

2– Teghannî that is forbidden, harâm, is to perform them melodiously and musically. This kind of teghannî causes mispronunciation; It distorts the phonemes and changes their meanings. Tunes produced by such performers sound pleasant and sweet to the nafs al-ammâra. They make people overcome by their own nafses weep, cry and frolic about, which in turn makes them unaware about the meanings and makes it impossible for their hearts and souls to get over oblivion and illness.

It is stated as follows in the hundred and sixty-second page of **Terghîb-us-salât** (written by Muhammad bin Ahmad Zâhid 'rahmatullâhi ta'âlâ 'alaih', d. 632 [1234 A.D.], India,) and in the thirteen hundred and forty-second page of the second volume of **Berîqa** (written by Muhammad bin Mustafâ Hâdimî 'rahmatullâhi ta'âlâ 'alaih', d. 1176 [1762 A.D.], Hâdim, Konya, Turkey,) and in the five hundred and eighty-ninth page of the second volume of **Hadîqa** (written by 'Abd-ul-Ghanî bin Ismâ'îl Nablusî, 1050 [1640 A.D.], Damascus – 1143 [1731], the same place:) "You should not ride an animal furnished with bells for the purpose of enjoying yourself, for it is makrûh to do so. For, bells are the devil's musical instruments. Angels of Mercy do not descend on caravans (with animals) furnished with bells." (However,) it is permissible to do so for some business or benefit.

There is a unanimous scholarly statement that it is harâm to read or recite poetry incompatible with Islam and ethics or to read or recite it at places of fisq where musical instruments are being played and alcoholic beverages are being consumed and/or men and women enjoy themselves together even if the poetry itself is compatible with Islam and ethics or to listen in mixed groups at such places to recitals of poetry that are performed at other places and which are being broadcast or televised or played on the radio or on television or on a tape-recorder or for women and boys to perform such recitals in mixed choruses.] It is permissible to read or recite proper poetry at proper places. It may infuse tenderness to (listeners') hearts and thereby cause Compassion of Allâhu ta'âlâ. Some scholars did not feel an attraction even to the mubâh (permitted) version of simâ' (singing). Their unwillingness to simâ' stemmed from the idiosyncratic repulsion inherent in their nature and which prevented it from appealing to them. This natural disinclination, however, did not induce the blessed scholars into repudiation or denial of their valuable colleagues who felt inclined towards simâ'." It is harâm to read or recite the Qur'ân al-kerîm or mawlids or ilâhîs (eulogies) or salawât-i-sherîfs (special prayers said for Rasûlullah and sent as a gift to his blessed soul) at places of fisq, even if it is performed with due respect. (Places of fisq are places where sins are being committed.) It is kufr (unbelief) if it is done for pleasure or amusement. It is written in the sixth page of **Durr-ul-ma'ârif**: "Musical instruments and voices of women and boys are ghinâ (sinful music) and harâm. Useful poetry is simâ' and mubâh, unless it is performed (in such manners and) with such voices."

72– Suicide, i.e. to kill oneself, is a sin graver than homicide. A suicide is subjected to torment of Hell in grave. If he does not die at once and makes tawba, all his sins will be forgiven. He will not be subjected to torment in his grave. [Validity (being sahîh) of tawba made for omitted namâzes is contingent on their having been (paid by being) made qadâ of. A person who begins to make qadâ (of namâzes which he omitted) has virtually made niyyat to perform prayers of qadâ till the end of his life. In return for this niyyat of his, all his debts of qadâ will be forgiven. Likewise, supposing an unbeliever becomes a Believer and makes tawba for having been an unbeliever or a heretic holding (a heresy called) bid'at makes tawba for having been a heretic, they have virtually made niyyat not to relapse into unbelief and heresy, respectively, and not to resume the evil deeds that they had been committing in those old days of nescience. In return for this niyyat (sincere intention) of theirs, all their sins are forgiven.]

AWRAT PARTS
and
WOMEN'S COVERING THEMSELVES

It is stated as follows in the chapter dealing with 'nikâh (marriage contract prescribed by Islam)' in the book entitled **Eshi'at-ul-leme'at** (written by 'Abd-ul-Haqq Dahlawî 'rahmatullâhi ta'âlâ 'alaih', 958 [1551 A.D.] – 1052 [1642]):

1– Abû Hurayra 'radiy-Allâhu 'anh' narrates: Someone came to Rasûlullah 'sall-Allâhu 'alaihi wa sallam' and said: "I want to marry a girl from the Ansâr." The blessed Prophet stated: "**See the girl** [once]**. There is something in the eyes of** (the people belonging to) **the tribe of Ansâr.**" This hadîth-i-sherîf is quoted in the book entitled **Sahîh-i-Bukhârî**. It is sunnat to see the girl to be married once beforehand.

2– 'Abdullah ibni Mes'ûd 'radiy-Allâhu 'anh' narrates: Rasûlullah 'sall-Allâhu 'alaihi wa sallam' stated: "**Women should not tell their husbands about the beauty and goodness of the other women whom they have been seeing. It will be as if their husbands saw those women.**" This hadîth-i-sherîf is quoted in the books entitled **Sahîh-i-Bukhârî** and **Sahîh-i-Muslim**.

3– Abû Sa'îd-i-Hudrî 'radiy-Allâhu 'anh' (d. 64 [683 A.D.]) narrates: Rasûlullah 'sall-Allâhu 'alaihi wa sallam' stated: "**A man**

should not look at another man's awrat parts, and a woman should not look at another woman's awrat parts!" As is seen, it is harâm for men to look at women and for women to look at men's awrat parts, and likewise it is harâm for men to look at other men's awrat parts and for women to look at other women's awrat parts. A man's awrat parts (which are harâm) for other men (to look at) are between their knees and navels. The same rule applies among women. As for a woman's awrat parts (that are harâm) for men (to look at); they are her entire body with the exception of her hands and face. Hence, women are called awrat(s). Regardless of whether a woman is a Muslim or non-Muslim, it is harâm to look at a nâ-mahram woman's face with shahwa (lust), and it is harâm to look at her awrat parts even without lust.

4– Jâbir bin 'Abdullah 'radiy-Allâhu 'anh' (martyred in 74 [693 A.D.]) narrates: Rasûlullah 'sall-Allâhu 'alaihi wa sallam' stated: **"Do not spend the night at a nâ-mahram woman's house!"**

5– 'Aqaba bin Âmir 'radiy-Allâhu 'anh' narrates: Rasûlullah 'sall-Allâhu 'alaihi wa sallam' stated: **"Do not stay with a nâ-mahram woman in private in a room! If a woman stays in private with her husband's brother or with the latter's son, she will be drifted as far as death.**" That is, she will cause fitnas, (which in turn means disastrous results.) No effort should be spared to avoid it. This hadîth-i-sherîf is quoted in **Sahîh-i-Bukhârî** and in **Sahîh-i-Muslim**.

6– 'Abdullah ibni Mes'ûd 'radiy-Allâhu 'anh' narrates: Rasûlullah 'sall-Allâhu 'alaihi wa sallam' stated: **"A woman's body is awrat.**" That is, it must be covered. **"When a woman goes out, the satan looks at her all the time.**" (That is, he uses her as a decoy to beguile men and to lead them to committing sins.)

7– Burayda 'radiy-Allâhu 'anh' narrates: Rasûlullah 'sall-Allâhu 'alaihi wa sallam' said to Hadrat 'Alî: **"Yâ 'Alî! When you see a woman turn your face away from her. Do not look at her again! It is not sinful to see her unexpectedly. Yet it is sinful to look at her again.**" It is quoted by Abû Dâwûd and by Dârimî.

8– 'Alî 'radiy-Allâhu 'anh' narrates: Rasûlullah 'sall-Allâhu 'alaihi wa sallam' stated: **"Yâ 'Alî! Do not expose your thigh, and do not look at someone else's thigh, dead or alive!**" This hadîth-i-sherîf is quoted by Abû Dâwûd and by Ibni Mâja. Hence, looking at a dead person's awrat parts is like looking at a living person's awrat parts. [We must do our utmost to avoid looking at sportsmen's and swimming people's awrat parts.]

9– 'Abdullah ibni 'Umar 'radiy-Allâhu 'anhumâ' (d. 73 [692 A.D.], Mekka) narrates: Rasûlullah 'sall-Allâhu 'alaihi wa sallam' stated: "**Do not expose your awrat parts**! [Do not expose them even when you are alone.] **For, there are creatures who never leave you alone. Be ashamed in their presence and respect them**!" They are the angels called Hafadha, who protect you against genies and who leave you alone only when you are in the toilet and during your conjugal activity.

10– Umm-i-Salama 'radiy-Allâhu 'anhâ' relates: Meymûnâ 'radiy-Allâhu 'anhâ' and I were with Rasûlullah 'sall-Allâhu 'alaihi wa sallam', when Ibni Umm-i-Mektûm 'radiy-Allâhu 'anh' asked for permission (to enter) and entered. When Rasûlullah 'sall-Allâhu 'alaihi wa sallam' saw him he said to us: "**Withdraw behind the curtain**!" When I said, "Isn't he blind? He won't see us," "**Are you blind, too? Will you not see him**," said the Best of Creation. In other words, he said: "His being blind will not make you blind as well." This hadîth-i-sherîf is quoted by Imâm Ahmad and by Tirmuzî and by Abû Dâwûd 'rahima-humullâhu ta'âlâ'. According to this hadîth-i-sherîf, as it is harâm for a man to look at a woman nâ-mahram to him, likewise it is not permissible for a woman to look at a man nâ-mahram to her. The imâms (scholars) of our (four) Madhhabs 'rahima-humullâhu ta'âlâ', taking other hadîth-i-sherîfs as well into consideration, said: "It is difficult for a woman not to look at a nâ-mahram man's head and hair. Commandments that are difficult to do are **'azîmat**s. A man's awrat parts for a woman are between his knees and navel. It is easy not to look at those parts. Commandments that are easy to do are **rukhsat**s.

[As is seen, the Ezwâj-i-tâhirât (the pure wives of our blessed Prophet, i.e. Muslims' mothers,) 'radiy-Allâhu ta'âlâ 'anhunna' and the Sahâba-i-kirâm 'radiy-Allâhu 'anhum' preferred the way of 'azîmats and avoided the rukhsats. The casuistry which argues that women "did not cover themselves during the time of the Prophet. Today's dramatic spectacles wherein we watch women covering themselves like ogres did not exist in that time. Hadrat 'Âisha, for one, went about bare-headed. The present custom of women's covering themselves was invented later by fanatics and people of fiqh," is a hideous slander spread by British plotters whose real purpose is to demolish Islam from within and by **zindiq**s. It is true that women's covering themselves was not an Islamic commandment formerly. It was sometime between the third and fifth years of the Hegira (Hijrat) when women were commanded to cover themselves. Babanzâda Ahmad Na'îm Begh

(1290 [1872 A.D.] – August 14th 1352 [1934], Edirnekapı, Istanbul) writes in his (Turkish) book entitled **Tecrîd-i-sarîh Tercemesi** that the âyats of hijâb (women's covering themselves) were revealed piecemeal at three different occasions.]

11– Behz bin Hakîm, one of the greatest people among the Tâbi'în, narrates on the authority of his father and grandfather: Rasûlullah 'sall-Allâhu 'alaihi wa sallam' stated: "**Cover your awrat parts! Do not let anyone see them, with the exception of your wife and jâriyas! Feel shame in the presence of Allâhu ta'âlâ as well!**" This hadîth-i-sherîf is quoted by Tirmuzî, by Abû Dâwûd, and by Ibni Mâja 'rahima-humullâhu ta'âlâ'. Jâriya is called **mulk-i-yemîn**, which means mulk (property) of the right hand. For, a jâriya is examined with the right hand during the purchase, and the money for the jâriya is paid with the right hand.

12– 'Umar-ul-Fârûq 'radiy-Allâhu 'anh' narrates: Rasûlullah 'sall-Allâhu 'alaihi wa sallam' stated: "**If a man makes halwat with a woman nâ-mahram to him**, (i.e. if he and the woman stay together in a room without anyone else with them,) **the Satan joins them as the third person**." This hadîth-i-sherîf is quoted by Tirmuzî. [It is harâm to make halwat with a nâ-mahram woman, i.e. for a man and a woman to stay in private in a closed place. Ibni 'Âbidîn states as follows in his discourse on being an imâm: "If there is another man or a woman who is one of the (first) man's relatives called zî-rahm-i-mahram, the event will not be halwat."]

13– Jâbir bin 'Abdullah 'radiy-Allâhu 'anh' narrates: Rasûlullah 'sall-Allâhu 'alaihi wa sallam' stated: "**Do not visit women whose husbands are away! For,** (if you do so,) **the Satan will circulate like blood in your veins**." When they said, "Will he circulate in yours as well," the Darling of Allâhu ta'âlâ stated: "**Yes. He will circulate in mine, too. Yet Allâhu ta'âlâ has helped me against him. He has made him a Muslim, so that he has surrendered himself to me**." This hadîth-i-sherîf is quoted by Tirmuzî 'rahima-hullâhu ta'âlâ'.

14– Umm-i-Salama 'radiy-Allâhu 'anhâ' narrates: Rasûlullah 'sall-Allâhu 'alaihi wa sallam' was with me (in my room). My brother 'Abdullah bin Abî Umayya's slave was in the room, too. That slave was muhanneth (effeminate). When Rasûlullah 'sall-Allâhu 'alaihi wa sallam' saw that muhanneth person and heard his voice he said: "**Do not admit people like this one into your house!**" This hadîth-i-sherîf is quoted in **Sahîh-i-Bukhârî** and **Sahîh-i-Muslim**. Muhanneth is a man (or boy) who behaves, acts, talks, sounds, and dresses like a woman. People who do so are accursed. A hadîth-i-sherîf states as follows about them: **"May Allah condemn men who make themselves resemble women and women who make themselves resemble men!"** Women who wear clothes like men's and have their hair cut like men and do things that are to be done by men and men who grow their hair long like women and adorn themselves like women, without an 'udhr compelling them to do so, are within the scope of this hadîth-i-sherîf. Misver bin Mahrama 'radiy-Allâhu 'anh' was born in the second year of the Hijrat (Hegira). He is the son of 'Abd-ur-Rahmân bin 'Awf's sister 'radiy-Allâhu 'anhumâ'. He relates: I was carrying a big stone, when the clothes I was wearing fell down. I failed to lift them up. Rasûlullah 'sall-Allâhu 'alaihi wa sallam' saw me in that state. **"Lift your clothes up! Do not go out without a cover!"** This hadîth-i-sherîf is quoted in **Sahîh-i-Muslim**. This hadîth-i-sherîf interdicts both men's and girls' being without something to cover themselves in streets or at beaches or in sports fields.

16– Abû Umâma 'radiy-Allâhu 'anhâ' narrates: Rasûlullah 'sall-Allâhu 'alaihi wa sallam' stated: **"If a person who sees a girl's beauty turns his eyes away from her, Allâhu ta'âlâ bestows on him thawâb for a new act of worship and he immediately relishes its flavour."** This hadîth-i-sherîf is quoted by Imâm Ahmad bin Hanbal 'rahima-hullâhu ta'âlâ'.

17– Hasan Basrî 'rahmatullâhi 'alaih' narrates the following hadîth-i-mursel:[1] Rasûlullah 'sall-Allâhu 'alaihi wa sallam' stated: **"May Allâhu ta'âlâ condemn a person who exposes his parts of awrat and one who looks at another's awrat parts!"** This hadîth-i-sherîf is quoted in Imâm Bayhakî's book entitled **Shu'ab-ul-îmân**.

18– 'Abdullah ibni 'Umar 'radiy-Allâhu 'anhumâ' narrates: Rasûlullah 'sall-Allâhu 'alaihi wa sallam' stated **"If a person makes himself resemble a certain tribe** (group of people), **he will become one of them!"** This hadîth-i-sherîf is quoted by Imâm Ahmad and Abû Dâwûd 'rahima-humullâhu ta'âlâ'. That means to say that if a person makes his behaviour, his acts, or the clothes he wears to those of enemies of Islam, he will become one of them. [This hadîth-i-sherîf should be a warning to people who keep up with unbelievers' fashions and who call harâms 'fine arts' and who call people committing harâms 'artists'.]

---

[1] Please see the sixth chapter of the second fascicle of **Endless Bliss** for kinds of hadîth-i-sherîfs.

19– 'Amr Shu'ayb narrates on the authority of his father and grandfather: Rasûlullah 'sall-Allâhu 'alaihi wa sallam' stated: **"Allâhu ta'âlâ likes to see the gifts which He has given His slave."** This hadîth-i-sherîf is quoted by Tirmuzî 'rahima-hullâhu ta'âlâ'. As is seen, Allâhu ta'âlâ likes (a person's) clothes to be smart and clean. He likes a person who makes them (and one who wears them) in order to show the gift. He dislikes one who makes them (and one who wears them) to flatter their own vanity. It is not permissible to conceal the gifts bestowed by Allâhu ta'âlâ. Knowledge, as well, is a gift bestowed by Allâhu ta'âlâ.

20– Jâbir bin 'Abdullah 'radiy-Allâhu 'anh' narrates: Rasûlullah 'sall-Allâhu 'alaihi wa sallam' came to our place. There was someone with dishevelled hair in the house. When the Prophet saw him he said: **"Has he been unable to find something to tidy his hair with?"** When he saw someone with dirty clothes he said: **"Doesn't he have something to wash his clothes with?"**

21– Abu-l-ahves, one of the Tâbi'în, narrates on the authority of his father: I went to Rasûlullah's 'sall-Allâhu 'alaihi wa sallam' place. My clothes were old and worn. **"Don't you have property,"** he asked. I said that I had property. He asked again: **"What kind of property do you have?"** "I have all kinds of property," I said. Thereupon the highest of all creatures said: **"When Allâhu ta'âlâ gives** (you) **property, He should see its tokens on you!"** This hadîth-i-sherîf is quoted by Imâm Ahmad and by Nesâî 'rahima-humullâhu ta'âlâ'. Here we end our translation from the third volume of the book entitled **Eshi'at-ul-leme'at**.

22– It is stated as follows in Yusûf Qardâwî's book entitled **al-Halâl-u-wa-l-harâm-u-fi-l-islâm**: The Islamic religion prohibits a woman from covering herself with material thin enough to show what is under it. It is stated as follows in a hadîth-i-sherîf quoted in the books entitled **Sahîh-i-Muslim** and **Muwattâ**: **"Women who are covered (but) naked and (women) whose heads bulge upwards like humps of camels shall not enter Paradise. They shall not even receive the smell of Paradise. On the other hand, the smell of Paradise reaches very distant places."** This hadîth-i-sherîf prohibits women from wearing thin, transparent and closely fitting dresses, stockings and headgears and from winding their hair into balls atop their heads. To dress like this is (as sinful as) going about naked. Muslim women and girls should not wear thin and tight dresses and should not wind their hair or the hair on the wigs that they are wearing into balls like camel-humps on their heads. They should know that these sinful acts are bad enough to take a person to Hell.

[That Qardâwî is a man of religion without a certain Madhhab has been stated earlier in the text. The Islamic religion declares that it is farz for women to cover themselves properly and describes the cover to be used. This description does not go into details as to the kinds of the material to be used or the dresses or skirts or coats to be worn. It is written in books of Fiqh that it is farz for women to cover themselves (in a manner described) and that kinds of the covers to be used and dresses to be worn are a matter of **sunnat-i-zewâid**, which in turn consists of sunnats that pertain to customs, rather than worship. For that matter, the kind of the cover to be used should preferably be one that has been customary. It is makrûh not to cherish the custom in something that does not pertain to worship. In fact, it is harâm if it arouses fitna. It is stated in **Hindiyya**: "It is permissible to look at a woman wearing something thick and ample. It is not permissible to look at a tightly dressed woman. It is harâm to look lustfully at the face of a woman who has covered herself (properly). It is makrûh to do so even without lust if there is no reason to do so. The same rule applies to looking at non-Muslim women. It is permissible to look only at their hair, according to a scholarly statement."

To wear an ample, thick, and dark-coloured overall-like coat that extends down to the heel-bones and which covers the arms and wrists is better than (wearing an overgarment called) a charshaf (and) which is made up of two parts. It is stated in **Halabî-yi-kebîr**: "A free (Muslim) woman's hair that hangs down to her ears is (within her) awrat (parts), according to unanimity (among Islamic scholars). So is the case with its part hanging down below the ears, according to a majority of scholars. According to some scholars, the hanging part is not awrat during namâz. However, it is not permissible for a man nâ-mahram to her to look at that part, either." She must cover her entire hair with a thick headgear. The front part of the middle of the headgear must stick to her forehead and extend down to her eyebrows, its both sides must be made to extend to the outer ends of he eye-brows, make a downward turn, extend down to her chin, being pinned together on her chin and their ends hanging over her breast; and the middele part of its back side must cover the upper part of her back. If it is likely that a fitna will arise, the cheeks also must be covered. She must as well wear thick and dark stockings. If one-fourth of the hanging part of a woman's hair remains exposed as long as one rukn (in namâz), the namâz she performs will not be sahîh. And it will be makrûh if a smaller part remains exposed (that long). Not a single Islamic book discriminates young from old concerning the woman's age. There are Islamic scholars who have stated that it is permissible to acknowledge an old woman's greeting or to make musâfaha (shake hands)[1] with her or to make halwat with her, (i.e. to stay together with her in a closed room;) yet not a single Islamic scholar has stated that it is permissible for an old woman to expose her hair or (for men who are nâ-mahram to her) to look at her (exposed) hair. Some Islamic scholars have said that it is permissible to look at a non-Muslim woman's hair. But none of them has said that it is permissible to look at an old Muslim woman's hair. The Islamic scholars who have stated that it is permissible for an old woman to enter a mosque or to visit a cemetery have stipulated that her hair must be covered properly.

It is not right to say, "It is stated in the fifty-ninth âyat of Ahzâb Sûra that Muslim women should cover themselves with a **jilbâb**. This âyat commands them to cover themselves with charshaf, which consists of two parts." If this âyat commanded (women) to wear charshaf, Rasûlullah's 'sall-Allâhu 'alaihi wa sallam' blessed wives and the wives of the Sahâba 'radiy-Allâhu ta'âlâ 'anhum ajma'în' would have worn charshaf. But no Islamic book reports any one of them to have worn charshaf. The Turkish book of Tafsîr entitled **Tibyân** explains it (this âyat) as a commandment that women "should cover their heads." It is stated in the book of Tafsîr entitled **Jelâleyn** that it, (i.e. jilbâb,) is a headgear which women wear in such a manner as it will hang over their face. Sâwî explains this, saying: "It consists of a headgear and a dhir', i.e. a piece of cloth laid over the garment." It is written as follows in the books of Tafsîr entitled **Rûh-ul-beyân** and **Abu-s-su'ûd**: "Jilbâb is a headgear that is laid on the gauze that is wrapped around the head so as to prevent the hair from becoming untidy; the jilbâb is wider than the gauze; it extends down to the breast and covers the jeyb, [i.e. the neck opening, bosom,] of the garment. In this âyat-i-kerîma, women are being commanded to cover their heads and their entire bodies." The books entitled **Zewâjir** and **al-Fiqh-u-'ala-l-madhâhib-ul-erba'a** quote a hadîth-i-sherîf showing that jilbâb is (a clothing which is) worn by men as well and explain that the jilbâb for men is a long garment called qamîs (chemise). A set of woman's outdoor clothing consisting of a long coat and a thick headgear and the kind of clothing called charshaf and made up of

---

[1] Please see the sixty-second chapter of the third fascicle of **Endless Bliss**.

two parts are equal in carrying out the commandment pertaining to women's covering themselves and which is cited above. Women should cover themselves compatibly with the local customs of their environment so that they should not arouse fitna. It is written in the twenty-sixth page of the sixth chapter of the book entitled **Sahîh-i-Bukhârî** that a part of the âyat-i-kerîma commanding women to cover their awrat parts was revealed on the day when the nikâh of Zeyneb 'radiy-Allâhu 'anhâ' was performed. The nikâh was made in the third year of the Hegira.]

A person who professes to be a Muslim has to know whether anything he is to do is agreeable with Islam. If he doesn't, he has to learn by asking a scholar of Ahl as-sunnat or by reading books written by such scholars. If what he is going to do is not agreeable with Islam, he will not be safe against sinfulness or irreligiosness. A true tawba should be made daily. A sinful or irreligious act will definitely be forgiven (by Allâhu ta'âlâ) if tawba is made for it. If tawba is not made, torment in the world and in Hell, i.e. punishments shall be experienced. The punishments to be inflicted are written at various places of the current book.

Men's and women's body parts that must be covered when performing namâz and elsewhere are called **awrat parts**. "**It is harâm to expose one's awrat parts or to look at others'** (exposed) **awrat parts.**" It is sunnat for a man to cover his feet (e.g. by wearing socks) when performing namâz. A person who says that there are no awrat parts in Islam becomes an unbeliever. Our religion commands us to cover our awrat parts. A place where there is a man or woman with exposed awrat parts or where musical instruments are being played and/or people are gambling and/or alcoholic beverages are being consumed and/or people are listening to women singing is called **a place of fisq**. It is harâm to go to places of fisq. The heart also must be pure. The heart's being pure means its being beautified ethically. The heart is purified by obeying Islam. People who disobey Islam cannot have pure hearts. If a person says, "halâl," about exposing one of the parts of the body that are said to be awrat by ijmâ' (consensus of all Islamic scholars), i.e. which are awrat in all four Madhhabs, or about looking at others' awrat parts, i.e. if he does not fear being tormented for that sinful act, he becomes an unbeliever. The same rule applies to women's exposing their parts of awrat, singing or performing Mawlid in the presence of men. Parts of a man's body between his knees and groin are not awrat in the Hanbalî Madhhab only.

A person who says, "I am a Muslim," has to learn the essentials of îmân and Islam and the farzes and harâms unanimously taught by all four Madhabs, i.e. taught by ijmâ' (consensus) and esteem them highly. It is not an 'udhr not to know them. That is, it is like knowing them and denying them. "**The entire body of a woman, with the exception of her face and hands, is awrat,** (that is, it must be covered,) **in all four Madhhabs**." If a Muslim indifferently exposes a part of his or her body on which there has not been an ijmâ', i.e. which is not awrat according to only one of the other three Madhhabs, he or she will have committed a grave sin according to his or her own madhhab, although they will not become a kâfir (unbeliever). An example of this is men's exposing parts between their knees and groins. It is farz for a Muslim to learn what he or she does not know. Once they have learned about it they have to make tawba immediately and cover that limb of theirs.

A BELIEVER'S QUALIFICATIONS

There are seven rights that a Believer has to observe with reference to another Believer:

To participate in his invitations.

Iyâdat, [i.e. to visit him when he is ill.]

To go and take part at his funeral.

To offer him advice.

To greet him (as is taught in the sixty-second chapter of the third fascicle of **Endless Bliss**).

To rescue him from a tyrant's oppression.

To say, "Ye-r-hamukallah," when he sneezes and thereupon says, "Al-hamd-u-lillah."

The good Believer is the one who has developed the following six faculties:

He performs worship. He learns knowledge. He does not do evil. He avoids harâms. He does not cast covetous eyes at anyone's property. He never forgets death.

A note: It is stated in a hadîth-i-sherîf: "**Everyone will like people who do them favours. This liking is inherent in the human nature**." A person who is indulgent towards the desires of his nafs like people who help him to attain the desires of his nafs. A wise and knowledgeable person, on the other hand, will like people who help him to become a cultivated person. In short, good people will like good people. Evil people will like evil people. How a certain person is will be judged by observing the people he likes and prefers to make friends with. We should treat everyone with a similing face and with sweet words, friend and foe alike, and Muslim and non-Muslim alike, with the exception of people of bid'at. The most useful favour to be granted to people and the most valuable present to be given to them is to talk pleasantly with them and to smile at them. When we see people worshipping an ox, we should feed straw to the mouth of the ox, thereby forestalling their enmity towards us. We should not dispute with anyone. Disputes will impair friendships and exacerbate enmities. We should not be angry with anyone. Anger will cause neuralgia and heart diseases. A hadîth-i-sherîf dissuades: "**Do not become wrathful**!" (In this hadîth-i-sherîf the blessed Prophet advises us to avoid anger.)

A person will be a good (and useful) one if he conceals four things:

1– His poverty;

2– His alms;

3– His afflictions;

4– His troubles.

Paradise pines after four people:

1– A person whose tongue makes dhikr.

2– A person who is a hâfid-i-kalâmullah.

3– A person who feeds people.

4– A person who fasts in the blessed month of Ramadân.

Every person should never cease from the seven utterances written below:

They should say the Basmala-i-sherîfa whenever they are to start doing something (good, useful, or permissible). (To say or make the Basmala means to say, "**Bismillâh-ir-Rahmân ir-Rahîm**.")

They should say, "**Al-hamd-u-lillah**," whenever they are through with something (good or useful or permissible).

They should add the utterance, "**Inshâ-Allah**," whenever they say, for instance, "I will go to (a certain place)."

They should say, "**Innâ lillah wa innâ ilaihi râji'ûn**," whenever they hear sad news.

They should make tawba and istighfâr whenever they say (or do) something wrong. (To make tawba means to repent for a certain sin, to be resolved and to promise Allâhu ta'âlâ not to repeat the sin. To make istighfâr means to say, "Estaghfirullah," and thereby to beg Allâhu ta'âlâ for forgiveness.)

They should often say the Kalima-i-tayyiba, i.e. say, "**Lâ ilâha il-l-Allâhu wahdahu lâ sherîka leh, lehul-mulku wa lehul-hamdu wa huwa 'alâ kulli shey'in qadîr.**"

They should often say the Kalima-i-sherîfa, i.e. say, "**Esh-hedu an lâ ilâha il-l-Allah wa esh-hedu anne Muhammadan 'abduhu wa Rasûluh.**"

They should say the following, day and night:

1– "**Estaghfirullah.**"

2– "**Subhân-Allâhi wa-l-hamd-u-lillâhi wa lâ-ilâha il-l-Allâhu wallâhu ekber wa-lâ-hawla wa-lâ quwwata illâ billâh-il'aliy-yil 'adhîm.**"

CONCERNING AKHLÂQ-I-HAMÎDA
(Laudable Moral Qualities)

There are some seventy-two moral qualities that would look lovely on a person:

Îmân; belief of Ahl as-sunnat; ikhlâs; ihsân; tewâdu'; dhikr-i-minnat; nasîhat; tasfiya; ghayrat; ghibta; sekhâ; îsâr; muruwwat; futuwwat; hikmat; shukr; ridâ; sabr; khawf; rejâ; bughd-i-fillah; hubb-i-fillah; hamul; istiwâ-i-dhem wa med-h; mujâhada; sa'y; qasd; 'amal; dhikr-i-mawt; tefwîdh; teslîm; talab-ul-'ilm; selâ-'ahd; injâz-i-wa'd; husn-i-khulq; zuhd; qanâat; rushd; sa'y-i-fi-l-khayrât; riqqat; sewq; hayâ; thebât-i-fî emrillah; unsu billah; shewqu ilâ liqâillah; waqâr; dhekâwat; istiqâmat; adab; firâsat; tawakkul; sidq; murâbata; murâqaba; muhâsaba; muâtaba; kadhm-i-ghaydh; hubb-i-tûl-i-hayâti li 'ibadatihi; tawba; khushû; yaqîn; 'ubûdiyyat; mukâfât; ri'âyat-i-huqûq-i-'ibâd.

Tewâdu' means modesty; dhikr-i-minnat means to know that every tâat (act of obedience to Allâhu ta'âlâ) is owing to guidance, assistance and kindness on the part of Allâhu 'adhîm-ush-shân and to be grateful (to Allâhu ta'âlâ) for that; nasîhat means to admonish one's Mu'min brother; tasfiya means to expel the akhlâq-i-dhemîma (wicked moral qualities) from one's heart and beautify it with the akhlâq-i-hamîda; ghayrat means perseverance in one's faith; ghibta means to yearn for the like of a blessing possessed by someone else; sekhâ and futuwwat (both) mean generosity; îsâr means to see to the solutions for the problems of one's Mu'min brothers; muruwwat means to be dutiful towards humanity; hikmat means to know one's 'ilm-i-hâl (Islamic teachings pertaining to Muslim's religious duties) and to practise one's knowledge; shukr means to use the blessings at places (and in manners) dictated (by Islam); ridâ means to be pleased with Allâhu ta'âlâ's prearrangements for you; and sabr means patience for disasters.

[Ri'âyat-i-huqûq-i-'ibâd means to be watchful about the rights of the slaves (of Allâhu ta'âlâ), (i.e. people.) The most important ones of the rights of the slaves are the parental rights. With sweet words and a smiling face, we should run to help them and do our best to win their hearts. Next after them come rights of our neighbours, rights of our teachers, conjugal rights, rights of our friends, and rights of our government. We should not lie to anyone or deceive anyone, and we should use measuring instruments properly and pay the worker's wage before his sweat dries off. It will be treason not to pay our debts on not to pay fares for our journeys by bus or the like. Not to pay taxes to the government is in effect to do injustice to thousands of people. Supposing the government perpetrates oppression and thereupon the oppressed people revolt against the state, that it is not permissible to help the rebels is written in the book entitled **Berîqa**, in its chapter dealing with fitna, and also in **Fatâwâ-i-Hindiyya** and in **Durr-ul-mukhtâr**. It is stated in a hadîth-i-sherîf: "**If a person betrays the government Allah will betray him**," i.e. He will abase the rebel and make him despicable [Nibrâs]. For that matter, we should not lend credence to subversive and destructive publications provoking Muslims into revolting against the government and which are authored by people without a certain Madhhab, such as Sayyid Qutb and Mawdûdî. Rebellion is not something justifiable, be it against an oppressive government, and nor is it advisable to support rebels. Ibni 'Âbidîn 'rahima-hullâhu ta'âlâ', as he explains that it is harâm for men to wear silk clothes, states: "It is permissible to lay silk materials or to exhibit gold and silver articles without using them during celebrations of occasions such as 'Iyd days and weddings for the mere purpose of carrying out the government's commandment rather than for ostentation. However, it is being a wasteful and needless use of property to put on lights, to burn candles or to run lighted advertisements during the day, it is not permissible to do so. It is permissible to do these things or to send your children to mixed schools where boys and girls are educated together, if the government commands the people to do so. Another place that is not permissible (for Muslims) to go to is one where men and women are mixed and people expose their awrat parts." It is written in **Ibni 'Âbidîn**, in its chapters dealing with 'Friday prayer' and 'Being a Qâdi', that it is not permissible to revolt against disbelievers' laws, either. It is stated (by Islamic scholars) that acts of worship performed in violation of rights of Allâhu ta'âlâ's slaves, (i.e. human beings,) will not be accepted and will not help the worshipper to enter Paradise. It is stated also that paying a non-Muslim's rights is more difficult than paying a Muslim's rights. We do good to everyone and should not react to evil doers in kind. A true Muslim will obey Allâhu ta'âlâ's commandments and the government's laws.]

A blessed Walî's company is hard to come by,
People who attain it won't let it go awry.

One must look far and near to find the right guy;
A money-changer knows the gem, not a daft guy.

If you put a closed jug by a source of water;
Be it there forty years, it will still be dry.

Sohbat makes a heart pure, to make heavens envy;
What makes a man sage is not his garb chest-high.

First of all, have îmân, and cease from the harâm;
What the soul feeds on is not almonds on a pie!

CONCERNING VIRTUES of the SAHÂBA

Of all the Sahâba, Rasûlullah's four Khalîfas 'radiy-Allâhu ta'âlâ 'anhum ajma'în' are the highest. Caliphates of all four of them lasted for thirty years. [It is a declared fact that all the Sahâba 'radiy-Allâhu ta'âlâ 'anhum ajma'în' shall go to Paradise. It is not permissible to speak ill of any one of them.]

The kerâmât of the Awliyâ are haqq, i.e. true.[1]

Hadrat Abû Bakr as-Siddîq 'radiy-Allâhu ta'âlâ 'anh' is the most virtuous and the highest of all Walîs (Awliyâ). His caliphate is haqq (rightful). That he is the first Khalîfa is a proven fact by the ijmâ' (consensus, unanimity of the Sahâba). He is Rasûlullah's 'sall-Allâhu 'alaihi wa sallam' father-in-law. He married his daughter 'Âisha 'radiy-Allâhu 'anhâ' to Rasûlullah 'sall-Allâhu ta'âlâ 'alaihi wa sallam'. He is well versed in the knowledge of Haqîqat. He spent his entire property in the way of haqq, (i.e. true way, Islam,) so much so that he did not have a scrap left. So he wrapped a cover made of date fibres around his waist. Jebrâîl 'alaihis-salâm' donned the same kind of clothing and visited the Messenger of Allah. When the blessed Messenger saw the Archangel clad in the unusual apparel, he said: "**O Jebrâîl, my sibling! I have never seen you like this before. I wonder what is happening**." Thereupon, Jebrâîl 'alaihis-salâm' explained: "Yâ Rasûlallah (O Messenger of Allah)! Now you see me in this state. All the angels also are in this state. Its reason is this: Allâhu 'adhîm-ush-shân declared: '**My slave Abû Bakr has spent all his property for My grace and in My way. So he is clad in a cover made of date fibres. O My angels. You be clad like him!**' So all the angels are clad like this." From then on Hadrat Abû Bakr has been called 'Siddîq' (by Allâhu ta'âlâ and for that matter by all Muslims).

The second most virtuous Walî after him is Hadrat 'Umar 'radiy-Allâhu 'anh'. His caliphate is rightly guided according to the ijmâ'-i-ummat (consensus of the Sahâba). He is well versed in the

---

[1] It has been Allâhu ta'âlâ's 'âdat-i-ilâhiyya (divine habit) to create things and events through means (sababs). For instance, something heavier than water sinks in water. Sometimes Allâhu ta'âlâ suspends His law of causation for the grace of His beloved slaves such as Prophets and Awliyâ, so that events that we call wonders and miracles happen through these blessed people. When a wonder happens through a Prophet it is a mu'jiza, and a wonder that happens through a Walî (pl. Awliyâ) is termed a kerâmat (pl. kerâmât).

Islamic branches of knowledge. One day a munâfiq[1] and a jew came to Hadrat Rasûlullah 'sall-Allâhu 'alaihi wa sallam', asking the blessed Messenger to adjudicate a dispute between them. Hadrat Rasûlullah 'sall-Allâhu 'alaihi wa sallam' listened to their claims. Justice came the jew's way, (so the blessed Messenger of Allah made a judgment in the jew's favour.) When the munâfiq did not acquiesce to the judgment, Rasûlullah 'sall-Allâhu ta'âlâ 'alaihi wa sallam' stated: "**O you people! Go to 'Umar, and let him adjudicate between you**!" So they went to Hadrat 'Umar 'radiy-Allâhu ta'âlâ 'anh'. When the blessed Sahâbî asked why they were there, the munâfiq said: "This jew and I have had a dispute." Hadrat 'Umar 'radiy-Allâhu ta'âlâ 'anh' said: "How can I adjudicate the dispute in comtempt of the Owner of Islam (Messenger of Allah)?" The munâfiq explained: "We went to Rasûlullah 'sall-Allâhu 'alaihi wa sallam'. He made a judgment in favour of the jew. I would not acquiesce to his judgment." Presently 'Umar 'radiy-Allâhu 'anh' said: "Wait here! I will be back with the solution," and went in. After a while he was back with a cleaver hidden underneath his garment, and no sooner had he drawn the cleaver than the munâfiq was beheaded. "This is the just deserts of someone who will not acquiesce to Rasûlullah's verdict," was the great Sahâbî's explanation. On account of this significal event was he called 'Umar-ul-Fârûq 'radiy-Allâhu ta'âlâ 'anh', and he has been called so ever since.

Hadrat Rasûlullah 'sall-Allâhu 'alaihi wa sallam' stated: "**It is 'Umar who distinguishes right from wrong.**"

The third most virtuous Walî after him is 'Uthmân-i-Zinnûreyn 'radiy-Allâhu 'anh'. His caliphate is rightly-guided, righful. It is a fact ascertained by the ijmâ'-i-Ummat, (i.e. by consensus of the Sahâba.) Rasûlullah 'sall-Allâhu ta'âlâ 'alaihi wa sallam' married two of his blessed daughters to him, one after the other. When his second daughter passed away, he stated: "**If I had one more daughter, I would give him that one as well.**"

When the blessed Messenger married his blessed second daughter to 'Uthmân 'radiy-Allâhu ta'âlâ 'anh', he praised his blessed son-in-law highly. After the tezwîj (matrimony, event of marriage), the valuable daughter said: "O my beloved father! You praised Hadrat 'Uthmân so much. He is not so good as (to

---

[1] A munâfiq is an unbeliever who pretends to be a Muslim, lives among Muslims, joins them in some of their acts of worship that they perform together (in jamâ'at).

deserve) your blessed praise!" Thereupon Hadrat Rasûlullah 'sall-Allâhu 'alaihi wa sallam' said to his daughter: "**O my daughter! Angels in heaven feel hayâ** (shame) **towards Hadrat 'Uthmân**!"

Because Rasûlullah 'sall-Allâhu 'alaihi wa sallam' gave him two of his daughters in marriage, (one after the passing of the first one,) he was called 'Uthmân-i-Zinnûreyn. Zinnûreyn means owner of two Nûrs. He is well versed in the knowledge of Ma'rifat (Spiritual knowledge pertaining to Allâhu ta'âlâ).

The fourth most virtuous Walî after him is 'Alî 'kerrem-Allâhu wejheh wa radiy-Allâhu 'anh'. His caliphate is rightful, a fact ascertained by the ijmâ'-i-ummat. He is Rasûlullah's son-in-law. The beloved Messenger of Allâhu ta'âlâ gave his daughter Hadrat Fâtima 'radiy-Allâhu 'anhâ' in marriage to him. He is well versed in the knowledge of Tarîqat. He had a ghulâm (man slave). One day his ghulâm intended to test his master. Hadrat 'Alî 'radiy-Allâhu ta'âlâ 'anh' was outdoors at that time. When he came in and asked the ghulâm for some service, the latter remained silent. Thereafter, Hadrat 'Alî 'kerrem-Allâhu wejheh' inquired: "O ghulâm! What wrong have I done to you to offend you and what on my part has hurt you?" The ghulâm replied: "You have done nothing wrong towards me. I am your slave. I have behaved so only to test you. You are a true Walî."

[Muslims who love all the Ashâb-i-kirâm (Sahâba) and who follow in their footsteps are called **Ahl as-sunnat** (or **Sunnî Muslim**s). Those who say that they love some of them and who hate most of the Sahâba are called **Shî'îs** (Shiites). Those who are inimical towards all the Sahâba are called **Râfidîs**. A person who claims to love all the Sahâba but who does not follow any one of them is called a **Wahhâbî**. **Wahhâbîism** is a mixture of the ideas of the heretical man of religion named Ahmad ibni Taymiyya and the lies of the British spy named Hempher. They call the Ahl as-sunnat Muslims 'disbelievers' because those true Muslims reject the Wahhâbî tenets of belief. [This stigmatization on their part bounces back on them, making them disbelievers themselves.]

The Wahhâbî doctrines were concocted by British plotters in the Arabian peninsula in 1150 [1737 A.D.] They shed a considerable amount of Muslim blood in their efforts to spread the British plans. Today also, they are establishing Wahhâbî centers which they call **Râbita-t-ul 'âlam-il-islâmî** in every country and hunting unlearned men of religion by showering gold onto them. Through these mercenaries they are misguiding Muslims. They are blackening the scholars of Ahl as-sunnat who have been defending Islam for more than fourteen hundred years and their protectors, the Ottomans. They are falsifying the true Islamic teachings which those blessed scholars extracted from the Nass (âyats and hadîths).

Some Wahhâbîs say, "We, too, are in a Sunnî Madhhab. We are in the Hanbalî Madhhab." This claim of theirs is similar to the claim of the adherents of the heretical group called Mu'tazila, who say, "We, too, are Sunnî Muslims. We are in the Hanafî Madhhab." They say so because they know that people who are not in the Sunnî group shall go to Hell. The fact, however, is that the harmonizing of the religious practices and acts of worship of a certain group of people with those of one of the four Madhhabs does not necessarily show that those people are in that Madhhab. Being in a certain Madhhab requires adapting oneself to that Madhhab both in tenets of belief and in practices. All four Madhhabs are identical in their tenets of belief. All four of them are in the Madhhab of Ahl as-sunnat in respect of belief. A certain person's being in the Hanafî or Hanbalî Madhhab requires his holding a belief agreeable with that of the (credal) Madhhab called Ahl as-sunnat. Wahhâbîs do not hold the Sunnî belief.]

CONCERNING FOOD and EATING

There are ten benefits in washing your hands before meals in an awareness that it is an act of sunnat (to wash your hands then):

If a person washes his hands before a meal and puts his wet (index fingers on the inner corners of his eyes and moves his fingers, gently in contact with the lids of his well-nigh closed eyes, backwards until they reach the outer corners of his eyes, that person, with the permission of Allâhu ta'âlâ, will not have a sore eye. The ten benefits are:

1– An angel below the 'Arsh-i-Rahmân will hail: As you have cleaned your hands, likewise you have been cleaned from your [venial] sins.

2– He will earn as much thawâb as he would if he had performed nâfila namâz.

3– He will be secured against poverty.

4– He will attain thawâb equal to that which is granted to Siddîqs.

5– Angels will make istighfâr for him.

6– In return for each and every morsel of food he eats, he will attain as much thawâb as he would if he had given the entire food as alms.

7– He will be cleaned from his sins if he also begins eating with the Basmala.

8– Benedictions that he pronounces after the meal will be accepted (by Allâhu ta'âlâ).

9– If he dies that night, he will attain thawâb equal to that earned by martyrs.

10– If he dies during the day, he will be recorded in the group of martyrs.

There are six benefits in washing your hands with the intention of performing an act of sunnat:

1– An angel below the 'Arsh-i-Rahmân will hail: "O you Believer! Rasûlullah 'sall-Allâhu ta'âlâ 'alaihi wa sallam' is pleased with you."

2– You will attain thawâb specially reserved for this blessing.

3– The thawâbs that you will attain will be as many as the hairs on your body.

4– You will have a share from the ocean of Rahmat (Compassion of Allâhu ta'âlâ).

5– You will earn as many thawâbs as the number of the drops that fall off your hands.

6– You will die as a martyr.

[Allâhu ta'âlâ's commandments fall into two main categories; Emr-i-tekwînî and Emr-i-teklîfî or Emr-i-teshrî'î.

Emr-i-tekwînî: It is His saying, "**Be**," to things that He wills to create. That thing comes into being as soon as He says, "Be!" No one can prevent that thing from coming into being. He has created certain things as causes for the creation of every being. As he has made certain substances causes for the creation of certain other things, likewise man's material and spiritual powers and various kinds of energy are causes for the creation of many (other) things. If He wills to bestow a gift or something good on a slave of His, He makes that slave attain the causes for that gift. When the causes take effect, if He, too, wills and says, "Be!" that thing (gift, ets.) comes into being. Nothing comes into being unless He wills it to. He has concealed His Hikmat and His Creating by covering them with causes. Many people see the causes only and fail to see the

Hikmat, His Creation behind the causes. This lack of understanding on their part causes them to end up in ruination.

Emr-i-teklîfî: It consists of the commandments which He has enjoined on human beings concerning what they should do and what they should avoid doing. These commandments of His are dependent on man's will and choice. He has set man free in his will and choice. However, it is Him, again, who creates the thing which man wills and opts to do. When man wills and opts to do something, He creates it if He, too, wills it. He does not create it if He does not will to create it. He, alone, creates all things and supplies substances with effectivity and various properties. There is no other creator besides Him. To believe that anyone besides Him has the attribute of ulûhiyyat (deity) means to attribute a partner to Him. He has declared that He shall never forgive in the world to come anyone who attributes a partner to Him (in this world) and that He shall inflict unending and bitterest torment on people who do so. When people opt to carry out His commandment and do good things, He, too, being merciful, wills and creates their obedience and good deeds. When people who deny and disobey Him want to do evils, He, too, wills and creates their evil deeds. When people who believe Him and beg Him want to do something evil, He, being compassionate, does not will that evil deed and does not create it. So, because all the (evil) wishes of His enemies come true, they fall into all the more vicious deeds and become all the more rampant.

Allâhu ta'âlâ's emr-i-teklîfîs have been graded in respect of their importance:

1– He has commanded the entire humanity to have îmân and to become Muslims.

2– He has commanded those who have had îmân not to commit harâms and not to do evil.

3– He has commanded those who have had îmân to perform the farzes.

4– He has commanded Muslims who avoid the harâms and perform the farzes and to avoid the makrûhs and to perform the sunnats and the acts of nâfila worship.

In the gradations above, it is not something acceptable to pass over a more important commandment and to do the one next after it in importance; it is not liked. It will not be useful. If a person avoids evils without having îmân or performs the farzes without avoiding evils and harâms or performs the sunnats and the nâfilas without performing the farzes, Allâhu ta'âlâ will not like him or accept what he has done. For the same matter, if a Muslim does not perform namâz or pay zakât or pay the rights of his parents or wife or children, Allâhu ta'âlâ will not like or accept his pious deeds such as alms and/or charities and/or donations and/or mosque-buildings and/or monetary supports and/or washing the hands before and after meals and/or performing 'Umra. As is seen, everyone should perform the ewâmir-i-teklîfiyya in the order of importance stated above. On the other hand, supposing a person performs something of lesser importance without performing the deeds in the upper class and if his doing so causes him, say, to omit an act that is farz or to commit a harâm; he will not earn any thawâb, that is true, but then he should not let himself do without that good deed, either. It is written in the book of Tafsîr entitled **Rûh-ul-beyân**, in the final part of its sixth chapter, that with the barakat of continuously performing that good deed, it is hoped, Allâhu ta'âlâ may mercifully bless him with performing the commandments in an upper class.]

There are four farzes in eating:

1– When eating and drinking, to know that satisfaction and satiation is granted by Allâhu 'adhîm-ush-shân.

2– To eat food that is halâl.

3– To spend the entire energy that you acquire from that food doing your duties as a slave of Allâhu ta'âlâ.

4– To be contented with what you have obtained.

When starting to eat you should make your niyyat to acquire energy to worship Allâhu ta'âlâ, to do things useful to the slaves of Allâhu ta'âlâ, and to make the religion of Allâhu ta'âlâ, the way to everlasting happiness and peace, reach all people. It is permissible to eat bareheaded.

Mustahabs in eating: To set a (wooden) tray on the floor (in lieu of a dining table); to wear clean clothes as you sit for the meal; to sit on your knees; to have washed your hands and mouth before the meal; to make the Basmala, (i.e. to say, "Bismillah-er-Rahmân-er-Rahîm,") when starting to eat; to taste a little salt before starting to eat; to eat bread made of barley flour; to break the bread manually; not to wast the crumbs of bread; to eat from the side (of the dish) nearest to you; to consume (a little) vinegar; to eat the bread in small morsels; to chew the food well; to eat with your three fingers; to wipe inside the dish with your finger; to lick your fingers three times; to make hamd after the meal; to use a toothpick.

Makrûhs in eating: To eat with left hand; to smell the food you are to eat; To neglect the Basmala; [The Basmala must be made whenever it is remembered, be it far gone into the meal.]

Harâms in eating: To continue eating after being sated; [if you have a guest, you should pretend to continue eating lest you should prevent him from eating; to be wasteful of food; according to some (scholars), to make the Basmala when eating food that belongs to someone else [unjustly]; to take part in a feast without having been invited; to eat someone else's food without their permission; to eat something that will undermine your health; to eat food that has been prepared with riyâ (ostentatiously); to eat something you have vowed.

Eating hot food causes the following harms: It causes deafness; it causes a pale face; it causes eyes to become lusterless; it causes teeth to turn yellowish; it causes mouth to lose taste; it causes insatiability; it weakens comprehension; it impairs your mind; it causes a physical malady.

Benefits of eating little are as follows: You will have a strong body; your heart will be filled with nûr; you will have a powerful memory; you will make an easy living; you will relish your work; you will have made dhikr of Allâhu 'adhîm-ush-shân very much; you will meditate over the Hereafter; you will get very much flavour from worship; you will have a deep insight and guidance in all matters; you will undergo an easy judgment (on the Judgment Day.)

> *When any person says, "I am a Muslim;"*
> *Daily five prayers are incumbent on him.*
> *On the Day of Rising that is soon to come,*
> *Raiment and crown, and a horse to carry him.*

CONCERNING MARRIAGE

There are many benefits in marriage.

First, it will shield your faith. You will form beautiful habits. There will be barakat in your earnings. You will have performed an act that is sunnat. As a matter of fact, our Prophet stated: "**Make nikâh**, (i.e. enter into a marriage by making Islam's marriage contract called 'nikâh',) **and have many children. For, on the Rising Day I shall take pride in the majority of my Ummat (Muslims) over the other ummats.**"

The husband and the wife have to observe each other's rights.

A person who plans to enter into a marriage should search well until he finds a girl (or woman) who is sâliha, (i.e. firm in her faith,) and who is not (one of his close relatives called) a mahram relative, and marry the girl (or woman) who fulfils the conditions stipulated. It is permissible to make nikâh with a woman who has become pregnant by way of fornication. If the fornicator is another man, waty (intercourse) before childbirth is not permissible (Fatâwâ-i-Fayziyya)[1]

Do not marry a girl on account of her beauty or property. Otherwise you will become despicable. Our blessed Prophet 'sall-Allâhu ta'âlâ 'alaihi wa sallam' stated: "**If a person marries a girl on account of her property or beauty, he will be deprived of her property and beauty.**"

If a person marries a girl on account of her piety and beautiful moral quality, Haqq ta'âlâ increases her property and beauty.

The wife should be lower than her husband in four respects: Her age and her stature and her kith and kin. In four respects the wife must be superior to her husband: She must be pretty and she must have adab and beautiful moral habits and she must avoid harâms and doubtful things and she must not show her hair and head and arms and legs to men nâ-mahram to her.

Young girls should not be married to old men. It may cause fasâd, (which means, lexically, malice.)

Before preliminary arrangements concerning the (marriage contract called) nikâh, families of the would-be couple should

---

[1] Written by Fayzullah Efendi of Erzurum, Turkey 'rahmatullâhi ta'âlâ 'alaih' (martyred in Edirne in 1115 [1703 A.D.]), the forty-sixth Ottoman Shaikh-ul-islâm.

make thorough investigations about the youngsters, which is sunnat and will help the continuation of marriage. According to scholarly statements, this will yield three benefits: First, there will be lifelong affection between the couple; second, there will be barakat (abundance, divine fruitfulness) in their rızq (living, sustenance, daily food); third, they will have done something which is sunnat.

Thereafter, legal matrimonial procedures in the municipality should be completed. It will be gravely sinful not to make a (marriage contract called) nikâh compatibly with the Sunnat. And it will be a guilt not to complete the legal matrimonial procedures.

After nikâh is performed in a manner agreeable with the Sunnat, the man's family should send beautiful and valuable gifts to the girl's family; it will cause affection to do so.

It is permissible for the wife to adorn herself well for her husband; it will yield much thawâb (rewards in the Hereafter).

It is sunnat to give a feast on the nuptial evening. [The dinner meal should be eaten after evening prayer, and after night prayer the bridegroom should be taken to the bride's place, and after the dictated prayers and benedictions the group should disperse.

An act of sunnat to be performed the first night is for the bridegroom to wash the bride's feet and sprinkle the water all around the house. He should perform a namâz of two rak'ats and and say prayers. Any prayer said on that night will be accepted (by Allâhu ta'âlâ). People who see the bridegroom should remind him of this. They should say, "**Bârekellâhu lek wa bârekellâhu 'alaihâ wa jeme'a beynekumâ bi-l-khayri,**" which means, "May Allâhu ta'âlâ bless you with it and may your wife be blessed with it, and may He unite you two with khayr!" Some people congratulate a newly married couple by saying, "May you get on well and may you have sons and servants!" It an ignorant and useless statement. It is sunnat to say the prayers prescribed for that time.

You should know the necessary religious teachings and teach them to your wife. For, you shall be questioned on them in the Hereafter. Not to know will not be an acceptable excuse. [It is farz to learn the farzes and the harâms and the tenets of Ahl as-sunnat belief and to teach them to your wife and children. And it is sunnat to learn the sunnats and to teach them to them.]

You should not take or send your wife to a place not permitted by Islam! You should not take her out or let her go out without covering herself properly. For, our blessed Prophet "alaihis-salâm" stated: "**If a woman comes to our mosque with a pleasant smell on her to perform namâz, that woman's namâz shall not be accepted** (by Allâhu ta'âlâ) **unless she goes home and makes a ghusl like making a ghusl to get out of the state of junub.**" Since it is not permissible for them to go to a mosque with pleasant smells on them, then we should make a mental picture of the gravity of the sin of going elsewhere and showing herself to people. We should make a comparison and then try to imagine the torment that she will be subjected to!

Our blessed Prophet states in one of his hadîth-i-sherîfs: "**Most of the people of Paradise are people who were poor** (during life in the world), **and most of the dwellers of Hell are women!**" Thereupon Hadrat 'Âisha 'radiy-Allâhu 'anhâ' inquired: "What is the reason for Hell's being occupied mostly by women?" The Rasûl-i-ekrem 'sall-Allâhu 'alaihi wa sallam' explained: "**They do not show patience when a disaster befalls them. When someone who has always been good to them and who has done them, (say,) ten favours behaves sourly towards them, they always mention that sour behaviour, completely forgetting about those old ten favours. They love worldly ornaments and do not work for the Hereafter and are particularly fond of gossipping.**"

All people with these evil habits are people of Hell, men and women alike.

Hadrat 'Alî 'kerrem-Allâhu wejheh' narrates: One day a woman entered the blessed presence of Rasûlullah 'sall-Allâhu ta'âlâ 'alaihi wa sallam' and said: "Yâ Rasûlallah (O you Messenger of Allah)! I want to marry a man. What is your blessed opinion?" Said the Most Happy creature of Allâhu ta'âlâ: "**A man has a number of rights over his wife. Will you manage to observe them**?" The woman said: "Yâ Rasûlallah! What are a husband's rights?" "**If you hurt him you will have revolted against Allah, and your namâz will not be accepted,**" was the blessed answer. The woman said: "Are there other rights?" "**If a woman goes out of her house without her husband's permission, a sin for each step will be recorded** (in her book of deeds)," replied Rasûlullah 'sall-Allâhu 'alaihi wa sallam'. The woman said: "Are there others?" "**If a woman hurts her husband with bad words, one the Rising Day they will make her tongue jut out from the back of her neck,**" was the Rasûl-i-ekrem's, the most beautiful, reply. The woman said: "Are there others?" "**A woman who has property and yet will not minister to her husband's needs will rise in the Hereafter with a black face,**" replied the Rasûl-i-ekrem (Blessed Messenger). The woman inquired: "Are there others?" The Rasûl-i-ekrem answered: "**If any woman pilfers from her husband's property and gives it to someone else, Allâhu 'adhîm-ush-shân shall not accept that woman's zakât or alms, unless she asks her husband to forgive her and he in his turn forgives her.**" The woman said: "Are there others?" Thereupon the blessed Messenger of Allah stated: "**If any woman swears at her husband or refuses to obey him, they will hang her by her tongue in the pit of Hell, and if any woman goes out and watches woman dancers and listens to musical instruments and spends a penny, all the twawâb which she has earned for her pious deeds since her childhood will be annihilated and the dresses she has been wearing will sue against her, saying, 'She did not wear us on sacred days or when she was with her halâl (husband); she wore us at harâm places where she went.' Thereupon Haqq ta'âlâ will declare: 'I shall burn such women for a thousand years.' "** [Hence also should we realize the bad aspects of the cinema, of the radio and television programs.] When the woman heard these answers she said: "Yâ Rasûlallah! I have never entered into marriage until now, nor will I ever."

This time the Rasûl-i-ekrem 'sall-Allâhu ta'âlâ 'alaihi wa salla' graciously offered their explanation: "**Yâ khâtûn** (O you woman)**! Let me inform you also about the blessings of marrying a man; listen! If a woman's husband says to her, 'May Allah bless you with His Grace,' she will be better off than having worshipped for sixty years. And her giving her husband some water to drink is a more meritorious service than fasting for one year. If she makes a ghusl after a conjugal relationship with her husband, she will attain as much thawâb as if she performed Qurbân. If she does not play tricks on her halâl** (husband), **angels in heaven will make tasbîh**[1] **on her behalf. If she frolics with her husband, she will be more blessed than for having manumitted sixty slaves. If she protects her husband's rizq and has mercy on her husband's kith and kin and performs namâz five times daily and fasts** (in Ramadân), **it is more meritorious than visiting the Ka'ba a thousand times.**" Fâtima-i-Zehrâ 'radiy-Allâhu 'anhâ' (Rasûlullah's blessed daughter, inquired: What will become of a woman if she hurts her halâl (husband)?" Thereupon the most blessed of all fathers stated: "**If a woman refuses to obey her husband, the curse of Allah shall stay**

---

[1] To make tasbîh means to say, "Subhân-Allah," which means, "I know Allah far from defects of any sort." Making tasbîh yields plenty of thawâb (rewards in the Hereafter).

upon her until she asks her husband to forgive her and he forgives her; if she shirks her conjugal duties she will lose all her thawâb; if she behaves haughtily towards her husband, she will become an object of Allâhu ta'âlâ's rage; if she says to him, 'Are you an officious meddler?' or, 'Have you ever been of any use to me?', Allâhu ta'âlâ will make His blessing harâm to her. If she licked her husband's blood with her tongue she would still have not paid her husband's right. If her husband lets her go out without properly covering herself, a thousand sins will be recorded in her husband's book of deeds for condoning her." This will help to imagine the gravity of a woman's sin for just going out without her husband's permission!

The Rasûl-i-ekrem 'sall-Allâhu ta'âlâ 'alaihi wa sallam' stated: "Yâ Fâtima! If Allâhu ta'âlâ had commanded human beings' prostrating themselves before others, I would command women to prostrate themselves before their husbands."

Hadrat 'Âisha 'radiy-Allâhu 'anhâ' narrates: I asked Rasûlullah to make a will for me. The blessed Messenger stated: "Yâ 'Âisha! I will make a will for you and you make that will to the women among my Umma! When people rise for judgment on the morrow: Questioning shall be made on îmân first. The second questioning shall be made on ablution and namâz. With women the third questioning shall be made on (the rights of) their husbands. If a man is patient with his wife's petulance, Haqq ta'âlâ shall reward him with thawâb equal to that which was granted to Prophet Eyyûb (Job). And if a woman is patient with her husband's cantankerousness, Allâhu ta'âlâ shall promote her to the grade of 'Âisha-i-Siddiqa."

"If a man beats his wife I shall sue against him on the day of Judgment," is another hadîth-i-sherîf uttered by the Rasûl-i-ekrem 'sall-Allâhu 'alaihi wa sallam'.

There are three reasons for which a man is permitted to beat his wife with the palm of his open hand or with an unknotted hankerchief: For ceasing from namâz or ghusl or for refusing to come to his bed or for going out without his permission. By no means is it permissible to beat her with a stick or to punch her with the fist or to kick her or to beat her with a knotted handkerchief or to hit her on the head or on the body. And she must never be beaten for other faults. She must be warned a couple of times. If she does correct herself, then she must be left to herself lest you should torment yourself.

[It is stated as follows in **Shir'at-ul-islam**: "If your wife begins to exhibit surly behaviour, you should blame yourself. You should say to yourself, "She wouldn't behave like that if I were good. If your wife is a sâliha (pious) one, you should not take a second wife. It is not permissible for a man short of rendering justice with respect to the maintenance of his family to marry a second wife. If he knows that he will be capable of rendering justice, then it is permissible for him (to take a second wife). However, it is more meritorious for him not to do so. When your wife leaves for places permissible for her to go to, she must wear a headgear and cover her body properly. It is harâm for a woman to go out with a smell of perfume and/or with her ornaments exposed. A sâliha (pious) woman is the most valuable of worldly blessings. To treat a Muslim with mercy and tenderness yields more thawâb than does an act of nâfila worship." It is written as follows in **Riyâd-un-nâsikhîn**: The eighteenth âyat of Nisâ Sûra purports: "**Behave well and tenderly towards your wives!**" The following hadîth-i-sherîfs: "**Yâ Abâ Bakr! If a person talks smilingly and tenderly with his wife, he shall be given as much thawâb as if he had manumitted a slave**." and "**Allah shall not have mercy on a woman who marries a fâsiq man**." and "**Let him who wants my shafâ'at not give his daughter as a wife to as fâsiq man**." and "**The best of people is one who is good to people. The worst of people is one who harms** [hurts] **people**." and "**To unjustly hurt a Muslim is worse than demolishing the Ka'ba seventy times**."

It is stated in **Durr-ul-mukhtâr**: "Once a Muslim man has married a woman by making a sahîh (valid) (marriage contract called) nikâh with her, (she becomes his wife and) it becomes farz for him to provide her (means of subsistence called) nafaqa. **Nafaqa** consists of food, clothing, and dwelling. He has to make his wife live in a house which is either his own property or one that he has rented. The wife may demand that none of her husband's relatives should be allowed into the house. The husband as well may demand that none of his wife's relatives should enter the house. Both of them possess this right. The house should be in a quarter where sâlih Muslims live. [The muazzin's own voice should be heard from the house (without having to use a loudspeaker, since it is an act of bid'at to use it in Islamic practices).] The husband cannot ban his wife from going out to visit her parents once a week. They might as well come and visit their daughter once a week. If one of them becomes ill and there is no one to look after them, the wife should go and tend on her parent even if her husband is opposed to her doing so. The husband cannot prevent her other mahram relatives from visiting her, or prevent her from visiting them, once a year. If he allows her to visit others or to go to sinful places, both of them will be sinful. He prevents her from doing work for others, in return for a payment or gratis, at home or elsewhere, from going out to school or to preaches. A woman should be busy doing housework at home; she should not sit idly. He should not let her go to places with people with exposed awrat parts, such as public baths [and beaches or to places where people watch sports activities. He should not keep a television set in his home lest such activities should be watched.] She should not be allowed to go out with an ornamented or new dress on her." He may take her out to places where Muslims who avoid harâms live, even if they are not her mahram relatives, i.e. close relatives who are harâm for her to marry; yet in that case men and women should be sitting in separate rooms. A woman's **mahram relatives** are the following eighteen men: Her father and grandfathers; her sons and grandsons; her brothers, only uterine or only paternal ones alike; her brother's or sister's sons; her paternal and maternal uncles. These seven men are mahram relatives when they are related to her by milk-tie or by way of fornication as well. And four other men become mahram relatives by way of nikâh (marriage entered into by way of a marriage contract prescribed by Islam). They are: Father-in-law and his fathers; son-in-law; stepfather; stepson(s). A man's children's daughters-in-law and a woman's children's sons-in-law are their mahram relatives. Mahram relative means a person with whom you cannot make a nikâh, (i.e. whom you cannot marry.) For instance, a man's sister is his mahram relative. Everyone's siblings' children are their mahram relatives. A man's brothers' wives or his paternal and maternal uncles' and aunts' daughters or his paternal and maternal uncles' wives are not his mahram relatives. Your maternal aunt's children and her husband are nâ-mahram, (i.e. they are not mahram relatives.) Your husband's or wife's siblings are nâ-mahram. That a woman's sister's or aunt's husband and her husband's brothers are nâ-mahram to her is written in the book entitled **Ni'mat-i-islâm**, in its chapter dealing with the essentials of Hajj (Pilgrimage). It is harâm for the wife to show herself to these men without covering herself in a manner taught by Islam or to stay with them in private in a closed room even if she has covered herself properly or to go on a (long-distance journey called) safar with them. Also, a woman's maternal and paternal mothers are her son-in-law's mahram relatives. A girl cannot marry one of her mahram relatives. It is permissible for her to sit in their presence without covering herself so strictly as she would do in the presence of men who are nâ-mahram to her. She can stay with one of her mahram relatives in private in a closed room or undertake a long-distance journey with him. When one of her relatives that are not mahram comes to their place, she says to him, "Welcome," in the presence of her husband or women who are her relatives and with her entire body covered with the exception of her face. She serves coffee, tea or the like. But she does not sit there. Muslims should adhere to books teaching Islam, rather than customs and etiquettes. Every Muslim should teach his wife Islam's credal and practical tenets; if he is not learned enough, he should send her to a woman learned enough to teach her and sâliha (pious) enough (for them to trust her). If he cannot find a woman who obeys Islam and avoids harâms, he and his wife should sit together and read books teaching Islam correctly and written by scholars of Ahl as-sunnat; thereby both of them will learn Islam, îmân, harâms and farzes well. He should not contaminate his home with heretical books of tafsîr written by men of religion without a certain Madhhab; books of that sort should not be read. He should not bring home radios and televisions with programs destructive to Islam and deleterious to ethics. They are worse than evil company. They will spoil the faith and moral behaviour of your wife and children. Wives and daughters should be busy doing housework; they should not be made to work in fields or factories or banks or companies or civil services. Wives and daughters do not have to help their husbands and fathers in arts and trade. It is the man's duty to do these chores and to buy their domestic needs at shops and markets and bring them home. If the woman is forced to do these things, her faith, her moral behaviour and her health will be impaired. The world and the Hereafter of both of them will be ruined completely. They will feel bitter remorse, yet to no avail. For, it will not rescue them from sins and disasters. A person who obeys Islam will attain comfort both in this world and in the Hereafter. We should adapt ourselves to books teaching us our religion and we should not fall for the smiles and the suave words on the part of evil company and the (hypocritical people called) munâfiqs. We should protect our daughters and sons as well against harâms. We should send our sons to schools employing Muslim teachers. The woman does not need to work among men in stores, shops, factories or civil services. If she does not have a husband, or if her husband is an invalid, the woman's mahram relatives have to provide all her needs. If these relatives of hers are poor, then the State has to grant her an ample allowance. Allâhu ta'âlâ places all the woman's needs at her disposal. He imposes the burden of making a living on the man. Although the woman does not have to work for a living, He gives her half the man's share from the inherited property. The woman's duties consist of indoor activities. And the first and foremost of these activities is to raise the children. The child's elementary murshid (guide) is its mother. Once a child has learned religious and ethical teachings from its mother, it can never be misguided by irreligious teachers, by evil company, or by the lies of zindiqs who are Islam's enemies. It becomes a true Muslim like its parents. Please see the twelfth chapter of the fifth fascicle, and also the fifteenth chapter of the sixth fascicle, of **Endless Bliss!** Munâfiqs who carry on inimical activities against Islam are called **zindiq**s.]

CONCERNING the TEJHÎZ and the TEKFÎN and the TEDFÎN of a JANÂZA
(How To WASH and SWATHE and BURY a DEAD MUSLIM)

To perform a namâz of janâza, to wash and swathe and bury a dead Muslim are, all, acts of farz worship.

To wash a dead Muslim's body, the corpse is made to lie flat on its back on a marble or wooden bench placed somewhere in solitude. Its shirt is taken off. It is made to make an ablution. The upper part of its body, from head to navel, is washed with lukewarm water. Then its part between the navel and the knees is covered and washed. The person doing the washing wears a glove on their right hand. They insert that (gloved) hand under the cover, pour water and wash that (covered) part. They should not look at the part under the cover. Then the corpse is turned leftward and its right side is washed; thereafter it is turned rightward and its left side is washed with the gloved hand. One of the three parts of the shroud is spread on the bench and under the corpse. Then the spread cloth and the corpse on it are placed into the coffin.

There are three kinds of shroud (kefen): The kefen-i-farz, [which is also called the kefen-i-darûrat;] the kefen-i-sunnat; and the kefen-i-kifâya.

The kefen-i-sunnat for men consists of three parts, and the one for women consists of five parts.

The kefen-i-kifâya for men consists of two parts and the kefen-i-kifâya for women consists of three parts.

It is stated in **Bahr-ur-râiq**: "The kefen-i-kifâya for women is the izâr, the lifâfa, and the himâr, i.e. headgear. For, women cover themselves with these three pieces of clothing (at the minimum) when they are alive." Izâr, in those old days, was a wrapper covering the entire body from shoulders or from top to feet. That lifâfa is a qamîs (chemise) is written in Ibni 'Âbidîn. As is seen, formerly women wore an ample overcoat and a headgear when they went out. It is written in Bahr-ur-râiq and in **Dur-ul-muntaqâ**: "The nafaqa which is wâjib for the husband to provide for the wife consists of food, clothing, and dwelling. Clothing consists of himâr (headgear) and milhâfa, which means outer wrapper. [It is called 'ferâja' or 'manto' or 'saya' today. As is seen, the woman's clothing consists of three pieces, and the charshaf is not one of these pieces. The charshaf came into fashion afterwards. It is permissible for women to wear the charshaf at places where it is customary to wear the charshaf and to wear an ample overcoat (manto) and a thick headgear at places where it is customary to wear them. To hold oneself aloof from others in common and customary usages will cause fitna, which in turn is harâm.]

The kefen[1]-i-farz consists of a single piece both for men and for women.

At places no material with the exception of silk is available, one piece for men and two pieces for women will do.

Priority in conducting the namâz of janâza as the imâm is as follows: President, if he is a Muslim; judge of the town; the khatîb authorized for Friday prayer; and imâm-i-hay. (Please scan the twentieth chapter of the fourth fascicle of **Endless Bliss** for minute details.)

The person called the imâm-i-hay is a learned Muslim about whom the deceased Muslim (for whom the namâz of janâza is to be performed) used to have a good opinion when he was alive. Next to come in priority is deceased's walî. If the walî is absent and the namâz is conducted by a Muslim who is not one of the aforesaid people, the walî will have an option. He may or may not have the namâz reperformed. Details are available from the fourth

---

[1] The lexical meaning of kefen (or kafan) is 'shroud'.

and fifth fascicles of **Endless Bliss**.

Supposing a person was cut in half (vertically) and one half of the corpse has been found, namâz of janâza need not be performed for that found half.

Supposing they found a corpse torn in pieces and the pieces are here and there; again namâz of janâza for the owner of the pieces need not be performed. However, the namâz should be performed if the pieces have been brought together.

If a corpse has been washed and yet they say that one of the limbs is dry; that limb must be washed if the corpse has not been shrouded yet. On the other hand, supposing they say, after the janâza has been brought near the grave, that one of the limbs of ablution of the corpse has been left dry; they wash that limb and thereafter perform the namâz of janâza. If they say so after the corpse has been interred; in that case the corpse must not be exhumed. If (it is found out after interment that) the corpse was not washed; then the corpse must be taken out and washed, if the burial has not been done yet.

Supposing you made the corpse make a tayammum and thereafter find water as you are carrying the corpse (in the coffin); you have an option.

Supposing a number of people are dead at the same time in a town; it is permissible to perform a single namâz for all of them. It goes without saying that it should be done in agreement with the Islamic rules. It is better, however, to perform a namâz for each and every one of them separately.

Niyyat for a namâz of janâza must be made like this: "(I make my niyyat **to perform namâz for the grace of Allâhu ta'âlâ, to pronounce benedictions over the male** [or female] **Muslim, and to follow the imâm who is present and** (who is) **to conduct the namâz**."

Supposing a person is arrested as he is robbing the travellers and killed upon the judge's or the walî's decision or a rebel is killed as he is fighting against the state or a person (is killed because he) has killed his own parents; namâz of janâza is not performed for the (killed) culprit in any of these three instances.

Namâz of janâza is performed for a suicide, i.e. for a person who killed himself (**Durr-ul-mukhtâr**).

Sunnî Muslims have ten characteristics:

1– The Sunnî Muslim will be a regular mosque-goer to join the jamâ'at (for the daily five namâzes).

2– He will join the jamâ'at and perform namâz behind an imâm [whose belief and fisq (sinfulness) are not so bad as to make him an unbeliever].

3– He will accept the permissiblity of making masah on the mests, (which is explained in detail in the third chapter of the fourth fascicle of **Endless Bliss**.)

4– He will not vilify any of the Ashâb-i-kirâm 'radiy-Allâhu ta'âlâ 'anhum ajma'în'.

5– He will not revolt against the state.

6– He will not struggle or quarrel unjustly over religious matters.

7– He will not entertain religious doubts.

8– He will know that everything, good or evil alike, is from Allâhu ta'âlâ.

9– He will not accuse any Muslim among the people of Qibla with disbelief [unless their ilhâd is certainly known].

10– He will give preference to the (earliest) four Khalîfas, (i.e. Hadrat Abû Bakr and Hadrat 'Umar and Hadrat 'Uthmân and Hadrat 'Alî,) over the other Sahâbîs.

CONCERNING the STATES of DEATH

O you poor weaklings, you run away from death! "So and so is dead. If I am near him, death may pass on to me by contagion," you say. When plague or another infectious and fatal disease spreads over a certain quarter, you flee to another place. It is harâm to hold such belief. A disease will pass on to you if Allâhu ta'âlâ wills it to.

O you poor weaklings, what place are you fleeing to! Death is an end you have been promised. Not even for a moment will death be postponed! When your time of death comes, Khallâq-i-'âlam (Creator of all beings) shall not allow you respite even as long as it would take a twinkle. It will take place neither sooner nor later than its predestined time.

Whereever a certain person's destination foreordained by Haqq ta'âlâ is, that person shall go to that place, leaving all his property, family, and children. And his soul shall not be ordered out unless he arrives in that place where his soil awaits him.

Everyone shall die when their time of death comes. The thirty-third âyat-i-kerîma of A'râf Sûra purports: "... when their term is reached, not a little can they cause delay, nor (a little time) can they advance (it in anticipation)."

Before a person is born, it has been foreordained how long they shall live. And it all has been written in the Lawh-i-mahfûz: where that person shall die, whether they shall die having made tawba or without having made tawba, what illness they shall die from (if any), whether they shall die with îmân or without îmân. In fact, this fact is pointed out in the final âyat of Loqmân Sûra.

Khallâq-i-'âlam created death. Thereafter He created life. Thereafter He created our rizq and wrote it in the Lawh-il-mahfûz.

Haqq ta'âlâ knows the number of the breaths you are to take. And He wrote it in the Lawh-il-mahfûz. Angels watch over it, and when the time comes they let the Melek-ul-mewt (Angel of death) know.

If you have spent your life believing the facts stated in the Qur'ân al-kerîm and practising the commandments declared therein, you will go (to the next world) as a happy person! Deem everything from Allâhu ta'âlâ! Do not cry out behind a person who has passed! Things of this sort cause a person to die without îmân. We take refuge in Allâhu ta'âlâ. Should we commit a sin or a fault, we should make tawba-i-nasûh.

Haqq subhânallâhu wa ta'âlâ orders Azrâîl ''alaihis-salâm' (Angel of death): **"Take away My friends' souls with ease, and My foes' souls harshly**!" Al-ayâz-u-billah, if one should be disobedient!

One day in the Hereafter is as long as one thousand or fifty thousand years. There are various explanations concerning this matter. This fact is understood from the fifth âyat-i-kerîma of Sajda Sûra and from the fourth âyat-i-kerîma of Me'ârij Sûra.

Thereafter angels extract the disobedient person's soul with torture. Language would fall short of describing it. We trust ourselves to Allah, who created us from nothing. Some dying people writhe and turn from one side to the other like a spring. As a matter of fact, Allâhu ta'âlâ describes them in Wa-n-nâziâti Sûra. The angels torment them bitterly, and in the meantime talk with one another. Jebrâîl ''alaihis-salâm' says unto them: "Do not show mercy!" The munâfiq's soul comes up to the point of his nose. Then the angels let it loose. So tightly do they squeeze all his limbs that the light of his eyes pour down. The angels say unto him: "You are not for Paradise! Have you forgotten the wrongdoings that you committed as you were living? O you good-for-nothing person! The torment that has been prepared for you is the torment for munâfiqs and unbelievers. For, you had nothing to do with namâz, with zakât, with alms, or with mercy for the poor. You did not avoid harâms, and all your doings were fasâd. You committed backbiting and then said, 'Allah is kerîm.' And now, bitter is the torment." Then Hadrat Haqq subhânahu wa ta'âlâ addresses: **"Those munâfiqs did not think of their death even for a day. They were arrogant. They did not observe farzes, sunnats, or wâjibs. So let them see My torment now**!" Again, Zebânîs (Angels of Torment) hold his nails by the bottoms and pull his soul through the veins of his chest, taking it up to his pharynx, and then let it go down back again. Again, another voices comes (from Allâhu ta'âlâ), saying: **"Didn't scholars tell you? Didn't you read Our Book? Didn't it say: Do not be caught unawares, and do not follow the devil? Didn't it say: Know that everything is from Allah**?" Do not pine for this world, the place for carcasses! Be contented with what Allâhu ta'âlâ has given you, have mercy over His poor slaves, and feed the miskîns! Allâhu ta'âlâ is such a sovereign that He created you and took over Himself to feed you, and if a disaster from Him befalls you ask and beg Him again, and ask Him again to rescue you. Do not say, "I have paid doctors and they have cured me!" Know that it is Allâhu ta'âlâ who has rescued you! Property that you claim to be yours is something trusted to your care. It is no remedy for your sufferings. If it has been obtained by a way that is halâl, you will be called to account for it. Whatsoever Haqq subhânehu wa ta'âlâ has decreed for you, you will take it; no help will come from your property or from your children or from your friends, and you will not escape your end no matter how much you cry and wail and to whatsoever wilderness you flee to. Eventually you will be buried at the place holding the soil of your foreordained grave. Unless the time of your death comes, no one will harm you. Only, you have been commanded to protect yourself against dangers and to adhere to the causes that will be remedy to your sufferings.

And whenever Haqq ta'âlâ gives you blessings such as health, property, and children, you rejoice in them and say, "Our Rabb has been kind to us." But when Allâhu ta'âlâ gives you something disastrous, i.e. when He sends a calamity unto you, you become sad instead of being patient and you forget about gratitude.

A voice from Haqq ta'âlâ says: **"O My angels! Hold him**!" The angels hold his soul from the bottoms of all his hairs, letting him go again thereafter. No one has the power of rescuing a person being tormented by Allâhu ta'âlâ.

When the person lying in his death bed sees this torment he laments: Alas, alas, how I wish I had performed the commanded (Islamic) practices as I was in the world, so that I would not be suffering from the policy being inflicted on me now! Again, a voice from Allâhu ta'âlâ says unto the people attending the invalid: "**O My arrogant slaves! Go ahead and rescue this friend of yours by spending property! In the world you do not show patience about the disasters coming from Me, and complain about Me. Here, this slave is in torment and his soul has reached his pharynx. Of My Power!**" The angels hear this voice and prostrate themselves, saying: "O our Rabb! Your torment is haqq (true, rightful)!" Haqq ta'âlâ informs us about these events in the Qur'ân al-kerîm. Thereafter, another voice comes, bidding the angels to "Hold him." So severely painful is their hold that not a single hair-root all over his body feels free from torment. The angels shout in tandem: "O the soul of Allah's disobedient slave! Come on and get out of your body. Today is the day of torment for you, because you had affection for beings other than Allâhu ta'âlâ and you were too arrogant to greet the poor and you did things that were harâm and you deemed wrong to be right, and right to be wrong." These events are narrated in the Qur'ân al-kerîm.

Thereafter that person says to the angels: Allow me a moment's respite so that I may pull myself together. Presently he sees the Angel of death standing at the bedside. As soon as he sees the Angel of death he begins to tremble, forgetting about the torment he has undergone. When he sees the Angel of death he says: Who are you amidst the torment being inflicted by all these angels, and why are you here? Thereupon death bellows with all the awe it inspires: I am the death which shall take you away from earth, making your children orphans and letting your loathsome worldly relatives inherit from your property.

When he hears these words from death, he shudders and turns his face here and there. For, this is the symptom pointed out by the Rasûl-i-ekrem 'sall-Allâhu ta'âlâ 'alaihi wa sallam' in the following hadîth-i-sherîf quoted in Sahîh-i-Bukhârî: "**When he hears the angels, he turns his face towards the wall and sees death standing before him.**"

Whereever he turns he sees death right there, and then he turns

– 259 –

backwards again.

The Angel of death shouts vehemently: I am that great angel who took away the souls of your parents; you were there then; what help did you give? And now all your kith and kin are watching. To what avail? I am that great angel, and the people I killed before you had more power than you do.

As this person lying in bed talks with the angels, the angels of torment withdraw and they are gone. When he sees Azrâîl ''alaihis-salâm' (Angel of death) with all the angel's awe-inspiring appearance, he loses his mind on the spur of the moment.

Azrâîl ''alaihis-salâm' enquires: How did you find the world? He replies: I indulged in tricks of the world. This is the result of my indulgence.

And the Khallâq-i-jihân (Creator of all beings) changes the world into a woman. With her injurious sky-coloured eyes, her teeth like the horns of an ox, and her hideous smell, she sits on his chest.

Then they bring that person's property before him. Despite his utter grievance and before his eyes, they give his property, which he earned without discriminating between halâl and harâm, to his inheritors.

Thereafter the property says unto its owner: **"O you disobedient slave! You earned me and then spent me unfairly without giving alms and paying zakât. And now I have gone out of your possession and become property of people you disliked. They have taken me without any gratitude from you."**

As he is in this state, he looks all around him with such thirst as it makes his heart feel like burning.

This state of his affords the accursed Satan the opportunity he would be so happy to grab: With a goblet in his hand he comes to the bedside of that person for the purpose of stealing his îmân. He shakes the goblet with icy cold water in it at the invalid's bedside. The invalid sees him and hears the water being shaken. That is the place and time where and when a poor person and a rich one are known from each other.

If that person is without sa'âdat, he says: "Let me have a drink of that water." What more could the accursed want! He says: Say that –hâshâ– the universe does not have a creater! If the invalid is a shaqî person, he says what he is asked to say, then –al– ayâzu billah–his îmân is gone. However, as hikmat belongs to Hudâ

(Allâhu ta'âlâ), people with such an invalid should keep some water close at hand. Frequently, the invalid's mouth should be opened ajar and he should be made to have some water.

If hidâyat comes to his rescue, he accurses the Satan and rejects the water he offers.

If his time is up –and if he is a Believer– Azrâîl ''alaihis-salâm' is ordered to take his soul out and the blessed angel carries out the order. Three hundred and sixty angels take that (fortunate) soul from Azrâîl's ''alaihis-salâm' hand and, all of them disguised in his friends and beloved acquaintances, they clothe his soul in Paradise garments and take it up to the Palace of Paradise and show it its place in Paradise and –immediately thereafter– take it back to where the corpse is.

As yet if he left without îmân, three hundred and sixty angels from the sijjîn bring leaves of (a tree of Hell called) zaqqûm from Hell, which are even blacker than tar, wrap his soul, which has left his body without îmân, in them, immediately take it down to Hell, show its place, and take it back to where the corpse is.

If a person reaches the age of puberty, leads a long life in the the world, disobeys the commandments, and leaves this worldly life without having made tawba –naûzu billah (May Allah protect us against such an end)– he sees all these punishments, undergoes all the shameful treatments, and ends up in Hell, unless hidâyat (guidance) from Allâhu ta'âlâ comes to his rescue or he is blessed with the shafâ'at-i-Muhammadî 'sall-Allâhu ta'âlâ 'alaihi wa sallam'. (Please see the thirty-fifth chapter of the second fascicle of **Endless Bliss** for detailed information about shafâ'at [intercession].)

CONCERNING (INNOCENT) CHILDREN'S DEATH

When a Muslim child becomes ill and goes into its deathbed, its abode is the Maqâm-i-illiyyîn, i.e. Paradise. Three hundred and sixty angels come from there, stand in lines before that child and say unto it: "Yâ Mâsûm (O you innocent child)! Glad tidings to you! Today is a day when you are to plead with Haqq ta'âlâ for your past, for your parents and grandparents and neighboùrs." Thereupon a hundred angels put a crown of shafâ'at on its head and another hundred angels make it wear a crown of love and another hundred angels make it wear a raiment of zeal and strength and sixty other angels raise the curtain and barrier from before it eyes. As soon as all the barriers are raised, it sees all the fathers and grandfathers of all the passed Believers since Hadrat 'Âdam, and also the torment prepared for some of them. When it sees these states and facts concerning those people, it cries, wails, and shudders, so that people who do not know the inner essence of the matter construe its convulsions as agonies of death.

When angels charged with taking out its soul come and see it crowned with and clad in shafâ'at and with the curtains before its eyes raised and yet they are unable to take its soul out, they say unto it: "Yâ Ma'sûm! The Khallâq-i-'âlam (Creator of all beings) sends His salâm to you (greets you and offers His best wishes to you), says to you: I created it, and let it come back to Me. For, I gave it its soul for safekeeping, and let it return it to Me. And let Me give it Paradise and dîdâr (seeing Me) in return for it. If you do not believe us turn your face towards heavens, so that you will see (for yourself)." Thereupon the cihld looks and sees the angels and the Beauty (Jemâl) of Allâhu ta'âlâ. It trembles, foams at the mouth, and reddens with joy. So great is its rejoicing that it is about to jump and rush forward to give its soul away, when, somehow, it catches sight of its forefathers in torment, and it refuses to surrender its soul. "Yâ ma'sûm," say the angels! "Why don't you surrender your soul?" The child says: "O angels! Request of Allâhu ta'âlâ on my behalf to forgive my relatives and ancestors." The angels say: "Yâ Rabbî! You know what we are having with this innocent child." Thereupon Hadrat Allah 'jalla shânuhu' addresses to them: "For the right of My 'Iz (Power, Glory), I have forgiven them." Then the angels turn to the child and say: "Yâ ma'sûm! Glad tidings to you! Allâhu ta'âlâ has forgiven the ones who had îmân and accepted all your requests." As the child rejoices in the grand glad tidings, Haqq ta'âlâ sends unto it two houris from Paradise. Disguised in its parents, they appear to it, open their arms, and say: "O our son, or daughter! Come along with us! We cannot do without you in Paradise." They hand an apple that they brought from Paradise to the child and say, "Here, take it." As the child smells the apple, Hadrat Azrâîl 'alaihissalâm' (Angel of death) becomes an innocent child as lovely as it and takes its life [soul] out instantly.

According to another narration, as the child smells the apple, its soul sticks on the apple and the Angel of death takes the child's life from the apple. Both narrations are permissible.

Thereafter the Angel of death takes the soul to Paradise, the soul watching the heavens on the way. There is a vast open country made of green chrysolite there. When they get there the child asks: "Why have you brought me here?" The angels explain: "Yâ ma'sûm! There the place of Rising. It is very hot there. This vast country contains seventy thousand fountainheads of mercy. Stand by Hadrat Rasûl-i-ekrem's "alaihis-salâm' blessed pond and see the glasses of nûr! When your parents come to the place of Rising, you fill these glasses with water and give them, and hold them here and do not let them go, lest they should go towards Hell and subjected to torment and reprehension. For, the prayers you say are acceptable in the view of Haqq ta'âlâ. And on Friday nights (nights between Thursdays and Fridays) go down to earth. When you go there take Allâhu ta'âlâ's salâm to the Ummat-i-Muhammad 'sall-Allâhu ta'âlâ 'alaihi wa sallam'. And sprinkle nûr unto them and take the berât of their gratitude to Allâhu ta'âlâ."

After making the child's soul tour these grades, they hurriedly bring it back and place it at the head side of the dead child. Throughout the procedures such as performance of the namâz of janâza, interment of the corpse, and questioning in the grave, the soul stays over the grave. If its parents die without îmân, there will be a curtain between the parents and the child. The child does not look for them or meet them anywhere, so that they long to see one another. These are the facts about Muslims' children who die before reaching the age of puberty.

CONCERNING MUSLIM WOMEN'S DEATH

If a woman dies from lochia or pregnancy or plague or internal suffering or, without any of these causes, dies of a natural death as she leads a life wherein she never shows herself to men nâ-mahram to her without properly covering her body, (i.e. in a way taught by Islam,) and wherein her husband is pleased with her, at the time of her death angels of Paradise come and make lines before her and make salâm to her with reverential respect, saying unto her: "O you, beloved and martyred maiden of Allâhu ta'âlâ! Come on out, what are you doing in this worldly palace? Allâhu ta'âlâ is pleased with you and He has forgiven you your sin at the pretext of your illness and has granted you His Paradise. Come on and surrender your safekeeping!" When that woman sees the high rank she is going to attain she wants to surrender her soul. However, she looks around herself and says: "Let Allâhu ta'âlâ judge my friends in the

world with compassion, and thereafter I shall surrender my soul."
The angels present her request to Jenâb-i-Haqq. Thereupon the
Word of Allâhu ta'âlâ manifests itself, saying: "For the right of My
Greatness, I have made all the prayers of this slave of Mine
acceptable." So the angels give her the glad tidings. Thereafter the
Angel of death and a hundred and twenty angels of mercy arrive
there. The nûr on their faces reach the 'Arsh, they wear crowns on
their heads, they are clad in raiments of nûr and shod in gold clogs,
and they have green wings. With fruits of Paradise in their hands
and scents as fragrant as musk dabbed on them, they come down
and make salâm with deep respect and kindness, and say: "The
Khallâq-i-'âlam (Creater of all beings) sends His salâm to you,
gives you Paradise, makes you a neighbour to His beloved Prophet
Muhammad ''alaihis-salâm' and a companion to Hadrat 'Âisha."

This woman with îmân hears what is being said to her, the
curtain before her eyes opens up, and she sees women with îmân
and the ones being tormented on account of their sins. So she
entreats: "Please forgive them their sins, Yâ Rabbî!" Thereupon a
voice comes from Jenâb-i-'izzat, saying: "O My jâriya! I have made
all your wishes come true. Now, do surrender your safekeeping
(soul), with My Beloved One's wife and daughter ready and
waiting." No sooner does she hear this voice than she attempts to
give her life, her soul trembling, her feet rushing forward, and she
in perspiration. She is about to surrender her life, when two angels
appear on the scene. Each of them holding a stick of fire in their
hands, they stand on her both sides, one of them on the right hand
side and the other one on her left. Meanwhile, the accursed Satan
runs to the scene, soliloquizing: "I do not expect much from this
one, but let me see!" He comes forward, showing her the pot made
of jewelry and to the brim with pure icy water. When those angels
see that wicked creature, they break the pot he is holding with the
sticks in their hands and scare him away. The Muslim woman
laughs as she watches them. Thereafter the maidens (of Paradise)
called houris offer her beverage (of Paradise) from the Kawthar
pond in bowls made of jewelry, and she drinks it. So delicious is the
beverage of Paradise that her soul jumps and sticks to the goblet,
whence the Angel of death picks it. Angels announce the death to
one another, saying: "**Innâ lillâhi wa innâ ilaihi râji'ûn** (Certainly
we are from Him, and to Him shall we certainly return)!" And
they take the soul up to heavens like a sightseeing tour, show her
her abode in Paradise, and come back with the soul in no time,
placing the soul at the headside of the corpse.

When they take off her clothes and undo her hair, her soul comes to the headside of her corpse presently and says: "O you, the person to do the washing! Hold it gently! For, it has received a fatal wound from the talons of Azrâîl. And my skin has become enervated after all the fatigue it has gone through." When the body is brought to the washing bench the soul comes again and says: "Do not make the water too hot! My skin is quite weak. Let me be saved from your hands the soonest possible, so that I may attain comfort!" When the corpse is washed and shrouded, the soul waits for a while and then says: "This is the last time I see the world. Let me see my kith and kin and let them see me, so that it should be a warning for them. Since they, too, shall die soon, like me, let them not cry and wail after me. Let them not forget me, and let them always remember me, read (or recite) the Qur'ân al-kerîm (and send the thawâb for that good deed of theirs to my soul). Let them not quarrel over the property I leave behind so that I should not be tormented in grave on account of their quarrel. Let them remember me on Fridays and on the days of 'Iyd."

Thereafter, when the coffin with the corpse in it is placed on the (bench called) musallâ (for the namâz of janâza), the soul calls: "Remain easy, o my son(s) and daughter(s) and parents! No other day of separation is like this one. We will be missing each other until we meet again, no sooner than on the day of Rising. Farewell to you, o you people who weep after me!"

When the coffin is lifted up to shoulders, her soul calls again and says: "Carry me slowly! If your purpose is (to earn) thawâb, do not cause me trouble! And let me take my pleasure (with you) to Allâhu ta'âlâ!'

When the coffin is placed by the grave, her soul calls again, saying: "See the situation I am in and let it be a warning for you! Now you will place me in a dark place and leave. I will be alone with my 'amal, (i.e. my deeds in the world.) Behold these desperate times lest you should not get carried away by the trickeries of this mendacious world!"

When the corpse is consigned to the grave the soul takes its place by its headside. By no means should a dead person be left in their grave without the telqîn (inculcation). [It is an act of sunnat for a sâlih Muslim to carry out the (inculcation called) **Telqîn**[1]

---

[1] Please also see the sixteenth chapter of the fifth fascicle of **Endless Bliss** for 'Telqîn'.

after interment. Wahhâbîs deny the fact that it is sunnat to carry out the telqîn. They say that it is bid'at to do so. They say that a dead person will not hear you. The scholars of Ahl as-Sunnat 'rahima-humullâhu ta'âlâ' wrote various books and proved that it is an act of sunnat to give telqîn, (i.e. to perform it.) One of these valuable books is **Nûr-ul-yaqîn fî mebhas-it-telqîn**, written by Mustafâ bin Ibrâhîm Siyâmî 'rahima-hullâhu ta'âlâ'. A hadîth-i-sherîf on the authority of Tabarânî and Ibni Menda is quoted in that book. That hadîth-i-sherîf commands to perform the telqîn. The book, i.e. **Nûr-ul-yaqîn...**, was printed in Bangkok, Thailand in 1345, and its second edition was brought out in Istanbul, Turkey, in 1396 [1976 A.D.]. With the command of Allâhu ta'âlâ, the corpse in its grave wakes up, like from sleep, to find itself in a dark place. She calls her servant or slave or the person who used to serve her in the world and says: "Fetch me a candle!" There comes no reply, not even a single sound or voice. The grave cleaves in two, and there appear the two questioning angels [named Munkar and Nakîr]. Raging flames come from their mouths, and their nostrils belch out heavy smoke. They get quite close to her and ask: "**Men Rabbuka wa mâ dînuka, wa men nebiyyuka**, (i.e. who is your Rabb and what is your religion, and who is your Prophet,)?" If she answers the questions correctly, the angels deliver her the good news of the mercy of Haqq ta'âlâ, and leave. Presently there opens a window on the right hand side of her grave and someone whose face is as bright as the full moon comes in through the window. As soon as this woman blessed with îmân sees that beautiful person by her side, she rejoices at the unexpected company, and asks: "Who are you?" "I have been created from your patience and gratitude in the world," replies company from felicity. "I shall be your companion until the day of Rising."

So long as the nafs carries on with harâms its affinity,
The heart shall never reflect the lights coming from Divinity!

CONCERNING THE DEATHS of the WRONGED, the PATIENT, and the GHARÎB–MARTYRS

Deaths of all these people are identical. We will describe one of them, so that the rest will be matched accordingly. There are two kinds of gharîb (lonely, forlorn, left alone) people: One of them is a person left alone in a far away land and who have no relatives or acquaintances with them. The other one is poor, although they live in their home land. Nobody condescends to go and see them. Both these kinds of Believers are gharîb people, who will be martyrs if they die (in that situation). Another Believer who will die as a martyr is one who is past the age of sixty and never omits the daily five namâzes. [A person who dies from committing an act of harâm will not become a martyr; an example of this is a person who imbibes alcohol and becomes poisoned. (This person will not become a martyr if he dies from poisoning.) However, if a person dies during alcoholic consumption and yet for some other reason, e.g. because the building where they are imbibing alcohol collapses, then they attain martyrdom. A woman's entire body, with the exception of her face and palms, is within her limbs of awrat. It is farz for her to cover her entire body, with the exception of her face and palms, (as she goes out or in the presence of men who are nâ-mahram to her.) A woman who does not attach due importance to this matter becomes an unbeliever. Another kind of martyr is a girl or woman who never goes out without properly covering her head, hair, arms and legs. Allâhu ta'âlâ's commandments and prohibitions, as an ensemble, are called the **Ahkâm-i-islâmiyya**. Parents who learn the Ahkâm-i-islâmiyya and teach them to their children are among martyrs.] None of these people will become martyrs unless they have îmân (as taught by the scholars of Ahl as-sunnat) and perform their namâz five times daily. As well, a Muslim who dies as he is being held captive by the enemy, becomes a martyr. An unbeliever who dies under torture shall not become a martyr. A person who dies as an unbeliever shall never enter Paradise.

The moment when the aforesaid martyrs put their heads on the cushion on their deathbed, the gates to heavens open and so many angels descend to earth that only Mawlâ (Allâhu ta'âlâ) knows their number. They hold crowns and garments of nûr in their hands. With profound reverence they invite that person's soul. As a matter of fact, Haqq ta'âlâ describes this state at the final part of Fajr Sûra.

Another martyr is a Believer who turns his face towards the Derghâh-i-'izzat and supplicates: "O my Ma'bûd (the One whom I worship)! As long as I have lived I have never placed my hopes on anyone but Thine Greatness! Nor have I ever hung my head before anyone (but You). And I have never gotten carried away by trickeries of the world or of the enemy. Yâ Rabbî! Presently, I hope that Thou wilt treat all the Ummat-i-Muhammadî 'sall-Allâhu ta'âlâ 'alaihi wa sallam' with 'afw (forgiveness) and maghfirat (compassion)". This person also is a martyr.

The blessed angels wrap that fortunate soul in the garments (that they have brought with them. At that moment a voice from Haqq ta'âlâ says: "Take that soul to Paradise! For, he (or she) used to perform namâz more than others did and he (or she) liked having guests, and forgave people their faults and guilts, and said 'Istighfâr' very often. And he (or she) made dhikr of Me so much. And he (or she) never went out without properly covering themselves. And he (or she) avoided harâms. And he (or she) obeyed Prophets and Islam, in the world."

Now, the two angels on a person's both shoulders and who are charged with recording that person's good and evil deeds supplicate: "Yâ Rabbî! You have made us responsible for this person in the world. And now, please give us permission to ascend to heavens with this person's soul. The voice coming from the Most Great says: "You stay by that person's grave, say tasbîh and tekbîr and make sajda and donate the thawâb (for all those acts of worship) to that slave of Mine." Thereupon they continuously make dhikr and tasbîh and record the thawâb in that person's book, and this process continues until the end of the world.

[AN IMPORTANT NOTE: The munâfiqs living in Egypt revolted against the (rightly-guided) Khalîfa 'Uthmân 'radiy-Allâhu 'anh' and came to Medîna to kill him. Their accomplices in Medîna supported them with lies and slanders. They vilified the Sahâba by spreading the gossip that "Muslims in Medîna did not help the Khalîfa." The fact, however, was that the Khalîfa's purpose was to attain the high ranks of martyrs in Paradise, and he was praying to Allâhu ta'âlâ for that greatest blessing. Other Muslims came to help him, but he requested them not to do anything about the matter. He sent them back. Taking advantage of this, the rebels martyred the Khalîfa easily. Thereby he attained his wish. His supplications had been accepted (by Allâhu ta'âlâ). Martyrs do not feel any pain as they die. The blessings to be given to them in Paradise are shown to them, so that they surrender their souls willingly to the angels as they rejoice at the rewards awaiting them.]

CONCERNING the DISBELIEVER'S DEATH

When a disbeliever or a murtadd (renegade) or an idiot who despises Islam and calls the Qur'ân al-kerîm 'desert law' and who is as ignorant and as immoral as to call Muhammad ''alaihis-salâm', –the highest and the most honourable human being and the master of all Prophets–, 'camel-herd' –may Allâhu ta'âlâ protect us against such an ignoble act–, and who stoops to saying that religions are unnecessary as the result of an evaluation of Islam, –the mainstay of social peace and happiness, the source of knowledge, ethics, cleanliness, health and justice, and the edifier of all cultures, –made under the niggardly criteria of an addle brain which is as noisome as a box of carcasses,– and who is no more than a plaything in the hands of his own nafs–, is about to die, the curtain before his eyes is raised. Paradise is shown to him. A beautiful angel says to him: "O you, disbeliever! O you, ignoble person, who used to call Muslims 'fuddy-duddies', and people who ran after their lusts and who trampled on ethical principles 'illuminated and modern people'! You have been in the wrong way. You have been despising Islam, right religion. People who have believed and respected the teachings which Muhammad ''alaihis-salâm' brought from Allâhu ta'âlâ shall enter this place, Paradise." He sees the blessings in Paradise. And the houris of Paradise say: "People who have îmân will be saved from the torment to be inflicted by Allâhu ta'âlâ." Thereafter the Satan appears in the guise of a priest and says: "O you, so and so, the son of so and so! Those who were with you a while ago are liars. Those blessings shall be all yours." Then Hell is shown to him. It contains mountains of fire, scorpions and centipedes as big as mules. He sees the torments stated in hadîth-i-sherîfs. Angels of torment from Hell, called Zebânîs (or Zabânîs), hit with sticks of fire. Flames exude from their mouths. They are as tall as minarets, and their teeth are like horns of oxen. Their call sounds like thunder. The disbeliever shudders at their voices and turns his face towards the Satan. So frightened is the Satan that he turns tail. The angels catch the Satan and knock him down. Accosting the disbeliever, they say: "O you, the enemy of Islam! In the world you have been denying the Messenger of Allah 'sall-Allâhu ta'âlâ 'alaihi wa sallaml'. And now you deny the angels, and once again the accursed Satan deceives you." They hang chains of fire on his neck, pull his legs up to his head, so that his feet are on the back of his head now, and make his right hand thrust into the left hand side of his chest and his left hand into his right flank, making his both hands jut out from his back. There is an âyat-i-kerîma informing us about these tragic events. He cries and calls his flatterers for help. The Zebânîs, instead, answer him: "O you, disbeliever; o you, idiot who mocked the Muslims! It is no longer time for begging. Îmân or prayers shall no longer be accepted. It is time for you to be punished for your disbelief." They pull his tongue out from the back of his neck. They scoop out his eyes. With many another way of very bitter torment they extract his abominable soul and hurl it into Hell. May Allâhu ta'âlâ bless us with the lot of surrendering our soul in the religion of Muhammad ''alaihis-salâm' and equipped with the creed written in the books of scholars of Ahl as-sunnat, who have conveyed the religion of that noblest Prophet correctly to us! Âmîn.

However long you may live, you shall die eventually. Our Prophet ''alaihis-salâm' stated: **"When a person's soul leaves his body, a voice says: O you, mankind, have you left the world, or has the world left you? Have you collected the world, or has the world collected you? Have you killed the world, or has the world killed you? When the washing of the janâza (corpse) starts, a voice asks three questions:**

1– Where is your strong body? What thing has weakened you?

2– Where is your lovely speech? What thing has silenced you?

3– Where are your beloved friends? Why are they gone, leaving you all alone?

When the janâza is wrapped in the shroud, another voice says: Do not set out without provisions! This journey is without return; you can never come back, eternally. Your destination is teeming with angels charged with torment. When the corpse is placed in the coffin another voice says: If you have managed to please Jenâb-i-Haqq, good news for you, for greatness and happiness are awaiting you! If you have incurred the Wrath of Jenâb-i-Haqq, then woe betide you! When the janâza is brought near its grave another voice says: O you, mankind! What have you prepared in your worldly life (that will be useful) **for you in the grave? What nûr have you brought with you for this dark place? What have you brought from your riches and fame? What have you brought with you to furnish and embellish this barren grave? When the janâza is placed in the grave, the grave starts to talk and says: You spoke on my back, and now you are silent in my abdomen. And, eventually, when the interment is finished and the people doing the service are gone, a voice coming from Hadrat Haqq ta'âlâ says:**

O My slave, you are alone now; they are gone, leaving you alone in that dark grave. They were your friends, your brothers, your children, and your devoted men. But none of them has been of any benefit to you. O My slave, you have been disobedient to Me; you have not carried out My commandment, and you have never thought of this situation. If the dead person died with îmân, it is hoped that Jenâb-i-Haqq blesses that person with His forgiveness, saying to him: O My slave who has been a Believer! It is not worthy of My Greatness to leave you gharîb (lonely) in your grave. For the right of My 'Izzat-u-jelâl, I will treat you with such mercy as will daze your friends and I will show you such compassion as will surpass parents' compassion over their son. With His unique Kindness and Favour, He forgives all the sins of that slave, so that his grave becomes a Garden of Paradise enriched with houris and blessings of Paradise. Allâhu ta'âlâ is so merciful that He forgives His sinful slaves. He is so merciful that He sees His slaves' sins numbers of times and covers them instead of casting their sins to their teeth. Then, we must perform the commandments and avoid the prohibitions of such a Creator and save ourselves from the imminent torment by doing the 'amal-i-sâlih."

All Believers, sinful ones as well as sinless ones, shall experience the questioning in grave. Torment also shall be inflicted on the ones who have not attained forgiveness, as well as on disbelievers. People who spread gossip among Muslims and those who splash urine on their clothes in toilet will be subjected to torment in grave. [Torment in grave will be inflicted not only on the soul, but both on the soul and on the body, i.e. physically as well. These facts are beyond the scope of mind. So we should avoid attempting to solve them by using our mind.]

If that person died without îmân, (i.e. as an unbeliever,) he (or she) will undergo bitter torment till mahsher, (i.e. day of Judgment,) [and thereafter as well, eternally in Hell.]

The following is the simplified English version of an Ottoman Turkish poem written by **'Abd-ur-Rahmân Sâmi Pâsha**, a retired Ottoman General, who passed away in 1295 [1878 A.D.], during his membership of the Senate:

O you, living visitor! Do not lose your heart to anyone but Allâhu ta'âlâ!

No one shall be left in the world. No one but Allâh can do anything. No one but Allâhu ta'âlâ shall continue to exist.

Everyone has cares, sweet and bitter days. This base world is not worth competing with anyone for it.

I, too, was one in my time, like a precious stone on a President's ring, like a sovereign's signature. But now destiny has turned all upside down.

Then my heart fell ill. My energy was all gone. At last the bird of my life [my soul] flew away. For, the cage [my soul] had gone to rack and ruin.

My health, like a candle, went out. Darkness was all around me. The sun of the Hereafter rose. All was enlightened with nûrs of Allah.

At that moment I attained my Rabb. My sins surfaced. When I begged for forgiveness, He met me with His endless mercy.

Yâ Rabbî! I have committed hundreds of thousands of sins. Yet I trust myself, with this black face of mine, to Your Gate Most High. Please do forgive me!

I have made Your Name Ghafûr date of this writing of mine [1286]. Its meaning will certainly come true. No one but Allah can do anything. No one but Allah shall continue to exist!

This life is a dream beset with sufferings;
Aren't we born to die eventually?
After a few hours in pleasures,
Cares chase each and every pleasure presently.

We dive every moment, in ignorance,
Into the depths of death so zealously.
In divers troubles and many hardships,
The world pushes us to insolvency.

And, poor us, seeing this edifice,
Ask whence its dwellers are all coming from.
Its Creator, His creatures, its secrets,
His hidden causes, so wonderfully.

But the secrets hidden by Haqq Himself,
Are beyond the slave's mind, definitely.
Man, with nescience, void, inability,
Will be made to err within fallacy.

TO VISIT GRAVES and TO READ (or RECITE) THE QUR'ÂN AL-KERÎM

Grave-visiting is an act that is sunnat. Graves should be visited weekly, or on 'Iyd days at least. A visit that yields more thawâb is one made on Thirsday or Friday or Saturday. It is written in the final pages of the book entitled **Shir'at-ul-islâm**, (and written by Muhammad bin Ebî Bakr 'rahmatullâhi ta'âlâ 'alaih', d. 573 [1178 A.D.], Bukhâra,) that it is sunnat to visit graves. The visitor will meditate on the fact that the corpses in graves rot away, which in turn will give him a warning. Whenever 'Uthmân 'radiy-Allâhu 'anh' walked by a grave, so bitterly would he weep that his beard would become wet. In addition (to the warning for the visitor), the dead person in the grave will benefit from the blessings pronounced over them. Rasûlullah 'sall-Allâhu 'alaihi wa sallam' would visit the graves of his relatives and those of his Sahâba 'radiy-Allâhu ta'âlâ 'anhum'. After making the salâm' and pronouncing the benedictions and saying the prayers, the visitor sits with his face towards the grave and his back in the direction of Qibla. It is Chirstians' custom to rub your hands and face gently on the grave or to kiss the soil on the grave. It is stated in a hadîth-i-sherîf: **"When a person visits the grave of an acquaintance of his and makes the salâm, his acquaintance in the grave recognizes him and acknowledges his salâm."** Ahmad ibni Hanbal 'rahima-hullâhu ta'âlâ' states: "As you pass by a cemetery, recite the Ikhlâs, the two Sûras beginning with Qul-a'ûdhu..., and the Fâtiha, and send the thawâb earned thereby to the dead people lying there. The thawâb shall reach them." A hadîth-i-sherîf quoted on the authority of Enes bin Mâlik 'radiy-Allâhu ta'âlâ 'anh' reads: **"When the Âyat-al-kursî is read (or recited) and its thawâb is sent to the dead people lying in graves, Allâhu ta'âlâ makes it reach all the dead people there."**

It is stated in the book entitled **Khazânat-ur-riwâyat** (and written by Qâdî Hindî 'rahmatullâhi ta'âlâ 'alaih'): "If certain scholars are being visited when they are alive, it is permissible even to make long distance journeys to visit them after their death. With respect to benefits, there is no difference between visiting Prophets ''alaihim-us-salawât-u-wa-t-teslîmât and visiting the Awliyâ or the 'Ulamâ (Islamic scholars) 'rahima-humullâhu ta'âlâ'. The difference is in their ranks and grades."

[If a Muslim hangs a signboard with the name of someone whom he loves on it on one of the walls of his sitting room or erects a stone with the name of that person on that person's grave, whenever Muslims who enter the room or visit the grave pronounce a blessing over that person, Allâhu ta'âlâ will bless the owner of the name with His Mercy and forgiveness. Writing the name on the wall or on the grave stone is not intended to remember the owner of the name. It is intended for Muslims to say the Fâtiha and to pronounce blessings over the owner of the name. For that matter, it has become customary in Muslim countries to write names on the walls of rooms and on stones erected on graves. If a Walî's name is written, when you read the name and ask the owner of the name for shafâ'at (intercession) and prayers and benedictions over you, the Walî will hear you and pray for the realization of your wishes pertaining to this world and to the Hereafter and his prayers will be accepted (by Allâhu ta'âlâ).]

Although grave-visiting is permissible for women as well, it is better for them not to visit graves other than that of Rasûlullah. Grave-visiting in a state of haid (menstruation) or junub is permissible, yet it is sunnat to have an ablution during the visit. It is stated in a hadîth-i-sherîf: "**When you visit a Believer's grave and say this prayer: 'Allâhumma innî es-elu-ka bi-haqqi Muhammadin wa âli Muhammadin an lâ-tu'adh-dhiba hâdhel mayyit,' the Believer will be saved from torment.**" Another hadîth-i-sherîf reads: "**If a person visits his parents' graves or that of either one them on every Friday, he shall attain forgiveness.**" It is permissible to kiss the soil on a grave only if it belongs to one of your parents. As is related in the book entitled **Kifâya**, someone asked Rasûlullah 'sall-Allâhu 'alaihi wa sallam': "I have taken an oath to kiss the threshold of Paradise. How can If fulfil my oath?" "**Kiss your mother's foot,**" said the Master of Prophets. When that person said that he did not have parents, Rasûlullah stated: "**Kiss your parents' graves! If you do not know their graves, then draw two lines with the intention of their graves and kiss those lines! You will have fulfilled your oath!**"

We should rather visit the graves of great people far away from our place when we go there for another business than specially make the long distance journey only for the purpose of visiting their blessed graves. However, it yields plenty of thawâb to make a long distance journey (specially) to visit our Master, the Prophet 'sall-Allâhu 'alaihi wa sallam'. A person who visits (the graves of) Prophets ''alaihim-us-salâm' and Awliyâ ''alaih-ir-rahma' benefits from their blessed souls. His heart becomes purified in direct ratio to his love and attachment to them. If sins are committed at the tombs of the Awliyâ, e.g. if they are visited also by women who do not cover themselves properly, this should not be grounds for ceasing from visiting those blessed places; if we cannot prevent violations of that sort, we should hate them with our heart. Likewise, we should attend a Believer's janâza (funeral) even if there are women or songs or eulogies are being chanted or speeches are being made.

If women's visiting graves is intended for mourning, crying and wailing or causing fesâd (sins) by mixing with men, it is harâm. Condemnations shower on women who do so. Although it is permissible for old women to visit the graves of their relatives or of the Awliyâ without mixing with men, even this conditional grave-visiting is makrûh for young girls. The same rule applies to women's attending a janâza (funeral).

It is stated in the book entitled **Jilâ-ul-qulûb** (and written by Zeyn-ud-dîn Muhammad bin 'Alî Birghivî, 928 [1521 A.D.], Balıkesir, Turkey–981 [1573] of plague, Birgi): A person who enters a cemetery says: "**Es-salâmu 'alaikum, yâ Ahla dâr-il-qawm-il-mu'minîn! Innâ inshâ-Allâhu 'an qarîbin bikum lâhiqûn,**" standing as he is. Thereafter he makes the Basmala and recites the Sûra Ikhlâs eleven times (making the Basmala at each time) and the Sûra Fâtiha once (making the Basmala before reciting it as well). Thereafter he says this prayer: "**Allâhumma Rabb-el-ejsâd-il-bâliyeh, wa-l-izâmin nâhira-t-illatî harajat min-ad-dunyâ wa hiya bika mu'minatun, edhil-'alaihâ revhan min 'indika wa salâman minnî.**" He approaches the grave from the right hand side [Qibla side] of the meyyit (dead Muslim in the grave), preferably closer to the meyyit's feet. He makes the Salâm, (i.e. he says, "Salâmun 'alaikum.") Standing or kneeling or sitting, he recites the initial and final parts of the Sûra Baqara, then the Sûra Yâsin, and then the Sûras Tebâraka and Tekâthur and Ikhlâs-i-sherîf and Fâtiha, and sends the thawâb thereby earned as a gift to the meyyit (or mayyit).

An important note: Our scholars state in their discourse over performance of hajj on someone else's behalf that it is permissible to donate the thawâb earned by performing acts of farz and/or nâfila worship and other pious acts and good deeds such as namâz, fasting, alms, reading (or reciting) the Qur'ân al-kerîm, dhikring, making tawâf, hajj, 'umra, visiting the graves of Prophets and/or Awliyâ, shrouding a dead Muslim, as a gift to someone else's soul. Both the person who performs the act of worship and donates its thawâb and the person to whose soul the thawâb is donated as a gift shall be given thawâb (by Allâhu ta'âlâ). For that matter, the Qur'ân al-kerîm should be read (or recited) during grave-visiting and elsewhere and its thawâb should be donated to the souls of dead Believers and immediately thereafter blessings should be pronounced over them and prayers should be said for them. For, rahmat and barakat descends on a place where the Qur'ân al-kerîm is read (or recited). Any prayers said at that place is accepted (by Allâhu ta'âlâ). When it is read (or recited) by a grave, that grave is filled with rahmat (mercy of Allâhu ta'âlâ) and barakat. According to the Hanafî Madhhab, when a Muslim performs nâfila fasting, namâz or alms or reads (or recites) the Qur'ân al-kerîm or says prayers and donates the thawâb to other Muslims, dead or alive, the thawâb will reach those Muslims. There are Islamic scholars who say that the same rule applies to acts of farz worship as well. The thawâb is not divided by the number of the meyyits. The entire thawâb is given to each and every meyyit. According to the Madhhabs of Mâlikî and Shâfi'î, acts of worship that are performed only physically, such as reading (or reciting) the Qur'ân al-kerîm, are not donated to other Muslims. Blessings are pronounced over them on account of the physical acts of worship performed.

It is written in the book entitled **Kitâb-ul-fiqh 'ala-l-medhâhib-il-erbe'a**: "Grave-visiting is an act of sunnat to be performed by men for the purpose of taking warning from the dead and meditating over the Hereafter. In the Madhhabs of Hanafî and Mâlikî, it is sunnat muakkad to do the visiting on Thursday, Friday and/or Saturday. In the Shâfi'î Madhhab it is sunnat muakkad to do the visiting between late afternoon on Thursday and sunrise of Saturday. The visitor should read (or recite) the Qur'ân al-kerîm for the mayyit and pronounce blessings on them. These things will be useful to the meyyit. When you arrive in the cemetery, it is sunnat to say this prayer: "**Es-salâmu 'alaikum, yâ Ahla dâr-il-qawm-il-mu'minîn! Innâ inshâ-Allâhu 'an qarîbin bikum lâhiqûn.**" Every grave is visited, far and near. In fact, it is sunnat to go long distance for the purpose of visiting Sâlih Muslims and Walîs 'rahima-humullâhu ta'âlâ'. It is one of the most valuable acts of worship to visit Rasûlullah's 'sall-Allâhu 'alaihi wa sallam' blessed grave. Grave-visiting is permissible for old women as well, provided they be properly dressed. It is harâm for old women as well if it should cause fitna and fesâd. It is not permissible to make tawâf around the grave or to kiss the soil or to ask for something from the dead during the visit." The Awliyâ 'rahima-humullâhu ta'âlâ' are asked for shafâ'at, for intercession for the blessing of Allâhu ta'âlâ.

There are two things whose missing,
Will burn all, regardless of who they are.
Eyes shedding blood will never pay their dues;
One is youth, other one: Muslim brother!

THIRD VOLUME, NINTH LETTER

The ninth letter of the third volume of the book entitled 'Maktûbât' and written by Imâm Rabbânî Mujaddid-i-elf-i-thânî Ahmad Fârûqî 'rahima-hullâhu ta'âlâ' was written for Mîr Muhammad Nu'mân. It explains the âyat-i-kerîma that purports: "Take what Rasûlullah has brought for you!" The letter is in the Arabic language. The following is its English version:

Bism-illâh-ir-Rahmân-ir-Rahîm! The seventh âyat-i-kerîma of Hashr Sûra purports: **"Take what Rasûlullah has brought for you. Avoid his prohibitions and fear Allah!"** [Doing the commandments and avoiding the prohibitions, in the aggregate, are called obeying Islam.] Allâhu ta'âlâ's adding, "... fear Allah," after saying, "Avoid his prohibitions...," shows that it is more important to avoid the prohibitions. For, to fear Allâhu ta'âlâ, i.e. taqwâ, means to avoid the prohibitions, (i.e. harâms.) Taqwâ is the the basis of Islam. It is called **wara'** to avoid the doubtful acts as well. Rasûlullah 'sall-Allâhu 'alaihi wa sallam' stated: **"Wara' is the mainmast of our religion."** He stated in another hadîth-i-sherîf: **"Nothing can be like wara'."** This importance which our religion attaches to avoiding harâms is on account of the greater number of the acts to be avoided and its being more useful to avoid harâms. For, doing a commandment contains a kind of avoidance as well. To do a certain commandment means to avoid not doing it. And its being more useful is on account of its entailing unyielding opposition to the nafs. When a commandment is being done, the nafs also has a share from the pleasure taken. The less the indulgence allowed for the nafs in doing something, the more useful will it be to do it. In other words, the faster will it make you attain the grace of Allâhu ta'âlâ. For, the Ahkâm-i-islâmiyya, i.e. Islam's commandments and prohibitions, are intended to oppress and undermine the nafs. The nafs is Allâhu ta'âlâ's enemy. It is stated in a hadîth-i-qudsî: **"Be inimical to your nafs! For, it is My enemy."** Therefore, of all the turuq-i-'aliyya (paths and orders of Tasawwuf), the one which tutors more strict obedience to Islam is the one which will guide closer to Allâhu ta'âlâ. For, that one contains more opposition to the nafs. And this, as is known to the connoisseurs of the matter, is the path we have been following. It was for that reason that the profound scholar Behâaddîn Bukhârî, our superior guide, stated: "I have found the shortest of the paths making one attain Allâhu ta'âlâ." For, this path instructs more opposition to the nafs. As for this path's championship in its strictness of obedience to Islam, it will be quite easy for an intelligent and reasonable person who studies the books written by our guides to realise this fact. That person will see the fact clearly. So clear a fact as it is, I have explained it in detail in a number of my letters. Allâhu ta'âlâ knows the truth of everything. His help will suffice for us. He is a very good wakîl. Salât (prayers and benefactions) and salâm (greetings, salutations, salvations) to our Master Muhammad ''alaihis-salâm', to his Âl and Ashâb 'radiy-Allâhu ta'âlâ 'anhum ajma'în', and to people following the right way!

THIRD VOLUME, EIGHTY-FOURTH LETTER

Hamd (praise and gratitude) be to Allâhu ta'âlâ, and salâm to His slaves whom He has chosen and loves! A person who wants to strive in this way [and to attain Allâhu ta'âlâ's love], first of all, has to correct his creed in light of the teachings of the scholars of the right way, [i.e. scholars of Ahl as-sunnat.] [These profound scholars acquired all their learnings from the Ashâb-i-kirâm. They should not be mistaken for their personal thoughts or for the ideas of philosophers.] May Allâhu ta'âlâ bless these great people with plenty or rewards [requitals] for their works! Thereafter, that person has to learn the knowledge of Fiqh necessary for every individual. Thereafter, he has to practise what he has learned. Thereafter, he has to make dhikr of Allâhu ta'âlâ all his time. [That is, he has to always think of Allâhu ta'âlâ and His (Attributes called) Sifât-i-dhâtiyya.] However, making dhikr is conditional on first learning how do so from a blessed person who is both kâmil, (i.e. who has attained perfection under the guide of another superior and blessed person,) and mukammil, (i.e. who has been authorized by his master and superior guide with an ijâzat [diploma] to guide other Muslims to perfection.) If he learns it from defective people, [especially if they are the so-called unlearned and heretical shaikhs,] he can never attain perfection. In the beginning he should make very much dhikr; so much so that after performing the daily five) farz namâzes and their sunnat parts, no acts of worship other than dhikr should be performed; even reading (or reciting) the Qur'ân al-kerîm and other acts of nâfila worship should be left until some time later. Dhikr should be made with or without an ablution. This duty must be done continuously, when standing, when sitting, when walking, and when lying. Not a single moment should be spent without dhikring when walking in the street, when eating, when going to sleep. A Persian couplet in English:

Make dhikr, as long as you live, all the time, and always!
With dhikr of Beloved is the heart clean, no other ways.

So much dhikr should he make that no other wish or thought than the object of dhikr, [i.e. Allâhu ta'âlâ,] should be left in his heart. No names of things other than Him, not even their traces, should come to his heart. Even if he forces himself to think of things other than Him, he should fail to bring them to his heart. This unawareness of the heart of things other than Allâhu ta'âlâ is the beginning of (the great fortune of) attaining Him. This oblivion is the glad tidings of attaining the Matlûb's (Allâhu ta'âlâ's) grace and love. An Arabic couplet in English:

How can we that high Su'âd attain,
With high hills and deep dales in between!

[Su'âd is the name of a ma'shûqa (sweetheart).] Allâhu ta'âlâ, alone, makes a person attain anything. Salâm to the travellers of the right way! [It is stated in the seventeenth letter of the third volume: "Making dhikr with the heart frees a person from affection towards things other than Allâhu ta'âlâ. Affection of that sort is a heart illness. Unless the heart rids itself of that illness, it will not attain true îmân and it will be difficult to obey the Ahkâm-i-islâmiyya, i.e. commandments and prohibitions of Allâhu ta'âlâ. It will be dhikr as well to make niyya when obeying these rules and not to think of the nafs's gusto when doing the mubâhs (permissions)." The heart's illness is its following the nafs. The nafs is Allâhu ta'âlâ's enemy. It does not want to obey Him. It is an enemy of itself as well. It relishes the heart's making all the limbs commit harâms and do harmful things. It wishes to be irreligious and without îmân so that it may attain these pleasures. It makes the heart ill to make friends with disbelievers and with people without a certain Madhhab, to read their books and newspapers, to listen to their radio programs and to watch their harmful television broadcast. What cures the heart's illness is to obey Islam. And it makes the nafs ill. It lessens its pleasures and desires and its power to affect the heart.]

Who on earth in enforcing their wishes attains victory?
Definitely cometh true whatsoever is in destiny!

HUNDRED and FOURTEENTH LETTER

There are a hundred and twenty-five letters in the book entitled Mekâtib-i-sherîfa and written by 'Abdullah Dahlawî 'rahima-hullâhu ta'âlâ', one of the greatest scholars of India. The following is the English version of the hundred and fourteenth letter, which was written for Hâdji 'Abdullah Bukhârî:

There is no deficiency in Allâhu ta'âlâ. He always tells the truth, and shows the right way to His slaves. May our salâms and prayers be over our highest guide and our beloved Prophet Muhammad Mustafâ 'sall-Allâhu ta'âlâ 'alaihi wa sallam' and over his blessed 'Âl (Family) and Ashâb (Companions) 'radiy-Allâhu ta'âlâ 'anhum ajma'în'! Men of Tarîqa living here, [i.e. in the city of Delhi,] are reading Esmâ and writing musqas (amulets) for the purpose of attaining their desires. Thereby they are alluring other people to themselves. They are holding the Emîr-ul-mu'minîn 'Alî 'kerrem-Allâhu wejheh wa radiy-Allâhu ta'âlâ 'anh' superior to the other three Khalîfas 'radiy-Allâhu 'anhum'. These people are called **Shi'îs** (Shiites). People who are inimical towards the three Khalîfas and towards the Ashâb-i-kirâm are called **Râfidîs**.

[Scholars of **Ahl as-sunnat wa-l-jamâ'at** 'rahima-humullâhu ta'âlâ' have stated in various of their books that Hadrat Abû Bakr and Hadrat 'Umar and Hadrat 'Uthmân are superior to Hadrat 'Alî 'radiy-Allâhu ta'âlâ 'anhum ajma'în', and proved this fact by adducing ample evidence and proof from âyat-i-kerîmas, from hadîth-i-sherîfs, and from the ijmâ', i.e. unanimity, consensus of the Ashâb-i-kirâm 'radiy-Allâhu ta'âlâ 'anhum ajma'în'. Two of these valuable books are **Izâlat-ul-khafâ 'an khilâfat-il-khulafâ** and **Qurrat-ul-'aynain** fî tafdhîl-i-shaikhayn, both of which were written by Waliy-yullah Muhaddîth Dahlawî 'rahima-hullâhu ta'âlâ' (1114 [1702 A.D.] – 1176 [1762], Delhi). The books are in a mixture of Arabic and Persian languages; the first one was translated into the Urdu language and the two versions were printed in Pakistan in 1382 [1962 A.D.], and the second one was translated into Turkish and thence into English. The English version occupies a major part of the final section of the book entitled Sahaba 'The Blessed', one of the publications of Hakîkat Kitâbevi of Istanbul, Turkey. It occupies also a part of the book entitled 'Documents of the Right Word'. The Arabic book entitled **Es-sawâiq-ul-muhriqa** and written by the great Islamic scholar Ibni Hajar-i-Mekkî 'rahima-hullâhu ta'âlâ' (899 [1494 A.D.] – 974 [1566], Mekka) was reproduced by offset process in Istanbul, Turkey, by Hakîkat Kitâbevi. A reasonable Muslim who reads that book will realize quite well that the lâ-madhhabî people have been in the wrong way. Some of those people are calling themselves Ja'farî as of today. They are deceiving young people with the lie that they are the followers of the Twelve Imâms. The fact, however, is that Muslims following the Twelve Imâms are called **Ahl as-sunnat** Muslims. Scholars of the true way called Ahl as-sunnat 'rahima-humullâhu ta'âlâ' have stated: "Loving the Twelve Imâms will cause a Muslim to die with îmân."

They are organizing funeral processions and feasts for the purpose of performing 'dawr'. [They are not performing namâz in jamâ'at. In mosques and] in gatherings of Mawlid they are having groups sing ilâhîs (eulogies) and mersiyas (dirges). They are listening to musical instruments such as lutes in convents. They are committing these acts of bid'at and many another heresies in the name of Tarîqat (Paths of Tasawwuf). In fact, they are adding the irreligious rites of Jukîsm and Brahmanism into their so-called practices of Tarîqat. They keep company with people who are after worldly advantages and with fâsiq (sinful) people. They do not attach importance to qawma and jalsa in namâz, (which have been explained in detail earlier in the current book,) to namâz in jamâ'at, and to Friday prayer. None of their rites and rituals exists in Islam. Such things did not exist in the time of the Salaf-as-sâlihîn. Scholars of **Ahl as-sunnat wa-l-jamâ'at** 'rahima-humullâhu ta'âlâ' avoided such acts and ways of bid'at. Thanks be to Allâhu ta'âlâ, none of these ugly acts of bid'at existed among the Ashâb-i-kirâm 'radiy-Allâhu ta'âlâ 'anhum'. A person who wants to be a Muslim and follow in the footsteps of the Salaf-as-sâlihîn (early Islamic scholars) 'rahima-humullâhu ta'âlâ' should flee such false men of Tarîqat. They are thieves of faith. They are demolishing the religion and îmân of the slaves of Allâhu ta'âlâ. Their dhikring and other practices set the heart and the nafs into motion. [These things should purify (the heart) from the mâ-siwâ (thoughts other than those of Allâhu ta'âlâ) rather than stir some states and actions.] Besides, such things as kashfs [karâmats, informing about lost things and communing with genies] have no value in Islam. Disbelievers such as Jûkis also display kashfs and karâmats. People with wisdom should be on the alert and distinguish right from wrong. Adhering to Islam and being fond of worldly interests are two polar opposites which cannot coexist in a person. It is not something a wise person will do to compromise his religious principles for the purpose of obtaining some worldly advantages. Scholars and shaikhs of the city of Bukhâra were people with tawakkul (putting one's trust in Allâhu ta'âlâ). They were not fond of worldly advantages. It darkens one's heart to give feasts and to gather together people who are fond of worldly interests. Those great people avoided things of this sort. They adhered fast to the correct belief taught by the Salaf-i-sâlihîn 'rahima-humullâhu ta'âlâ' and to Rasûlullah's 'sall-Allâhu ta'âlâ 'alaihi wa sallam' Sunnat. In everything they did they preferred the way of **'Azîmat**. They avoided bid'ats. They avoided things coming by ways that were either harâm or makrûh. When mubâhs (permissions) cause harâms, they, too, become harâms. **Dhikr-i-khafî**, i.e. to make dhikr silently (innerly), is better than **dhikr-i-jehrî**, i.e. to make dhikr loudly. They made this (first) type of dhikr. They had attained the grade of 'ihsân' mentioned in a hadîth-i-sherîf. Their hearts were always turned towards the source of fayz, [i.e. Allâhu ta'âlâ.] If a faithful and true devotee attains the tawajjuh of such a superior man of Tasawwuf, his heart, and all his latîfas as well, will immediately start dhikring. He will attain hudhûr, i.e. the heart's containing nothing but Allâhu ta'âlâ, which is a state also called **mushâhada**, jadhbas and fayzes called **wâridât**, which are blessings wherein the fortunate devotee bathes in nûrs both in his zâhir (outwardly, physically) and in his bâtin (innerly, spiritually). Once the devotee starts receiving fayz from his murshid's heart, no thought except that of Allâhu ta'âlâ will come to his heart. All his limbs will act compatibly with Sunnat and with 'azîmat. What great happiness these blessings are. Yâ Rabbî! For the grace of Your Beloved Prophet Muhammad Mustafâ 'sall-Allâhu 'alaihi wa sallam' and for the grace of the meshâikh-i-kirâm 'rahmatullâhi 'alaihim ajma'în', who are the followers of that noblest Prophet, do make this extremely valuable blessing our daily food. Fayzes of Imâm Rabbânî mujaddid-i-elf-i-thânî 'rahmatullâhi 'alaih' make all a person's latîfas attain this blessing. (Please scan the thirty-ninth chapter of the first fascicle, and the twenty-third and twenty-sixth chapters of the sixth fascicle, of **Endless Bliss** for 'latîfa'.)

May my life be sacrificed for your way,
Beauty in name and essence, Muhammad!

Please do intercede for your humble servant,
Beauty in name and esence, Muhammad!

Believers suffer much in this life,
They shall be rewarded in next life.

Choice of eighteen thousand worlds in life,
Beauty in name and essence, Muhammad!

One who travels over seven heavens,
Who strolls above Kursî and heavens,

Who begs Haqq for his Umma at Mi'râj,
Beauty in name and essence, Muhammad!

What, for Yûnus, are two worlds without you?
With no bit of doubt, true Prophet are you!

People against you pass without îmân;
Beauty in name and essence, Muhammad!

FINAL REMARKS FROM
BOOKLET FOR WAY TO PARADISE

We observe that all beings, living ones and lifeless ones alike, are all in a systematic order. We learn that there is an unchanging arrangement and some mathematical connections in the make-up of every substance, in every event, in every reaction. We classify these arrangements and connections under categories such as laws of physics, chemistry, astronomy, biology, and so forth. Making use of this unchanging order, we develop industries, open factories, make medicines, travel to the moon, and establish connections with stars and atoms. We make radios, televisions, computers, and networks. Were it not for this order in creatures, and if everything were on a haphazard basis, we would not manage any of these things. Everything would collide with every another, they would get out of order, and disasters would happen. All the existence would cease to exist.

This systematic regularity, codified orderliness and interrelation among beings indicates that they did not come into existence on their own or by chance, and that everything has been created by an omniscient, omnipotent, all seeing, all hearing being who does whatsoever He wishes to do. He creates and annihilates everything at will. He makes things causes and means for His creating other things. If He created without causes and means, there would not be an established order among beings. Everything would be in a dire mess. There would be no signs to show His existence. Into the bargain, no sciences or civilizations would exist.

He has not only made His existence manifest through this order, but also announced His existence to His slaves, which in turn shows His great magnanimity towards His slaves. In every century, beginning with 'Âdam ''alaihis-salâm', He has chosen one person from every community the world over, created him as the best and highest among his people, sent him His angel, let him know His existence and His Names, and instructed him on what people should do and what they should avoid so that they lead a comfortable and prosperous life in this world and in the Hereafter. These chosen and superior people are called **Prophets**. Commandments and prohibitions that they conveyed to people are called **Dîn** (religion) and **Ahkâm-i-dîniyya** (religious rules). Because the human nature is forgetful of past information and because evil people, who always exist among people, have interpolated the Prophets' ''alaihim-us-salawât-u-wa-t-teslîmât' heavenly books and changed their utterances, past religions have been forgotten and defiled. What is even worse, evil people have made up and concocted bogus religions.

Because Allâhu ta'âlâ, Creator of all, pities human beings very much, He has sent them a final Prophet with a new religion. And He has given them the good news that He shall protect this religion till the end of this world and spread it intact far and near despite the evil people's attacks and attempts to change and defile it.

We express our profound gratitude to Allâhu ta'âlâ that we have had belief in the existence and unity of the Creator since we were only a small child, when we attained the fortune of learning that the Name of this Creator is Allah, that Muhammad ''alaihis-salâm' is His final Prophet, and **Islam** is the religion conveyed by that beloved Prophet to His slaves, (human beings.) We wanted to learn this Islamic religion correctly. Throughout our years of education in high school and in university, we searched for a source to learn it from. But the youth of our nation had been surrounded by a virtually insurmountable barrier of sham scientists who had hawked themselves to freemasons and communists and hirelings who had been suborned by wahhâbîs into becoming eclectics without a certain Madhhab. So cunning had been the behind-the-scenes activities carried on by the renegades and heretics who had bartered their faith for worldly interests that it was next to impossible to sort the correct way out. There was no way out but to beg Allâhu ta'âlâ. Our Allah, most high, blessed us with reading books written by scholars of Ahl as-sunnat 'rahima-humullâhu ta'âlâ'. Yet the convictions we had been imbued with in the name of scientific knowledge by **sham scientists** passing as modern people and in the name of translations of the Qur'ân al-kerîm by **sham men of religion** who had been exploiting Islam for their personal interests had penetrated deep into our soul. May infinite gratitude be to Allâhu ta'âlâ for blessing us with an awakening owing to the admonitions on the part of true men of religion, so that we began to distinguish between good and evil. We were able to realize that what our mind had been saturated with was sequinned poison, rather than knowledge, and that our heart had been darkened with their deleterious effect. Had we not seen the books written by scholars of Ahl as-sunnat, we would have been unable to distinguish between friend and foe, and we would have been deceived by the tricks and lies of our nafs and of enemies of religion. We would have been unable to escape from the snares set by those insidious enemies who had been touting irreligiousness and immorality as 'advancement'. We would be mocking our parents, true and pure Muslims, and the Islamic teachings we had acquired from them. Our beloved Prophet 'sall-Allâhu ta'âlâ 'alaihi wa sallam' warns us against falling into the traps set by enemies of Islam: "**Learn your faith from the mouths of rijâl!**" When we can't find any rijâl, i.e. true scholars of religion, we will learn from their books. Religious books written by bid'at holders or by unlearned men of religion without a certain Madhhab are very harmful like books written by disbelievers.

It is harâm for women and girls to expose their heads, hair, arms and legs and for men to expose parts of their bodies between their navels and knees in the presence of others. In other words, Allâhu ta'âlâ has prohibited them. The four true Madhhabs, which teach the commandments and prohibitions of Allâhu ta'âlâ, differ from one another in their accounts of men's awrat parts, i.e. their limbs that have been forbidden for other men to look at and for them to show other men. Every Muslim has to cover his awrat parts defined by the Madhhab he is in. It is harâm for others to look at these parts of his if they are exposed. It is stated in the book entitled **Kimyâ-i-se'âdet**: "It is harâm for women and girls not only without covering their heads, hair, arms and legs, but also by wearing thin, ornamented, tight and perfumed dresses. If their parents, husbands and brothers allow them to do so, approve of their doing so and condone them, they will share their sin and the torment that they are going to be subjected to." In other words, they shall be tormented together in the fire of Hell. If they make tawba, they shall be pardoned and shall not be burned. Allâhu ta'âlâ likes people who make tawba. It was in the third year of the Hijrat (Hegira) that girls who had reached the ages of discretion and puberty and women were prohibited to show themselves to men nâ-mahram to them. We should not believe the falsification that women's covering themselves is a later invention concocted by scholars of Fiqh. It is a deceit on the part of British spies and some unlearned people trapped by them by putting forth the fact that women did not cover themselves before the revelation of the âyat commanding the hijâb (women's and girls' covering themselves).

We will say it again: When a child becomes 'âqil (discreet) and bâligh (pubescent), i.e. when it reaches an age to tell good and evil apart and enter into a marriage, it becomes farz for that child to immediately learn the six tenets of îmân (belief) and thereafter to learn the **Ahkâm-i-islâmiyya**, i.e. the farzes, the halâls and the harâms, and to lead a life in keeping with these rules and principles. A girl becomes 'âqil and bâligh when she becomes nine years old, and a boy becomes so at the age of twelve. It becomes farz for them to learn these tenets, rules and principles by asking their parents, kith and kin, and acquaintances. Likewise, a disbeliever who has converted to Islam to immediately go to a man of religion, to a muftî, and acquire these teachings from them, who in turn will have to teach that person, either directly or by giving him or her a true Islamic book as a present. It is farz for both parties to do their part, i.e. for the new Muslim to learn, and for the requested person to help them learn. If the latter party merely says, "Very good, very good," and does not help them by teaching them or by giving them true Islamic books, they will have disobeyed the (commandment called) farz. A person who disobeys a farz shall be tormented in Hell fire. Once the former party starts searching for the man of religion or the religious book, it will be an 'udhr for them not to learn those teachings until they find the source of the teachings. (An 'udhr is something, e.g. an excuse, which absolves a Muslim from having to do an Islamic commandment or from having to avoid an Islamic prohibition. As these commandments and prohibitions have been dictated by Islam, likewise 'udhrs for all Islamic commandments and prohibitions have, again, been prescribed by Islam. As the source for learning Islamic commandments and prohibitions is the books written by scholars of Ahl as-sunnat, likewise 'udhrs can be learned only from scholars of Ahl as-sunnat or from their books. Hakîkat Kitâbevi of Istanbul, Turkey, is today's Islamic treasury department where one could find all the books one needed in multifarious languages.)

For the purpose of letting the younger generations hear about the true Islamic teachings we have read and thereby serving the people all the world over so that they should attain comfort and peace in the world and endless bliss in the Hereafter, we shall, inshâ-Allah, carry on with our business of publishing selections and valuable writings from books written by scholars of Ahl as-sunnat.

The following prayer, called **Salât-an-tunjînâ**, should be recited for attaining wishes: "Allâhumma salli 'alâ sayyidinâ Muhammadin wa 'alâ âl-i-sayyidinâ Muhammadin salât-an-tunjînâ bihâ min jamî'ul ahwâl-i-wa-l-âfât wa taqdî lenâ bihâ jamî'al hâjât

wa tutahhirunâ wa tubellighunâ bihâ min jamî' is-seyyiât wa
terfe'unâ bihâ a'l-ad-derejât wa tubellighunâ bihâ aqsa-l-ghâyât
min jamî'il khayrât-i-fi-l-hayât-i-wa ba'd-al-memât."

It is stated in hadîth-i-sherîfs that it is very useful to recite the
prayer of Istighfâr for protection against all sorts of trouble and
danger and for escaping harms and attacks of devils and enemies.

> *My life came and went by like a wind passing.*
> *To me it is nothing but an eye twinkling.*
> *Haqq bears witness: Body is soul's dwelling.*
> *One day it will fly off its cage, a birdling.*

HUNDRED and TWENTY-THIRD LETTER

**This letter of Hadrat Imâm Rabbânî's 'quddisa sirruh' was
written for Tâhir-i-Bedahshî. It states that an act of nâfila worship,
be it a hajj, will be good for nothing if it causes an act of farz
worship to be missed:**

My wise brother. The valuable letter sent by Molla Tâhir, who
is as cleanly as his name, has arrived here. My brother! It is stated
in a hadîth-i-sherîf: **"Allâhu ta'âlâ's disliking a slave of His will be
known from that slave's sparing time for frivolities."** To perform
an act of nâfila worship instead of performing an act that is farz
means to work in vain. Therefore, we should study what we are
spending our time with. We should know what we are busy with.
Are we doing nâfila worship or farz worship? A number of
prohibitions, harâms are being committed for performing a nâfila
hajj. You should think well! A mere signal will do with a wise
person. I send my salâm to you and to your friends.

[It is understood from this letter as well that the sunnats of four
of the five daily namâzes, with the exception of the sunnat of
morning namâz, should be performed with the niyyat (intention)
of (making) qadâ.]

HUNDRED and TWENTY-FOURTH LETTER

**This letter, again, was written for Tâhir-i-Bedahshî. The wujûb
(being wâjib) of hajj is conditional on possessing travel funds. To
go on a hajj without having money to spend for the journey means
to waste time despite other duties. The blessed letter explains this
fact:**

The valuable letter sent by my brother Khwâja Muhammad Tâhir-i-Bedahshî has arrived here. Hamd (praise and thanks) and gratitude be to Allâhu ta'âlâ (for His blessing) that there has been no laxity in (your) love for the faqîrs and attachment to them. Lingering of the days of separation has not paved the way for that (changing for the worse). This state of yours is a harbinger of great happiness. O my brother, who loves us! You have decided to go and asked (us) for permission. As we were parting, we said that perhaps we would attain the blessing of joining you en route. However, the istihâras[1] that we made thereafter did not come up with signs of approvel. It was not been concluded, therefore, that this journey would be permissible. So we changed our mind. Before that, your going had not been considered approvable, either. Yet, so enthusiastic had you appeared that a clear-cut displeasure had been held back. Setting out (for that journey) is conditional on having money for the journey. If a person is unable to fulfil that condition, he would have spared time for frivolities by going on a hajj. [It is one of conditions for wûjub for hajj to have the money for the journey. (In other words, among other conditions to be fulfilled, it is wâjib for a Muslim to have the money so that hajj may be farz for him.) Going on a hajj will not be farz for a person unless he has the money needed for the journey for a hajj. If he still goes on a hajj (without having that money), he will have performed a nâfila (supererogatory) hajj. As a matter of fact, it is not an act of farz or wâjib to go on an 'Umra. That is, it is an act of nâfila worship. And doing an act of nâfila worship, in its turn, when causes the omission of an act of worship that is farz or causes the performer to commit a harâm, loses its identity as an act of worship. It degenerates into committing a sinful act. [Please see the twenty-ninth letter, (which does not have an English version as of today!)] It will not be appropriate to do something that is not farz at the cost of neglecting an act that is farz. I stated these facts in a few letters of mine. It is not known whether you have received them. We rest our case. You know what to do with the rest. Wa-s-salâm. [There is information concerning hajj also in the two hundred and fiftieth (250) letter, (which has not been translated into English as of now.)]

---

[1] 'Istihâra' is touched upon in the last paragraph of the twenty-fifth chapter of the sixth fascicle of **Endless Bliss**.